Mac® OS X 10.3 Panther
Little Black Book

Gene Steinberg

PARAGLYPH
P R E S S

President
Keith
Weiskamp

Editor-at-Large
Jeff
Duntemann

Vice President,
Sales,
Marketing, and
Distribution
Steve Sayre

Vice President,
International
Sales and
Marketing
Cynthia
Caldwell

Production
Manager
Kim Eoff

Cover
Designer
Kris Sotelo

Mac® OS X 10.3 Panther Little Black Book

Paraglyph Press, Inc.
4015 N. 78th Street, #115
Scottsdale, Arizona 85251
Phone: 602-749-8787
www.paraglyphpress.com

Paraglyph Press ISBN: 1-932111-86-7

Printed in the United States of America
10   9   8   7   6   5   4   3   2   1

PARAGLYPH
P R E S S

The Paraglyph Mission

This book you've purchased is a collaborative creation involving the work of many hands, from authors to editors to designers and to technical reviewers. At Paraglyph Press, we like to think that everything we create, develop, and publish is the result of one form creating another. And as this cycle continues on, we believe that your suggestions, ideas, feedback, and comments on how you've used our books is an important part of the process for us and our authors.

We've created Paraglyph Press with the sole mission of producing and publishing books that make a difference. The last thing we all need is yet another tech book on the same tired, old topic. So we ask our authors and all of the many creative hands who touch our publications to do a little extra, dig a little deeper, think a little harder, and create a better book. The founders of Paraglyph are dedicated to finding the best authors, developing the best books, and helping you find the solutions you need.

As you use this book, please take a moment to drop us a line at **feedback@paraglyphpress.com** and let us know how we are doing - and how we can keep producing and publishing the kinds of books that you can't live without.

Sincerely,

Keith Weiskamp & Jeff Duntemann
Paraglyph Press Founders

Paraglyph Press, Inc.
4015 N. 78th Street, #115
Scottsdale, Arizona 85251

email: **feedback@paraglyphpress.com**
Web: **www.paraglyphpress.com**
Phone: 602-749-8787
Fax: 602-861-1941

I wish to pay special thanks to my "muse" (she knows who she is) for always helping me to find the right things to say and the means to say it.

≈

About the Author

Gene Steinberg is an award-winning technology journalist. He is the author of more than 30 books on computing, the Internet, and telecommunications and he has written articles for such diverse sources as CNET, Gannett News Service, ZDNet, *MacAddict*, *MacHome*, and *Macworld*. His voice is heard weekly on the syndicated radio show, *The Mac Night Owl LIVE*, and his weekly Mac commentaries are published by USAToday.com. In addition his support and information site, The Mac Night Owl (**www.macnightowl.com**) is regularly visited by tens of thousands of Mac users each day. In his spare time, Gene and his teenaged son, Grayson, are developing a science fiction adventure series, *Attack of the Rockoids*.

Acknowledgments

Panther is both a simple yet an extraordinarily complex operating system, and there is no way to complete a project of this scope without outside assistance. During the course of researching and writing this book, I've been pleased to receive the help of a number of folks who have made this daunting task far more pleasant.

First and foremost, I want to thank the folks at Apple's corporate communications department for letting me see the future of the Mac OS and answering all my questions, whether simple, complex, or just downright silly. I'm particularly grateful to Anuj Nayar for his able assistance. In addition, Mike Shebanek, the "handler" Apple selected to guide me through the development process for Panther, was especially helpful in delineating the key aspects of Panther for both this book and my ongoing online articles on the subject.

In addition, an author cannot work without a publisher and editors, and the terrific folks at Paraglyph Press were especially helpful in putting up with my quirks and demands without protest. I'm particularly thankful to Keith Weiskamp, Cynthia Caldwell, and Kim Eoff for ensuring that the words I wrote were understandable to all of our readers, and for making this book look good.

Finally, I am especially thankful for the help and support from my little family, my beautiful wife, Barbara, and my brilliant son, Grayson, for putting up with the long hours I spent at the keyboard in order to deliver the manuscript for this book on schedule.

—*Gene Steinberg*

Contents at a Glance

Contents

Chapter 5
Panther Desktop Management 109

Chapter 6
Setting Up Panther for Multiple Users 127

Chapter 17
Security and Panther 387

Chapter 18
Troubleshooting Panther 407

Contents

Introduction

Apple has a history of confounding the skeptics. One Mac support site is busy counting up the number of times the company has been pronounced dead and buried. Despite everything, the company continues to develop insanely great products and making enough money to keep its stockholders happy.

For years, the issue of developing a modern operating system for the 21st century was especially irksome. I hesitate to imagine how many millions of dollars Apple wasted trying to do the job itself. In those days, the company suffered from what some regard as the "not invented here" syndrome, which simply meant that another company's technology, even if it was proven to be better, would remain unwelcome.

But the arrival of Mac OS X in March 2001 proved that this was a new Apple Computer. Incorporating a clever mixture of tried and tested Unix-based software with the fit and finish and, in fact, elegance that only Apple can create, the new operating system was as much a homage to the past as a portrait for the future.

In October 2003, Apple released its fourth major upgrade to Mac OS X. Code-named Panther, which is the name I'll use most often in this book. Panther arrived with a claimed 150 new features. Even more surprising is that it appeared a mere 14 months after the previous release, known as Jaguar, which also touted a similar number of enhanced capabilities.

It's hard to believe the company has come so far and so fast. The first release of Mac OS X was something meant for power users and corporate customers to explore the possibilities, not actually get any work done. Each successive upgrade has brought restored lost features, added new ones, and delivered better and better performance.

The Mac OS X 10.3 Panther Little Black Book is designed to be your companion as you upgrade to Apple's latest Unix-based operating system. From installation to setup to troubleshooting, you'll find the information you need is readily available, all tested with the release version of the software for maximum accuracy.

The Bill of Fare

Since this book is part of The Little Black Book series, it covers the essential information you need to install, configure and use Panther. There are no frills and no fluff. Useless tips and tricks that will satisfy one's intellectual curiosity or perhaps trigger a chuckle, but not enhance your productivity, aren't included.

The 22 chapters here are meant to cover all the essential areas of your Mac user experience. There are even sections about hardware configuration and setup, so you can get the most value from this book.

In the first ten chapters of this book, I run through the important new features, and then help you plot installation strategies. You are then taken step-by-step through the actual installation and configuration. From here you'll be introduced to the Panther's Finder, the Dock, multiple user features, search features, plus the big changes in the networking architecture. This part closes with information about AppleScript and how to install and use your programs. You'll even find a section covering Panther's Finder-like Open and Save dialog boxes, which are sure to simplify file management.

Two chapters cover hardware. If you planning to install Panther on a new Mac, or just one you've upgraded with extra memory, drive space, and other additions, you'll find that the critical subjects will really help you. You'll also learn how to add peripherals, such as printers, scanners, and removable drives, on your Mac. Finally, you'll find a section on using Panther with one of Apple's iBooks or PowerBooks.

In the next seven chapters, you'll discover some of the new Panther applications, how to run older "Classic" software on your Mac and how to handle fonts, perform backups, and check for computer viruses. Finally, a comprehensive section on troubleshooting is included, plus you'll encounter a visit to the Unix command line of the new operating system to perform regular system maintenance and to navigate through the underbelly of the new operating system.

The last part of this book covers Internet access from stem to stern. You'll have a birds-eye view of the newest Web browsers, Apple's Mail application with its terrific junk mail feature, and other Apple digital hub applications, such as iPhoto. You'll even get a look at iChat AV, Panther's chatting application that includes support for both audio and video.

How to Use This Book

(Although I don't particularly mind it if you do it all in a single sitting) the *Mac OS X 10.3 Panther Little Black Book* isn't designed to be read from cover to cover as you might read a novel. You'll probably just want to read the chapters that answer your questions about Panther.

As part of the Little Black Book series, each chapter is divided into two sections. The first, *In Brief*, gives you the basics and theories about the subject. The second, *Immediate Solutions*, offers step-by-step instructions on how to accomplish tasks, along with guides on what to do if something goes wrong.

Although the Panther user interface is ultra simple and smooth, Panther is a highly sophisticated operating system, one that will be updated regularly as time goes by. If you were one of the early adopters to the new operating system, you can see the vast number of changes between the original release and the subsequent upgrades. As a result, a book of this sort is also a developing process, and future updates for this book will reflect those changes, plus what I've learned as I continue to use Mac OS X.

I also welcome your comments, questions, and suggestions for future editions. If you have a problem with the new operating system, or discover something totally unique and utterly cool, let me know. You can email me directly at the address below.

Gene Steinberg
Scottsdale, AZ
Email: **gene@macnightowl.com**
 www.macnightowl.com

What's Hot About Mac OS X.3—Panther

Mac OS X is extremely young as operating systems go, yet it has received numerous minor bug fix updates and three major upgrades since its release in March 2001. The first version, 10.0, was primarily designed for early adopters who wanted to give the new operating system a try. By September, Mac OS X 10.1 came along, with speedier performance, interface improvements, better networking, and expanded support for peripherals. In 2002, Mac OX X 10.2 (Jaguar) was released, which took the popular operating system to new heights.

As you'll learn in this chapter, Apple's latest offering is Mac OS X 10.3— Panther. We'll dive right in and explore the new features of Panther and you'll quickly learn why this new operating system is a must have. If you have not yet used one of the versions of Mac OS X, such as Jaguar, you'll be in for a real treat as you start using Panther. If you have been a Jaguar user, on the other hand, and you are upgrading to Panther, you'll be pleasantly surprised with the approximately 150 new features that have been added to Panther.

A Brief Look at Panther's New Features

The striking new look of the Mac OS X interface, called Aqua, has undergone slight but noticeable revisions. The sometimes glaring impact has been softened. The menu and title bars have a light gray color, similar to the platinum look of Mac OS 8 through Mac OS 9. The pinstripe effect has been minimized. Such changes, and others you'll encounter as you explore Panther, have greatly refined the look and feel of the operating system. The watchwords are: less garish, more productive, and definitely more stable.

Under the surface Panther incorporates a tremendous number of changes designed to provide improved support and make your Mac run more reliably than ever. Some of the critical new features that we'll be covering in this book include:

- Audio and video conferencing

- Background downloading of software updates

- Better help with context sensitive links

- Customizable keyboard shortcuts

- Drag and drop printing

- Easier network preferences

- E-mail message threading

- Enhanced networking and printer sharing with Windows computers

- Exposé window management

- Fast User Switching

- FileVault Home directory encryption

- Finder-based Open and Save panels

- Font management software

- Improved PDF rendering

- Journaled file system

- Microsoft Exchange support

- More powerful spam filter

- More built-in printer and scanner drivers

- Label printing and mailing list support

- Fax support

- Speedier, user-centric Finder

- Super-fast file searching

- Superior font anti-aliasing

- Updated application switcher

- Zip compression

I'll be showing you the importance of these new Panther features in more detail, but first let's look at some of the core components of Mac OS X in general. This will help you better understand what Panther brings to the table, especially if you have never used one of the earlier versions of Mac OS X, such as OS X 10.1 or Jaguar.

Darwin

The open source core of Mac OS X is called *Darwin*. Darwin is based on a Unix microkernel, consisting of the Mach 3 microkernel and FreeBSD. The Apache Web server, which powers a majority of Web sites, has been refined and forms the basis of the new operating system's Web-sharing capabilities. Even better, you can create a basic Apache server with just a few mouse clicks.

NOTE: *Apple's Darwin is also an open-source project, where the core components of the operating system are made available free of charge to software developers, with Apple retaining full rights to the code. These developers can test and debug the software and then make available bug fixes and enhancements to the entire developer community. For more information about this feature, visit Apple's Darwin Web site at **www.apple.com/darwin**.*

Although its Unix underpinnings are well hidden beneath Aqua's striking user interface, they are not invisible. Power users can easily access Unix directly, bypassing the graphical user interface, and run regular Unix-based applications under Mac OS X via a command-line interface. Apple has even provided a Terminal application in the Utilities folder (see Figure 1.1) that lets power users acces the command line and run core Unix commands. I'll be showing you how to do this in Chapter 19.

In addition, Mac OS X offers the same industrial-strength features that are the hallmark of Unix:

- *Protected memory*—Each Mac OS X native program you run resides in its own address space, walled off from other programs. If a single program crashes, that application is shut down, along with the memory address space it occupies. You can continue to run your Mac without the need to restart. This feature will help to

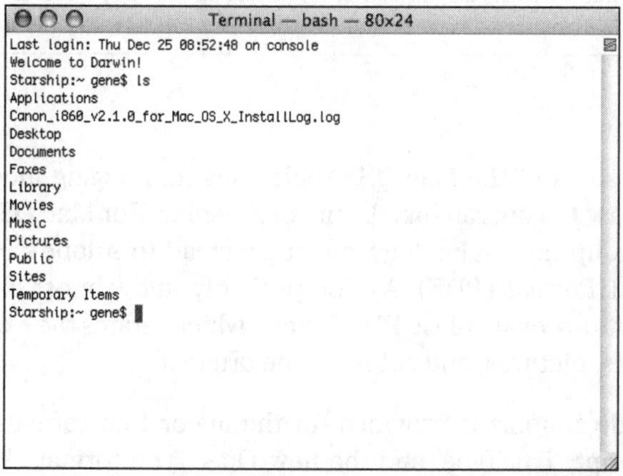

Figure 1.1   Mac OS X provides a command-line interface that allows you to make changes right in the underbelly of the system.

sharply reduce the operating system's tendency to crash at the least sign of a software conflict.

- *Preemptive multitasking*—Apple's previous multitasking method was cooperative, meaning that each application would, in effect, have to share CPU time with other programs. This meant that if you were working in a program, such as typing in a word-processing document, background tasks, such as printing or downloading a file, could come almost to a screeching halt, particularly if a program hogged processor time unnecessarily. With Mac OS X, the operating system serves as the traffic cop, performing the task management and allowing programs to run more efficiently and with fewer slowdowns when multiple processes are running.

- *Advanced virtual memory*—Prior to the release of Mac OS X, virtual memory meant slower performance, poor performance with multimedia programs, stuttering sounds, and other short-comings. Under Mac OS X, virtual memory management is dynamic. Programs are automatically given the amount of memory they require, via either RAM or virtual memory disk swapping. Performance is optimized, so you get the maximum possible performance from your programs.

NOTE: *Virtual memory in Mac OS X is super-efficient, but it can't do miracles. To get the best possible performance, you should have sufficient RAM to run your memory-intensive programs (such as Adobe Photoshop or Apple's Final Cut Pro). Fortunately, you no longer have to visit the Get Info window to constantly change a program's memory allocation to meet your needs (except, of course, for Classic applications). Mac users have grown accustomed to having 1GB systems, with more than 2GB becoming the hallmark for the Power Mac G5, Apple's popular 64-bit desktop computer.*

Quartz

In previous versions of the Mac OS, Apple used an imaging model called QuickDraw to generate pixels on your display. For Mac OS X, Apple has given up this technology, moving instead to Adobe's Portable Document Format (PDF). As you probably know, most electronic documents are available in PDF format, which retains the exact formatting, fonts, pictures, and colors of the original.

Full system-wide support is provided for the major font formats—bitmap, PostScript, TrueType, and the new OpenType format. As a result, Adobe Type Manager (ATM) is no longer needed to render fonts crisply on the screen, although font management is not quite as extensive as the Deluxe version of ATM.

NOTE: *ATM still works from Mac OS X's Classic environment, including the font-management features for the Deluxe version. ATM, however, was not upgraded to Mac OS X. Chapter 15 covers the subject of font handling with Panther and includes information on the available options for font management, which include Apple's own software solution.*

The Quartz 2D graphics system is extremely powerful, with speedy rendering of images and anti-aliasing, providing sharp screen display. You'll see some of this elegance in the illustrations provided in this book, but you have to see the real thing to get the flavor of the effects of this unique technology. OS X also provides system-level support for PDF, which makes it easy for Mac software developers to provide built-in support to save documents in this format. In addition to PDF, Apple includes support for ColorSync to ease color management from input to display to output; the industry-standard OpenGL, which provides superlative performance for many 3D games and graphic applications; and Apple's famous QuickTime, used worldwide for generating multimedia content.

If you have the correct video hardware on your Mac, you'll experience the joys of Quartz Extreme, a souped-up version of Quartz that harnesses the power of OpenGL to offload 2D and 3D graphics to the video hardware. It's no free ride, though, as it requires a Mac with AGP-based graphics, using a graphic card from NVIDIA, or one of ATI's Radeon products and a minimum of 16MB of video memory.

NOTE: *If your Mac isn't equipped with the correct video hardware, don't despair. Apple can also use the G4 processor's Velocity Engine, the chip's vector processing capability, to provide some performance improvement. There are also performance optimizations for Macs with a G3 processor, so older Macs, including those millions of vintage iMacs, aren't abandoned. I have personally verified speed improvements on all Macs capable of running Mac OS X so don't feel you have to buy a new computer just to run Panther. You'll experience performance boosts even if previous versions of Mac OS X proved disappointing.*

Cocoa

Cocoa is one of the technologies inherited from NeXTSTEP, which forms the basis for a large part of Mac OS X's capabilities. This is the name for an advanced object-oriented programming environment that allows programmers to develop new applications much more quickly than with other programming tools. In one spectacular example, Stone Software's integrated illustration program, Create, which features drawing, HTML, and page layout capabilities, is largely the work of one programmer. With traditional programming tools, a large, highly skilled team would be required to perform the same work.

NOTE: One possible downside to this flexibility is that programs created in this fashion cannot run on older Macs. However, that situation may be of less significance as more Macs are shipped with or upgraded to Mac OS X in the years ahead.

Carbon

Carbon is a set of application programming interfaces, commonly referred to as APIs, which can also be used to build a Mac OS X application. Apple designed Carbon to make it easier for software publishers to develop Mac OS X applications. Most major Mac developers, including such heavyweights as Adobe, Macromedia, Microsoft, and Quark, have updated their applications using these APIs.

NOTE: Even though Carbon greatly simplifies conversion of software to Mac OS X, developing software for the Mac is not a cakewalk. The final Classic version of Microsoft Office, for example, consists of millions of lines of computer code. Microsoft has the largest Mac programming team outside of Apple Computer and yet it took approximately a year to build Office v. X. QuarkXPress 6.0 didn't reach the dealers until the summer of 2003, having been under development for two or three years.

The main advantage of an application that is "Carbonized" is that it supports the major features of Mac OS X, such as preemptive multitasking, protected memory, and advanced virtual memory, plus the eye-catching Aqua interface. In addition, when Apple's CarbonLib extension (which first appeared as part of Mac OS 9) is installed, many of these programs can run on older Mac operating system versions—though, of course, without the advanced features of Mac OS X.

NOTE: Not all Carbon applications have backward-compatibility. In order to maximize performance, many software publishers have given up on Classic support. This means that Adobe's Creative Suite, QuarkXPress, and the latest and greatest from other big publishers no longer run under Mac OS 9.

Classic

Although thousands of Mac OS X–savvy programs have shipped since the release of the new operating system, you may still want to use some of the thousands of older programs. Fortunately, you can do so by virtue of the Classic feature.

Classic is, in effect, Mac OS 9.1 and later (9.2.2 is the version that was in use when this book was written) running as a separate application under Mac OS X. You can think of it as being somewhat similar to running Microsoft Virtual PC to emulate the Windows environment on a Mac. But it goes further than that. Apple's Classic feature runs almost transparently under Mac OS X after a brief startup process. The feature lets you run most of your older applications with amazingly good performance and a high level of compatibility, but without taking advantage of the Aqua user interface or the robust underpinnings of the new operating system. It is designed to ease the transition to the new Mac computing paradigm.

NOTE: *The Classic environment is not a panacea. Some cherished system extensions, particularly those that modify Finder functions and hardware drivers for such peripherals as scanners and CD writers, won't run. You'll need to get Mac OS X–compatible drivers for all these products.*

Aqua

The Macintosh user interface is reborn with Aqua (see Figure 1.2). Although at first glance Aqua clearly comes across as eye candy—a software interface that is consistent with the striking industrial designs for Apple's latest computers—much more is involved here.

Aqua's translucent, shimmering, ocean-blue look is designed to address many of the usability problems with older graphical user interfaces (both Mac- and Windows-based). It is designed to be relatively easy for novice computer users to master; such users form a large percentage of purchasers of Apple's consumer-level products (the eMac, iBook, and the iMac). But Aqua is also intended to provide the power that will appeal to the sophisticated computer professional.

Figure 1.2   After you boot a Mac with Panther installed, you will witness a bold, new, eye-catching user interface.

> **NOTE:** Apple is also offering a slightly more subdued graphite version of its user interface as an appearance option, paying attention to professional users who might consider Aqua just a bit too imposing for an office environment. You'll learn more about setting this option in Chapter 3.

From large, photo-quality icons to translucent menus, drop shadows, and real-time object dragging (without a performance penalty), Aqua provides all Mac users, regardless of skill level, with a convenient, easy-to-manage user experience. The standard single-window mode, which keeps Finder displays to one window, helps reduce the clutter and confusion of previous operating system versions. However, the new Mac OS X Finder has many adjustment options, so you can easily configure it to spawn additional Finder windows when you open a folder, just like the Classic Mac OS.

One common interface problem addressed with Mac OS X is the Save dialog box. Even experienced Mac users have had trouble navigating through complex folder hierarchies; some don't even bother. Under Mac OS X, however, when you're ready to save an open document for the first time, the Save As dialog box opens as a sheet of paper right below the title bar of the document in question (see Figure 1.3). You can simply switch to another document window and the Save As dialog box remains anchored to the document you want to save. Then, you just return to it when you're ready to save the document. In addition, column and list view arrangements provide Finder-like navigation of folder hierarchies.

The Finder

The core of the Mac user experience is the Finder, an application that runs full-time on a Mac, providing the desktop appearance as well as performing file- and disk-management chores. For Panther, the venerable Finder has undergone its second complete redesign (see Figure 1.4), ending up as a composite of technologies from the original Finder and the NeXTSTEP file viewer. The combination is designed to make it possible to access your applications, files, and disks easily without having to dig deep into numerous nested folders, scattered icons, and directory windows.

To the left of the Mac Finder window is a Sidebar displaying icons that take you directly to the most frequently accessed areas on your Mac, and that includes the ones you add yourself. The top half of the Sidebar displays your mounted disks, those available for file access,

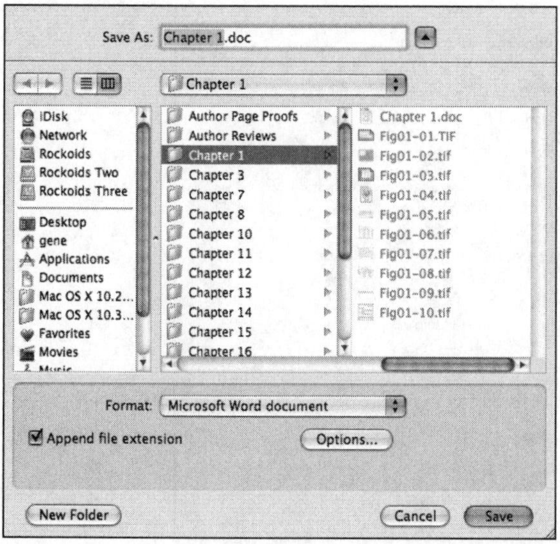

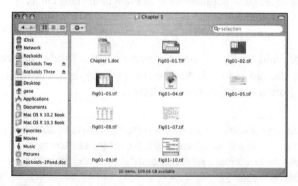

Figure 1.3   The new translucent Save As dialog box, known as a "sheet,"
remains hooked to the document window you're going to save.

Figure 1.4   The new face of the famous Mac Finder has striking differences,
yet retains some familiar elements.

and network connections. The bottom half displays your Applications
folder and other common locations. At the top of the Finder window
is a toolbar that provides for a browser-like navigation scheme. It also
incorporates a integrated Search feature, which allows you to locate
the contents of a Finder window. However, that is just the beginning.
You can further customize the toolbar and Sidebar with a variety of
stuff (see Figure 1.5) and size the Finder as necessary. You can even

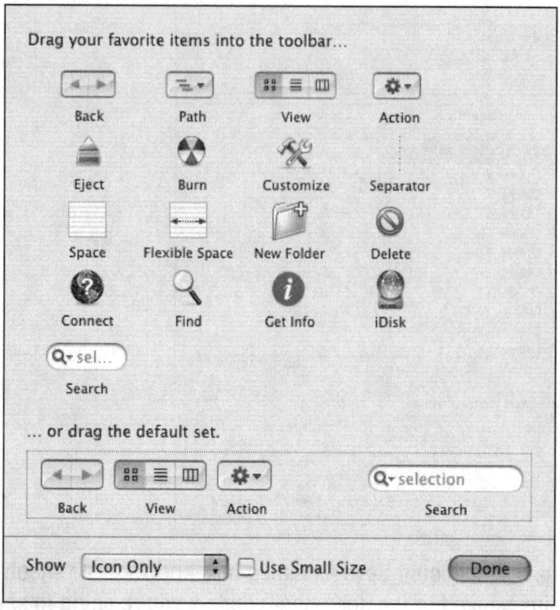

Figure 1.5   A wide range of possibilities is inherent in the new Finder toolbar setup window.

hide the Sidebar and toolbar altogether and have the Finder behave very much like the old Mac OS, despite the daringly different look. I will show you how to do all of this in Chapter 4.

TIP: *Combining local, network, and Internet access in a single interface is part of Apple's Internet integration efforts. These also include the .Mac feature at Apple's Web site, a subscription-based service that provides a set of Web-based tools for Mac users. I'll cover the subject in more detail in Chapter 22.*

The Finder offers not only new, more colorful variations of the list and icon views that exist on the original Finder, it also offers a new column view that makes locating deeply nested items easier (see Figure 1.6). You single-click on a folder or disk and the contents quickly display in the window at the right. Reminiscent of Greg's Browser, a popular Mac shareware program, this file-viewing feature allows you to more easily locate anything from a file to a networked drive.

TIP: *Mac OS X also features spring-loaded folders. When you drag a file on top of a closed folder, the folder will pop open, after a short delay, to reveal its contents. This helps you more easily find the proper place to put an item. The Finder also supports Labels, which allow you to attach a color and title to specific files and folders for easier access to important projects.*

Figure 1.6   The Finder's column view option speeds navigation through even complex file directories.

The Dock

In the old days of the Mac, the Apple menu was the principal repository on the Mac for your frequently accessed files, folders, and disks. Apple's Control Strip was a floating palette of control panels and other programs, offering one-click access. The latter is history, replaced (at least in part) by the Dock (see Figure 1.7). This picturesque taskbar puts a set of colorful, almost "cartoonish" icons at the bottom of your Mac's display (or at the side, if you prefer). It contains files, folders, disks, programs—whatever you choose to store there. The icons are designed to easily reflect their contents. For example, a picture file contains a preview of the image so you can recognize it immediately. If you prefer to view titles, you'll be pleased to see the title of an item displayed as soon as the mouse passes over it.

To access an item on the Dock, just click once on it and it will open in a new window. When you minimize a window it transfers to the Dock in a flashy motion that looks like a sheet of paper being folded (in a sense, the end result is similar to the way a minimized window is moved to the Microsoft Windows taskbar). The motion is sometimes known as the *Genie Effect*. With the standard single-window mode, you'll find that your previous open window is closed and moved to the Dock. You can also use the Mac's drag-and-drop feature to add items to the Dock.

TIP: *If the Genie Effect is too distracting, Panther now includes a scaling option that drops a minimized window to the Dock or returns it to full size with much less flourish.*

Even the venerable Mac trashcan is now part of the Dock, although it performs precisely the same functions as in previous Mac operating system versions.

Figure 1.7   The Dock automatically resizes to accommodate additional items.

Desktop

The famous Apple desktop isn't left untouched by Mac OS X. Although on the surface it looks very different, looks can be deceiving. The versions of Aqua that were first displayed during Apple's Mac OS X previews showed a clear desktop, without even a disk icon to clutter the landscape. Apple answered the call of devoted Mac users and has restored much of the desktop behavior of previous versions of the Mac OS. As Mac OS X matures, even more of the older features are expected to return in full force.

Panther vs. Jaguar

This book covers Panther (Mac OS X 10.3), which first appeared in October, 2003. With this new release, Apple has incorporated 150 new features. Some of these features are hidden away and some are very obvious and beautiful to look at. As you'll see shortly, many of these features will actually make you more productive.

NOTE: Just to drive the point home, MacAddict writer Deborah Shadovitz concluded, in the January, 2004 issue, that the various performance boosting features in Panther could save you up to $7,680 per year. This is more than enough to buy Apple's most expensive Power Mac, a great monitor, and leave enough change for a new iBook or PowerBook. I won't confirm the math, but her point is an interesting slant on what Panther might do for you.

If you gave up on earlier versions of Mac OS X because of performance or the lack of cherished features from the Classic Mac OS, Panther may make you reconsider the new operating system. Here are some of the most significant changes that have been added since the release of Jaguar (and I'm only covering the basics here):

- *Audio and videoconferencing*—Apple's latest instant messaging client, iChat AV, (see Figure 1.8) can be used to exchange messages with members of AOL, CompuServe, users of AOL Instant Messenger, subscribers to Apple's .Mac Web services, and users of your local network. In addition, if you have a broadband hookup to the Internet and a FireWire-based camera, such as Apple's iSight, you can communicate via audio or video to fellow iChat users with similar setups.

Figure 1.8   Apple's iChat instant messaging client can put text in fancy balloons or as simple text blocks. It can also be used for audio and video chats.

- *Exposé*—If you open lots of applications on your Mac, you are probably plagued by screen clutter. Exposé lets you display all open windows, or just those open in a single application, in a reduced size, leaving them a click away from action. You can also push them aside to easily access the contents of your desktop. This feature exploits the power of the Quartz imaging technology, but it still functions pretty well on the slowest Macs that support Panther.

- *Enhanced cross-platform networking*—Apple's built-in SMB/CIFS (SAMBA) software now provides near seamless browsing of Windows file shares, access to your Microsoft Exchange Inbox, and makes the Mac readily available for easy networking via a Windows PC. New for Panther is also the ability to browse shares from the Finder and share printers in either direction, which may reduce the need for a third-party program to accomplish this task.

- *Fast User Switching*—Apple sometimes "borrows" a feature from the Windows platform, but when they do, they always add an element of spit and polish. In the case of Fast User Switching, this feature allows another user to jump to his or her account on your computer, but it leaves your working programs intact, so you can get back to work almost instantaneously without enduring a regular login process. On Macs that support Quartz Extreme, you'll even see a rotating 3D cube heralding the switchover.

- *Faxing*—You no longer need to depend on a third-party program to use your Mac's modem as a fax machine. Panther's built-in fax drivers are integrated with the Print dialog box. A simple setup panel in System Preferences can be used to configure your Mac to receive, store, e-mail, and print the faxes you receive.

- *FileVault*—Security is improved with Panther. You can now encrypt the files in your Home directory, using the latest 128-bit security measures. Once the feature is engaged, your files are secured on the fly when saved. This feature is tailor-made for a work environment, or where different users must work on your Mac.

- *Font Book*—The new tool for font management, Font Book (see Figure 1.9) provides smooth installation, activation and deactivation of your fonts, and fast, interactive font previews. While it may not replace some of the third-party font programs, such as Alsoft's MasterJuggler, Extensis Suitcase, or Insider Software's FontAgent Pro, Font Book will get the job done for most users.

- *New Finder Interface*—The Panther Finder sports a brushed metal interface and includes a Sidebar to list mounted disks, network shares, and frequently used folders. It provides a more user-centric view of the contents of a drive. It's also noticeably faster than previous versions, especially when you need to navigate through folders with hundreds of files inside. The new Action icon mirrors, Apple's context menus feature for speedier access and Finder labels, have returned.

- *Sherlock 3.6*—Apple's Internet search tool comes with a large number of third-party "channels" to access Web content. It's also faster than the version that shipped with Jaguar.

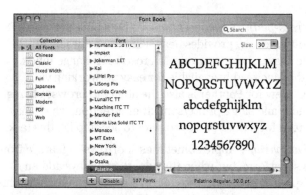

Figure 1.9   Font Book lets you bring a little organization to the Mac OS font management situation.

- *Simplified System Preferences*—The System Preferences application, used to adjust all sorts of settings for your Mac, has been enhanced to make it easier to use. For example, the Login Items pane is now part of an expanded Accounts panel. A new Print & Fax panel is used to configure your printers and set up your Mac to receive faxes.

- *Journaled file system*—This feature stores drive changes in a database, which makes recovery to the last saved state a simple process in the event of a crash or the need for a forced restart. It can also reduce the possibility of drive directory problems.

- *Mail's Smarter junk e-mail filtering*—The bane of every PC user's experience is spam. Apple's update to its Mail application includes a more powerful e-mail filter, extending the features of the one that first premiered in Jaguar, which checks the contents of a message, not just the subject line, for evidence of spam. Apple has also added threading and loads of convenience features to Mail. I'll cover these features in more detail in Chapter 21.

NOTE: Mail and Address Book have also been updated to work with Microsoft Exchange Server installations to provide cross-platform communications in corporate environments. If you need to synchronize your corporate calendars and schedules, however, you'll need an Exchange compatible client, such as Microsoft Entourage X.

- *More beneath the surface*—Apple touts over 150 features so I've only covered the highlights here. As you read through this book, you'll learn about all the important features in full detail. In most cases, you'll also see a healthy performance boost, because Apple has spent a lot of time optimizing key elements of the system to make them run more efficiently. If you have been on the fence about upgrading, Panther may be sufficient reason for you to finally make the switch.

Are You Ready for Panther?

If you're ready to take the plunge into a whole new world of ultra-reliable, speedy Macintosh computing, you should make sure that your Mac is ready for the upgrade.

Here are some points to consider when moving to Panther:

- *System requirements*—Panther will work on any Apple Macintosh computer that shipped with a PowerPC G3, G4, or G5 CPU so long as it includes built-in USB. This includes even the original Bondi Blue iMac. However, the beige-colored G3 and some of the earlier versions of the PowerBook G3 are excluded because of lack of a built-in USB port—add-ons don't count, unfortunately. In addition, Apple specifies a minimum of 128MB of RAM. However, this is a minimum, and Panther really does work better if you have 256MB of RAM or greater. My feeling is that 512MB is the sweet spot, after which you only get performance gains if you use resource hungry programs, such as Adobe Photoshop CS. You'll also want to allow 3GB of disk storage space for the installation.

NOTE: *Panther does not include a copy of Mac OS 9. If you need a copy, you can use the "Proof of Purchase" coupon that comes with the package to order a copy at low cost using Apple's "Up-to-Date" program at its Web site.*

TIP: *If you have a very large hard drive, you might want to consider making a separate partition for Panther. Check the ReadMe file that comes with Panther to find out about any partition limits, such as putting it on the first 8GB of a drive.*

- *Peripheral compatibility*—If your Mac has a non-Apple expansion card of any sort, such as a graphic card, SCSI accelerator card, or video capture card, contact the manufacturer about driver software that might be required for full compatibility with Panther. Although the Classic feature lets you run older Mac software, it doesn't provide the hardware-level support you need for unsupported hardware.

- *Software compatibility*—Most older programs should run fine in the Classic mode under Panther. You should contact the publishers directly, however, to be sure that your programs will run without a hitch. System extensions, for example, are not part of the Mac OS X architecture but might, within limits, work under Classic. However, programs that directly access the hardware, such as a CD writing program or hard disk formatter, will need an update to work properly—more than likely a Carbon version that's tuned to recognize Apple's updated hardware driver model.

- *Printer and serial devices*—Regular PostScript laser printers should work well under Panther. Other printers, especially ink jets, will need driver updates to function with the new OS. Printer drivers from such major companies as Canon, Epson, HP, and Lexmark are included with Panther. In addition, Gimp-Print drivers, a third-party set of printer software, can support hundreds of devices, including older models where the manufacturers have stopped producing driver updates. As far as other peripherals are concerned, in each case, you'll need to check with the manufacturer about compatibility. Apple Computer has provided tools to help developers make its products Mac OS X– aware, but how quickly this is done depends on each particular company, its priorities, and the amount of work required.

NOTE: Even though Panther is the fourth major release of Mac OS X, some older peripherals are still awaiting a driver update to be compatible. At this point, you might want to consider other options, rather than wait for the end of the rainbow.

WARNING! Apple doesn't officially support Macs or Mac OS clones upgraded from older PowerPC CPUs to G3s or G4s. If you decide to take the risk anyway, you might be able to install Panther on one of these unsupported models, and the G3 Macs that don't have USB. It would require use of a shareware application, XPostFacto, which "tricks" the Panther installer into working on those computers. (I'll discuss this in more detail in Chapter 2.) If you take this route, don't depend on Apple for support. Also be prepared to make a full backup of your data, in case you run into a disk-related problem or want to return to your previous Mac OS version. Some of the companies that make G3 and G4 upgrades promise Mac OS X support, but it doesn't come with Apple's blessings. You will have to depend on those companies to provide help if something goes wrong when you use their products.

Upgrading to Panther

In Brief

You now should be ready to install Panther (if you haven't already). As you learned in the previous chapter, Panther is much superior to the older generation of the Mac OS. Panther also really offers a lot over previous versions of OS X, including Jaguar. If anything, Panther has more in common with high-end workstations that are used to power Web and network servers around the world.

Don't be put off by all this sophistication, however. Despite the complexity of the underlying software, Apple has gone the extra mile to simplify installation. But don't be lulled into a sense of complacency by the ease of the process. A lot of complicated things will happen very quickly when you install the new operating system. During that time, the Panther installer will copy tens of thousands of new files to your Macintosh. It's not something to take lightly, and you will want to take a few precautions to make the process as seamless as possible.

Preparing for Panther

Before you attempt to install Panther, you should make sure that your Mac is ready for the installation. First, you should review Chapter 1 to see if your Mac can run the new operating system.

WARNING! *Take the warnings about attempting an installation on unsupported hardware very seriously. If you want to take a chance, you should use Ryan Rempel's XPostFacto tool. This software provides a highly-successful method of performing such an installation, although there are a few limitations, depending on which hardware you're using. You can find the latest version of this shareware application at http:// eshop.macsales.com/OSXCenter/XPostFacto framework.cfm?page=XPostFacto.html. If you try this type of installation, consider installing Panther on a secondary machine, one you don't use for work or that contains important files you need for your job. You'll learn the basics of how such an installation works at the end of this chapter, which was prepared with Ryan's assistance.*

NOTE: *If you install Panther on an unsupported Mac, be guided by the instructions provided with the software you use, which are apt to change as Panther itself is updated. The information in this chapter assumes you will be doing your installation on a Mac that is officially supported by Apple for Panther.*

In the following pages, I will cover the basics of preparing for a few types of installations. Once you're ready, proceed to the "Immediate Solutions" section for step-by-step instructions that walk you through the entire installation process and let you know what to expect along the way.

Make Sure You Have Mac OS 9.1 or Later for Classic Applications

There are literally thousands of Mac OS X applications, including the ones produced by major publishers. Unfortunately, a fair number of the Mac OS programs you'll be running may be of the older Classic variety. Therefore, you'll need an installed copy of Mac OS 9 on your Mac. Basically, any Mac made since 1999 has 9.1 or later installed (even the models that no longer boot under the older operating system). You can keep your older Mac operating system version on the same disk volume as Mac OS X, just the way it's done on your new Mac. If you choose to install it on a separate partition, be guided by the instructions later in this chapter in the section "Panther: Hardware-Related Issues."

NOTE: If you have Mac OS 9.1 installed, you aren't forced to upgrade to a later version for Classic to function. But the later versions of Mac OS 9 are more stable and offer better performance in the Classic environment, so you'll want to consider the upgrade seriously. In addition, Panther will "suggest" you upgrade to a later version of Mac OS 9 the first time Classic runs. Panther users can order a copy from Apple at a special upgrade price.

Check Your Hard Drive

During the installation process, the Panther Installer has a lot of work to do. Whereas older versions of the Mac operating system generally consisted of hundreds of files, this time literally thousands of files (taking up over two gigabytes of storage space) are required. This installation work is done behind the scenes in minutes, which means your Mac and its disk storage system will be taxed to the limit to keep up.

As a result, you should make sure that the target drive for your computer is working properly. Fortunately, this isn't hard to accomplish. Apple provides a free hard drive diagnostic and repair utility—Disk First Aid (see Figure 2.1)—in the Utilities folder of every Mac. This program, although not as full-featured as the commercial alternatives, should be able to detect and repair basic drive directory problems. Although the Panther Installer will be able to check your drive during the setup process, you should consider running an extra verification for your piece of mind.

2. Upgrading to Panther

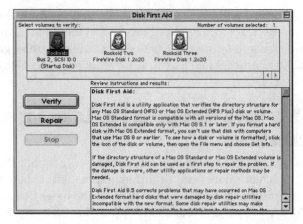

Figure 2.1   The best part of Disk First Aid is that it's free with every new Mac and included with every Panther installation.

NOTE: If you are upgrading from a previous version of Mac OS X, you'll want to run Disk Utility from the Panther installation disk. I'll cover how it's done in this chapter.

If you want to make doubly sure that your drive is in tip-top shape, you may want to look at one of these commercial alternatives:

- *Norton Utilities*—This is the oldest existing hard drive utility package. You will need to use the installation CD that comes with this product (or run it from another drive) for the most effective diagnosis and repair. Norton Utilities is also included as part of Norton SystemWorks (shown in Figure 2.2).

- *TechTool Pro 4*—MicroMat's upstart utility application (see Figure 2.3) performs many of the same tasks as Norton Utilities. In addition it can run an extensive set of hardware checks on your Macintosh, including several levels of RAM tests. The most interesting feature of TechTool Pro is eDrive, a feature that creates, in software, a special partition on your drive containing the application. You don't need to reformat your drive as you'd have to do with a disk formatting utility. The great part of the eDrive feature is that you don't need a separate CD or another drive to boot from to launch TechTool Pro. Just launch the program and set it to restart from your eDrive and you're ready to roll.

NOTE: A limited-feature version of TechTool Pro—TechTool Deluxe—is provided under Apple's AppleCare extended service policy. However, this version of the program doesn't offer disk drive maintenance, nor does it offer virus protection.

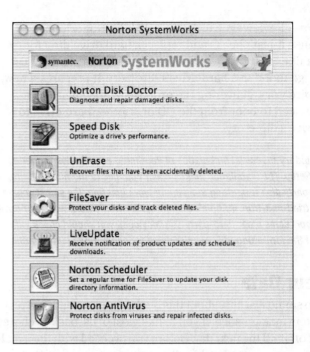

Figure 2.2   Norton SystemWorks includes disk diagnosis and virus
protection as part of its bag of tricks.

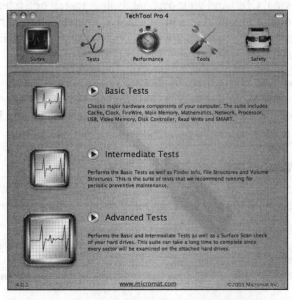

Figure 2.3   You can use TechTool Pro 4 to check a hard drive for directory
damage prior to the Panther installation.

- *DiskWarrior*—Reviewers call Alsoft's DiskWarrior a "one-trick pony" because it just checks and replaces hard drive directories. However, it does that task extraordinarily well. Rather than just fixing damage found in a hard drive's directory, it prepares a new, optimized directory, delivering the promise of speedier performance. You need to boot from the CD or another hard drive to rebuild a drive's directory.

WARNING! You should try to restrict installation of Panther to a hard drive formatted with Apple's Drive Setup. The installation makes major changes to the file structure, and although third-party disk formatting tools might work just fine, the safest course is to stick with the tried-and-true. If Apple's disk formatter won't work with your drive (and it doesn't support some older third-party SCSI devices), you should check with the manufacturer of the formatting utility you're using for compatibility information.

Back Up Your Data

I don't want to sound alarmist about this but backups should be a regular part of system maintenance. If you're like most of us, backup chores tend to be put off until the next day. Before you proceed with the installation instructions presented in this chapter it is super-critical that you back up your data. The most effective backup is a complete one that back ups all your data. If you have backups of all your applications (such as the original CDs) and your original System Install or System Restore optical discs for your Mac, you can, as a time-saver, restrict the backup to the documents you've created with your software, along with critical program settings, such as your Internet preferences.

However, having your entire drive backed up on a single set of disks is far more convenient, and it makes the process of restoring your files much easier. I'll cover the subject of backups in more detail in Chapter 16.

Panther Hardware-Related Issues

You should consider some hardware issues and strategy suggestions before proceeding with the installation. Doing so will avoid problems and confusing performance later on.

NOTE: This information is based on the release notes for Panther (Mac OS X 10.3). As Apple updates its operating system, some of the limitations are apt to be addressed and perhaps new ones will appear.

Here's a list of primary concerns:

- *Firmware*—You should make sure the firmware is current. All the Macs officially supported by Apple for Panther installation have firmware (a boot ROM) that can be upgraded by software. Because the updates enhance the boot process and stability of your Mac, you'll want to stay current for the best experience with your new operating system. The first Panther installer CD includes a selection of firmware updates for various Macs, but you'll also want to check Apple's support Web site (**www.info.apple.com/support/downloads.html**) to be sure that the firmware on your computer is up to date.

WARNING! *Take this requirement seriously: Don't assume the Panther Installer is perfect even though it should alert you about incompatible firmware. On some of the early slot-load iMacs, for example, trying to install Panther can result in loss of video. The video can come back, but getting the video back is a tricky process.*

- *Rev A through D iMac (those with pop-up CD trays)*—For these vintage iMacs, if you choose to divide your hard drive into multiple partitions or volumes, make sure that the Panther installation is performed on the first 8GB of the drive (it will appear first in your list of available volumes in the Panther installer). Fortunately, the Installer will usually put up a warning message if the Mac has the wrong drive partitioning scheme.

NOTE: *You could install Panther on a drive with a single partition and have it coexist with Mac OS 9.2.2. In fact, Apple ships all its new Macs this way. Partitioning a drive can be done for protection, as a way to start your Mac if the other partition goes down, or just to more easily organize the contents of your drive. However, it's not required.*

- *FireWire and USB drives*—Most FireWire drives will work fine under Panther. However, don't think of using a standard USB (1.1) device, even if the installation takes, because it is just too slow. Many Macs now also ship with USB 2.0, and performance should be close to that of the original, or FireWire 400, standard.

WARNING! *Apple and Oxford Semiconductor identified a problem with firmware used on some FireWire 800 drives that could cause loss of data under Panther. It actually happened to me once, so take the warning seriously. Although Apple fixed its share of the burden, beginning with the 10.3.1 update, you will also want to update your drive's firmware as well. You'll want to check with the drive maker's Web site for details and a downloadable updater. The affected firmware for the Oxford 922 bridge chip-set is 1.02 or earlier. Unfortunately, you can't easily detect this version using Apple's System Profiler. If you have a newer drive it should be okay because the vulnerable drives pretty much all shipped before the winter of 2003. However, it doesn't hurt to confirm that fact with the manufacturer.*

- *Third-party SCSI cards*—If you can't boot your Mac after Panther is installed, place a drive or terminator on one of the ports of your third-party SCSI card.

WARNING! Check your card maker's support Web site for information about compatibility between your SCSI card and Panther. You may need to upgrade software, flash ROM, or a ROM chip, or perhaps even replace the card to avoid trouble with your new operating system. For example, Adaptec is not supporting many of its older cards with Mac OS X.

- *AirPort and AirPort Extreme*—Apple's fancy wireless networking hardware, based on the 802.11b or 802.11g Wi-Fi standards, works fine under Panther. If you're using a third-party 802.11b wireless networking card, such as the Asante AeroLAN or the Farallon (now Proxim) SkyLINE, check with the manufacturer about updated drivers for Panther. Central access points, which are similar to the AirPort Base Station, are configured via a browser interface and should work well with Panther.

NOTE: The latest versions of Apple's AirPort software supports a number of third-party Wi-Fi cards but the support isn't official. The best thing to do is try the software you have and see if it works. If it doesn't, you'll want to check with the manufacturer for updates.

- *Third-party graphics cards*—If you have a Mac card from ATI and NVIDIA, you should be okay, though you might need an update for an earlier ATI product. Officially, no other graphic cards are supported, so don't be surprised if you run into difficulty. Even if you do get a usable picture, hardware acceleration and OpenGL support may not be available and you'll be disappointed with performance. Fortunately, ATI has some low-cost Mac products that serve as useful replacements if you run into any difficulty here.

- *Processor upgrade cards*—Again, it's the responsibility of the product manufacturers to make a processor card function. Some of these products use special software to activate a G3's or G4's backside cache. Even if they worked, there might be a severe performance penalty. However, most existing products from such makers as PowerLogix, Sonnet Technology, and XLR8 work fine under Panther, although software updates may be necessary. In addition, the Sonnet processor cards designed for the Blue & White Power Mac G3 line do not require software.

WARNING! Let me remind you that Apple's official support policy for Panther requires a Mac that shipped with a G3, G4, or G5 processor and built-in USB. While you can add processor and USB upgrades to older Macs, the Panther Installer won't care unless you use an unsupported solution such as XPostFacto.

Immediate Solutions

Final Steps for Installation

Before you install Panther, you'll need to make a few decisions about how to proceed:

- *Determine where to install*—You can install Panther on the same drive partition as Mac OS 9 or on a separate partition. Be guided by the instructions in the previous section about partitioning a hard drive supporting hard drives on certain Macs. If you plan to install Panther on a separate partition, the Panther Installer can handle the job of erasing the partition for you.

- *Install Mac OS 9.2 or later*—If you need to run Classic applications, you should install the Classic system first before proceeding with Panther. That way, if something goes wrong with the Panther installation, you can still return to the older operating system to remove Panther files or just to use your Mac until you decide to reinstall the new system. A copy of the installation CD is available at a special "Up-To-Date" price directly from Apple for Panther users.

- *Copy Internet and networking setups*—During the installation of Panther, you'll need to enter information manually to get access to a local network or the Internet. This information is not cataloged during the Panther installation process, unless you're updating from a previous version of Mac OS X. If you were running Mac OS 9, you'll then need to copy all these settings from the Modem, Internet (see Figure 2.4), Remote Access, and TCP/IP control panels.

NOTE: *If you are an EarthLink member, you can use the Mac OS X Setup Assistant, which appears right after the installation of Panther, to pick up your account settings. If you are upgrading from an older version of Mac OS X, you can pick up the previous settings by a simple upgrade installation or by one of the clean install options I'll detail in the next section. AOL, MSN, and United Online (Juno and NetZero) members can simply install the Mac OS X version of the software for these services.*

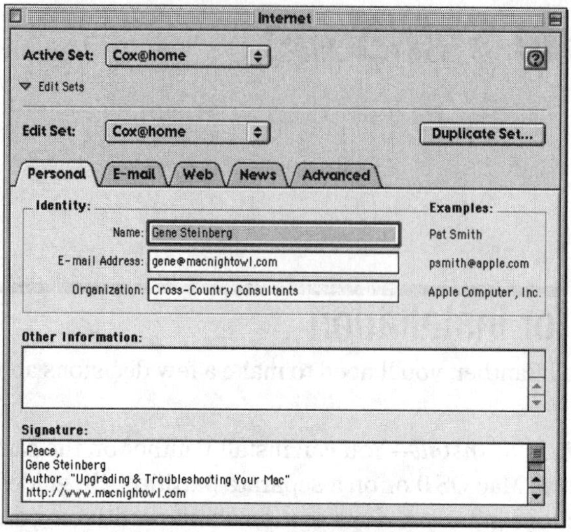

Figure 2.4   The Classic Internet Control Panel has several tabs you need to check to pick up all your configuration information.

TIP: You can quickly capture the Internet and networking settings with a screenshot. To take a picture of just the Control Panel window (rather than the entire screen), press Command+Shift+4+Caps Lock. Then, click on the window that you want to capture to complete the action. You'll hear the sound of a shutter clicking in confirmation. Each file will be identified by the name Picture plus the number (1, 2, and so on). You can then open these files in SimpleText and print them so you'll have a copy to refer to when needed for Mac OS X's Setup Assistant.

Installing Panther

These instructions will take you through the entire installation process, including how to restart your computer after the contents of the first CD have been loaded:

NOTE: These instructions are based on the installer screens used for Mac OS X 10.3. As the operating system is updated, the setup dialog boxes may change, but your basic choices will be essentially the same as described here.

---

1. Insert Disc 1 from your Mac OS X 10.3 upgrade package into your Mac's drive.

NOTE: What are the two other CDs used for? They contain additional system software and applications for Panther and will be used after the first stage of the setup process is complete. Depending on your installation options, you may only need Disc 2, but some setups will require Disc 3. The Installer will let you know with an onscreen message before it begins, so you can get everything ready.

2. Restart your Mac, holding down the C key, so that it boots from the CD. After you restart, the Installer will take several minutes to begin, so be patient. During each step of the process, you'll have to click a button or click a checkbox or pop-up menu to make a choice before proceeding. Therefore, read the onscreen instructions carefully in case they've changed from those present when this book was written.

NOTE: If you just double-click the Installer after the CD mounts, it will put up a prompt that lets you click the Restart button to automatically restart from the Installer CD. There's no other way to do the installation.

3. The first screen that appears, labeled Select Language, allows you to select the default language kit used for the installation. You're not restricted to English. After you've made your selection, click Continue to proceed. As you set up installer options, you'll see a Go Back screen that allows you to recheck settings. You can back out at anytime until you actually click Install on the final screen.

4. Before you actually go through the installation, you should choose Disk Utility from the Installer screen. This will allow you to give your hard drive one final diagnostic run before you install Panther. It is better to be safe than sorry. When you launch Disk Utility, you'll see the window shown in Figure 2.5.

5. Select the name of the target drive, the one which you plan to install Panther, and select Repair Disk. If you have several drives or partitions on your Mac, I suggest you select all of them before running the repair operation.

NOTE: If the repair process reveals problems with any of your drives, keep running the utility until you get a clean bill of health. If you don't clear up the trouble, quit the Installer and run a third-party disk repair utility before trying to install Panther. Any problems now could damage data on your drive if you don't first fix the problems.

6. Next, select just your destination drive, and click Repair Disk Permissions. Since Panther sets up a complicated arrangement

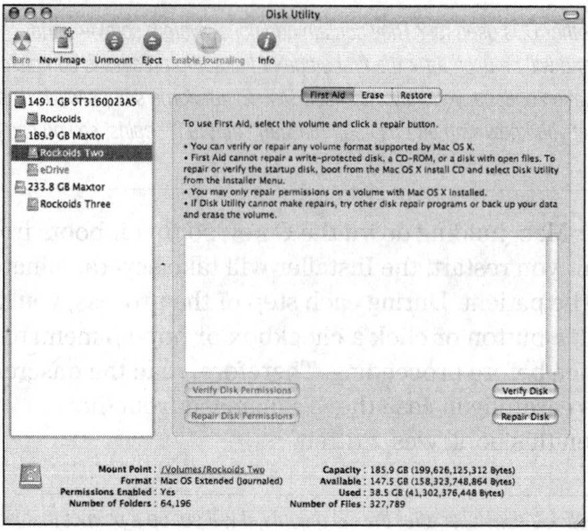

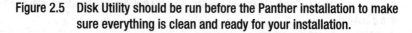

Figure 2.5   Disk Utility should be run before the Panther installation to make sure everything is clean and ready for your installation.

of read and write privileges for the installed files, anything that is set improperly may cause trouble later on.

7. When you're finished, quit Disk Utility, which will return you to the main Installer screen, where you'll continue the setup process.

NOTE: *Because the Panther Installer takes over a Mac during the setup process, I could not capture illustrations of the process in the usual way, except for one picture Apple gave me when I begged them for it. If you follow the steps precisely as described, however, you'll get through the process like a champ.*

---

8. The Welcome to the Mac OS X Installer screen appears. All you'll find here is a message telling you to get ready for the main event. Click Continue to move on to the next step in the process.

9. The Important Information screen appears next. You should consult this information to see if you must consider any additional factors before proceeding with the installation, or whether something in your setup might conspire to hurt the process. Spend a few moments reading this document. If it looks like you might have a problem, you can back out here and quit the Installer to restart; then, just hold down the mouse key to eject the CD and you'll reboot under your previous version of the Mac OS. If everything looks okay, click Continue to proceed, or click Go Back to review the previous screen.

10. The next screen shows the License for Mac OS X 10.3 Panther. This is a fairly standard agreement covering Panther. Click Continue after reviewing the information. You'll see a dialog box in which you must click the Agree button and accept the agreement to continue with the installation; if you click Disagree, you'll end the process then and there. You have no other choice. Click Agree to continue.

11. The Select A Destination screen appears, showing the available drive volumes that can support a Panther install. Click the icon representing the drive on which you want to place Panther. The standard installation process will install a fresh copy of Mac OS X 10.3 or upgrade your existing installation, but you have other options worth checking, especially if you have an older Mac OS X version already present on your Mac. To see the choices, click the Options button, which gives you the following alternatives (as shown in Figure 2.6):

* *Upgrade Mac OS X*—As it says, this option will simply replace all the updated components of your existing Mac OS X installation with the new versions. Under most circumstances, this choice should work fine. However, if you have

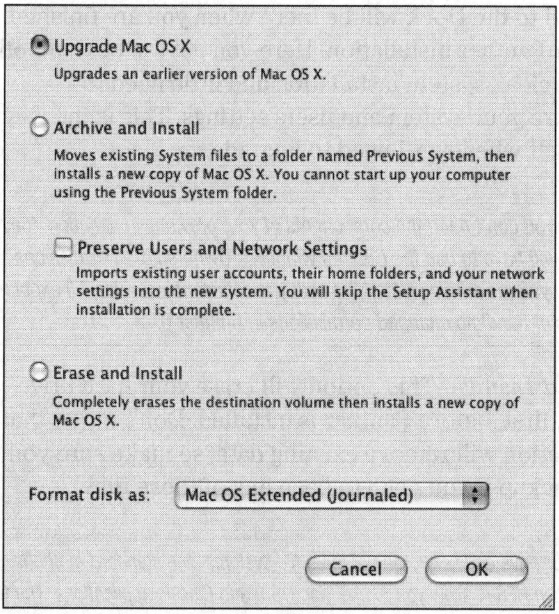

Figure 2.6   Pick the installation option you prefer.

run into trouble with a previous Mac OS X setup, you will probably want to consider the next option.

- *Archive and Install*—This is the Mac OS X equivalent of the clean installation. All your existing Mac OS X system files will be placed within a folder labeled Previous System and your new system will be installed fresh and clean. You'll have to reenter all your user settings, including your ISP access information, in the Mac OS X Setup Assistant. By leaving the old system around, you can access such things as third-party peripheral drivers that may not have been picked up by the new installation, although it's better to install them from scratch.

NOTE: Sorry, once the older system is archived, you cannot boot from it again, even if you move the files to their original locations. This doesn't work the same as it does when you do a clean install under Mac OS 9.

- *Preserve Users and Network Settings*—This is the most convenient clean installation because it picks up virtually all of your users and network settings, including application preferences and Internet configurations. Even the extra items you added to the Dock will be there when you are finished with your Panther installation. Here you get the best of both worlds: a clean system installation and little need to reconfigure your system and users settings. This is the way I do it myself whenever I need to upgrade my Macs.

TIP: When you are sure you don't need the components of your previous installation, they can be deleted but you will have to use the Get Info window's Ownership & Permissions screens to give you, as systems administrator, the ability to remove those files. I'll explain more about the process of handling changed permissions in Chapter 6.

- *Erase and Install*—This option will erase your hard drive partition, first, before Panther is installed. Don't forget that this operation will remove existing data, so make sure you have a backup if you need to keep any of those files.

NOTE: You can erase your drive and set up one of three file systems. The standard methods, HFS+ (Journaled) and plain HFS+, allow you to use Mac OS 9 and Classic applications. The third, UFS (for Unix File System), is best for UNIX-based application development and is otherwise not really necessary. I recommend HFS+ (Journaled) because it sets up a database system that tracks changes to your drive and minimizes the possibility of data loss or drive directory damage in the event of a system crash.

WARNING! *Formatting a hard drive can be a destructive process. If you select that option, all the data on the selected volume will be wiped out with little or no chance of recovery. Be certain that this is the decision you want to make. You can't go back once you format a drive.*

TIP: *If you cannot locate the correct startup volume on the Select A Destination screen, go to the Installer application window and quit the Installer so you can cancel the process and reboot your Mac. You should then verify that the drive on which you want to install Panther is indeed available. After everything has been rechecked, you can attempt installation again by restarting from the CD.*

12. After you click Continue, the Install screen appears. If you click Customize, you'll see a dialog box where you can remove some of the Panther installer components to save drive space, such as the extra printer drivers, applications, and unused foreign language kits. Usually it's best just to leave well enough alone, unless you are really tight on disk space, in which case you may want to consider putting Panther on a larger drive or drive partition if one is available.

NOTE: *If you plan on using Apple's X11 software to run Unix applications designed to work in that windowing environment, you should choose that option here for convenience. You can run the installer file directly (it's on Disc 3) later on, but I prefer to get everything out of the way at once, and maybe you'll agree with me.*

Once you click Install, you'll see a progress Install Software screen, where you'll observe the entire process, as various components of Panther are placed on your Mac's drive. You should expect the first part of the installation to take anywhere from 30 minutes to an hour, depending on the speed of your Mac's processor, the speed of your CD (or DVD) drive, and the speed of your hard drive. The time estimate in the progress bar will vary considerably until it settles down about halfway through he process. When the installation of the contents of CD 1 is complete, your Mac will restart automatically under its new operating system version, but you'll have more to do.

After the restart, an Additional Software screen will appear and your CD will be ejected. Put Disk 2 in the drive, and, in a short time, installation will resume. Depending on your installation choices, you may also encounter a request for Disk 3, but in most cases you won't. Once the process is over, you'll see a brief multimedia presentation, and you'll be guided through the Setup Assistant, where you'll be asked to make some very basic system settings to get Panther up and running to your satisfaction. These steps include registering your copy of Panther, optionally registering Apple's iTools feature, plus setting up your Mac for Internet access. I cover these and other settings in Chapter 3.

NOTE: If you opted for an upgrade installation or a clean installation in which you choose the Preserve Users and Network Settings option, you may not see a Setup Assistant, as all the settings it requests will already be present and accounted for. If you do see the Setup Assistant, it'll only ask you for your registration information and nothing else.

Related solutions:	Found on page:
Configuring the Setup Assistant	42
Configuring System Preferences Under Panther	47

Notes on Performing an Unsupported Installation

It is possible to install Panther on a computer that it wasn't designed to run on. This process requires the clever efforts of third-party programmers who know their UNIX and have managed to, shall we say, induce the Installer to run.

One method that has proven successful for thousands of Mac users is Ryan Rampel's XPostFacto, which is being distributed by Other World Computing, a large Mac retailer. Although the program is free, the author requests a $10 goodwill donation if you get it to work. When you download the software, you'll receive plenty of documentation that takes you through the process but I want to cover a few of the basics here, so you know what you're getting into:

- *Consider a new or refurbished Mac*—The easiest thing to do is buy a Mac that can run Panther successfully without help. But if you have a large investment in a system and memory and want to save some cash, an unsupported installation is worth trying, with appropriate care.

- *Check the instructions before proceeding*—At the time this book was written, XPostFacto only worked on a Mac with a G3 or G4 processor upgrade, although the author was working on a way to get Macs with the original 603 or 604 processors to accept the Panther installation. Also bear in mind, that performance on these older processors is apt to be rather slow anyway, so you may not want to proceed without a faster processor.

- *Expect less stable performance than a supported installation—* Some basic functions, such as the Sleep mode, may not be supported. The third-party peripheral cards that don't officially work under Panther will not operate under an unsupported installation either. So if you have a SCSI scanner or another older peripheral that is not likely to be upgraded for Panther, expect to have to restart under Mac OS 9 from time to time.

- *Backup your files*—You should do it anyway, and I discuss the process in more detail in Chapter 16. But if something goes wrong that affects your files, you'll need to consider reformatting the drive and starting over.

- *Some components won't run*—Although there is an unofficial driver for floppies from **www.darwin-development.org/floppy/**, there's no standard support for such drives, unless installed as a USB peripheral. In addition, not all serial modems will run, so you'll want to check the latest documentation from Ryan on supported devices.

- *What does it involve?*—In order to induce the Panther Installer to work on an unsupported Mac, XPostFacto places some kernel extensions on the drive on which you want to install Panther, plus a modified version of BootX, which allows your Mac to restart with the Panther Installer and put Mac Panther on that computer.

WARNING! *Since special files are required for Panther to be installed, do not erase the drive after running XPostFacto on it.*

If you are willing to take the chance after knowing the risks, examine the instructions for XPostFacto or any other unsupported installation utility you try very carefully, especially the troubleshooting information. While it does indeed work for many, don't be surprised if your specific installation doesn't take. At worst, consider the process a useful learning experience and perhaps a good incentive to acquire that new Mac you've been lusting after.

Chapter 3

Panther
User Preferences

In Brief

Once your Mac OS X installation hits the finish line, you'll be ready to take the setup process to the next level. As soon as the new Mac desktop appears, you'll be introduced to a pleasant multimedia presentation, providing a musical introduction to the new operating system, followed by the appearance of Apple's Setup Assistant. You use the Setup Assistant to register Mac OS X with Apple, and then configure a basic set of user and networking settings for Mac OS X.

As is typical of a Unix-based operating system, Mac OS X is designed for multiple users, which allows each person who works on the Mac to have a separate user account and a different level of access. If you find the concept a little strange, consider this: In almost every installation, more than one person is using a Mac. Even in a home setup, the family computer may be used by parents and children, each of whom may have a different set of requirements—and an equally diverse need to restrict certain elements of user access. (I cover the subject of configuring your Mac to work in such an environment in much more detail in Chapter 6.)

NOTE: There's an exception to this rule. If you opted for an upgrade installation or used the "archive" or clean install option that picked up your previous network and users settings, the Setup Assistant will be bypassed, except for the registration steps, and you'll be greeted with the Panther Finder shortly after the installation process is over.

This chapter first discusses the preference settings you'll make right after installing Panther using the Setup Assistant. In large part, they cover access to your Mac by you as administrator of your system. You'll also configure basic network setups, including your Mac's network name and various types of Internet access. In addition, time zone adjustments are necessary so that your Mac will put the correct time on your documents and email messages.

NOTE: Did I say administrator? Yes, even if you are using your Mac at home and you will be the only person to work on the computer, you will still need to install new software, including Panther updates from Apple. So you're elected as the administrator or chief user of your Mac.

Control Panel Settings: A Mixture of the Old and New

After you've completed the basic setups, you can use your Mac and your favorite programs without making a single change. However, to get the optimum performance from your computer, you'll also want to tackle the preference panels. Rather than offer each item as a separate control panel, as was the case with the Classic Mac OS, Mac OS X merges them all into a single System Preferences application. This arrangement greatly simplifies the setup process, because you don't have to hunt down multiple applications from the Control Panel's submenu in the Apple menu or directly from that folder to enter the settings you want. For convenience, the preference panels are divided into four distinct categories: Personal, Hardware, Internet & Network, and System.

If you add extra preference modules to add custom features to your Mac, you'll find them lodged in a fifth category, called "Other."

NOTE: *Although the Apple menu is still present, it is a rather different breed from the one with which you're familiar from the Classic Mac OS. For one thing, it replaces the functions of the Finder's Special menu, and it adds a few elements from the original version. I cover that subject in more detail in Chapter 4.*

In some ways, Mac OS X's design is a throwback to the way system setups existed under older versions of the Mac operating system prior to System 7. Even though control panels were separate items then, they all displayed in a single window. Apple has apparently taken the simplicity of this design to heart, except for organizing the icons in a horizontal Finder-like display rather than the vertical array of icons you clicked to get to a particular setting.

Click an icon just once to activate the labeled function, which will launch essentially as a separate application within the Preferences window. You'll see how the System Preferences application is set up in the "Immediate Solutions" section of this chapter.

Before I discuss the various preference settings and the ones you'll probably want to configure, let's look at some new Finder-level features of Panther that you'll need to work with. The rest are explained in Chapter 4. Unlike previous Mac OS versions, you don't click a square box to close, minimize, or maximize Finder windows. Instead, three separate traffic-light-colored buttons mounted at the left provide these functions:

- *Red ("X" symbol)*—Close the window. Clicking this button may or may not quit the application (in most cases, it won't).

- *Yellow ("–" symbol)*—Minimize the window. When you click this button, the window is collapsed and appears as an icon on the Dock.

- *Green ("+" symbol)*—Maximize the window. This command expands the window to the largest size necessary to encompass its contents, limited only by the size of your Mac's display.

NOTE: *When you pass your mouse over any of these buttons, you'll see a symbol inside representing its function. If you choose the Graphite interface as an Appearance preference, as described in the "Setting General Preferences" section later in this chapter, the button colors will all switch to the same color (graphite), but the symbols will still appear whenever the mouse is brought to the vicinity of these buttons. There are also some third-party "theme" enhancers for Panther that you can use to make further alterations of the interface. Some even offer a Windows-style motif, if that's what you want.*

If you are new to Mac OS X, you'll notice that you no longer quit an application from the File menu (unless the publisher of that application defied convention, of course). Apple Computer decided to move that function to the Application menu (the one in bold at the left end of the menu bar, next to the Apple menu). The standard Command-Q shortcut still works, however. A few other shortcuts have been changed, as you'll learn in the next chapter.

Mac OS 9 Features: Where Did They Go?

As much as Panther resembles previous versions of the Mac OS, as you explore the landscape, it's clear some things are quite different. Functions that you expected to find in one place are performed differently, or are simply no longer around. In some cases, preferences have been combined, so you no longer have to visit separate programs to perform a single set of settings. The International and Network preference panels are prime examples.

Throughout this chapter I will be covering many of those differences in more detail. But here is a table that lists the component of Mac OS 9 and where it went, using the most common equivalent. Features not specifically listed here are either not present in Panther, or there are alternatives you'll want to experiment with.

Classic Mac OS Component	Mac OS X Solution
Chooser—setup printers	Printer Setup application (Utilities Folder)
Chooser—shared volumes	Network globe in Finder Sidebar or Connect to Server (Finder's Go menu)
Fonts folder (System Folder)	Fonts folder (Library folder and Library folder for each user, plus other locations)
Sounds	Sounds folder (Library folder within Home folder)
Utilities folder	Applications and Applications (Mac OS 9) folders
Apple Extras folder	Applications (Mac OS 9) folder
Internet folder	Applications (Mac OS 9) folder
Mac OS 9 applications	Applications (Mac OS 9 folder)
Desktop items (Mac OS 9)	Desktop (Mac OS 9) folder
Documents folder	Same location and Documents folder for each user
Sleep, Restart, Shut Down	Apple menu
Special menu	No longer needed
Finder preferences	Finder's application menu
Application preferences	Application menu within each application
Control panels	System Preferences
File Sharing	Sharing preferences (System Preferences)
Software Update control panel	Software Update (System Preferences)
SimpleText	TextEdit
TCP/IP control panel	Network preferences (System Preferences)
AppleTalk control panel	Network preferences (System Preferences)
Modem control panel	Network preferences (System Preferences)
Remote Access control panel	Network preferences (System Preferences)
Location Manager	Network preferences (System Preferences)
Multiple Users control panel	Accounts (System Preferences)
Numbers	International (System Preferences)
Text	International (System Preferences)
Startup Items	Startup Items in Accounts preference panel (System Preferences)
Extensions Manager	No longer needed
Disk Copy	Disk Utility (Utilities folder)
Disk First Aid	Disk Utility (Utilities folder)
Drive Setup	Disk Utility (Utilities folder)
Favorites in Apple menu	Favorites in Go menu

**3. Panther
User Preferences**

Immediate Solutions

Configuring the Setup Assistant

As you explore the setup screens in the Setup Assistant, check the instructions carefully. They will change from time to time as Apple updates Mac OS X. As you progress through the setup process, click the right arrow at lower right to move to the next setup screen, and click the back or left arrow to review or change a previous setting. At the top left of the screen, you'll see the title of the setup category you've entered.

NOTE: *After the Setup Assistant runs during the initial Mac OS X configuration process, it is no longer needed. From here on, you can use System Preferences to configure your Mac; except for the initial registration process, you can configure all the same settings, and much more, as you'll see later in this chapter.*

The introduction will consist of a short multimedia presentation, punctuated by music with a nice beat (as the music reviewers are apt to say), but you don't need to dismiss it. Soon, you'll see the message, "We'll have you up and running in no time." Follow these steps:

1. *Welcome*—When you see the Welcome screen, select the country in which you're located from the list. Click Show All to see more options. After you've checked the appropriate country, click Continue.

2. *Registration Information*—There are several screens where you will enter the information needed to register your product with Apple Computer. The first screen asks for your name, address, phone number, email address, and so forth. The next screen inquires about some simple marketing information (you don't have to answer). You can even opt not to receive any mail from Apple Computer. No doubt your mailboxes are filled up enough as it is. Then, click Continue to receive an acknowledgement that your registration information has been recorded and will be sent to Apple when you have connected to the Internet.

NOTE *You won't have to toil through the registration process again if you reinstall Mac OS X, unless you've removed the original installed files (in other words, only if you're doing a clean installation).*

3. *Create Your Account*—Enter your user name as owner or administrator of the Mac. For convenience, press the Tab key to move to the next text field; press Shift+Tab to return to the previous field. You also need to enter a short name or nickname for yourself. Once your user name is created, the Mac OS X's Setup Assistant will create a shortened version of your name by default, but feel free to change it. In the next three text fields, enter a password, reconfirm your password, and enter a password hint—a word or phrase that will remind you of the password in case you forget it. You will also have the option to choose a picture for yourself that will appear at Panther's login prompt; don't worry, it can be changed later.

NOTE: If you are using your Mac in a home or small office, a secure password probably doesn't matter. However, if you want the utmost in security, try to use what is considered a strong password: a password that consists of random numbers and mixed upper- and lowercase letters so that it cannot easily be guessed by anyone who might try to break into your computer. An example is 0Bfusc8. However, you should pick a password that is easy for you to remember (or at least write it down and put it in a safe place).

4. *Get Internet Ready*—After you've created a user name and password, you'll move on to a setup screen where you can configure your Mac for Internet access (see Figure 3.1). Click the button to indicate whether you already have an ISP or want Apple to set you up with an EarthLink account or retrieve your EarthLink settings from its servers. While you will enjoy more of the benefits of Mac OS X with an Internet account, such as the Sherlock Internet services application, you aren't forced to establish an account right now. You can make that decision later on. Assuming you are already connected and select the option to add your existing settings, you'll have the following options:

NOTE: This particular range of settings can be separately duplicated in the Network preference panel later on, but doing so now is simple because you get the proper range of dialog boxes you need depending on the type of connection you specify. When you set up your new Mac, you'll usually find EarthLink sign-up software in the Utilities folder; otherwise you would need to install a copy from EarthLink's Web site or from an installation CD.

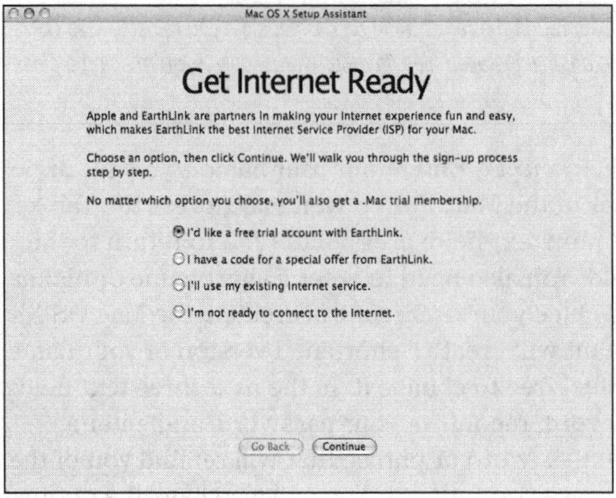

Get Internet Ready

Apple and EarthLink are partners in making your Internet experience fun and easy, which makes EarthLink the best Internet Service Provider (ISP) for your Mac.

Choose an option, then click Continue. We'll walk you through the sign-up process step by step.

No matter which option you choose, you'll also get a .Mac trial membership.

○ I'd like a free trial account with EarthLink.
○ I have a code for a special offer from EarthLink.
○ I'll use my existing Internet service.
○ I'm not ready to connect to the Internet.

Go Back   Continue

Figure 3.1   Follow this setup to handle your initial Internet settings.

- *Telephone Modem*—This option is for a standard, garden-variety, dial-up connection to an ISP. When you check this option and click Continue, you'll be greeted with a Your Internet Connection screen where you enter the basic login information required to connect to your ISP. These settings include the service's phone number and your standard user name and password for a particular ISP.

NOTE: Unfortunately, the Setup Assistant will not work with AOL or CompuServe 2000 because their client software must be separately configured to access these services. You can download the latest versions from the ISP's Web sites, but, of course, you must be online to do that, which is sort of a vicious circle. You can also just locate one of those ubiquitous AOL sign-up CDs or download from a friend's computer.

- *Local Area Network*—If you log on to the Internet via your local area network (perhaps using a server for the connection), choose this option. In the next screen you see, enter your network setup information.
- *Cable Modem*—This setting is used for high-speed Internet provided by a cable service. Click Continue to see a setup screen where you enter your setup information. You might have to put in a DHCP client ID number to allow your cable modem to connect, or PPP over Ethernet (PPPoE) settings, as required.
- *DSL Modem*—Another connection option for high-speed Internet service is accessing the Digital Subscriber Line broadband option. Again, if you click Continue after

selecting this option, a setup screen will appear for you to enter the required information.

NOTE: You'll need to check with your ISP for the specific settings you need, if you haven't recorded them from a setup book or your Mac OS 9.x installation. Sorry, but the Panther installer doesn't grab this information for you.

- *AirPort*—When you use Apple's AirPort or Airport Extreme wireless networking system, click this option to access the wireless network.

NOTE: Because the AirPort system is based on international standards, such as 802.11b (802.11g for the AirPort Extreme product line), or Wi-Fi (wireless fidelity) for short, you can use your Mac's AirPort system to connect to a number of third-party wireless devices, which greatly increases your flexibility when it comes to connecting to a Mac or cross-platform network.

5. *Get .Mac*—Depending on whether you want to pay the annual subscription rate, this may be one of Apple's better ideas to move the platform beyond the box. .Mac is a set of special features at the Apple Web site that enhances the user experience, including a mac.com email address, online disk storage and Web page publishing. The package also includes backup and virus protection software, online training courses, discount coupons, and lots of other "Member Extras." In this settings screen, choose whether you want to set up a .Mac account (a free 60-day trial is offered for new subscribers) or use the one you already have, by entering the appropriate information.

NOTE: If you need to set up a new .Mac account, be sure your Mac has been set up to connect to your ISP so that Apple's Web site can be checked to establish your account and make sure your user name hasn't already been taken (in which case you'll be given a chance to try a different one).

6. *Now You're Ready To Connect*—Click Continue to send your registration to Apple via your ISP and do the next stage of setups for your Mac. A progress screen indicates that you're connecting to Apple. Once you're done, continue to the next screen to perform the last setups.

7. *Set Up Mail*—Mac OS X's Mail application offers great speed and reasonably powerful mail-handling features. Indicate whether you want to use your iTools account or choose the option Add My Existing E-mail Account. The setup screen will ask for your email address, incoming mail server, account type

(POP, IMAP or Exchange), user account ID, password, and outgoing mail server. These settings are the same ones you've always used for your email.

NOTE: Don't have the settings? If you didn't follow my suggestions in Chapter 2 to copy your ISP settings from your Classic Mac OS, you'll need to refer to the documentation provided by your ISP or just ignore this setting right now. You can add them later on in the System Preferences application.

8. *Select Time Zone*—In order for such things as your e-mail and documents to display the proper time, you first need to locate the part of the world in which you live on the map. Then, choose the time zone or city nearest you from the pop-up menu if a special time setting is required (such as in Arizona, which doesn't observe daylight savings time).

NOTE: Don't be surprised if Panther has already figured out your time zone, based on existing settings when you fill out your registration information. After all, you expect a computer to do some of the thinking for you.

9. *Thank You*—This final setup screen gives you one last chance to recheck all the entries you've made before they are stored in Mac OS X. You can use the back arrow to return to any setting and change it now. If you accept the setup, click the Go button to move on.

NOTE: Once again, your setups aren't set in stone. Feel free at any time to change everything from networking to passwords in the System Preferences application. I explain how later in this chapter.

10. *Logging In*—Once you're done, your Mac will finish the startup process. When you first see the Panther desktop for the first time (see Figure 3.2), you'll feel for a moment as if you've visited an alien environment. The new Aqua interface has familiar elements, but there are unfamiliar elements as well. In the next few chapters, I cover every aspect of the revised look of the Mac OS. For now, get comfortable, and get ready to explore the system setup and printer setup options.

NOTE: This is the last time you'll need the Setup Assistant under Mac OS X, unless you want to reinstall the operating system on a different volume. If you launch the application again (it's located in a folder called Core Services, within the folder path System>Library), you'll return to your Internet setup screens but you can configure the very same settings in the Internet and Network preference panels.

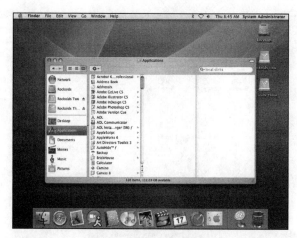

Figure 3.2   Your first exposure to Mac OS X, with your computer already given based on your user name.

Related solutions:	*Found on page:*
Preparing for Panther	20
Setting Up Multiple-User Access	133

Setting System Preferences Under Panther

Once you've configured your basic Mac settings with the Setup Assistant, you can compute without having to change any other settings. However, if you want to make adjustments to the look and feel of your Mac, use the System Preferences application (see Figure 3.3).

You'll find the System Preferences application on the Dock when you've done a normal installation of Panther. If for some reason the program isn't where you expect it to be, click the Applications icon on the Finder's sidebar (or use the same command in the Go menu) to locate and launch the application.

TIP: If a program isn't already on the Dock, drag its icon to the left side, and the Dock will expand to accommodate it; icon sizes will be reduced as needed, should the Dock expand to the ends of your screen. Applications go on the left and documents appear at the right, separated by a dark vertical line. Don't worry if you miss the separator line—sometimes you have to glance twice to notice it.

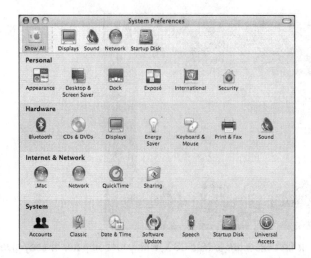

Figure 3.3   Click an icon to access a specific system setting.

To switch from one program setting pane to the next, click the icon you want. If the icon isn't shown in the application's toolbar, click Show All to see the entire lineup. After making your settings, press Command+Q to quit the program, or just click the close button. This is one of those rare applications that always exits gracefully when a window is closed.

Depending on the settings you make, such as ones involving your network or ISP connection, you may see an additional confirmation dialog box with a Save or Apply Now button you have to click to store your settings. Some system-critical functions can be secured by clicking the padlock, in which case only users granted "administrator" status will be able to change those settings after entering the correct user name and password.

NOTE: If you've used previous versions of the Mac operating system, you'll find some of these preferences are quite familiar. Aside from the flashy interface, they work pretty much the same as in the previous versions.

You do not have to set all the settings in the Preferences application right now. You can try each one for size or experiment with one setting without changing any of the others. If the setting isn't what you like, you can quickly restore it to the previous one. In addition, depending on your specific Mac setup, you may find additional preference components to adjust.

Although System Preferences components are divided into categories, I've opted to dump them in alphabetical order so that you can
easily find the one you want without having to concern yourself over
what category it's in.

TIP: *To quickly bring up the settings pane you want, click the application's View menu and
choose from the pop-up menu. That's the way I do it. You can also opt to Organize Alphabetically, which will present you the very same picture I'm offering up here.*

Setting Accounts Preferences

Bring up this screen to change your login password, add additional
users to your Mac, to take advantage of its multiple-users features
and to add startup items (see Figure 3.4). To alter your personal settings, click the password button. You'll see a dialog where you must
enter your current password and click OK to proceed. Now enter the
new password in the Password and Verify text fields, and then enter
the appropriate hint, if you want a reminder. The changes go into effect immediately. You can also alter login options to provide extra
features, such as disabling automatic login, activate the FileVault encryption feature, and add or remove Startup Items. Once these items
are added, the files, programs and servers that launch right after your
Mac boots. When you set up new users, you can customize access to
various parts of your Mac. For example, the Simple Finder option
that sharply limits access to various Mac features. Chapter 6 covers
this subject in more detail.

Figure 3.4   Modify your account and startup settings here.

Related solution:	Found on page:
Setting Up Multiple-User Access	133

NOTE: If you used previous versions of Mac OS X, you'll notice that the Panther version of System Preferences consolidates some settings such as including Startup Items, formerly called Login Items, in the Accounts pane. It becomes, at once, easier and more complicated, depending on your point of view and whether you're a creature of habit.

Setting Bluetooth Preferences

If your Mac is equipped with a Bluetooth wireless networking device, this preference panel will appear; otherwise you won't see it. This panel allows you to configure how such devices are discovered and authenticated. You can also control file sharing settings. For now, Bluetooth is generally limited to cell phones, handhelds, input devices (such as Apple's Bluetooth keyboard and mouse), and printers.

Setting Appearance Preferences

This preference was called General in previous versions of Mac OS X. It is, in part, the Aqua equivalent of the Classic Appearance control panel, which was used to customize the look of your Mac in a somewhat limited fashion. It also includes a pair of settings for the Apple menu, which required a separate control panel under Classic. So much for consistency.

Seven sets of appearance-related settings are provided in the Appearance pane (see Figure 3.5) from which you can set the following:

- *Appearance*—If the default Blue (or Aqua) color isn't to your liking, click the pop-up menu to choose the Graphite setting to adjust the look of buttons, menus, and windows.

NOTE: When you switch the appearance to Graphite, the colorful buttons at the left of a Finder or document window become gray when they can be used. The only visual indication of what they do is a symbol within each clear button when the mouse is brought near it.

- *Highlight Color*—This option sets the color you see when you select text. Feel free to experiment with different settings to see which colors set off highlighted text to your liking.

- *Place Scroll Arrows*—You can set the position of scroll arrows at the top and bottom or all together at the bottom (this option may be easier on the mouse and your wrist).

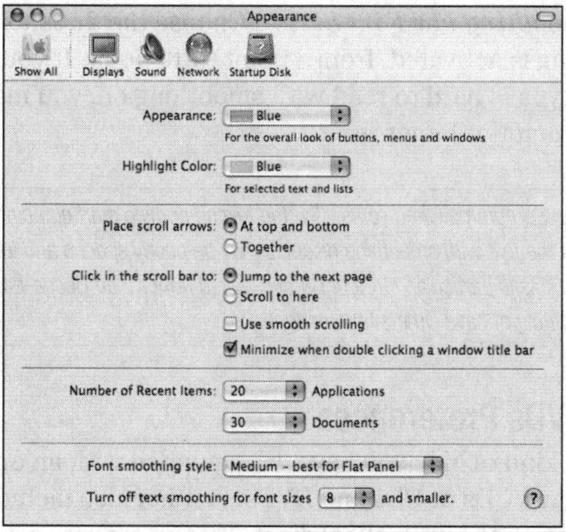

Figure 3.5 Choose your Mac's appearance settings on this panel. In this picture, I've increased the number of recent items and selected a text smoothing option to support my digital flat panel monitor.

- *Click In The Scroll Bar To*—This setting is supposed to direct how far a screen jumps when you click in the scrollbar (to the next page or to the point at which you click). For most programs, however, there will be no difference, so the setting is best left at its default.

- *Number Of Recent Items*—This is, in a small part, the Mac OS X equivalent of the Apple Menu Items Control Panel under the Classic OS. Click a pop-up menu to pick the number of applications and documents displayed in the Apple menu's Recent Items list. The default is 10, but I'd suggest you increase the number of documents to 20, since you're more likely to open lots of documents than lots of applications.

- *Font Smoothing Style*—Apple offers four options from the pop-up menu. The first and default setting, Standard, is recommended for a CRT display. The second choice, Light, is for folks who don't like the smoothing or anti-aliased effect. The third, Medium (the one I use), is optimized for flat panel displays. The final effect, Strong, may be too much of a good thing. But the differences are really subtle and you may have to blink twice to see the differences.

NOTE: *Even though Apple now only sells LCD displays, the Font Smoothing Style is set by default to the Standard configuration. Don't ask me why, but if you're not satisfied with the way text looks on your Mac's LCD display, this could be the reason.*

- *Turn Off Text Smoothing For Font Sizes*—Choose the threshold at which smoothing is activated, from 4 point to 12 point. If you find that smaller type is hard to read with smoothing on, you may want to choose 9 point or larger.

NOTE: *I suggest you check a few programs when you switch the text smoothing starting point. You may find, for example, that the text with smoothing disabled may be poorly spaced and look worse than with smoothing on. This is particularly true of Carbon-based rather than Cocoa-based applications, some of which do not yet have Quartz text rendering.*

Setting CDs & DVDs Preferences

Depending on what kind of Mac you have, it's equipped with an optical drive that reads just CDs or CDs and DVDs. Panther also includes software that allows you to burn optical discs. This preference panel, shown in Figure 3.6, is used to tell the operating system how to handle blank or recorded optical discs when inserted. By default, inserting a music CD will launch iTunes, a picture CD will deliver iPhoto and a DVD video will open Apple's terrific DVD Player application. You will be given a dialog box with options when blank optical media is inserted. Feel free to click on any pop-up menu to change the default selections (such as running a different jukebox application, such as MusicMatch, for music CDs, even though it is no longer being revised for the Mac), but they work quite well as they are.

Setting Classic Preferences

The Classic mode lets you use traditional Mac OS applications by opening the older version of the operating system within Mac OS X. In a sense, it's similar to running Windows applications on a Mac using Microsoft Virtual PC. The major difference is that the Classic mode runs applications transparently, without inheriting the Aqua interface, using the Mac OS X Finder. What's more, performance is better than any of the emulation programs, because you're not emulating a foreign processor.

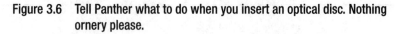

Figure 3.6   Tell Panther what to do when you insert an optical disc. Nothing ornery please.

NOTE: *In order for you to use the Classic environment, you need to install Mac OS 9.1 or later, if you don't already have it on your Mac. While 9.1 is just fine, later versions offer better compatibility and performance. You can update from 9.1 via a free update from Apple's support Web site, at **www.info.apple.com/**. If you don't have Mac OS 9 installed, you can order a copy at a special price for Panther users from Apple's customer service or from its upgrade Web site, at **www.apple.com/macosx/upgrade/**.*

The Classic preferences panel (see Figure 3.7) lets you specify the startup volume for the Classic operating system, which is especially important if you have more that one volume with a System Folder installed. If your Mac has Mac OS 9.1 or later on another hard disk (or partition), you'll see the drive's name displayed in the list (drives without a 9.1 or later partition will be grayed out). You can click the disk from which you want to run the Mac in Classic mode, and then specify whether you want to have the Classic environment automatically start when you boot (log into) your Mac. This is not an essential selection unless you want to begin using Classic applications without having to wait for Classic to boot. (This can take from 30 seconds to more than a minute, depending upon your configuration.) You can also choose Restart or Force Quit Classic. The Advanced preference tab is used to configure additional options, such as whether to rebuild the Classic Mac OS system's desktop, restart with extensions off, or bring up Extensions Manager when Classic opens; I cover this subject in more detail in Chapter 14. You can monitor the amount of memory used by Classic applications by clicking the Memory/Versions tab.

TIP: *If a preference panel is already open, you can access another panel by its icon on the top of the screen; if that icon isn't there, click the Show All button to see the rest of the list. It's also possible to drag an icon to the top toolbar so you can have it always available if it's earmarked for frequent changes.*

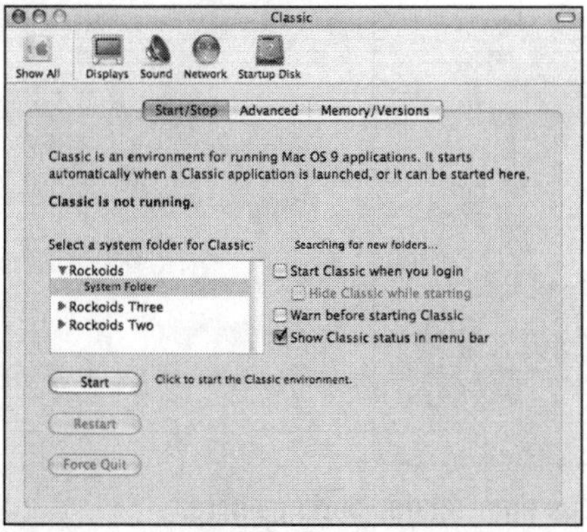

Figure 3.7   Choose your startup disk for Classic mode on this screen.

NOTE: Readers of previous editions of this book will notice the absence of a ColorSync preference panel. It's still around, but has been changed to an application that you'll find in the Utilities folder. Chapter 13 provides more on this subject.

Setting Date & Time Preferences

In effect, the settings you create here (see Figure 3.8), in many respects, mirror the ones you've already configured in the Setup Assistant. However, these settings have a new wrinkle. At the bottom left of the settings screen, you'll notice a button labeled Click The Lock To Prevent Further Changes. You can protect this panel and any other panel with a padlock icon so that only users with administrator's permissions can access them. Other system-related preference panes bear the same lockbox motif, which helps protect those settings from access by folks who don't have administrator access, assuming you want to keep the lock shut.

TIP: If you plan to access a particular preference panel often, and it's not already part of the standard listing, simply drag its icon to the top of the System Preferences window.

You can access any of the four settings categories by clicking on the appropriate tab:

- The first tab (Date & Time) and the second (Time Zone) offer essentially the same settings you already performed in the Setup Assistant. You can leave them alone or make further adjustments now. The only additional feature of significance is the Set Date & Time Automatically checkbox, which will synchronize your Mac

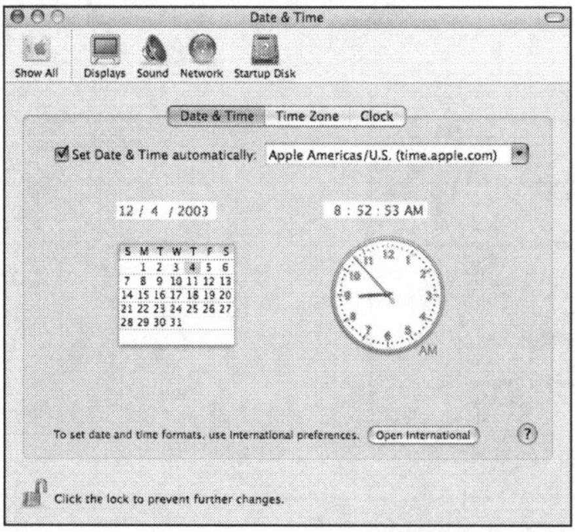

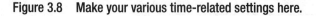

Figure 3.8   Make your various time-related settings here.

during startup, using an Internet-based NTP time server, if you're online at boot time.

• The third tab—Menu Bar Clock—allows you to specify whether you want to show the clock in the menu bar (it's on by default) and whether you want it to display seconds, AM/PM, the date of the week, or flashing time separators. Other selections let you choose an analog clock, or have the time displayed in a separate movable window. You can also opt to have the time announced on your Mac using one of the voices available under Panther's Speech Manager. If you like computerized voices, go for it. If not, I'd avoid this particular feature.

TIP: *If you're not happy with the limitations of Apple's menu bar clock, check for a shareware alternative. One resource is VersionTracker.com, a popular Web site that includes information about software plus links to download sites.*

Setting Desktop & Screen Saver Preferences

Don't like the default Aqua Blue ocean-blue backgrounds for Mac OS X? The Desktop & Screen Saver preferences panel (shown in Figure 3.9) can be used to change it to your liking and also configure the built-in screen saver feature. The setups for either feature are essentially the same. Click on a name representing the category of desktop backdrop or screen saver you want. Under screen saver, you'll also need to click the Activation tab to set the idle time before the screen saver activates. The intervals are in 5-minute jumps up to 60 minutes. The Hot Corners option lets you automatically activate a screen saver when moving the mouse to the selected corner.

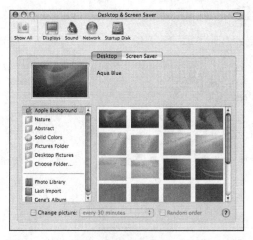

Figure 3.9   Pick another desktop backdrop from Apple's collection or yours.

NOTE: By default, the screen saver interval is activated when you install Panther, but you can change the interval or switch it to Never if you're not a fan of screen savers. On the other hand, you can also opt to password-protect your screen saver in the Activation pane, using your regular user name and password to unlock it and dismiss the display. You will also want to coordinate this setting with your Energy Saver settings, so your Mac doesn't drift into sleep mode when you really want to see a fancy screen effect.

TIP: You can also use the contents of your iPhoto library as both desktop background and screen saver, or both, using the Desktop & Screen Saver preferences pane. That way you can be entertained with family photos when you're not busy, or even if you are busy and need a short break from the action to pour over your favorite photos.

Setting Display Preferences

The Display screen (see Figure 3.10) is used to configure the size (resolution) of the images on your Mac's display and the color depth setting. The Resolutions setting specifies the number of pixels that are shown on your Mac's display. When you make this adjustment, you should weigh the range of your Mac's desktop against the clarity of the items it shows. To change the resolution, click the setting you want.

WARNING! If you're using an LCD monitor, you'll want to try to stick with the default or "native" resolution for the sharpest picture. When you set a different resolution, the monitor interpolates the resolution (a sophisticated form of guesswork), and the results aren't quite as crisp. In fact, they can be downright fuzzy on some monitors. Most computer games, such as Quake 3 Arena, will

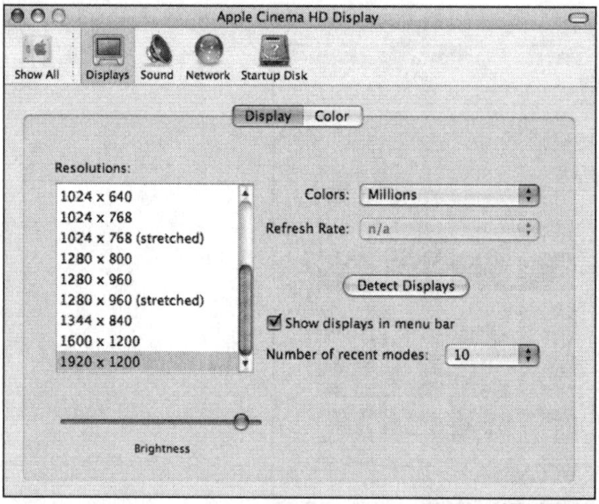

Figure 3.10   Choose your Mac's display preferences from this setup screen.

usually have their own resolution settings that revert to your system settings when you quit the program.

NOTE: On some Mac displays, you can configure contrast and brightness settings directly from the Display pane; on others, the settings will be grayed out. CRT-based iMacs, eMacs and some models equipped with an Apple display also have a tab labeled Geometry, where you can make sure your display's image is as wide as possible and that the shapes are straight and true.

To change color depth, click the Colors pop-up menu. For most purposes, the difference between thousands and millions is slight. But if you do graphics work, configure your Mac for the latter (unless you have a Mac with a slower graphics processor, such as a first-generation iMac, where the thousands setting will deliver noticeably better graphics performance).

NOTE: Click the checkbox to put a display system menu in your Mac's menu bar.

Click the Color button (see Figure 3.11) to adjust the color balance or calibration of your display. These settings take advantage of Apple's ColorSync technology so that your display more nearly matches the color balance of your printer or other output device.

NOTE: The model number of your display will be shown in this screen. If it's not one of Apple's, expect to see an arcane set of numbers that may not always be easy to decipher. Don't ask me why it's that way, because I'm not a marketing or product person.

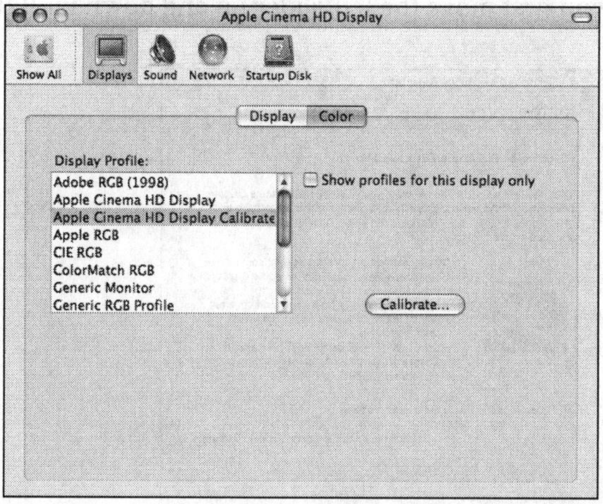

Figure 3.1   You can create a calibrated color profile to give your Mac a more accurate color balance.

The settings on the Color tab are quite different from that of previous versions of the Mac OS, although the starting point is very similar:

1. To establish a color profile for your Mac's monitor, select the model display you have or choose a generic profile from the Display Profile scrolling list. Then, click the Calibrate button. Apple's Display Calibrator Assistant (see Figure 3.12) will be launched.

NOTE: A change from previous versions of Mac OS X: The Display Calibrator Assistant application is no longer available, separately, in the Utilities folder.

---

2. Before proceeding, take a quick look at the introductory text in the Assistant's dialog box. For the most accurate color calibration, click the Expert Mode checkbox, if it's not already selected. Click the right (forward) arrow to proceed, and the left (back) arrow to review a setting. When you click the right arrow, you'll move to the Set Up screen, where you will set the brightness of your display, except for Apple LCD models and laptops (see step 3).

NOTE: Apple has totally revised these settings for Panther. They are more comprehensive and, frankly, a little harder to adjust, but the end result is superior in terms of color accuracy. You can even fine-tune your Apple LCD display in this fashion to deliver better results.

---

3. When you click the right arrow, you'll see the Native Gamma screen (see Figure 3.13). This setting lets you calibrate the gamma (center point) for the three RGB (red, green, blue) colors of your display, and involves a five-step process. For each setting, you first move the left slider up and down until the

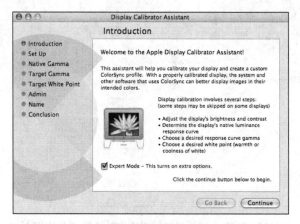

Figure 3.12   Apple's Display Calibrator Assistant helps you create a ColorSync profile for your monitor.

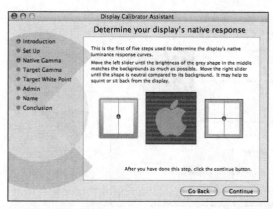

Figure 3.13   The native gamma or luminance response curves require a
little extra attention to set properly.

gray Apple shape in the middle square nearly disappears into
the background. Then you move the slider on the right until the
Apple shape's color matches that of the background as closely
as possible. Be patient, because it may take a little back and
forth and up and down movements to get this adjustment right.
One consolation is that the settings appear to become easier to
perform as you progress towards step five.

---

*TIP: It's a good idea not to sit too close to your display when making these adjustments. You get
the most accurate view of gamma settings if you sit back from the display as far as possible.
Otherwise, you might find that the inner and outer portions of the square never seem to merge.*

---

4. Once you've attained part three of the process (and congratula-
   tions by the way), the next click of the right arrow brings up the
   Target Gamma setting (see Figure 3.14). Move the slider to
   configure the setting and observe the picture in the preview
   screen to see the end result. If you work in a mixed-platform
   environment, you might want to choose the PC Standard
   setting. Otherwise, use Mac Standard.

5. You are near the finish line. Click the right arrow to see the
   Target White Point screen (see Figure 3.15). The slider will set
   white point (or color temperature) for your display. D65, or
   6500 degrees Kelvin, is normal. A setting of 9300 will brighten
   the display somewhat.

---

*NOTE: You may find that some displays benefit from one setting as opposed to another,
depending on their design characteristics. Apple's LCD monitors, for example (such as the 17"
and 23" models), seem to provide a brighter, more brilliant picture at the 6500 settings, as does*

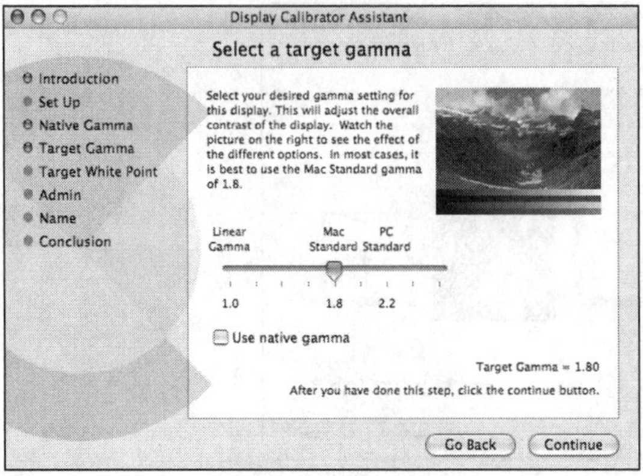

Figure 3.14   When Native Gamma is done, Target Gamma is next.

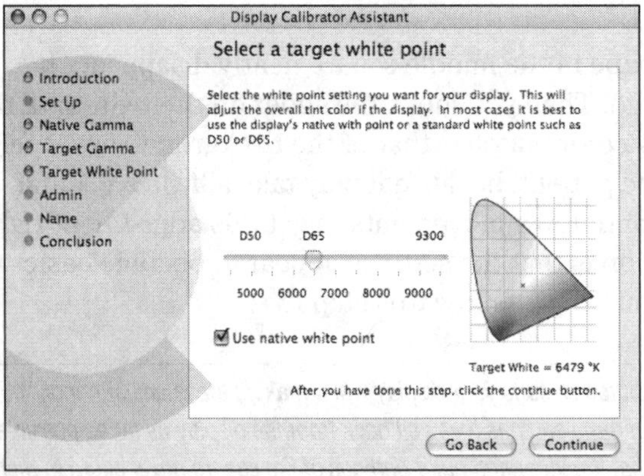

Figure 3.15   Choose the white point setting and you're almost finished.

a Planar WS231,23-inch display I've reviewed for my "Mac Reality Check" column. Other LCD displays I've used, such as the ViewSonic ViewPanel VP181 (18.1-inch) and the Sony SDM MD-81 (also 18.1") work best at 9300. Feel free to experiment.

6. If your office consists of other Macs with the same type of monitor, you might want to let them access the same calibration settings. Why put them through all the agony (or then again, why not)? When you click on the Administrator options screen, you'll have a checkbox that lets others access the setting.

7. Click the right arrow to name your profile (see Figure 3.16). The default setting will include the name of your monitor in addition to the word Calibrate. Then, click Continue to move on to the summary or Conclusion where you can observe a summary of the havoc you've wrought. When you click Done, you've quit the calibrator.

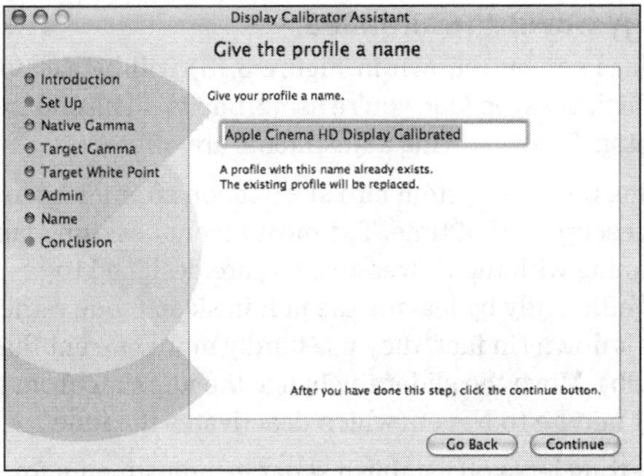

Figure 3.16 Name your calibration profile and click Continue to see a summary of your settings.

NOTE: By default, the Display Calibrator Assistant will simply overwrite a previous setting with the same name without warning. So, be careful about naming your profile.

Setting Dock Preferences

Apple's Mac OS X taskbar (see Figure 3.17) can be configured in several ways to adjust the display. I'll cover these settings in more detail in Chapter 5.

Related solution:	*Found on page:*
Using the Dock	120

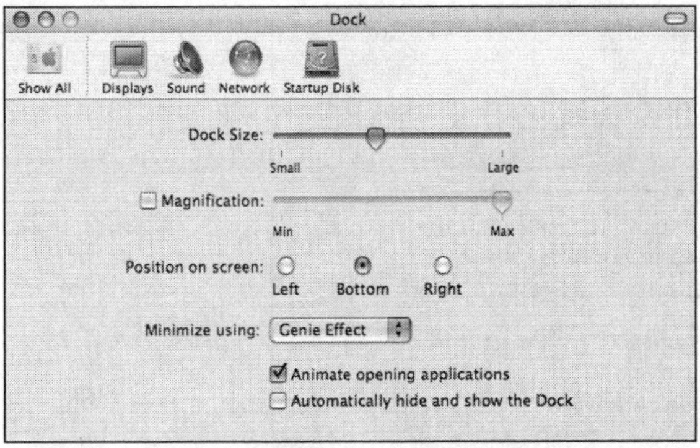

Figure 3.17 Adjust how you interact with the Dock here.

Setting Energy Saver Preferences

The Sleep settings screen (shown in Figure 3.18) will be the same regardless of which desktop Mac you're using, but it will be collapsed on an Apple laptop. The following adjustments are offered:

- The first setting puts the system into sleep mode after it's been idle for the preset period of time. The most recent desktop Mac models, beginning with the Power Mac G4, are designed to operate most efficiently by leaving the unit in sleep mode rather than shutting it down (in fact, they use hardly more current than a tiny light bulb). Move the slider to change the idle time from the minimum of 1 minute to Never (which deactivates the function).

- The second setting lets you establish separate adjustments for your display, to preserve screen life and put it into sleep mode when not in use for a specific interval.

NOTE: The Achilles heel of an LCD display is the backlighting, which has a finite life and is expensive to replace. If you allow your display to go to sleep when it's not in use for a while, you'll be able to enjoy top performance for a lot longer (no I won't make any estimates).

- The final setting puts the hard drive to sleep when possible. To activate this or the previous option, click the checkbox.

WARNING! Some older displays are not Energy Star–compliant and will not go into sleep mode, even though you've activated that setting. If you're not certain whether your display supports the feature, check the manufacturer's documentation, the shipping box, or the manufacturer's technical support division. Some displays ship with front panels peppered with all sorts of compliance information, but most users

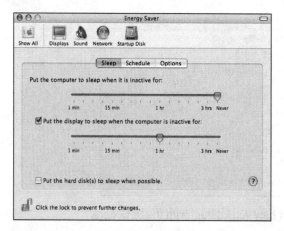

Figure 3.18   Use the slider to adjust your Energy Saver options here.

rip off these decals before putting the products into use. If it's any consolation, CRT monitors are so cheap these days that you're probably ready for a new one if the one you have isn't Energy Star-compliant.

NOTE: *Some programs make continuous demands on the hard drive, and thus putting the drive into sleep mode won't work efficiently. The best time to use this feature is when you do not intend to work on your Mac.*

Another set of preferences appears when you click the Schedule button. Here you can specify when your Mac starts and when it should go to sleep or shut down. You don't have to remember a thing, and this is one particular setting I use often.

The final button, Options, covers the rest. Your first choice, Wake Options, will bring your Mac to life when the modem detects a ring (useful if you use your Mac for faxing and don't want to waste electricity) or when a network administrator needs to access it. Your other choices depend on the kind of Mac you have. The first, Restart Automatically After A Power Failure, is useful if you need to keep your Mac on all the time (otherwise you can uncheck it and not worry over it). Some Macs afford you the ability to use the power button to engage Sleep mode. If you have an iBook or PowerBook, there will also be an option labeled Show Battery Status In Menu Bar on both screens, which is enabled by default if you install on an Apple laptop. You will also have the option to reduce processor performance on some models to conserve battery life. Even the Power Mac G5 offers a processor cycling feature to make it as energy efficient as possible. Those babies can consume a lot of power if the processor is set to run at its highest setting all the time.

NOTE: *Whenever you see a lock icon at the bottom of a preference panel, as you do with the Energy Saver preferences, it requires administrator access to change.*

Setting Exposé Preferences

Apple's Exposé is an ultra-clever, flashy approach to dealing with multiple application and document windows. By default, if you press F9 on your keyboard, all the windows will shrink and become neatly arranged so you can see all of them at once. When you press F9 again, your desktop returns to normal. The F10 key lets you see all the windows in the current application in the same fashion. F11 moves all the open windows to the corners of the screen so you can have a clear path to the desktop. This preference pane simply lets you change the keyboard shortcuts, or invoke hot corners, where moving the mouse to one corner of the screen or another activates an Exposé function. I'll cover this in more detail in the next chapter.

Setting International Preferences

Mac OS X is designed to be a worldwide operating system, with built-in support for some of the major languages. Under older system versions, you had to install separate modules for different parts of the world or buy a different product and use the Keyboard, Numbers and Text control panels to configure the settings. But Apple has moved to selling a single operating system version, and the preferences available (see Figure 3.19) are designed to localize keyboard and language settings as needed. You have settings for Language, where you can move a language to a different position by dragging and dropping it to set its priority. Separate buttons also let you adjust display formats for Date, Time, and Numbers. The final tab—Input Menu—lets you choose whether to put up a menu bar label from which you can quickly switch from one keyboard layout to another.

NOTE: *If you opted not to install some of the language packages during the initial installation of Panther, you may find fewer options available. Don't be concerned, unless you really need to switch to those languages, in which case you'd have to break out your system CDs and install them.*

Setting .Mac Preferences

This settings pane (see Figure 3.20) used to allow you to select a default mail and browsing client, but not for Panther. Now it's strictly use for configuring your .Mac access.

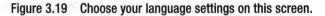

Figure 3.19   Choose your language settings on this screen.

Figure 3.20   Configure your .Mac settings here.

- *.Mac*—Put in your .Mac member name and password. If you don't have an account, click the Sign Up button; you'll be connected to Apple's Web site to set up your account.

NOTE: *Although you get a free .Mac trial with Panther or a new Mac, after that you will have to pay an annual subscription fee to continue use of any of the .Mac services.*

- *iDisk*—Examine the status of your iDisk, which is the online storage feature offered by Apple's .Mac service. You can use this preference screen to order up additional storage space or set access privileges to the files you have posted.

NOTE: *So where do you set your default e-mail and browser applications, now that there's no Internet preference panel available? Both Apple's Mail and Safari applications have preference settings for just that, even if you end up using different programs for mail and surfing. Don't ask me why they did that. I asked, and never really got an acceptable answer.*

Setting Keyboard & Mouse Preferences

Beginning with late versions of Mac OS X Jaguar, Apple combined the keyboard and mouse preference panes. You can configure four types of settings here. Under Keyboard, you can select the Repeat Rate, which affects your Mac keyboard's Automatic Repeat modes. Here's the list of the available choices:

- *Key Repeat Rate*—Specifies the time you hold down a key before it repeats.

- *Delay Until Repeat*—Specifies the speed at which a key repeats.

Move the sliders to make the needed changes. You can also enter text in the text box to get a feel for the changes you'll be making.When you click the Mouse pane (labeled Trackpad on an Apple laptop), as shown in Figure 3.21, you can increase the cursor speed to whatever is comfortable for your needs. Generally, you will find that the standard speed setting is just too slow, especially if your Mac has a large screen display. The Mouse Speed slider adjusts the tracking speed; the Double-Click Speed setting is used to configure the ideal interval for a double-click to activate a Mac OS function. There is no correct setting. It's entirely up to your taste, and you can experiment with different adjustments to see which ones are the most comfortable. You'll also find that the ideal settings change as you move from one Mac to another, or to a different brand of pointing device. If you have a two-button mouse with a scroll wheel, there will be yet a third option, scrolling, which strictly addresses how the scroll wheel performs.

NOTE: Some non-Apple input devices, such as those from Contour, Kensington, Logitech and Microsoft, come with special software to allow you to access extra button features plus custom tracking routines. While Apple's own adjustments may suit you, you'll need to use the manufacturer's own software to access all the features the product offers.

The final set of preferences can be accessed by clicking on the Keyboard Shortcuts button (shown in Figure 3.22). It is used to put you in control over which shortcuts control a particular function. Even the

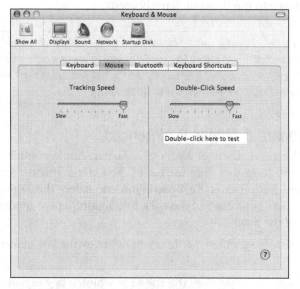

Figure 3.21   Adjust input device settings here.

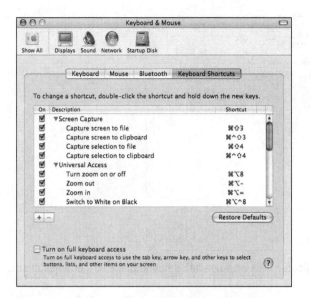

Figure 3.22   Add or alter keyboard shortcuts in this preference pane.

ever-popular Command-Shift-3, the venerable shortcut for taking a screen shot, can be altered. All you need to do to alter a shortcut is to double-click on the listing for that shortcut, and then hold down the new keyboard combo. Feel free to change as often as you need.

TIP: *To add a shortcut, simply click the plus button, and in the dialog box that appears, choose the application it applies to, choose the menu label, and then enter the shortcut you want to use. The minus button is used to delete a selected shortcut, and Restore Default does what it promises—it sets things back they way they were when you installed Panther.*

WARNING! Individual programs have keyboard shortcuts that might work in place of the various shortcuts you might want to set. This is especially true if the program has its own brand of function key support, such as the various applications in Microsoft Office. So you might want to look over an application's manual (if there is one) or Help menu before becoming too inventive.

Setting Network Preferences

This configuration screen (see Figure 3.23) controls various aspects of your network settings, including those connected with access to your ISP. As you saw above, in the section entitled "Mac OS 9 Features: What Happened to Them?," earlier in this chapter, this preference panel replaces the functions of several in your Classic Mac OS, which should make your configuration go faster and easier. You can make several types of settings. One is for your internal

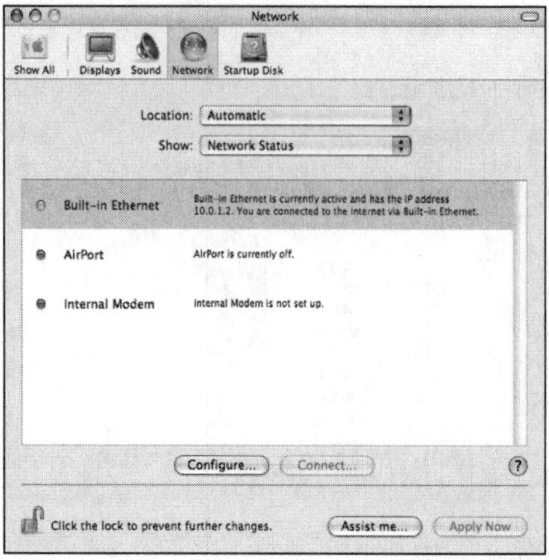

Figure 3.23   Double click on a network setup to make further adjustments.

modem, used for connecting to your ISP. (I cover those in more detail in Chapter 8.) The other, under the Built-in Ethernet category,
includes four buttons to configure different settings (these are mirrored in the settings panels for an AirPort card, if one is installed).

To give you an ever-so-brief picture of the sort of adjustments you
can make (I'll give you some more information in Chapter 8), let's
double click on the Built-in-Ethernet, which delivers the options shown
in Figure 3.24.

- *TCP/IP*—The settings you make here, labeled Manually using
  DHCP Router, BOOTP or DHCP, are for TCP/IP-based connections,

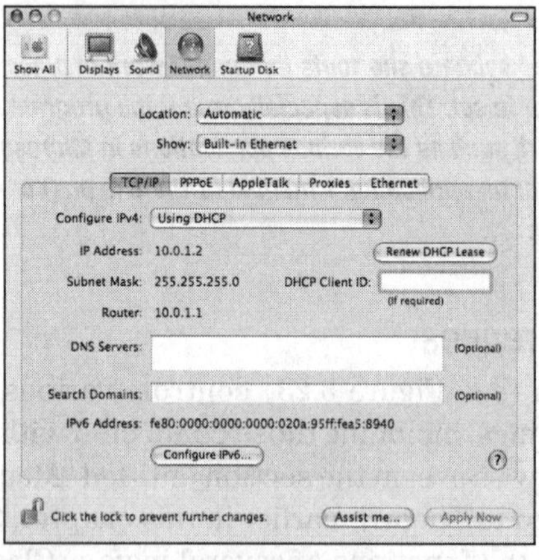

Figure 3.24   Each button takes you to a wide world of configuration
options.

if you have one. They activate these services for a local network, cable modem, or DSL. They're very similar to those used in the TCP/IP control panel of older Macs. The required settings will come from either an ISP or network administrator.

NOTE: To access a dial-up connection to the Internet, you'll make your settings in the Internal Modem category, available from the Show pop-up menu. AirPort users will find a category devoted to that product (with settings pretty much the same as the Built-in Ethernet category) if an AirPort card is installed on your Mac.

- *PPPoE*—Some broadband ISPs, such as those using cable modems or DSL, use PPP over Ethernet (PPPoE) software or settings. When you click this button, you'll be able to enter information for Service Provider, PPPoE Service Name, Account Name, and Password. You can also save your password and click the PPPoE Options button to make settings that might be required by your ISP.

NOTE: Your ISP is the source for updated information about the settings required for the PPPoE panel. The settings will vary from service to service. In addition, before installing anyone's software to make this connection, try the settings screen in the Network preference panel. It should accommodate the needs of the vast majority of ISPs that require this setup. You may have to argue the point with your broadband ISP's technical people, but you can definitely do it yourself in just a few minutes, tops, once you get the setup information.

- *AppleTalk*—To access Macs and network printers on a standard AppleTalk network, select the checkbox to activate AppleTalk.

NOTE: On or off? On some Macs with Panther installed, AppleTalk is turned on automatically, sometimes it isn't. It never hurts to double-check. In addition, to the limitations of the operating system, as of the time this book was written, you cannot activate AppleTalk on both Ethernet and AirPort at the same time. It's one or the other. Sorry folks!

- *Proxies*—Depending on the requirements in your network or for your ISP, you might have to enter proxy settings to access the Internet. A proxy is, loosely speaking, an intermediary server that intercepts Web traffic before it is retrieved by the end user. Some ISPs use this to cache frequently visited sites for speedier access, or to compress Web artwork to make it display faster. Other installations provide this function as an added measure of security. Contact your network administrator or ISP for the appropriate settings information.
- *Ethernet*—This is an automatic function but there may be times when you need to fine-tune your network for special purposes.

Most of you will leave it in its default or automatic condition. If you have specific issues with your installation, you'll probably want to call in your network administrator or an outside expert to let you know what works best.

After you've made your changes to your network services, click Apply Now to store your settings. If you quit System Preferences without saving your settings, you'll see a prompt asking if you want to save your settings before you move on. If you don't click Save, the network changes will be discarded.

TIP: *If you don't want to go through the drudgery of figuring out what settings to use, click on Assist me... and let Panther guide you through the proper setups. This largely mirrors the Setup Assistant you used after installing your operating system, but there are times when you might need to fix or alter a few things, especially if you've changed ISPs, perhaps moving from dial-up to broadband.*

Related solution:	*Found on page:*
Using Internet Connect for Dial-Up Networking	185

Setting QuickTime Preferences

Apple's QuickTime is a multimedia standard around the world. Use this settings pane (shown in Figure 3.25) to establish five sets of user preferences:

- *Plug-In*—These settings determine how your Web browser works with the QuickTime plug-in. The Play Movies Automatically checkbox turns on a QuickTime movie as soon as it's downloaded.

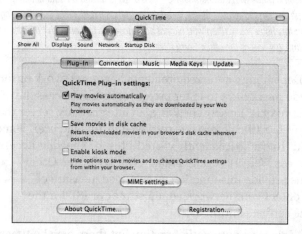

Figure 3.25   Choose your QuickTime user preferences from this pane.

Save Movies In Disk Cache stores a movie in the browser's Web cache (not a good idea if it's a big file). Enable Kiosk Mode turns on Kiosk mode, which allows you to save movies and adjust your QuickTime settings from within the browser.

- *Connection*—Click this button to optimize QuickTime to work best with your specific ISP connection. Choose the speed at which you access your ISP and whether to allow multiple streams of net traffic (this option is best only with broadband Internet access). The Transport Setup button should be left to network administrators.

NOTE: By default, the Connection settings are configured for a 56K modem. Although QuickTime Player will remind you to change the settings if you activate that program with a faster network hookup, it's better to save a little time and do it now.

- *Music*—Use this setting to choose a music synthesizer package. You don't need to use it unless you've added such a package from a music program.

- *Media Keys*—Use this setting to store passwords to access secured multimedia files. Specify the fashion in which Mac OS X's built-in QuickTime features are used.

- *Update*—The final button lets you check for updates to QuickTime from Apple's Web site. You can also enter your registration information, in the event you've opted to purchase QuickTime Pro (and get rid of those annoying messages about doing so when you try to view multimedia content on the Internet).

NOTE: The upgrade to QuickTime Pro, which costs $29.95 in the USA, gives you more options with which to edit and export movies in the QuickTime Player application. It also allows you to save at least some of the movie trailers that you download from the Internet. In some cases, you may not be able to access a larger movie trailer without buying the Pro license. This was true, for example, with Star Wars: Episode Two.

Setting Security Preferences

This preference pane (shown in Figure 3.26) combines the functions of the Security pane of Accounts with additional options that affect everyone using your Mac. You can activate FileVault, after setting your Master Password, and choose four options that protect your Mac from access by others. They require passwords for waking or disabling the screen saver, disable automatic login, lock secure system preferences, and provide for automatic log out after a specified idle period.

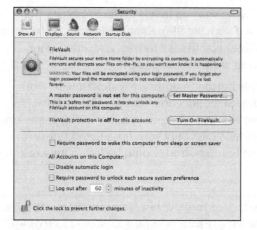

Figure 3.26   Enforce additional security for your Mac here.

Setting Sharing Preferences

Peer-to-peer file sharing is one of the delights of the Mac OS. You don't need a network administrator to set up a network over which you can share files with other users. You just have to open this pane (see Figure 3.27), select the service you want to share and click the Start button to activate the feature. The display at the top shows your Computer Name, which is used to identify your Mac on the network,

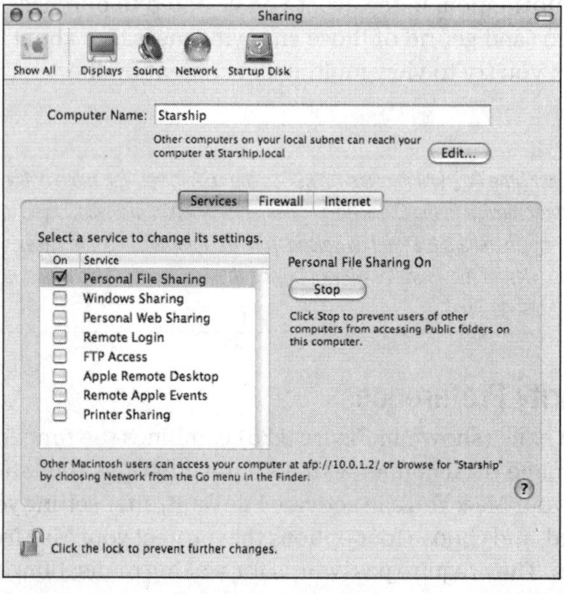

Figure 3.27   Choose whether file sharing and other sharing services will be availab
on your Mac.

and the corresponding name used for Apple's Rendezvous networking technology, along with its IP address for TCP/IP connections. I'll cover this subject in more detail in Chapter 8.

The following sharing preferences are available, selected just by clicking the appropriate button:

- *Services*—Use this to turn on sharing for Personal File Sharing, Sharing with Windows (which allows a Windows PC to see your Mac as just another computer in the network), personal Web sharing, Remote Login (allowing connection from a program that takes over your Mac, such as Timbukto, FTP Access, Remote Apple Events (used for Apple Scripts) and Printer Sharing (for personal or USB printers).

NOTE: You do not have to turn on Sharing with Windows to access files from a Windows PC. It's only required to allow the Windows user to access the files from your Mac. You will also have to engage the option to allow Windows logins for a specific user in the Accounts preference panel.

NOTE: If you want to network with an older Mac that cannot share files via TCP/IP, you'll need to turn on AppleTalk in the Network preference panel before activating file sharing here.

WARNING! The FTP sharing feature is, like Web sharing, a potential security hole, so use this feature with caution. If you must share files in this fashion, be sure to turn on the Firewall feature to protect your Mac.

- *Firewall*—Click the Start button on turn on this feature. If you need to allow access to specific network communication ports, click the service from the Allow list. You'll find they mirror all the sharing features in the Services preference pane. If you need to add other services, such as instant messaging or Timbukto access, click the Edit button and choose the services you want to allow.

- *Internet Sharing*—You can use this feature to share your ISP over your network connection. Just click the checkbox to activate this feature.

NOTE: Your Mac must be on whenever another computer on your network attempts to access the shared connection. You may be better off checking into a separate ISP router, such as Apple's AirPort Base Station, which allows any connected computer (be it wired or wireless) to share an ISP without requiring any specific Mac to be left on.

Related solution:	Found on page:
Setting Up a Web or FTP Server on Your Mac	193

Setting Software Update Preferences

Let me be blunt here: Mac OS X undergoes constant change. Not just the annual upgrade packages, but frequent maintenance revisions that you can expect every month or two during the life of Panther. The Software Update feature (see Figure 3.28) is an essential part of your Mac OS X user experience.

You can opt to update your software manually whenever you want, or select the Automatically option to have Apple's Web site checked on a daily, weekly, or monthly basis for needed updates. The status display will show the last time you attempted the update. Click Update Now whenever you want to recheck for updates. When an update is available, a separate Software Update application will launch, and that's where you can select the updates you want to install from the list (yes, sometimes there's more than one). If you want to see the list of previously received updates, click on the Installed Updates button.

NOTE: If you have a dial-up connection to the Internet, or just don't want to be bothered, check the box labeled Download Important Updates in the Background. This is similar to the Windows software update feature, and allows the updates you need to be retrieved whenever they are available, without your personal intervention. All you have to do is OK the installation and enter your administrator's password to start the installation.

TIP: When you access the Software Update application, choose Save As from the Update menu to store a copy of the update on your drive right after the updates are installed. This is a great way to ensure that the update is available should you need to reinstall it later (perhaps after reinstalling Mac OS X), without having to access the Internet to retrieve it again.

Setting Sound Preferences

Your Mac is, at heart, a multimedia computer with the ability to create and play audio and video productions (with the right additional software for making such productions, of course). There are several categories of settings. Alerts (see Figure 3.29) perform the following:

- *Choose an Alert Sound*—Select the audible warning you get when an alert is displayed. When you pick a sound from the scrolling list, you'll hear it played in your Mac's speaker.

- *Play Alerts and Sound Effects Through*—Do you have an extra set of speakers on your Mac? If you do, you should select the appropriate option here.

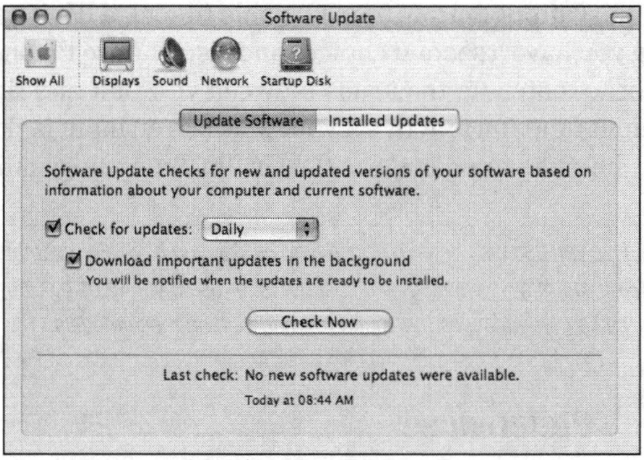

Figure 3.28   Use this feature to update Mac OS X.

- *Alert Volume*—Choose the level at which the Mac plays alert sounds, such as those warning you of a problem with your Mac. If the little beeps and blurbs irritate you, you can make them lower than the overall volume.

- *Checkboxes*—This is the Mac OS X 10.3 equivalent to the system sounds you could activate under Mac OS 9. I disabled both checkboxes after they became a little annoying (they are activated by default), but the first plays a sound when you access a different element of the Aqua interface, such as the Finder or Dock. The other checkbox adds a little click or thumping sound when you press the volume keys on the Apple Pro keyboard.

- *Output Volume*—This setting controls the system volume. The checkbox puts a system menu volume control on your Mac's menu bar.

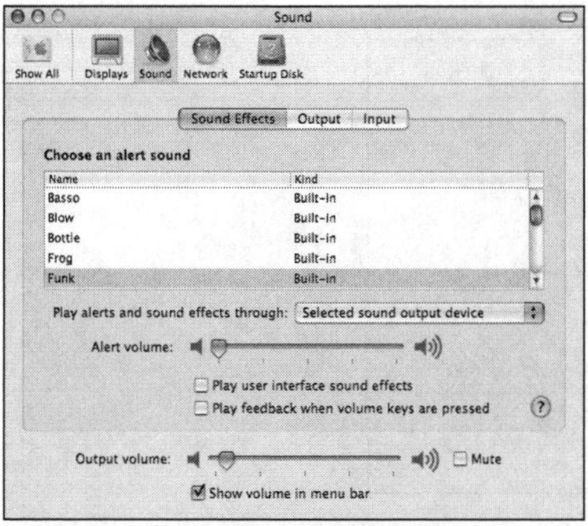

Figure 3.29   Set your volume and choose alert sounds in this pane.

When you click the Output button, you'll be able to pick a device for audio (assuming you have a second choice) and also choose Balance, moving the slider to match up the levels between your left and right speakers. The Input function is active if your Mac has an input jack or a separate audio input adapter, such as the Griffin Technology iMic.

NOTE: The Sound preferences you see also depend on the kind of Mac you have. For example, if you have a slot-loading iMac, you may see additional adjustments for use if you're using Harman Kardon's iSub, a woofer module that enhances the sound reproduction on these models.

Setting Speech Preferences

Some Mac programs support Mac OS X's Speech Manager, which allows you to activate Mac functions via spoken commands and have text read back to you. In the first Speech settings pane, Speech Recognition (see Figure 3.30), you can decide whether to activate the feature. Turn Apple Speakable Items on to specify whether to activate the feature. The standard setup calls for saying "computer" prior to a command. With recognition turned on, you'll be able to access the Speakable Items folder to see the available commands. The Listening and Commands buttons allow you to configure speech recognition options to tailor the feature to your needs.

NOTE: It's not a good idea to be overly dependant on Apple's speech features, unless you have a handicap that makes manual labor difficult. The "recognition" feature won't support all possible Mac commands and doesn't work terribly well in a crowded room. The Text-to-Speech feature works after a fashion, but many words simply are not pronounced correctly. To use speech recognition for dictation, you may want to look for a separate program, such as IBM's ViaVoice or MacSpeech's iListen, both of which allow you to verbally access some of your Mac's commands—but it's still a far cry from the way it is done on Star Trek.

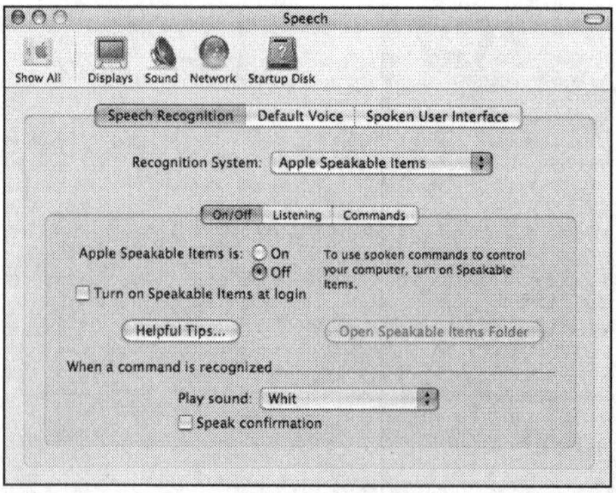

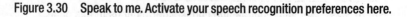

Figure 3.30   Speak to me. Activate your speech recognition preferences here.

The Default Voice and Spoken User Interface buttons allow you to specify the voice for text-to-speech and whether talking alerts will be allowed. Again, this is a personal preference, and most Mac users prefer to leave the features off unless absolutely needed.

Setting Startup Disk Preferences

This setting lets you switch startup disks, if you have additional volumes with system software on them on your Mac. In Figure 3.31, you can see selections representing the names of the volumes connected to my Mac when I wrote this book and the system versions they contained. For most of you, the option will be to switch from Mac OS X back to Mac OS 9, assuming you have an older Mac that supports that feature. In some setups, you might be using the NetBoot feature, present in Panther Server, which allows you to access your operating system from a networked computer. To change the startup disk, follow these steps:

1. Click the icon representing the name of the volume from which you want to boot your Mac.

2. Click the Restart button.

3. You'll see an acknowledgement prompt; click Save and Restart to boot from a different startup volume. Click Cancel to simply save your settings, in case you want to restart at a later time. This choice will produce a dialog in which you'll be asked if you want to save the new settings (even they are the old settings).

4. If you opt to restart later, choose Restart from the Apple menu to boot your Mac from the previously selected startup volume.

WARNING! *For your Mac to boot properly from another startup volume, it must contain system software that's compatible with your computer. The Startup Disk preferences screen only displays the disks on which a Mac OS System Folder is present; it won't always know whether your Mac can run from it. Should your Mac not be able to boot from the specified volume, it will, instead, boot from another volume with a compatible version of the Mac OS (perhaps the one from which you just switched).*

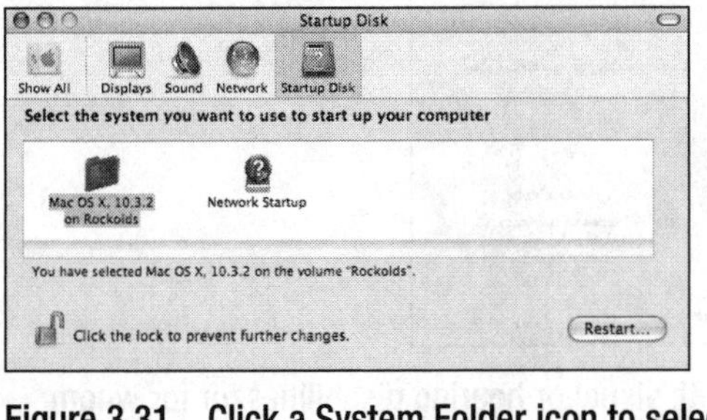

Figure 3.31   Click a System Folder icon to select another startup disk.

5. When you're finished setting your Mac's preferences, choose Quit from the application menu. The changes you make go into effect as soon as you apply them.

Setting Universal Access Preferences

This settings panel (see Figure 3.32) is a direct descendant of the EasyAccess feature of the Classic Mac OS. It's designed for those who are physically disabled, or anyone for whom the keyboard and mouse are difficult to use. The Seeing panel, shown in the figure, activates the Zoom feature, which blows up lettering for easier reading.

The Hearing button activates a visual alert, for those who are hearing impaired. Click the Keyboard button to access a sticky keys feature, to make it easier to handle sequential keystrokes, such as Command+S for Save. You may also choose to play a beep sound when you type the modifier key and see visual confirmation. The Mouse button allows you to use the numeric keypad on your keyboard to emulate the functions of the mouse, using just the number keys to control mouse action.

TIP: To quickly access the Sticky Keys function, press the Shift key five times in a row (repeating the action turns the function off). The Mouse Keys function is activated by pressing the Option key five times in a row (repeat the action to turn the feature off).

NOTE: According to Apple, the accessibility features provided in Panther meet or exceed the requirements of the U.S. government's Section 508 Accessibility statute.

Figure 3.32   For those with visual or hearing disabilities, or for whom mouse and keyboard movement is painful, Mac OS X has a possible solution.

Introducing the
Finder

In Brief

The showpiece of the Macintosh experience is the Finder—Apple's file browser. It has remained a constant since the Mac debuted in 1984. Although it has been enhanced and refined over the years, its basic look and goals have persisted substantially unchanged until Mac OS X appeared on the scene.

The Panther Finder (shown in Figure 4.1) has metamorphosed into a totally new application, bearing more than a passing resemblance to the file viewer for the NeXT operating system and even some of the Mac shareware programs that have been introduced over the years. In fact, it can even find the stuff on your Mac without launching a separate program. At the same time it retains characteristics of the Finder you know and love, although some features appear in a very different form. For Panther, Apple performed still another Finder overhaul, but the differences aren't as extensive as you might realize at first glance.

Aside from the function of the Panther Finder, there's a lot to be said about its form. Using Apple's Quartz imaging technology, as enhanced by Quartz Extreme on Macs with high-energy graphic cards, the Finder is carefully crafted from an artistic standpoint, with a brushed metal motif that bears similarities to such applications as iPhoto, iTunes, and the Safari Web browser.

Despite the surprisingly new look and feel, however, you'll see more than a passing resemblance to the traditional or Classic Mac OS Finder.

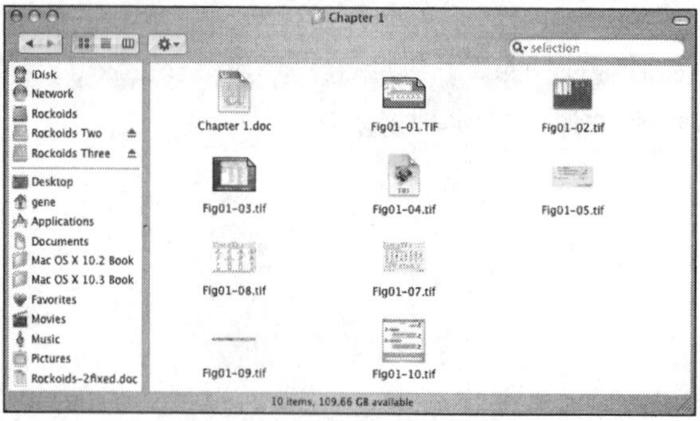

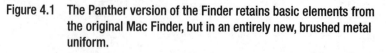

Figure 4.1   The Panther version of the Finder retains basic elements from the original Mac Finder, but in an entirely new, brushed metal uniform.

The basic functions—viewing the contents of a hard drive, as well as opening, copying, and moving files—are not very different despite the highly altered interface. But in some respects, the way you look for files may be substantially changed; and, as you'll see later in this chapter, you have more options with which to customize the Finder's look and feel. To start, look at the ways in which you can now view your files with Panther's Finder. To change the display motif, simply click one of the three small View buttons on the toolbar at the left end of the Finder window. Here's what they do, from left to right:

- *Icon View*—This view option is extremely close to the way you'd examine files with the original Mac Finder. Each Finder item is identified by a unique icon, ranging from the simple folder picture to a far more complicated rendering for some applications. You just double-click any item to open it.

- *List View*—The icons in List View (see Figure 4.2) are small (unless you change the Finder option to make a larger icon, as explained in the "Immediate Solutions" section titled "Setting Viewing Preferences," later in this chapter). As with previous versions of the Mac OS, the contents of a disk or folder are displayed as a list, in four distinct categories: Name, Date Modified, Size, and Kind. You can use the Finder List View preferences to add or remove categories. To open an item, just double-click it.

TIP: *You can easily change the sorting order in List View by clicking the title of the category under which you want the listings sorted. Normally, items are sorted by name; but if you click Date Modified, Size, or another category, the list will be organized in the manner that you select. Click the arrow at the right of the Name or Date Modified category to reverse the sorting order. I use this feature often because it helps me locate the most recent files at a single glance.*

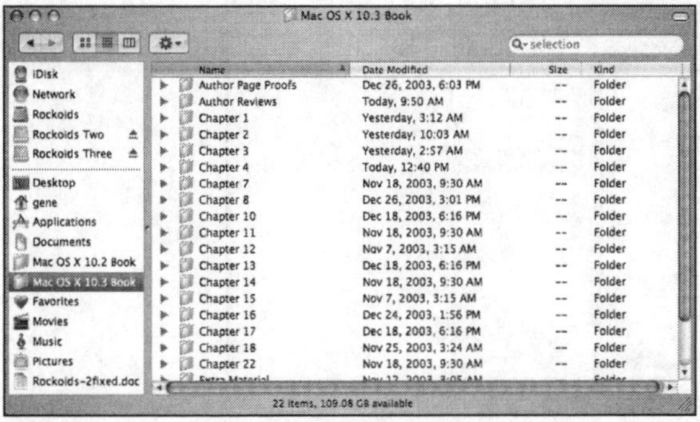

Figure 4.2   You see more items in a Finder window when you choose the List View option.

- *Column View*—The column view option may become your preferred method of file navigation. It gives you a full hierarchical view of the contents of a folder, from left to right (see Figure 4.3). Just click an item to see its contents, which are displayed at the right. If you click a file or application icon, a graphic preview describing the item you selected is displayed. This viewing method is ideal for navigating deeply into nested folders without having to produce endless numbers of open folders on your Mac. In addition, if you click a folder in one of the two rightmost columns, the view shifts to the left.

TIP: Other file browsers are available if you decide the Finder's not your cup of tea. Among the selections, SNAX offers an enhanced viewing interface. Macintosh Explorer X more or less mimics the file viewing features of Windows. You can find these programs and other offerings at www.versiontracker.com.

Additional Finder Navigation Features

After you've opened a folder, you can Command+click the title bar to produce a pop-up menu to see the direction (path) of your folder navigation and access the higher-level folders through which you've traveled. This feature is a carryover from earlier Mac OS versions. You can also move back through previous folders one at a time (regardless of the path) by clicking the back arrow. This operates like the back arrow of a Web browser.

TIP: The back arrow takes you to the previously viewed window and the forward arrow takes you to the next window. It is grayed out if there is no next window. If you prefer the Classic Mac OS Finder, just click the little rectangular button at the upper right and the picture will

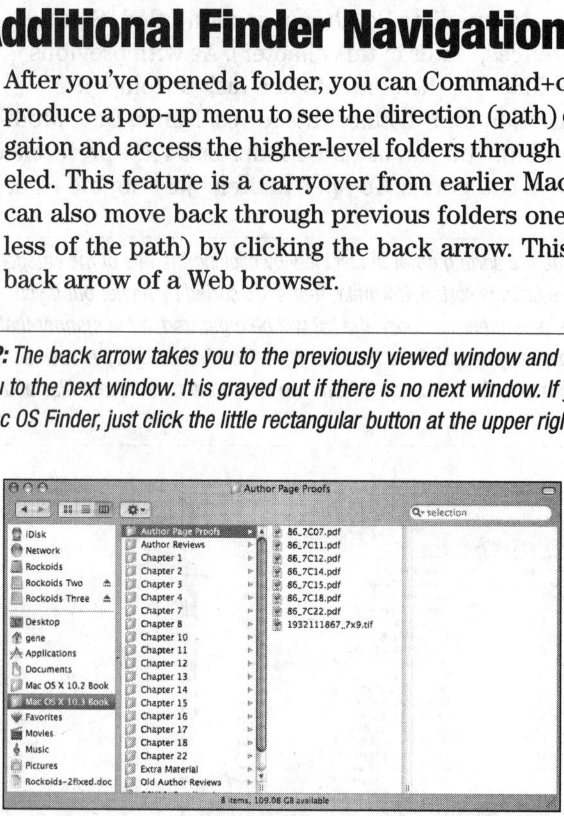

Figure 4.3   Click once on an item at the left to see the contents at the right.

change. The brushed metal look is gone, the Sidebar and toolbar vanish, and the Finder will spawn new windows whenever you open a disk or folder.

Visiting the Finder's Sidebar

In updating the Finder for Panther, Apple didn't just give it a new interface. They also made it more user-centric. With the previous Finder, you could use the horizontal scroll bar to navigate a drive from top to bottom. With Panther, the navigation scheme has changed and clicking an icon on the Sidebar (see Figure 4.4) uses that location as the starting point.

This navigation features is especially helpful if you add a folder to the Sidebar that is many levels deep. Once you become accustomed to the setup, you'll be able to get to the files you need much faster.

You also can easily customize the Sidebar the way you want. If you click and drag an icon away from the Sidebar, the icon will vanish just as it does when you remove something from the Dock. If you drag an icon to the Sidebar, the icon goes wherever you place it. The existing icons adjust in size to accommodate the new entry.

4. Introducing the Finder

Figure 4.4   The Finder's Sidebar is a new feature for Panther and one you'll get used to very quickly.

The Sidebar is a convenient replacement for the Favorites feature, which hasn't completely disappeared. You'll notice this if you take a close look at the illustrations in this chapter. Favorites is just harder to get to as you'll see in the Immediate Solutions part of this chapter.

Visiting the Finder's Toolbar

Another highly useful feature of Panther's Finder is a customizable toolbar, a carryover from previous versions of Mac OS X. The toolbar has been changed a bit with Panther. While it's basically used for Finder window navigation and view settings, it offers more features:

- *Browser-like navigation arrows*—Click the left arrow to move to the previous window and click the right arrow, if not grayed out, to advance to the next window.

- *View options*—As I said before, you can use this option to toggle through the three standard Finder views.

- *Action menu*—This new Panther feature (see Figure 4.5) allows you to perform a task associated with a specific item. When you click on the Action menu you'll see a pop-up menu, showing commands that relate to any item you've selected, be it a file, folder, or drive. The Action menu is identical to the context menus you see when you Command-click or right-click a Finder item.

- *Search*—If you know a file's name but you don't know where it is, just enter the name in this text entry field and you'll see a display of the files that match your search request as you enter the file name.

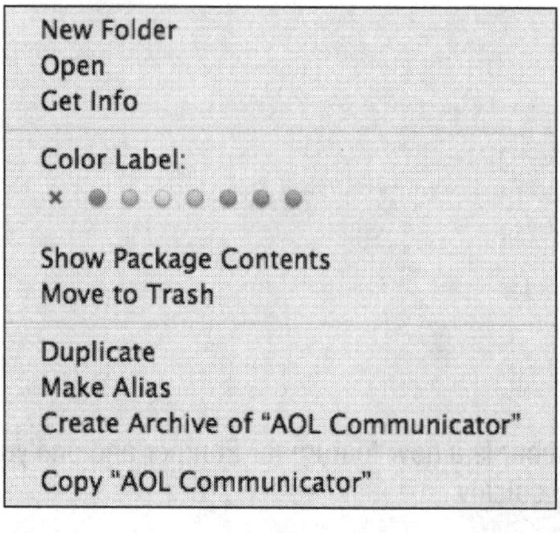

Figure 4.5   The Action menu is a real keystroke saver.

TIP: *Click the tiny arrow next to the magnifying glass and you'll be able to fine-tune your search using one of the following options: Local Disks, Home (your User directory), Selection, and Everywhere.*

The Panther Finder Menus

The Mac OS Finder has had essentially the same display options from day one. But certain elements have changed in Panther, although they aren't as drastic as the Finder's new look. There is, for example, an Apple menu (shown in Figure 4.6), which hasn't changed much since the original Mac OS X release back in March 2001.

Although the Apple menu looks the same, you'll notice some changes in its contents, particularly if you're upgrading from Mac OS 9. Part of this is the result of the elimination of the Finder's Special menu. All those commands, and some extras, are now available system-wide in the Apple menu. You now don't have to return to the Finder to activate these functions.

4. Introducing the Finder

NOTE: *If you use a Classic application, the Apple menu you see is the old one, from your Classic Mac OS System Folder. It can be configured just as before by dropping items into the Apple Menu Items folder, within that System Folder. That capability doesn't extend to the Mac OS X variant.*

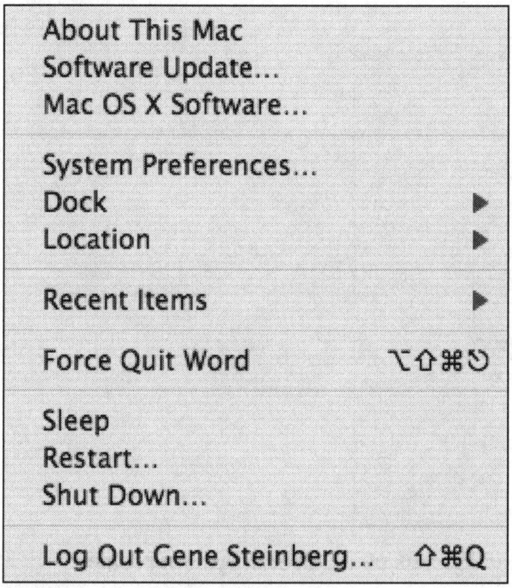

About This Mac
Software Update...
Mac OS X Software...
System Preferences...
Dock ▶
Location ▶
Recent Items ▶
Force Quit Word ⌥⇧⌘⌫
Sleep
Restart...
Shut Down...
Log Out Gene Steinberg... ⇧⌘Q

Figure 4.6 A familiar menu, but in a different guise.

Here's the list of the Apple menu features:

- *About This Mac*—Choose this command to see a window displaying the Mac OS X version you are using, the amount of memory installed, and the kind of processor your Mac has (see Figure 4.7). The amount of virtual memory is no longer listed because virtual memory is a full-time function and is never turned off. A button is provided to take you to the Software Update application. You can also access the More Info dialog, which launches System Profiler, an application that can display information about all of your installed hardware and software.

TIP: *Mac OS X version numbers are also classified by build numbers, which are used by Apple's Mac OS X system software team to catalog the development process. Just click the version number in the About This Mac window to see the actual build number. On some Macs, a third click will produce your computer's serial number. Either way, once you've gone through the options, the next click takes you back to where you started.*

- *Software Update*—This important feature can be configured to check Apple's Web site at periodic intervals for the latest Panther updates.

- *Mac OS X Software*—Select this command to be taken to a page on Apple's Web site where you can download Mac OS X software. You can also check out links to purchase new commercial applications.

Figure 4.7   The first screen focuses on the overall system profile.

- *System Preferences*—Access the System Preferences application from here.

- *Dock*—Configure the settings for the famous Dock, such as whether you'd like to hide it, magnify the icons when you pass the mouse over them, anchor the Dock in a different position, and so on. Chapter 5 covers this subject in more detail.

- *Location*—Location may be the watchword for realtors, but it's also a Panther feature that lets you customize network and Internet setups for different places. It is especially helpful if you move your Mac from place to place (invaluable with an iBook or PowerBook). Chapter 8 covers this feature in more detail.

NOTE: *Panther is multihoming by default, which means it can automatically switch among a single set of network and ISP hookups, including an AirPort network, Ethernet network, and dial-up connection.*

- *Recent Items*—*This feature is* a carryover from the Apple Menu Options software of previous Mac OS versions. It displays up to 10 recent applications and documents in the submenu by default, or up to 50 each, courtesy of the Appearance preference panel in the System Preferences application.

- *Special menu items*—The remaining five items—Force Quit, Sleep, Restart, Shut Down, and Log Out—are Special menu–type commands moved to the Apple menu for convenient access without returning to the Finder. You can also access the Force Quit dialog box via the Command+Option+Esc keystroke.

TIP: *Commands shown with one or more letters beginning with the Command (or Apple) key are keyboard shortcuts you can use to access a feature without using the mouse.*

Following is a list of the basics of the remaining Finder menus:

- *Application menu*—As with previous versions of Mac OS X, you'll see the name of an application in bold (see Figure 4.8) for clear identification. One important feature of any application menu is the Services submenu, which provides direct links to programs that extend the features of the one you're using. You can, for example, take a selected text passage that's actually a URL and open the site in a Web browser window. You can use the various hide options to hide the program in which you're working or to hide other programs for a cleaner desktop. The Finder's application menu adds Secure Empty Trash, which overwrites a deleted file with lots of ones and zeros, so you can't get it back, even with one of those file recovery utilities.

Figure 4.8   The Finder's application menu has new Panther features.

NOTE: Older, Classic Mac applications still have their Quit commands in the File menu, and their application menus will still appear in the original spot at the right side of the menu bar. This is likely to be confusing to some of you but you should get used to it after a while.

TIP: If you hold down the Option key while selecting another application's window, all windows for other programs will be hidden from view. The exceptions are applications that run in the Mac OS 9 or Classic environment. The Show All feature in the application menu reverses the effect. This feature works the same as it did with earlier versions of the Mac OS.

- *File menu*—The Finder's File menu (see Figure 4.9) isn't much different from the one in prior versions of Mac OS X. There are, however, a few notable exceptions. One exception is Create Archive, which will use industry-standard Zip technology to compress selected files or folders. The Color Label feature restores a cherished Classic Mac OS feature, which adds a color to a file or folder. Some users set Labels to mark important projects that need to be worked on first.

Figure 4.9   A built-in Zip compression tool and Finder labels are welcome additions to Panther's Finder.

- *Edit menu*—Some things never change. The Edit menu, shown in Figure 4.10, is functionally identical to the Edit menu of older versions of the Mac OS, except for one big addition: You can actually copy a file or folder from the Finder in addition to text or a picture object. You do so in the same way you would in Windows. This technique lets you copy these items without having to navigate or manipulate Finder windows to allow for a normal drag-and-drop operation. What's more, the Undo command also affects the last copy or move operation.

- *View menu*—The first three options (see Figure 4.11) simply mirror those available in the Finder itself. You can select to view items as icons, a list, or as columns. The other choices let you hide a Finder window's toolbar, customize the Finder's toolbar, or set view options. I'll explain the latter in detail later in this chapter.

- *Go menu*—This menu inherits some elements of the original Apple menu in Mac OS X (see Figure 4.12). Four of the first five choices mirror the standard toolbar options in the Finder, plus add the ability to bring up your iDisk, part of Apple's .Mac suite of online subscription services. The Recent Folders option provides a submenu of recent Finder folders you've accessed. Another new command to the mix—Go To Folder—lets you type the actual path of a folder in order to bring it up. An example would be "/

4. Introducing the Finder

Can't Undo	⌘Z
Cut	⌘X
Copy "AppleWorks 6"	⌘C
Paste item	⌘V
Select All	⌘A
Show Clipboard	
Special Characters...	

Figure 4.10   The contents of Panther's Edit menu have not changed very much from the menu in Mac OS 9.

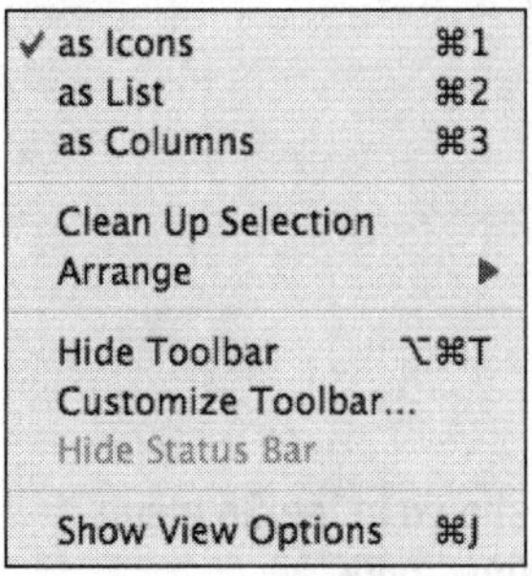

✓ as Icons	⌘1
as List	⌘2
as Columns	⌘3
Clean Up Selection	
Arrange	▶
Hide Toolbar	⌥⌘T
Customize Toolbar...	
Hide Status Bar	
Show View Options	⌘J

Figure 4.11   Choose the manner in which Finder contents are displayed from this menu.

users/<*your username*>," which would immediately transport you to your Home directory. The Connect To Server option is an alternate method of accessing remote servers, such as FTP sites. But you'll be using the Network globe for most of your access to file shares, as I'll explain in Chapter 8.

- *Window menu*—This menu is also found in most applications. The second option—Minimize Window—shrinks an application or the Finder window to the Dock. Bring All To Front makes all open Finder windows accessible (you'll use this option if the windows were previously hidden from view). The items at the bottom of the display are the names of the Finder windows presently open. Select the one you want to bring to the front.

NOTE: Among the applications that don't sport a Window menu is Ready,SetGo, a Mac OS X port of an aging desktop publishing application.

- *Help menu*—Most of the information that Apple provides about Panther is available here, brought up in a convenient browser window rather than in a printed document. To access a lot of this material, you'll need to know the what to search. (But at least you have this book to learn the rest.) In addition, just about every Mac application has some sort of Help support. With Panther, Apple has sped up performance considerably, and you no longer have to wait 20 to 30 seconds or more to bring up a Help window.

NOTE: Apple's printed documentation for Panther is very slim and hardly covers the basics. The company expects you to seek out the Help menu and Web site for more information.

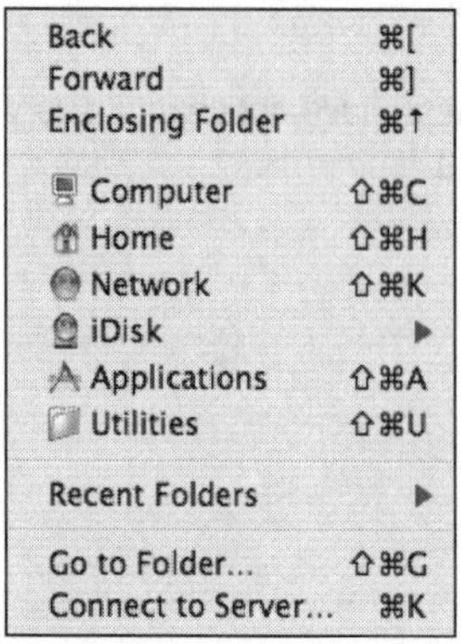

Figure 4.12   The Forward and Back features shown in the Go menu operate in the Finder's Column View mode.

Immediate Solutions

Setting Finder Preferences

Frankly, you really don't need to customize or alter the Panther Finder. You can continue to use it in its pure form if you prefer, running applications on your Mac, surfing the Net, and so on, without needing to alter its appearance. But there are many ways to customize its look and feel.

By default, the Panther Finder displays its contents in single-window mode. You open the contents of a folder in the Finder, and the Finder replaces the contents in the window with the contents of the opened folder. This is pretty much the way Web browsers work, unless a page is set to open in a new window. If you want to change this functionality to the way it worked with the previous Mac OS, where opening a folder opened a new Finder window, you can take any of the actions described in the following sections.

Keeping Folder Views Consistent

This preference dialog establishes the default behavior when you double-click a folder icon to open it. Just follow these instructions:

1. Choose Preferences from the Finder's application menu, and click the General icon to bring up the Finder Preferences window shown in Figure 4.13.

NOTE: I will cover the desktop-related preferences in Chapter 5, so don't be concerned that they aren't all tackled in this chapter.

2. If you need to change a Finder preference, click on the appropriate checkbox to select or unselect an item. The following Finder preferences are available:

   - *Show these items on the Desktop*—Do you want to see the icons for mounted disks or network shares or not? It's all up to you.

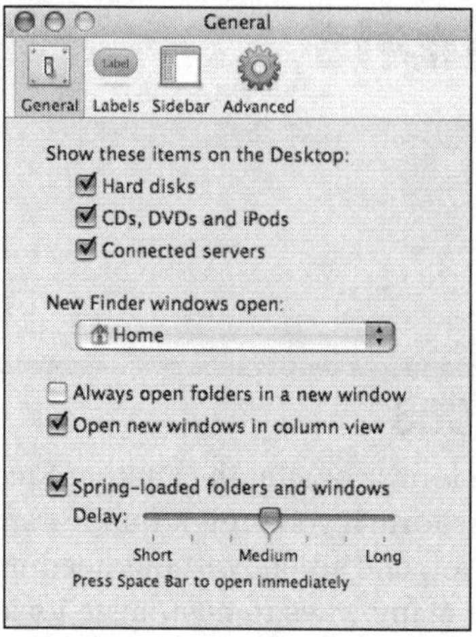

Figure 4.13   Select the way the Finder displays the contents of an opened folder.

- *New Finder Window open*—Choose among such options as Home, Computer, or Documents, or click the Other command to select the folder you prefer. If you use a different folder for current projects, you can specify that location here, and each new Finder window will point there, just like that.

- *Always open folders in a new window*—This option makes Finder behavior similar to what you had in the Classic Mac OS (what some call the spatial Finder). Opening a new folder will spawn a new Finder window, one that applies strictly to that folder. Although you will probably prefer the Mac OS X way of doing things when you get used to it, you aren't forced to stay with single-window behavior.

- *Open new windows in Column view*—Take your choice. Leaving this box checked supports the new viewing option available in Panther, but you can stick with icon or list view like the Mac OS of old if you prefer.

- *Spring-loaded folders and windows*—Move the slider to adjust the delay. When you drag an item over a folder, it'll open after a short delay, allowing you to see the contents. Holding the item over a folder within the parent folder will soon open that as well. Regardless of the interval you set, and it's a matter of personal taste, you can use the spacebar key to open it immediately.

Other Finder Preference Settings

As you noticed in the previous section, three more icons representing various Finder preferences are available in Panther:

- *Labels*—You can apply specific names to the various label colors. By default, Apple names them by color. But if you would rather have Red mean Priority or Avoid (my favorite), for example, go for it.

- *Sidebar*—This is a simple list of checkboxes (see Figure 4.14), which lets you configure the default icons that appear on the Finder's Sidebar. I tend to think there is nothing wrong with removing something you aren't going to use, such as Network, if you don't log into file shares.

- *Advanced*—There are three choices that confront you when you click the Advance icon. The first is whether file extensions, such as myfile.doc for a Word document, are always displayed. Unfortunately, this can be confusing, as some files show these extensions even if this choice is left unchecked. The best bet is to leave well enough alone. There's also the option here to disable the warning before you empty the trash. If you are confident that you don't need a warning, uncheck it. The last option allows you to select which languages to use when searching a file for content. Click the Select button to make your choice from the ones you've installed.

TIP: *Another way to avoid the Finder's warning about emptying the Trash is simply to click the Trash icon in the Dock and, while it's held down, choose Empty Trash from the pop-up menu. You can't change your mind later. The only way to keep from removing a file is in the event you do not have permission to trash that particular file.*

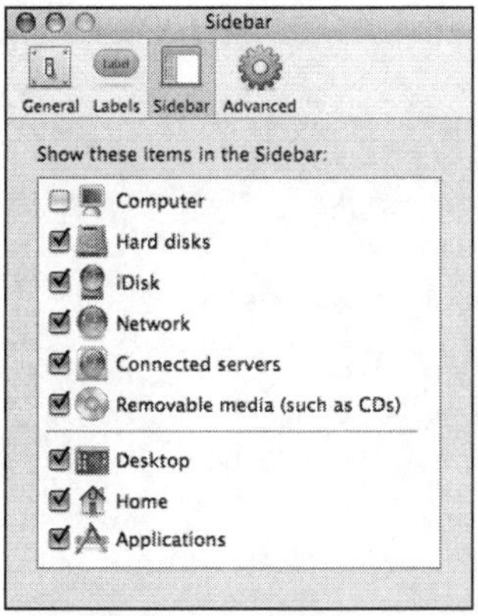

Figure 4.14   Customize the default look of the Finder's Sidebar with these options.

When you're finished configuring the Finder, click the red light button to close the window and save your preferences. From here on, all folder windows opened within a Finder window will inherit the same view setting, whether Icon, List, or Column View.

NOTE: *I didn't skip the other preference settings. I'll discuss the remaining Finder Preferences options in Chapter 5 because they relate to how the desktop is displayed.*

If you don't want to make a permanent change in the way an opened folder displays, just hold down the Option key to reverse the behavior when you double-click a folder icon. That way, you can decide on the fly whether a new Finder window is opened.

Related solution:	Found on page:
Setting Finder Preferences	91

Setting Viewing Preferences

You can easily set the way items appear in the Panther Finder. Settings can be made on a global basis, so they apply to all open Finder windows and all display categories, or to a specific Finder window. The options you have depend on the view setting, so each will be explained separately:

1. With a Finder window with Icon View selected open, go to the View menu and choose Show View Options, or press Command+J. The window shown in Figure 4.15 appears.

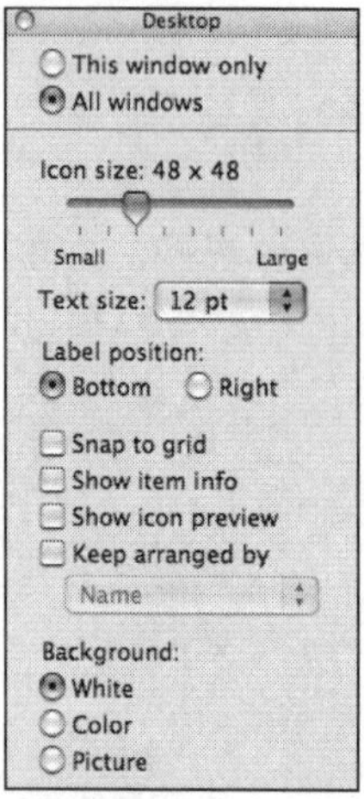

Figure 4.15   Choose a global or individual preference here.

2. Click the All windows if you want all Finder windows to inherit your changes or This window only to affect just the selected Finder window. You can choose from the following changes:

- *Icon Size*—By default, icons are fairly large—at least compared to older versions of the Mac OS. You can move the slider to change their size as you look on.

- *Text size*—Is 12 point too large for you? You can select from 8 point to 16 point.

- *Label position*—At the bottom or to the right of the icon? Your call.

- *Icon Arrangement*—Whether you like your desktop automatically arranged or not, the choice is yours. Just click the appropriate radio button. The default—None—means you can place your disk, file, and folder icons as you wish, anywhere in a Finder window. The Always Snap To Grid option is similar to what you find in some drawing programs. The icons are spaced by an invisible grid, at fixed distances apart. The Show item info option will display the size of a picture file and the number of items in a folder. Show icon preview does what the name implies, providing preview images of picture files. The final option—Keep Arranged By—gives you a pop-up menu of sort sequences: Choose from Name, Date Modified, Date Created, Size, and Kind.

- *Background*—This Finder feature is available in icon view. You can leave it set at White if you prefer the default background. Otherwise, you can give your Finder background a unique color by clicking the Color radio box, then on the box at the right to bring up an Apple Color Picker (see Figure 4.16). After you click the kind of color adjustments you want, moving the sliders with the mouse changes the selected colors. When you click the final Background option—Picture—you'll see a Select button that you click to bring up the Open dialog box. There, you can choose a picture.

After you've made your settings, you can click the close button to activate the changes. Or, go to the next section if you want to make further Finder changes.

NOTE: *Remember that a background color or picture you select will apply only to the selected Finder window unless you click All windows.*

Figure 4.16   Drag the sliders to produce a color scheme that suits your taste.

3. If you prefer the Finder's List View, the View Options window is different (see Figure 4.17). You can choose an icon size, and text size, just as in Icon View. Under Show Columns, choose which categories you want displayed. The most interesting option here is Comments which allows you to sort by the Finder comments you place in the Get Info window, a useful way to keep tabs on documents that require special priority or

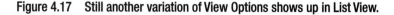

Figure 4.17   Still another variation of View Options shows up in List View.

are needed to meet a deadline. The Use Relative Dates option gives you such selections as Yesterday and Today (but never Tomorrow—that was a bad joke!). Calculate All Sizes will give you the size of items in a folder, but at the expense of slowing down performance; the same issue was true with the Classic Mac OS. The final option is Icon Size. Make it small or make it large—those are all the choices you have

---

TIP: *You can still view the size of an item without checking it in the View Options window. Instead, select a folder and choose Get Info from the Finder's File menu. You'll then see a visual display of the size in the first or General category.*

---

4. When you're finished setting Finder preferences, click the close button.

Changing Finder List View Columns

To change the sort order, simply click on a column title; when an arrow appears, you can reverse the sort order. The Panther Finder can be customized extensively in List View. In addition to adjusting preferences as to which categories are displayed, you can further modify it in two ways:

- *Resize Category Lists*—Move the mouse between the columns, and you'll see the cursor change to reflect two opposite pointed arrows. Then, simply click and drag the column to resize it. The change you make is reflected in all new Finder windows.

- *Change Order Of Categories*—You can also move an entire category into a new position in the Finder window. Just click and drag the Finder category to its new location, and let go of the mouse button. This change can be made in all categories except Name. After a category is in a new position, the change is reflected in all new Finder windows.

Resizing Columns in Column View

If you opt for the Finder's Column View, you aren't locked into the default size either. Just click the two vertical lines at the bottom in the space between columns and drag back and forth to resize the columns. If you hold down the Option key, the change is confined to the column at the left.

The changes you make in this fashion will affect all the new Finder windows you open in Column View, if you close the window first.

NOTE: You may have to open and close a Finder window a time or two for the new settings to take. This is not something you did wrong. It's a quirk of the Panther Finder that might, perhaps, be fixed in an update.

Customizing the Finder's Toolbar

You can simply hide the Finder's toolbar, if you prefer the old ways of the Mac OS—the ability to open a folder and spawn a new Finder window. If you decide to keep the toolbar open, you can customize it in a variety of ways. Here's how it's done:

1. Choose Customize Toolbar from the Finder's View menu to bring up a convenient window displaying additional navigation icons (see Figure 4.18).

2. To add an icon, drag it to the toolbar. You can use the Separator icon to categorize your selections.

NOTE: If you add too many icons, you can drag the resize bar to the right to make the Finder window wider; otherwise, you can click the arrow at the end of the toolbar to access the remaining icons.

3. To limit the toolbar icon to either the icon or the text, make your choices from the Show pop-up menu at the bottom of the screen.

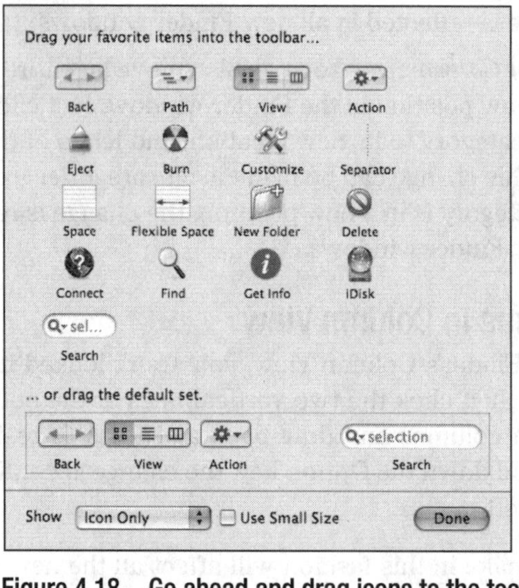

Figure 4.18 Go ahead and drag icons to the toolbar.

TIP: *If you make a mistake and put the wrong icon in the toolbar, you can click and drag it to a new position.*

4. Click the Done button to complete the process.

TIP: *To restore the toolbar to factory issue, click the default set on the Customize Toolbar screen and drag it to the toolbar. It will replace the contents.*

NOTE: *Even though Apple expects you to add icons to the Sidebar, you can also add them to the Finder's toolbar. But the process is slower. You first have to drag an icon to the toolbar, wait a few seconds (be patient now!), and you'll see a rectangle appear where you can place the icon.*

After you've altered the toolbar, you can remove an icon by holding down the Command key and dragging the icon off the toolbar. The default toolbar icons, however, cannot be removed this way. They can be removed only when you bring up the Customize Toolbar screen.

TIP: *The Path icon in the Customize Toolbar screen is useful. When you add it to the toolbar, clicking it will show the folder path of the item you've selected, which lets you quickly move to higher folder levels. Of course, holding down the Command key and clicking the title of a Finder window gets the same result.*

Using the New Finder on a Day-to-Day Basis

After you have configured the Panther Finder the way you want, you'll find that it's real easy to get accustomed to the new way of handling your Mac's files and even the somewhat restricted organizational requirements. In the next few pages of this chapter, I discuss basic file management techniques. For the most part, you'll see they aren't terribly different from earlier versions of the Mac OS.

Moving a File

To move a file from one folder to another, simply click to select the file, and then drag it to the new folder. You might need to open another Finder window to move between widely disparate folders.

Copying a File

To copy a file from one folder to another, hold down the Option key as the file is being dragged to its new location. This copying function is automatic if you are moving an icon from one drive's folder to a folder on another drive.

TIP: *If the folder you want to copy a file to is buried deep and not easily accessed, just use the Copy command in the Finder's Edit menu to copy the entire file or folder. Now open the folder into which you want to copy the item, and then choose Paste from the Edit menu to put a copy there. This is, of course, similar to the way it happens in the Windows platform. You can also simply drag the file atop a folder or Finder toolbar icon, and hold it, and it'll spring open. Then you can place it inside or put atop another folder within the parent folder.*

Making an Alias

An *alias* is a pointer to the original file that aids in file navigation (it's similar to a shortcut in Windows or a symbolic link under other Unix-based operating systems). You can put the alias where you want without having to depend on Panther's organizational structure for applications and other files. Many Mac users place aliases for files on the desktop, putting them a double-click away from launching without having to burrow deep through nested folders.

To make an alias, simply select the item, and then choose Make Alias from the Finder's File menu or press Command+L. The alias can then be moved or copied to your preferred location.

TIP: *To make an alias of an item and move it at the same time, simply drag it to its new location while holding down the Command and Option keys.*

Finding a File

Why call it Finder if you don't use it to find something? That's an old argument, since the search tools were always available as a separate function. However, with Panther, there's an integrated Search function in the toolbar (you can remove it if you customize the toolbar icons, of course). To locate an item in the folder or disk you've opened, just enter its name or part of the name, in the search field. A list of likely candidates will appear (see Figure 4.19) in a browser window, labeled by relevance.

NOTE: *You can still bring up a search screen via Command+F, with more elaborate searching options. I'll cover that topic, plus Apple's redesigned version of the Sherlock search application, in Chapter 7.*

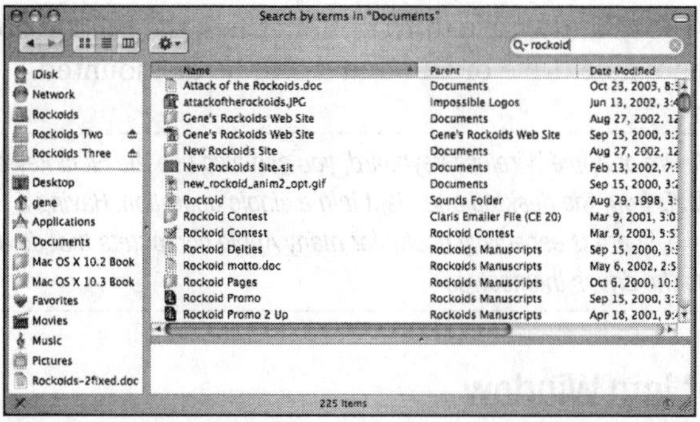

Figure 4.19   Here's a search window with likely responses to your search request.

A Fast Way to Add Items to the Sidebar

You don't have to simply drag items to the Sidebar. Just select the item, press Command-T and it'll jump there right away, to the bottom of the list. You can still drag and drop the item to a different position.

TIP: *If you missed the Favorites feature of previous versions of the Mac OS, here's a way to restore it, more or less. Look inside the Library folder, within your personal Users folder, and you'll find a folder named Favorites. When you drag it to the Finder's Sidebar, it'll bear the familiar heart-shaped icon. You can now drag an alias to an item into the Favorites folder, for fast Panther Finder access.*

Accessing the Action and Contextual Menus

This feature, whether from the Finder toolbar or via the common keystrokes, produces a pop-up menu related to the item selected. It's quite similar to the right-click feature of Windows. To access the contextual menu, select an item and hold down the Control key.

NOTE: *Some third-party input devices, from such companies as Contour, Kensington, MacAlley, and Microsoft, have extra buttons that you can program to access the contextual menus. This will be familiar territory for Windows users.*

Ejecting a Disk

This function works the same as it did in previous versions of the Mac OS, with a small exception. The normal behavior is to drag the disk icon to the Trash. You can also press Command+E after the drive has been selected. When you drag a disk icon to the Trash, the icon for the Trash changes to an eject symbol, no doubt a response to complaints from user interface experts that you aren't trashing a disk when you eject it. New for Panther is a third option: Click the Eject icon at the right of a removable drive or CD, and it will be dismounted.

TIP: *If you have an Apple Pro or Apple Wireless keyboard, you can also use the Eject key or F12 to remove a CD or DVD from the desktop and eject it in a single operation. Having a drive access key on the keyboard is especially useful for many Apple computers that do not have CD eject buttons on the drives themselves.*

Using the Get Info Window

Panther's Get Info window (see Figure 4.20) allows you to learn more about a file and configure several options, such as changing file privileges and altering the application used to open a file. What you see depends on the kind of item selected. A document will provide one set of options, an application another. Here are the basic features, each disclosed or hidden by a click of the triangle:

NOTE: *When you use the Get Info command with a Classic application, you will see a Memory option, which you can use to control allocation of memory for that application. Mac OS X's superior memory management doesn't help your older Mac applications.*

- *General*—Expanded by default, it displays general information about a selected item, including its location and size. If you've selected an application, it shows the version information. You can also lock a file in this pane so that it can't be modified.

WARNING! *It is a bad idea to lock an application or application support file. Many of these programs modify themselves as you use them, and locking the file can cause weird behavior problems, or even make the program refuse to run. If you're not sure, don't do it! There are other ways to protect your documents, such as Panther's FileVault feature. Chapter 6 has more information on Mac OS X security and setting up your computer for multiple users.*

- *Name & Extension*—For documents, this option lets you change the file's name and specify whether the file extension that applies to that document will appear.

NOTE: *The Get Info window is context sensitive, and will have options that depend on the kind of file that's selected. For example, if you bring up a Get Info window for a folder or disk, you'll have a Content index option with an Index Now button that will catalog text for the Finder's search feature.*

- *Open with*—If you've selected a document, this option lets you change the application that launches that document, or all documents of the same type.

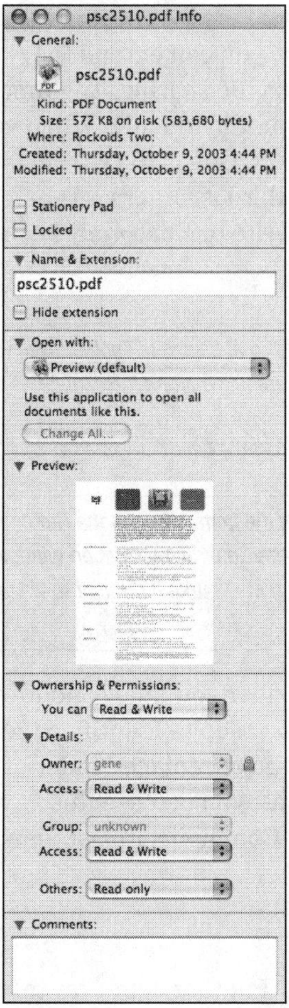

Figure 4.20   This is the Get Info window, with all its categories expanded.

- *Languages*—This window (available for Mac OS X applications only) shows the languages supported by an application. You can uncheck some of them, if you wish; doing so might improve performance at the expense of limiting the application's ability to handle multilingual material.

- *Preview*—This feature appears only when you select a document icon. You can use it to view a preview image of the document.

NOTE: If the icon you've selected belongs to a Classic application, all you'll see is an enlarged picture of its icon.

- *Ownership and Permissions*—Use this window to set access privileges to the selected item. That way, you can extend the range of users who can view that item via file sharing. The first listing explains your rights to open and modify the file. When you click Details, you'll see categories of users. One is the Owner (you), the second is the Group, and the third is Others. In each case you can set privileges for Read & Write or Read Only access to a disk, folder or separate file.

NOTE: On some items, such as files reserved for the system or that belong to another user, you will have to click the lock and enter an administrator's password into a prompt to change privileges.

TIP: You can easily change the icon for an item. Just select the item, bring up the Get Info window, and paste the new icon atop the previous icon in the General Information window. This is best done for drives and folders. Changing a file icon may make it difficult to visually identify which application opens the file.

- *Comments*—Like the Classic Mac OS Finder you knew and loved, you can place comments here that can be used to identify a file, or specify a priority. Although it doesn't quite replace Finder Labels from Mac OS 9 and earlier systems, you can use this feature, along with the ability to sort by Comments in List View, to keep tabs on important files.

Taking Screenshots

As in previous versions of the Mac OS, Panther lets you take a screenshot of the contents of your desktop or a selected item via simple keyboard shortcuts. The captured images are saved in PDF format and placed on your desktop. They bear the name Picture 1, Picture 2, and so on.

Here's a brief run-through of the built-in screen capture capabilities:

- *Command+Shift+3*—This is the original shortcut. When you press this combo, a picture of your entire screen is captured.

- *Command+Control+Shift+3*—This awkward combination also captures the entire screen, but puts the data in the clipboard, so you can paste it within an open document window via the Paste command.

- *Command+Shift+4*—This combination changes the cursor to a crosshair. Just drag the cursor across the area you want to capture. When you release the mouse, the area is captured as a screenshot.

TIP: *Press a spacebar after typing this combo and you'll be able to automatically select a specific window to capture without having to manually drag the cursor around it (a process very easy to do incorrectly). The cursor will take on the image of a camera, and when you click on a window, only that window will be captured.*

- *Command+Control+Shift+4*—This combination also lets you select an area for capturing. The saved area is stored in the clipboard for pasting into another application.

TIP: *Panther includes Grab, in the Utilities folder, which can also do timed screen grabs and save the results with the file name you choose. However, if you do lots of screen captures, my personal recommendation is Snapz Pro X, a shareware application available from Ambrosia Software (**www.ambrosiasw.com**). I used this program to capture all the illustrations in this book.*

NOTE: *If you want to convert your screen shot to a different format, just use Apple's Preview application, in the Applications folder, to convert to any of the popular image formats, such as JPEG and TIFF.*

Using the Finder to Burn CDs and DVDs

When Apple got the message and added built-in CD burners, it also added a feature that lets you burn your CDs from the Finder. Under Panther, it works essentially the same as in your Classic Mac OS:

1. Insert a blank CD, CD/RW, or DVD-R disc into the drive. After a short time in which the optical media is analyzed, you'll see a screen prompt where you can prepare the media for copying data (see Figure 4.21).

NOTE: *If you need to format the CD/RW, Disk Utility will open to the proper screen, where you can erase it.*

WARNING! *The Finder's CD burning feature works primarily with Apple's built-in CD and DVD burners (DVD-R support requires the SuperDrive), and a moderate selection of supported third-party devices. If you want to see the current supported list, check with Apple's iTunes site at **www.apple.com/itunes**. Whatever drives are supported by iTunes will, in large part, work with Finder-level disk burning as well.*

2. Name your CD or DVD and then choose what you want to do next from the pop-up menu. For data CDs, you'll want to open the Finder, so you can move files to the CD icon that will be created. If you want to make a music CD, you can select the option in the menu to open iTunes.

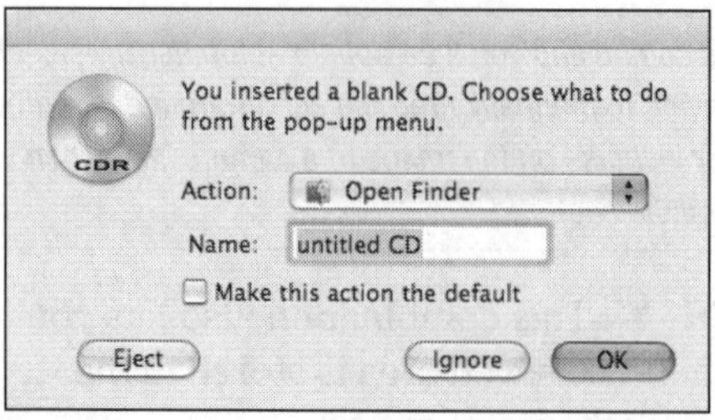

Figure 4.21   What do you want to do with the blank optical media you inserted?

3. With your selections made, click OK to complete the initial setup process. In a few seconds, you'll see an icon on your Mac's desktop identified by the type of media you prepared.

4. Drag the files you want to copy to the optical disc's icon.

WARNING! Depending on the kind of media you use, you'll be limited to 700MB for an 80-minute CD, 650MB for a 74-minute CD, and 4.7GB for a DVD-R. You will receive a Finder warning if you attempt to copy over too many files.

5. If you want to organize the layout of the optical media before it's burned, open its window and reorder the icons as you like and the position of the window. This will simplify locating the material on the disc later.

6. After the layout is set up, choose Burn Disc from the Finder's File menu to begin the process. You'll get a final warning from the Finder to confirm that you really want to burn a disc.

7. After you OK the prompt, the disk burning process will begin, followed by a verification procedure in which the data will be read back to make sure that the data is good.

8. When the disc burning process is complete, you can insert more media and continue to create CDs or DVDs.

WARNING! Not all optical media work with all drives, even if the labels say they're compatible. If you run into consistent problems with a specific brand, where burning is halted or the media isn't successfully verified, try another brand. If you're using a third-party CD or DVD burner, contact the drive manufacturer for additional help, because Apple won't provide direct support for its disc burning feature except with an Apple computer that shipped with a factory CD or DVD burner.

Restoring Classic Mac OS Application Switching

When Mac OS X was first unveiled, sharp criticisms were leveled at the disappearance of the oh-so-useful application-switching menu, which was located at the right end of the menu bar. Although the Dock (see Chapter 5) is meant as a substitute, an alternative is provided in the form of a donationware utility (meaning you send a voluntary donation). ASM is installed as a System Preference component. Once installed, it can be configured to restore an application-switching menu in its accustomed spot.

Two of the most interesting features of ASM are the ability to hide other applications automatically courtesy of its Single Application Mode, so you see only the active application. This is a sure way to reduce screen clutter and confusion, especially if you have a smaller display on your Mac. The other key feature is Classic Window Mode, in which all windows in an open application come forward, rather than just the one you select (the Mac OS X way).

ASM also sports an extensive array of adjustments to the way the application menu looks, from icon size to whether labels and icons appear, or just one or the other. You can also suppress application hiding for individual programs, in case you need to see both applications at the same time (or even use a modifier key such as Shift to suppress the feature altogether).

Related solution:	Found on page:
Using the Dock	120

Panther
Desktop Management

In Brief

If you're new to Mac OS X, you'll see that it consists of a bit of the old and a lot of the new. For example, the Panther desktop looks similar to the one you might be familiar with from Mac OS versions. It has a decorative background pattern and the familiar icons for your hard drive are present. But something appears to be missing. Where's the trash? Panther users must become accustomed to the fact that the trash has migrated to the Dock. As you'll learn in this chapter, the Dock is one of the main file and application navigation components of Panther.

The pristine desktop is part of the normal behavior of Panther, but as you'll see in this chapter, it's not necessary to keep things neat and clean. One of the rights of the Mac user is to arrange, even clutter, a desktop to suit your taste. Fortunately, Panther gives you lots of freedom to change background images and clutter it with icons to create the Desktop that serves your needs.

The Dock Dissected

If you have used Mac OS X 10.1 or 10.2, you'll see that, for better or worse, the Dock hasn't changed all that much, except for the subtle shadings of the background. So if you're comfortable with using the Dock, you may want to simply skip to the next chapter.

The Dock (see Figure 5.1) incorporates such features as application switching, application launching, and other features into a single taskbar. Notice that it is a colorful, almost cartoonish, and almost infinitely resizable palette of icons that resides at the bottom of your Mac's display (or elsewhere if you prefer, as you'll see shortly).

NOTE: If you have used Windows, you might notice some similarities between the Dock and Windows' taskbar. The Dock, however, is more closely aligned to the original application-launching palette used for the NeXT operating system, on which Panther is based.

Compared to the Classic Mac OS, the Dock replaces:

- *Control Strip*—The Control Strip was essentially a floating palette that offers one click access to some common system functions.

Figure 5.1   The Dock is a single location where you check and open applications, documents, and folders.

- *Application menu*—The original application menu that appeared at the right end of the Classic Mac OS's menu bar. The Dock puts all your open applications a click away and it's always displayed, unless you opt to hide it as you will learn later in this chapter.

NOTE: *If you prefer something more akin to the Control Strip of old, don't despair. Independent programmers have plenty of opportunities to get in the game. The OpenStrip shareware program is meant to replace some of the functions of the original Mac OS Control Strip. One popular application menu replacement is ASM, which deposits the same sort of application menu on the right side of the menu bar that you'd see in the Classic Mac OS. As with all such useful Mac OS X enhancements, you can find a good collection at the VersionTracker Web site (www.versiontracker.com/macosx).*

- *Apple menu*—As you learned in the previous chapter, Panther's Apple menu has very limited customization options, so you use the Dock to store the applications and other files you frequently use.

The Dock consists of two parts, separated by a thin vertical line. Here's a description of how they work:

- *Left side*—Application icons, including those representing open programs, stay here (see Figure 5.2).

- *Right side*—Icons representing documents, folders, servers, Web sites, QuickTime TV channels, and the Mac OS Trash exist on the right end of the Dock (see Figure 5.3).

5. Panther Desktop Management

Figure 5.2   The items at this end of the Dock consist strictly of applications. Icons with the triangles beneath are open.

Figure 5.3   The rest of the icons you put in the Dock reside at the right, regardless of content.

111

- *Finder*—Click this icon (see Figure 5.4) to open a Finder window.

- *System Preferences*—As part of the Dock when you install Panther, this icon allows you to set your Mac's preferences (see Figure 5.5). It replaces the Control Panels, at least in part.

TIP: *Missing an icon? Although several application and document icons are part of the standard installation of Panther, you can easily drag them off the Dock accidentally. To get an icon back, just locate the original icon for that item, which will usually be in the Applications or Documents folder, and drag it to the Dock.*

- *Mail*—This icon represents Apple's powerful new e-mail software (see Figure 5.6). When you receive e-mail, you'll see a display on the Mail icon indicating the number of unread messages waiting for you. I'll cover this program in detail in Chapter 21.

NOTE: *Many applications allow you to display messages about the applications in the Dock. For example, if you're an AOL member and you're using the latest version of Panther, you'll see numeric displays of the number of e-mail and instant messages that await you. A printer icon will appear with a document hanging from it while a job is being processed, and there will be a warning exclamation mark if there's a problem with the print queue.*

- *Document*—This icon represents a document that's been placed in the Dock (see Figure 5.7).

Figure 5.4   This icon represents the Finder.

Figure 5.5   Click this icon to launch the System Preferences application.

Figure 5.6   This icon represents Apple's exclusive e-mail software.

Figure 5.7 When you add documents to the Dock, they'll look something like this.

• *Web Sites And Servers*—Another great feature of the Dock is the ability to store icons that link you to your favorite Web sites or provide direct access to a networked server (see Figure 5.8).

• *Minimized window*—When you click the Minimize icon in an open document window, the document shrinks to the Dock. It remains there until you click it to restore or maximize the document window. Pressing Command+M, by the way, will also minimize a window.

TIP: *To view an ultraslow Genie Effect, hold down the Shift key when minimizing a document. You'll see the reverse effect with the same keyboard shortcut when you click an icon representing a minimized document in the Dock.*

• *Trash*—Panther's trash sits at the right end of the Dock (see Figure 5.9).

• *Pop-up menus*—Click any item in the Dock and hold down the mouse button to see a pop-up menu related to that item. (This is not the same as the contextual menus you see when you Control+Click an item.) Pop-up menus are really useful for allowing you quick access to certain commands. For example, you can use a pop-up to directly access any open document window for an application like Microsoft Word. The best effect occurs when you click a disk or folder icon displayed on the

Figure 5.8 A networked server or a favorite Web site can be just a click away in the Dock.

Figure 5.9 The Trash received can be found on the Dock.

5. Panther Desktop Management

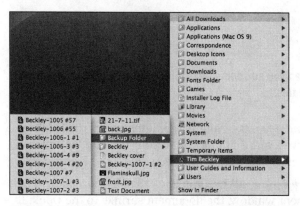

Figure 5.10 Multiple levels of pop-up menus can be displayed when you click and hold a folder or disk icon in the Dock.

Dock (see Figure 5.10). You'll see a pop-up menu with lots of submenus. Click the icon to access a Show In Finder command. If the application is open, you'll be able to quit it from the pop-up menu.

TIP: *Some applications, such as Apple's iTunes, display application controls in the Dock-based pop-up menus. That way, you can access functions without going to the program itself. Apple has opened the programming interface for this feature, so you can expect to see a number of programs supporting it over time.*

NOTE: *The pop-up menu you see when you click a Dock item is similar to what you get when you command click an item to see its contextual menu, but it doesn't require a modifier key and it's strictly limited to items placed in the Dock.*

Immediate Solutions

Panther's desktop is ripe for customization, and you'll be pleased to know you can organize it in many ways depending on your needs. In the following pages, I'll describe the various desktop preferences and then show you how to tailor your Mac's desktop to resemble the one used in prior versions of the Mac OS, or in ways you might not have imagined before. I'll also present a third-party utility that will take the desktop farther than you might have expected.

Setting Dock Preferences

In Chapter 4, I discussed the Finder preferences. We used some of these preferences to setup your desktop. Now I'll give you, as long-time radio broadcaster Paul Harvey says, the rest of the story. You can use the following steps to change the way your Mac's desktop and the Dock function:

1. To change Dock settings, choose Dock from the Apple menu and select Dock Preferences from the submenu. Doing so brings up the Dock settings pane from the System Preferences application (see Figure 5.11).

2. Set all or some of the following six Dock preferences:

   • *Dock Size*—This setting lets you configure the size of the icons by moving the slider. You're apt to find that the Dock is just too imposing on your Mac's screen unless you have a very large display, so you'll probably want to make it smaller.

TIP: *You can also resize the Dock by clicking the bar on the Dock that separates applications from documents and dragging it up or down. If you hold down the Option key while resizing the Dock, the Dock will default to fixed-sized icons, such as 32, 64, or 128 pixels. Otherwise, the adjustments are infinitely variable. When you Control-click the Dock, you'll have immediate access to its preferences.*

   • *Magnification*—Select this checkbox to make the Dock magnify the icons as you drag the mouse over them (see Figure 5.12). It looks flashy, but it may be a little bit much after you use it for a while. The slider bar lets you decide how much the icons will expand.

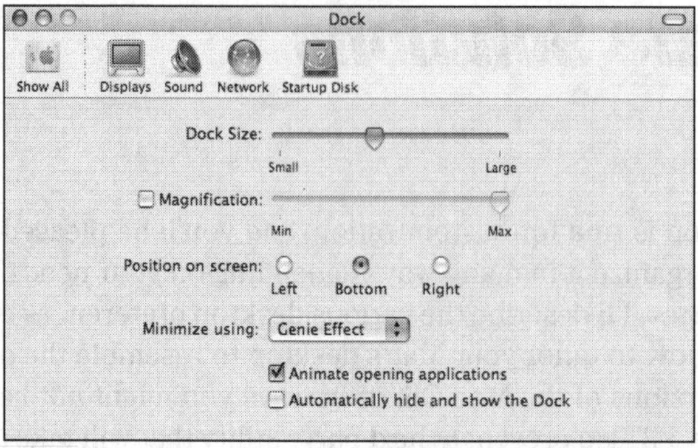

Figure 5.11 Change the look and actions of the Dock here.

Figure 5.12 The Dock's icons magnify when you drag your mouse over them.

- *Automatically Hide And Show The Dock*—Because the Dock sits above your open application windows and you cannot grab anything beneath it, this adjustment may be a great convenience. It's also a good way to save screen real estate. The Dock stays hidden unless you drag the mouse to the bottom of the screen to make it visible. You'll find this adjustment particularly useful for a smaller Mac's display.

TIP: *You can also make the Dock hide itself when the mouse isn't near by pressing Command+Option+D. Repeating the command will undo the change. This shortcut won't work if you're in a Classic application or in a program that has a keystroke that duplicates this one.*

- *Position On Screen*—This is feature is used to move the Dock from its bottom position. You can center it at the left or right end of your screen, if you prefer (see Figure 5.13).

NOTE: *As you'll see later in this chapter, you can use a third-party utility called TinkerTool to pin the Dock at the end of the screen or even at the top. This handy System Preferences add-on also can change other Dock settings, such as the one that follows.*

- *Minimize Using*—The Genie Effect can be really cool or totally annoying, depending on your perspective. This setting lets you choose a scaling effect instead, which rapidly reduces an item in size and puts it on the Dock. You may

Figure 5.13 You can move the Dock right or left to where you want.

prefer this option if you have a slower Mac and the Genie Effect slows things down even more.

- *Animate Opening Applications*—When this feature is shown at a presentation, it looks cool. However, having an application's icon bounce up and down in the Dock may grow tiresome. You can switch off the option here and wait for programs to open for you without warning.

NOTE: *The Dock provides another level of animation, where an icon bounces up and down to alert you that another application is calling for your attention. It may mean there's a problem with the application or, for example, that a Web site opened in Internet Explorer cannot be retrieved. This option can't be switched off (although some programs, such as your printer status display, manage to limit alerts to an icon that doesn't bounce).*

---

3. After you've set your Dock preferences, you can quit the System Preferences application or make further settings, such as the one that comes next.

Setting Desktop Preferences

In addition to modifying the Dock in various ways, you can change your Mac's desktop backdrop or control a handful of Finder preferences to make your desktop take on more of the look and feel you like. To begin with, let's change the desktop pattern:

1. To change your Mac's desktop settings, launch System Preferences and click the Desktop & Screen Saver preference panel. Click the Desktop button to reveal the dialog box shown in Figure 5.14.

2. Click one of the collection folders at the left, which include your iPhoto Library, or choose a folder to specify a different set of pictures for your desktop.

3. When you see the thumbnails of available pictures, click one of the images to immediately change the desktop background.

TIP: If your new background doesn't appear right away, log out and log in again. This time, the changeover should work as you expect.

4. When you've made your selection, you can quit System Preferences or choose another preference icon for further changes.

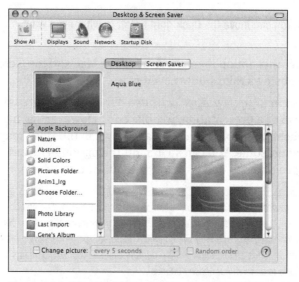

Figure 5.14 Alter the Mac's desktop backdrop here.

NOTE: You should be able to use just about any JPEG or TIFF image file as a background but remember that a large or complicated image may take longer to display on your screen. This will likely happen if you don't have the latest and greatest Mac with the fastest graphics accelerator. Should screen refresh slow down, pick a simpler image (or just try a few and see which work best).

TIP: If you really want to amaze your friends, click Change Picture and specify an interval ranging from five seconds to every day. With a fast change interval, you can entertain yourself and others by watching the background change at regular intervals, even at random if you pick that option. Just bear in mind that all of this screen-rendering skullduggery exacts a bit of a performance penalty, because it keeps your Mac's graphics card working overtime. If your Mac isn't quite the fastest on the block, you'll want to use this feature judiciously.

Related Solution:	Found on page:
Setting Desktop Preferences	55

Setting More Finder Preferences

Once you've established the way you want the Dock to look and the desktop background that meets your needs, returning to your Finder preferences is the final step of the equation. Here's how it's done:

1. Click the Finder.

2. Choose Preferences from the Finder's application menu to bring up the dialog box shown in Figure 5.15.

3. Click a checkbox or button to establish your personal settings. Here are the changes you can make:

   • *Show These Items on the Desktop*—If you don't want certain items to appear automatically on the desktop, just uncheck the options for hard disks, removable media, or connected servers. Even if you turn them all off, you can click the Computer icon in the Finder to show a display of available disks and servers.

   • *New Finder Windows Open*—Choose the folder where you want the newly opened windows to go from the pop-up menu. Any folder on any available drive is open season here, which is especially helpful if you need to jump to a special project quickly.

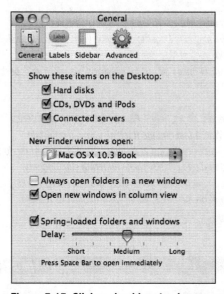

Figure 5.15 Click a checkbox to change your preference.

- *Always Open Folders in a New Window*—When you check this option, the Finder will operate like the Finder in the Classic Mac OS, in which opening a folder spawns a new Finder window rather than displaying the contents in the existing Finder window. Checking this option is a sure way to increase desktop clutter.

These options control how your Mac's desktop is populated under Panther. If you want to go further and set the entire range of Finder preferences, including those nifty spring-loaded folders, refer to Chapter 4 for more information. When you're done, click the Close button to dismiss the Finder Preferences screen.

Related solution:	Found on page:
Setting Finder Preferences	91

Using the Dock

The Dock is highly intuitive. It provides clear status messages about your open applications and documents, and it can be, as explained previously, customized in many ways for your convenience. Here are some basic hints and tips for getting the maximum value out of the Dock:

- *Adding icons*—Because the Dock expands dynamically to accommodate the number of icons you've added, you just need to drag an icon to the Dock to display it. (The actual file, of course, remains where it was.) The left side of the Dock carries your application icons. The right side handles the rest, such as documents, folders, links to servers and Web sites, and QuickTime channels. You can't put the wrong icon in the wrong side; the icon will only be accepted in the proper side of the Dock.

NOTE: *Icons in the Dock are not automatically sorted for you. You can click and drag them to new positions, depending on whether you prefer alphabetical order or some random sequence.*

- *Application switching*—As explained earlier, open applications are indicated by a black triangle below the application's icon in the Dock. Click the icon of any opened application in the Dock to move directly to that program.

TIP: *To hide all other open application windows when opening a new one from the Dock, hold down the Command+Option keys while clicking any application icon. Hold down the Option key to hide just the application window from which you're switching (but not all windows opened with that application). The Show All command in the Desktop application menu brings back the windows.*

- *Single-click access*—Just like the Launcher in older versions of the Mac OS, you can access any item in the Dock with a single click.

TIP: *You can use the keyboard to switch between open applications. Press Command+Tab to open the next application icon, as shown from left to right. Repeat the action to select other applications. To reverse the process, press Command+Shift+Tab.*

- *Reordering icons*—To change the order of an icon in the Dock, click and drag it to its new position. You cannot, of course, put application icons on the right end of the Dock; but otherwise, feel free to reorder items as you prefer.

NOTE: *Did the application icon disappear? Some applications, such as Panther's print queue display, stay open only as long as the print queue has a job being processed. After the processing is finished, the application automatically quits (except, however, if you double-click the print queue, in which case it stays open until you close the print queue window). It may take a few moments, however, for the actual document to finish, depending on the speed and the need for extra processing by the output device itself. The same vanishing effect holds true for the Classic environment; the Mac OS 9 icon vanishes when Classic has loaded (even though it remains active).*

---

5. Panther Desktop Management

- *Removing icons*—Did you change your mind? You can discard a Dock icon you no longer need. Just click and drag it away from the Dock. In just a second, it will disappear in a puff of smoke, like magic.

NOTE: *You cannot remove the icon for an open application.*

- *Pop-up menus*—When you click and hold a Dock icon, you'll see a menu related to the contents of that icon. For Panther applications, you have the option to jump to an open document window, to display the folder in which the item is located in the Finder, or to quit the application. In addition, some applications, such as Apple's iTunes, let you access additional control functions courtesy of the Dock, such as playing a song from your playlist or moving to other tracks on the list. This feature is optionally available to program developers, and you may see it in a specific application from time to time.

- *Dock notifications*—Are you trying to access a Web site while working in another program, and the browser needs to tell you the site can't be found or you have to OK a security window? Or, is there a problem with an application you need to know about? If you see a bouncing icon from an open application, click the icon to see what's up. Some applications, such as AOL, Mail and printer icons, will simply alter the Dock icon to present a notice, such as the number of messages waiting to be read in your mailbox or how many pages are still to be processed in a job queue.

NOTE: *Sorry, you cannot turn off the bouncing icon feature, even if you switch off the Dock preference to animate the process of opening applications.*

- *Dock icon shortcuts*—The Dock gives you a fast way to gain access to your hard drive. Drag a drive icon to the Dock and then click the Dock to see a hierarchical menu of the drive's contents. If that seems to be overkill, just drag a folder's icon to the Dock (such as your Favorites folder in your personal Users directory). The contents of that folder, up to five levels deep, are now just a click away from fast access.

TIP: *Another way to speed access to the Dock is to use the Full Keyboard Access feature, which is an option in the Keyboard panel of the System Preferences application. With this feature enabled (see Chapter 3 for details), the Control+F3 command will highlight the Dock for instant access to any Dock icon.*

Related solution:	*Found on page:*
Setting Keyboard Preferences	65

The TinkerTool Alternative

If Apple hasn't implemented a feature, you can bet a third party will find a way. TinkerTool is a useful alternative (see Figure 5.16); it's a shareware utility that can configure a whole range of default preferences for Panther. It runs as a simple application and the changes it makes remain even after the application is quit.

The Desktop settings in TinkerTool include the following features that will enhance your desktop control far beyond the standard range of Panther:

NOTE: As with most System Preferences settings, TinkerTool can be configured to offer a separate set of options for each person who has a user account on your Mac.

- *Finder Options*—The option to Show Rectangle Animation When Opening Files may make things slower on an older Mac, so you may want to turn it off. Another useful feature is the ability to set a maximum number of label lines from two to three. This helps in displaying lengthy Finder labels. Some features, though, simply mirror your regular Finder preferences.

- *Dock*—Even though Apple allows you to place the Dock at the left or right sides of your screen, TinkerTool adds the ability to place the Dock at the top or at any corner of the screen. In addition, a new Minimizer Effect called Suck-In displays a rapid shrinking motion when an open window is minimized. The Use Transparent Icons For Hidden Applications option will make it

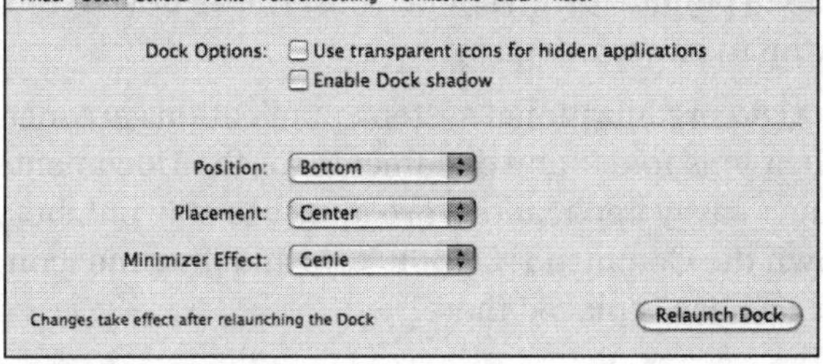

Figure 5.16 Click a button to access one of TinkerTool's powerful features.

easier to see background applications that may be open on your Mac. You can also configure scrollbar arrangement beyond the two choices available in the General preference panel (at top and bottom and together).

NOTE: *Many TinkerTool settings require a logout and a login (or a regular restart) to take effect. You'll see a message at the bottom of a TinkerTool settings window if this is required.*

- *Other TinkerTool options*—Click a button to see additional settings for TinkerTool. Other available options let you choose different default system fonts and sizes (another feature that not all applications support) and configure font smoothing beyond the 8 to 12 point range offered in Panther.

WARNING! *Don't assume your system enhancer is compatible with Panther simply because it worked a previous version of the operating system. Such utilities as ASM, Default Folder, an Open and Save dialog box utility, Mac Reporter, and TinkerTool were all modified for Panther as a result of various incompatibilities. You'll always want to be sure you have the latest versions, especially after a major system upgrade.*

Making Your Panther Desktop as Cluttered as Ever

One of the good or bad features of Panther, depending on your point of view, is the desktop. It can be clean and uncluttered when you remove the disk and network volume icons. However, if you leave them intact, you are well on your way toward producing the requisite degree of disorder.

Apple has made a concerted effort to organize your desktop and file organization patterns under Panther. The desktop is clear as water, unless you decide to pollute it with some icons. Here's how to return your Mac's desktop to its former glory:

1. In Panther's rigid organizational system, applications are meant for the Applications folder and documents for the Documents folder. Panther–savvy applications are meant to stay put, but if you hold down the Command+Option keys and drag the icon to the desktop, an alias is placed there.

NOTE: *The Command+Option shortcut also works with all files and Classic applications.*

---

2. After your application icons are on the desktop, go ahead and locate your favorite document files and place them there as well. A few minutes of clicking and dragging and, presto (see Figure 5.17), your Panther desktop can be as cluttered as you wish, precisely as it was in previous versions of the Mac OS.

Reducing Desktop Clutter

If you decide you're simply fed up with a crowded and messy desktop, you can clean things up to lessen the misery and confusion. Here's a brief overview of some quick solutions to this dilemma:

- *Use the Dock*—You can add regularly used applications and documents to the Dock. The only disadvantage here is that if you add too many items, the Dock will become so small as to be unmanageable, unless you have excellent eyesight, so look at the next solution too.

- *Organize your files*—Apple sets aside special folders in your home directory for such things as documents, movies, music, and photos. Take advantage of these repositories, which are a mere click or two away when you click your user name in the Finder's toolbar. If that isn't fast enough for you, drag the folders to the

5. Panther Desktop Management

Figure 5.17 If your taste is for a busy Mac desktop, don't worry. Panther will not prevent you from messing it up the way you want.

Dock and click and hold to see sub-menus showing the contents of that folder.

- *Get rid of unneeded aliases*—Common Mac practice, from previous operating system versions, was to make an alias to many of your favorite applications and place them in the desktop. With the Dock and immediate access to your Applications folder from the Finder's Sidebar, you may not need the aliases. Go ahead and trash them but make sure you are dumping an alias, and not the original file. (You'll notice that the alias has a tiny arrow pointing to the file's icon.)

TIP: Here's my personal solution to that confusing desktop: I have made one folder, called Desktop Overload, and stuffed all the odds and ends inside it. You can go one step further, though, and drag that folder to the Dock, so you can occasionally keep tabs on what's inside without having to go through file searches to find something you need.

---

5. Panther Desktop Management

Chapter 6

Setting Up Panther for Multiple Users

In Brief

The words "personal computer" connote a device for a single person. But that's a rarity these days. Whether you use your Mac in your home or your office, it's highly likely others will also use it. Panther's Multiple Users feature not only gives each user his or her own account, but lets you grant each person a custom work environment. This includes a Simple Finder for novice users who might have trouble finding their own way on a computer desktop.

The great value of the Multiple Users feature is that it provides each user with a personal workspace. As a result, those who work on your Mac can customize their Mac's desktop and Finder appearance to their needs without impacting the settings made by other users. They can also have a separate set of applications, documents, fonts, and other items. In addition, they can use their own user settings, from mouse tracking speed to Dock location and keyboard options.

Panther's Multiple Users Features

Panther inherits the multiple-user capabilities of Unix but Apple has given the feature a typically warm and friendly interface. Once you get accustomed to the simple setup routine, you'll be able to create a fairly secure working environment with lots of options to help you set it up for all the people who will use your Mac.

Here are some of the basic features of Panther that provide customized user environments and security:

- *User as administrator*—When you first install Panther, you establish your user account as the administrator or owner of the computer. After you've set up your username and password, you can add or remove users from your system, and you can unlock and use certain system-wide preferences that are available only to the administrators (see Figure 6.1). These preferences include Accounts, Date & Time, Energy Saver, Login Window, Network, Sharing, and Startup Disk. Chapter 3 covers more on using these preference settings.

NOTE: *Items in the System Preferences application that can be accessed only by the administrator are always identified by a padlock icon. In large installations I recommended you set up a dummy account, separate from the administrator's real user account, and create it for system administration. Doing so provides even greater security.*

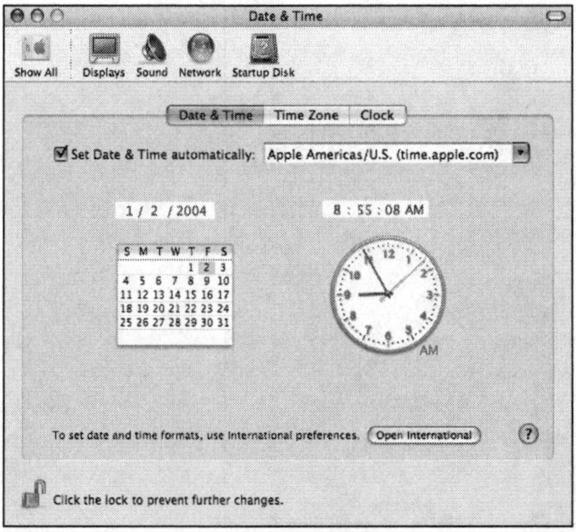

Figure 6.1   When you click the padlock icon, you must enter your administrator's username and password to gain access to certain Panther features and System Preferences settings.

- *Keychains*—If you use a number of different passwords to access your Internet accounts, online ordering, banking services, and various applications and server connections, keeping a record or having to memorize many passwords can be a dreadful chore. It's easy to forget those passwords and thus lose your access to programs and services. This happens to me from time to time, so I'm forced to make new accounts. Fortunately, Apple's Keychain Access application (see Figure 6.2) lets you store all those disparate passwords in a single location—called a *keychain*—and enter a single password to access all of them. Only you or someone with your password can unlock those passwords. When the passwords are unlocked, applications and services that need them can get them, but casual users cannot see them. When you finish using them, you just lock your keychain. The Keychain Access application is located in the Utilities folder.

NOTE: *By default, a keychain is automatically set for you when you set up Panther, so you may seldom need to visit the application unless you need a special setup. Also, in order for a keychain to work, the application for which you want to store a keychain must support that feature. Not all do, so you'll want to check the appropriate documentation to see which Panther features are supported before you attempt to use passwords stored in a keychain.*

- *Shared folders*—All users who have accounts on your Mac have their own personal user or Home folder for their own sets of applications, documents, system-related preferences, fonts,

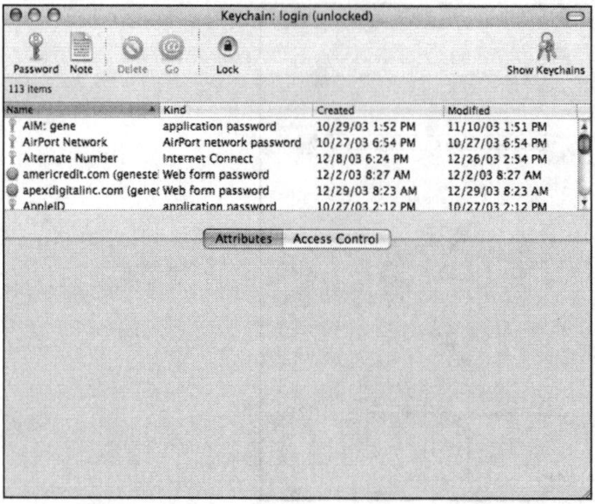

Figure 6.2 **You can use the Keychain Access application to set up additional personal accounts and store all your user passwords.**

Internet accounts, and so on. These files are available only to the individual user who logs in to that user account, unless additional sharing privileges are granted by that user or the administrator courtesy of the Ownership & Permission's feature of Finder's Get Info window. The Shared folder, however, serves as a place where you can put files and make them available to anyone who accesses your Mac. That way, those users do not need special access privileges. You can also create a Drop Box folder, where other users can place files, but only the individual user (who created the Drop Box) or the administrator can access the files inside.

NOTE: *The Shared folder is also used as a reasonably safe location where users who access your Mac from across a network can send and receive files. You'll want to read Chapter 8 for information on how to configure network file-sharing privileges so that access to your Mac is restricted.*

- *System logins*—When you log out, only a user with a valid username and password can use your Mac. That rule provides the maximum possible degree of security for system-related access. However, if you are usually the sole user of the Mac and you have no qualms about letting others—perhaps family members or coworkers—work on your Mac and possibly change the landscape or file setup, you can continue to bypass the Login prompt at startup. Because this is the default setting, nothing needs be changed.

WARNING! Although you need the proper password to access a Mac under Panther, if you have an older Mac that still boots under Mac OS 9, you could encounter a potential security leak. This is because nothing prevents you from restarting your computer under Mac OS 9, or with a Mac OS 9 or Mac OS X startup disk, and then gaining access to files in that environment. If maximum security is important to you, you'll want to set up the Multiple Users feature of Mac OS 9 as well so that users cannot casually access your Mac. It is also a good idea to store system startup CDs (and third-party utilities, such as Norton Utilities, that come with bootable CDs) in a safe place, so that access cannot be gained in that fashion.

- *FileVault*—New for Panther is built-in 128-bit encryption for your Home directory. This means that you can protect your personal stuff with a powerful security feature. Files that you save are secured on-the-fly and opened just as quickly when you use your password. In a sense, FileVault operates without you being aware of it. I will show you how to setup FileVault in Chapter 17.

- *Dedicated security software*—When this book was written, few third-party general-purpose security software tools were available. Intego's DiskGuard and FileGuard were still under development for Panther. A few shareware utilities are available that can protect folders and such. The most promising entry is MacPrefect from High Resolution Systems. The company also publishers MacAdministrator for network setups. Another workable solution is Apple's free Open Firmware Password application, available from Apple's support Web site. You can use this program to prevent startups from any volume other than the one set as a Startup Disk, even from a CD, unless the user enters the appropriate password. It works with all Macs officially supported for Panther.

WARNING! Because of changes in the file structures of Panther, do not even consider using a Classic security program with the new operating system. If you must secure your Mac to a level beyond what is available via the combination of Mac OS 9 and Panther Multiple Users settings, you may want to delay deploying Panther until dedicated security software is available for the new environment.

Using Strong Passwords

If you are running your Mac in a family environment or in a small office, you might not feel you should be overly concerned about your choice of passwords. This might not be a critical issue if another user in your environment works on your Mac. But if you need the maximum amount of security, you'll want to use a password that is difficult for others to guess. The best password is a random combination of uppercase and lowercase letters intermixed with numbers. Such a password is extremely difficult for anyone to guess, and thus you have the maximum level of security. An optimal password should contain at least eight characters to provide a good level of security.

WARNING! *Once you set up your Mac with Panther, there is no way to gain complete user access without the proper password. Even if you use the Login preference panel to bypass a password request at startup, some features, such as the ability to install some new applications, will not be available to you until you can manually enter that password. Should you forget it, you will have to reset your password using the Password Reset utility available in the Mac OS X Installer application. Chapter 18 explains how, and this is why you should also keep your Mac OS X installer CDs in a safe place.*

Immediate Solutions

Setting Up Multiple-User Access

Each user of your Mac can be given his or her own personal password and user environment, which allows each user to set, within the guidelines you establish, a custom font collection, user preferences, desktop layout, applications, and documents.

Follow these steps to create a new user account:

1. Launch the System Preferences application. You'll find it on the Dock or in the Applications folder.

2. Click the Accounts icon to bring up the settings panel (see Figure 6.3).

3. If the padlock is closed, click the padlock to open it, and enter the username and password for your administrator account.

NOTE: If you are logged in under your administrator account, the padlock normally remains open. You might want to consider closing it in various system settings until you can establish separate user accounts for others who are going to use your Mac.

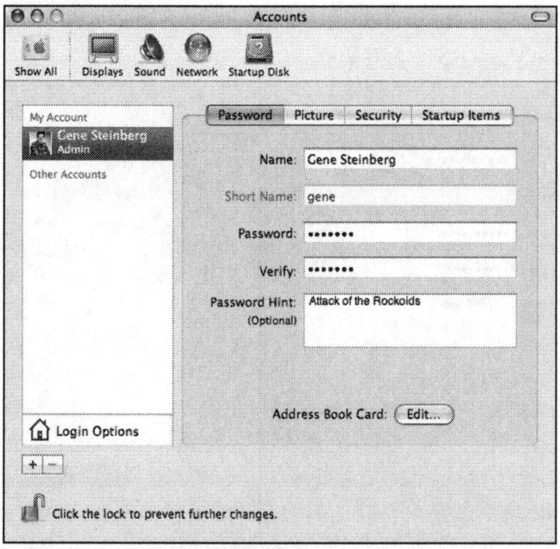

Figure 6.3   You can establish and configure user accounts from this preference panel.

4. With the padlock open, click the plus (+) button at the bottom left which will produce a dialog box with four buttons, as shown in Figure 6.4.

5. In the Name field, type the actual name of the new user.

6. In the Short Name field, type a username (nickname). By default, Panther will suggest an alternate username that usually consists of the same name in lower case, minus the word spaces. Feel free to shorten it further to just your first name, or a totally different name, if you prefer.

7. In the Password field, type a password containing at least four letters (although I really recommend eight or more characters). Then, retype the password in the Verify field. If the password isn't accepted, retype it again. It must be entered the same way (both upper- and lowercase letters) in both places.

8. If you want a helpful reminder about a forgotten password, enter a question in the Password Hint text field (but don't make it so obvious that a third party can guess the answer).

9. Click the Picture button (see Figure 6.5) and choose a Login Picture from those provided. A single click is all you need to select a photo. You can also click Edit and select a JPEG or TIFF picture in an Open dialog box from among the ones you might have on your Mac.

NOTE: *The picture you select here does additional duty in your Address Book and in iChat, so choose wisely. However, if you're dissatisfied with your choice, you can always change it later on.*

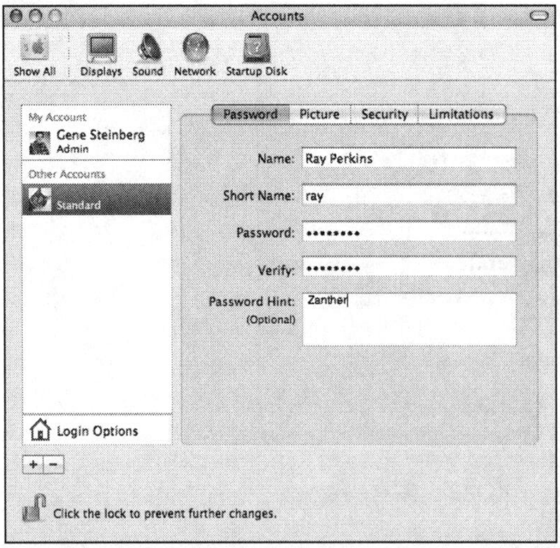

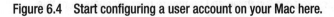

Figure 6.4   Start configuring a user account on your Mac here.

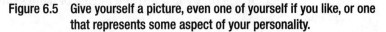

Figure 6.5 Give yourself a picture, even one of yourself if you like, or one that represents some aspect of your personality.

10. The next step is to click the Security button (see Figure 6.6). If you want to give the new user the authority to act as administrator for the Mac, select the checkbox at the bottom of the dialog box. As you'll notice, this preference pane mirrors the Security preference panel, and here you can also set a separate, Master Password, for use with FileVault. I'll cover this feature of Panther in Chapter 17.

6. Setting Up Panther for Multiple Users

Figure 6.6 Decide if the new user's files will be secured or not.

11. You can simply close the Accounts panel at this point and you're done. If you prefer to add limits to the new account, check out the next section of this chapter where I'll tell you more about what lurks behind the Limitations button. I bet you can't wait!

WARNING! *Before allowing another user to act as administrator for your Mac, consider carefully whether you really want to grant those access privileges to someone else (other than a family member, of course). Remember that any user who can log in as administrator will have the same authority that you do as owner of the Mac.*

12. When you create your initial administrator's account when setting up your Mac, Auto Login is set by default. If you want to change that setting, select the account name, click Login Options to specify whether a specific user will still be able to login by default, or whether you'll just see the list of names on the login panel.

13. Once you make your final changes, you can repeat these steps for each additional user. If you want to set access limits, tune into the next section.

Related solution:	*Found on page:*
Setting System Preferences Under Mac OS X	47

6. Setting Up Panther for Multiple Users

Customizing a User Account

If your children are using your Mac, or you simply want to restrict access to certain files and features for other users at your office, you can use the Limitations feature (see Figure 6.7) to simplify the user environment or set restricted access.

NOTE: The Limitations feature only functions with accounts that do not have administrator's access. If you want to change the user's rights, you'll need to select the Security pane under Accounts to switch off the ability to administer your Mac.

1. To customize the user, launch System Preferences from the Dock or Applications folder.
2. Click the Accounts icon to launch the settings panel.
3. Click the padlock (if it's not already open) and enter the username and password for your administrator account.

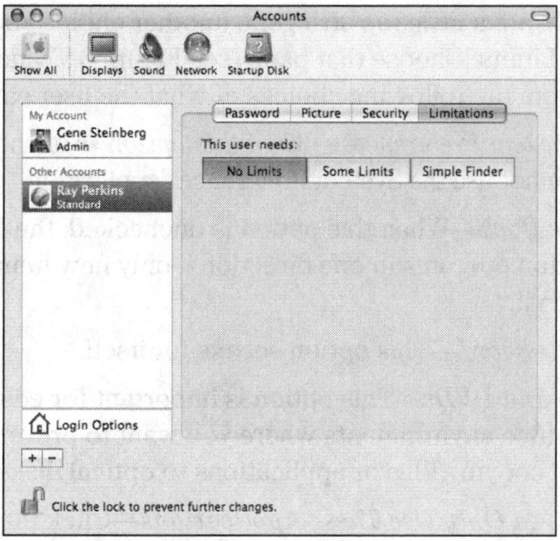

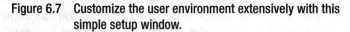

Figure 6.7   Customize the user environment extensively with this
simple setup window.

4. With the padlock open, click a user's name and click Limitations to bring up the settings screen. You'll be confronted with
   three choices: No Limits, Some Limits, and Simple Finder.

5. For children or other users who haven't mastered your Mac,
   click the Simple Finder option and specify what programs the
   user is allowed to access (see Figure 6.8). When that person
   logs in, only those applications will be permitted.

Figure 6.8   For young ones or others who aren't ready to enjoy the full
Mac experience, you can simplify the environment here.

6. If those limits are a little too stringent, another choice you can use is Some Limits. Choose that pane (see Figure 6.9) and you can select from the following choices of what the user can do:

- *Open all System Preferences—When this option is* unchecked, the user cannot use the System Preferences application.

- *Modify the Dock*—When this option is unchecked, the Dock configuration operates in one direction—only new items can be added to it.

- *Change Password*—This option speaks for itself.

- *Burn CDs and DVDs*—This option is important for educational or office environments where you want to prevent users from copying files or applications to optical disks.

- *The User Can Only Use These Applications*—Click the disclosure triangles under each category to bring up a list of available applications fitting that category. You can allow all applications, or just the ones that are checked, separately. This way, for example, if you don't want someone to use your financial management software, you can leave it unchecked.

NOTE: *The buttons at the bottom of the Some Limits window can be used to check or uncheck everything in a single operation. You can use the Locate button to select an application that is not listed or just drag the application icon to the list.*

Figure 6.9   There are lots of things you can do to set boundaries on a user account.

7. Click the close button to store the settings and quit System Preferences. The next time that user logs in, the privileges you established will be honored.

Editing a User Account

A user account can be changed easily at any time. If you need to reset a password or change other user information, follow these steps:

1. Launch the System Preferences application from either the Dock or inside the Applications folder.

2. Click the Accounts icon to launch the settings panel.

3. Click the padlock (if it's not already open) and enter the username and password for your administrator account.

4. With the padlock open, click a user's name, which will display that person's account information, neatly divided into four categories.

5. Make the appropriate changes to the user's name and password information and enter a password reminder question if you wish.

6. Go through each of the remaining categories to change the user's picture, FileVault options, and the needed Limitations on the account.

7. If you intend to grant this user the authority to act as administrator for the Mac, click Login Options and make the appropriate changes.

8. Exit System Preferences by clicking the red button.

If you need to remove a user account, follow these steps:

1. Launch the System Preferences application and click Accounts.

2. Click the padlock if it's closed and enter the username and password for your administrator account.

3. With the padlock open, click the name of the user account you want to delete.

4. Click the minus (–) key to respond to the acknowledgment prompt (see Figure 6.10). The Delete Immediate option will remove that user's directory from your Mac. Pressing OK will save the contents of that user's directory in a disk image file that can be opened later on, if necessary. This is one decision

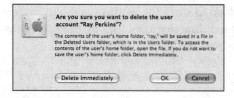

Figure 6.10 Deleting a user account.

you might want to consider carefully. When in doubt, just click OK and review the files later on at your leisure.

5. Quit the System Preferences application.

Configuring Keychain Access

Your Mac's keychain is a valuable feature that helps simplify management of all your passwords by storing them in a single place. By default, it's turned on and used every time you store a password in Panther Mail, Safari, Microsoft Entourage, and a host of other programs that support this password repository.

You will probably rarely need to actually use the Keychain Access application to customize the settings, but if you do, here's how to alter them, or create an additional keychain:

1. Locate the Keychain Access application, which is located in the Utilities folder inside your Applications folder.

2. Double-click the Keychain Access application to launch it and display the screen shown in Figure 6.11.

NOTE: *As you recall, a keychain is set up for you when you set up Panther for the very first time.*

---

3. Choose New Keychain from the File menu and name your new keychain (see Figure 6.12).

4. Type a name for your keychain and then click the Create button.

5. On the next screen, type a user password, and then retype the password to confirm the password. Use a strong password, as explained earlier in this chapter.

6. After you create a keychain, you'll need to populate it. Go to the File menu and Click New Password Item and type a name for

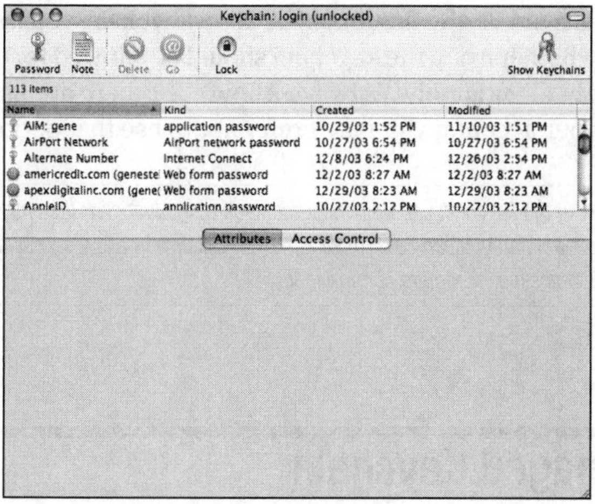

Figure 6.11 Here's your existing keychain.

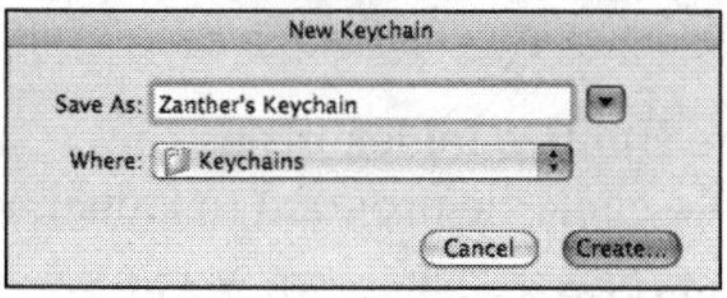

Figure 6.12 Give your keychain a name.

the item you want to add. (Use a name that identifies the item's contents.)

NOTE: *If you are entering a Web site, be sure you include the exact access URL in the Name field. Otherwise, you won't be able to use that password to access the site.*

TIP: *A quick way to enter a complicated password is simply to access a Web site using your Web browser and then copy the address in the URL field. You can then paste it into the Keychain Access application.*

---

7. Type the user password you need for that particular program or service.

8. Repeat Steps 6 and 7 for each password you want to enter.

9. When you're finished using Keychain Access, quit the application by choosing Quit from the application menu, pressing Command+Q, or clicking the Close button.

NOTE: *You can easily create multiple keychains, each of which stores a different set of user passwords. This method may help you from an organizational standpoint.*

---

6. Setting Up Panther for Multiple Users

With your keychains active, the first time you use a keychain, you'll see a prompt asking whether using the keychain should be allowed for this one time only or in all situations (Always Allow). If others are using your Mac under your account, you may prefer not to use that option.

NOTE: Access to each entry in the keychain can be configured separately. Just click the entry, and then the Access Control tab, and you can confirm whether you will always allow access to an item when your keychain is unlocked, or require confirmation.

Fixing a Damaged Keychain

On occasion, you might encounter trouble with your passwords being properly remembered, and have to enter them repeatedly. If you observe this or any other strange symptom, try these steps to fix the problem.

1. Locate Keychain Access in the Utilities folder, inside the Applications folder, and double-click the program to launch it.

2. Go to the Window menu and choose Keychain First Aid.

4. Enter your user password and click Repair and then Start. Over the next few seconds, the contents of your keychain will be examined and repairs, if needed, will be performed (see Figure 6.13).

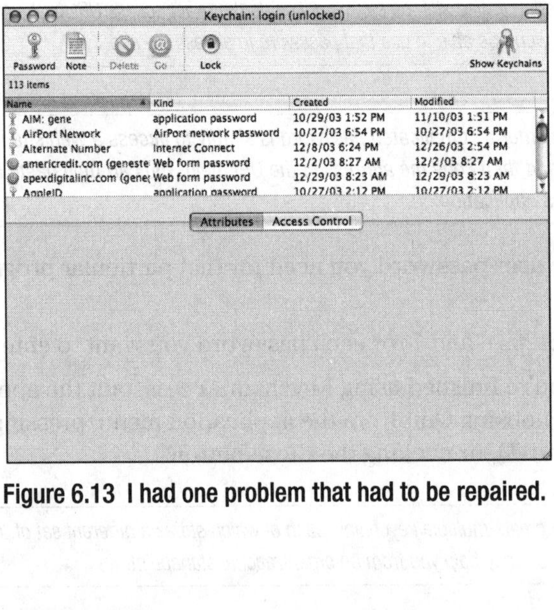

Figure 6.13 I had one problem that had to be repaired.

NOTE: I've opted to go right to the Repair option, since Verify will only confirm the problem and not fix it. You'd still have to perform the second step. I like to simplify my life.

Once you're done, you can repeat the process with other keychains if you have them or quit Keychain Access.

Coping with Problems Involving Keychains and Multiple Users

Panther's multiple users features are quite straightforward and usually work without a hitch. They just require a little attention to detail. But if you run into trouble, here are some likely problems and solutions:

- *Password isn't recognized*—Are you sure you entered the password correctly? Did you leave the Caps Lock key engaged by mistake? If you followed my suggestions about using a strong password, the keyboard combination might not be something you readily remember. It would be a good idea to write it down somewhere and put it in a safe place. Type the password again, just in case you made a mistake the first time (which you wouldn't see because the only feedback on your screen are the bullets in place of the characters you type). If you cannot get your keychain or a particular user's password to work, you may want to consider using the Reset Password feature, which can be accessed when you reboot your Mac with your first Panther installer CD. The application is available from the Installer menu, and I'll explain more about it in Chapter 18.

WARNING! Being able to reset a password via the Panther installer CD represents a potential security issue. If you are in an office environment, you may want to keep this CD under lock and key and accessible only if you need to reinstall Mac OS X or reset a password. The other issue, of course, is that individual users can bring in their own CD and do the deed, but this is an issue between you and your employees and beyond the scope of this book.

- *Keychain doesn't work with a program*—Not all applications support keychains or other multiple-user features. Check with the software publishers about their plans to support these features.

- *User forgets password*—Log in as administrator and recheck the user's account. You should keep a written record of all user accounts in a safe place, so you can access the users' computers whenever necessary or simply give them a lost password. As administrator, you can easily log in via the Multiple Users feature, open the user's account, and reset the password with a new one, if necessary.

NOTE: You cannot readily reset a password for your keychain. The best solution is just to trash it and start again if you forget the password.

- *User doesn't have permission*—If you used early releases of Mac OS X, perhaps you ran into a problem with not having permission to access, copy, or move a file. One sure way to fix this problem is to modify the permissions via the Owners & Permissions feature of the Finder's Get Info window. The options are described in more detail in Chapter 4. If you prefer to do it via the command line (and impress your co-workers), simply launch Terminal from the Utilities folder. With Terminal open, type "sudo chmod –R u+rw nameoffile". Press Return, and then enter your password at the password prompt, followed by another press of the Return key. In this command, **sudo** calls up your super user access. The **chmod** command and the subsequent instructions tell Panther to give you both read and write access to the named file.

WARNING! From a security standpoint, when you set up an administrator's account, it's never a good idea to leave a password setting blank. If nobody else will access your Mac, or only friends and family, you can just as easily create a password identical to your username.

Related solution:	Found on page:
Solving Panther Installation Problems	412

Suggestions for Setting Up Multiple Users for Use with Children

Many new Macs are purchased for home or small business use, where they'll be used frequently by children, ranging from those barely out of the toddler stage to those in the teen years. Parents are often surprised that young people take to personal computers far more easily than they did. My son, for example, was actively trying to trash all my files from my Mac's desktop when he was three or four years old. But more seriously, they learn mouse skills and develop good typing skills (with a little parental or school-based direction) far more speedily than the older generation. As a result, they can get on the Internet more easily and perhaps get into trouble more easily, as well.

Here are some considerations for setting up Panther for use with children:

- *Keep passwords hidden and hard to guess*—Just as you would hide your password from outsiders, consider making your user password difficult for children to detect. Today's kids have a remarkable ability to figure out such things if you make your password too easy to guess. Make sure they cannot log on to your administrator's account and do mischief (even if unintended). That way, they will be limited to system preferences that are padlocked or secured.

- *Consider AOL for a kid's Net access*—AOL partners with Apple on iChat and iTunes, so it stands to reason that the service has pretty good Mac OS X–savvy software available. AOL boasts a powerful set of Parental Controls (see Figure 6.14) that allow you to restrict your child's access to various features of the service, such as instant messages, e-mail from strangers, and various Web sites. This family-friendly approach is one reason AOL still occupies the top rank among ISPs, even though it has experienced some erosion in membership in recent years.

NOTE: Microsoft's MSN for Mac OS X also has Parental Controls available, though the settings are a little more general than those offered by AOL. MSN is a useful alternative if you seek a family-friendly online service.

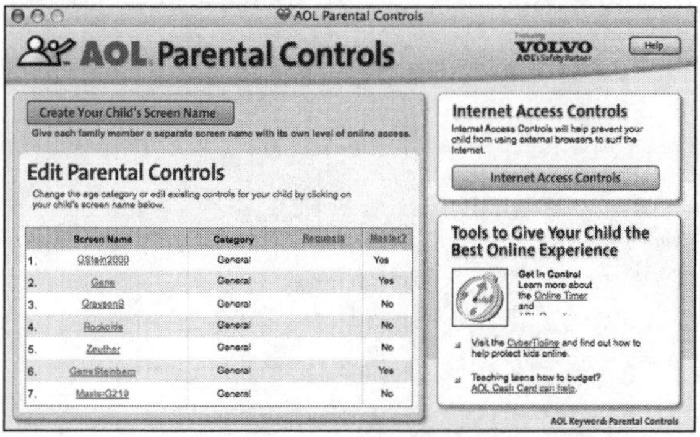

Figure 6.14 Here's AOL's user-friendly Parental Controls feature.

- *Use e-mail filtering*—Apple's Mail application and the other alternatives have filtering options that let you prevent e-mail from specific locations from arriving. The junk filters in Mail, however, are first-rate and can catch an extremely high percentage of received spam. In addition, when you use custom rules in your e-mail software, you can restrict a user to receiving e-mail only from approved locations, such as family members or friends. That way, unacceptable material will be blocked entirely. A number of ISPs also feature server-side spam filters, which will also keep your environment fairly free of junk mail. These services include AOL, AT&T WorldNet, EarthLink, MSN, and many others. You'll want to check with your ISP to see if it offers such a feature.

6. Setting Up Panther for Multiple Users

Chapter 7

Panther's
Search Feature

In Brief

"Where did that darn file go?" That's a common refrain when you're trying to locate a missing file. Hard drives are constantly getting cheaper and bigger, which means you can store more of your stuff on them. However, with so much data (and some new drives with capacities greater than 250GB), it gets increasingly difficult to find the files you want. In addition, the World Wide Web contains literally millions of sites, with content that dwarfs the largest libraries in the world. With so much material out there, what can you do to find the information you want without spending endless amounts of time in the process?

For Panther, Apple delivers two different search tools. One is a Finder-level search feature, which allows you to find the stuff on your drive, any drives connected to your Mac or accessed via a network. In addition, there's an enhanced (or at least changed) Sherlock search utility (see Figure 7.1), which has become a powerful tool to provide Web services, such as business phone numbers and movie listings, in a single application, often without the need to jump to a separate browser. This approach makes it much easier to find the information you want without having to know special search techniques or arcane instructions.

A Look at Apple's Search Utilities

Last night you finished an important document for your business, but today you just can't recall where you placed it. Or perhaps you recall writing material on a specific subject, but the content is buried in a document and you can't remember its title.

What to do?

The Panther Finder's toolbar includes a Search field. You can search the contents of whatever folder or disk to which the open Finder window applies by word or phrase. Press Return or Enter and, in seconds, the Finder window is updated with a screen showing the Search field (see Figure 7.2).

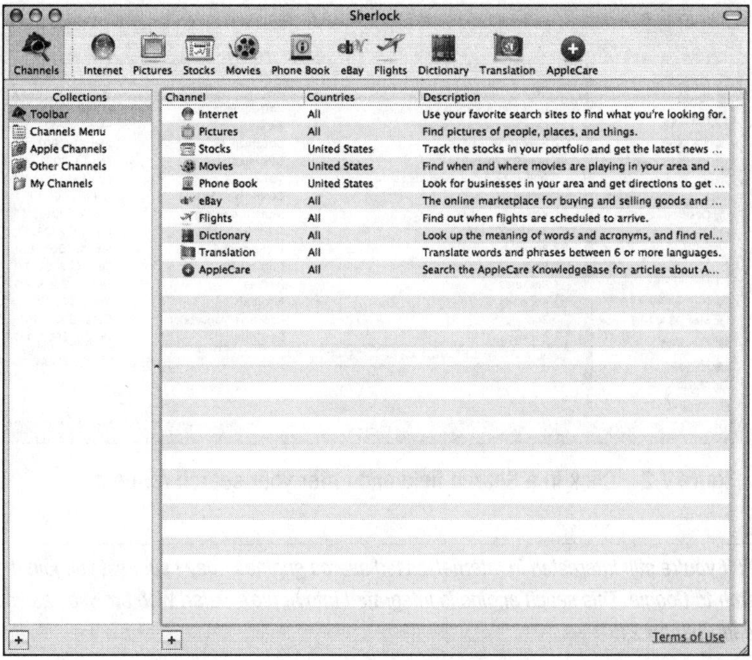

Figure 7.1   Apple's fancy search utility handles Internet searching with aplomb.

NOTE: The biggest improvement for the Finder's search feature in Panther is live searching. As you enter a search request, Panther begins to go to work to find what you want. You will, by the way, find a similar feature in the Search field in Mail.

However, searching the files on your drive is only part of the equation. What if you need to find information that isn't saved on your Mac? How about a news story about your favorite movie star or how Arnold is doing as "governator" of California? Are there online resources where you can search for new homes in the city to which you've been transferred?

Before Apple created its highly flexible Internet search tool, Sherlock, no central resource existed to access these kinds of information. The Internet has a number of popular and powerful search engines, but knowing which one will work for your specific range of requests is a matter of trial and error. In addition, you have to learn the right search syntax for any but the most simple information requests.

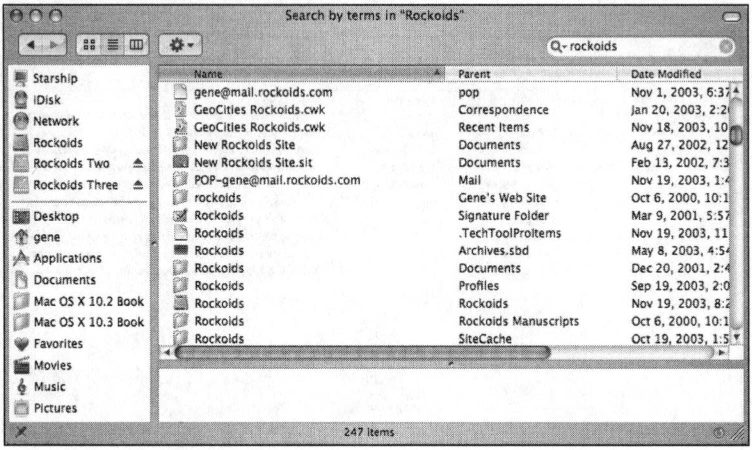

Figure 7.2   Click in a Search field and enter your search request.

TIP: If you're still interested in Internet-based search engines, may I suggest you join the march to Google. This seach engine is integrated into Apple's Safari Web browser, as you'll see in Chapter 21.

For Panther, Apple has overhauled Sherlock extensively, so it not only presents links to Internet content, but some of it is presented in a convenient multipaned interface. You can now see the information without having to jump to your browser.

Sherlock divides its search feature into channels, each of which accesses content in a specific category or from a specific resource. Here's a brief description of what they do; I'll cover all these features in detail later in this chapter:

NOTE: In addition to Apple's standard Sherlock channels, a number of third party entries come along for the ride, such as Google and VersionTracker, but since those items are apt to change as Apple's marketing agreements are revised, I'll only suggest that you explore them at your own leisure to see what they do.

- *Internet*—Use the resources of popular Web-based search sites (see Figure 7.3) to search for almost any accessible Internet-based content.

- *Pictures*—Are you looking for photos of a particular person, place or object? This feature brings up a window with thumbnails of pictures that match your description, and it requires double clicking on the image to see the result in your browser.

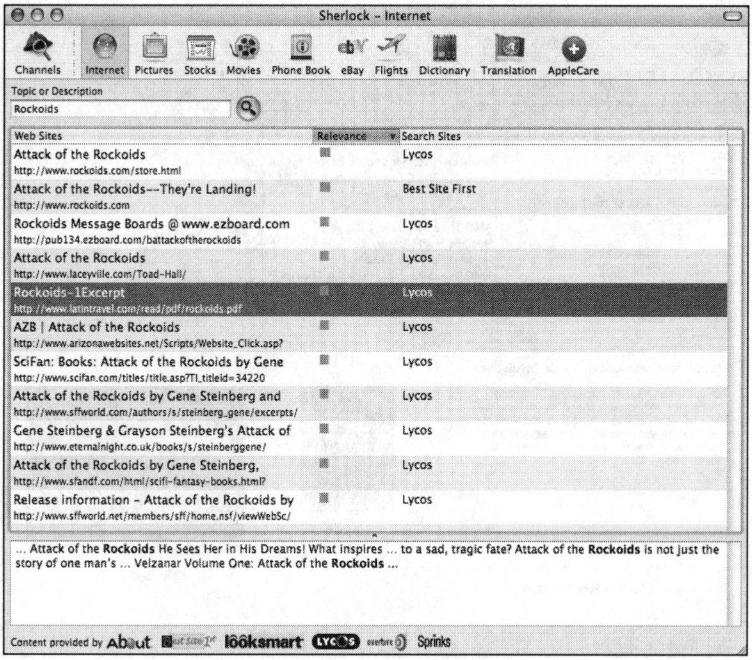

Figure 7.3 Check a number of Internet search engines in a single step.

- *Stocks*—Find out how the companies that move and shake our economy are faring. You'll not only see the recent price, delayed by up to 15 minutes during the trading day, but links to the latest news about a company and its stock price history.

- *Movies*—One of my favorite features. You can check by movie or theater in your area, get a list of when it's playing along with a brief description of the plot. In most cases, you can even check out a movie trailer (see Figure 7.4) and order your tickets.

- *Phone Book*—You can look up a residential or business phone number anywhere in the USA and, in most cases, see a map and get driving directions from your home, office, or whatever location you specify in Sherlock's preferences (I'll get to this in the Immediate Solutions section).

- *eBay*—Whether you want to participate in an online auction, or just check out the prices for a product of interest, this is going to be a very useful component of Sherlock.

- *Flights*—No, it's not a reservation's tool. It's a way to check on flight arrivals and departures.

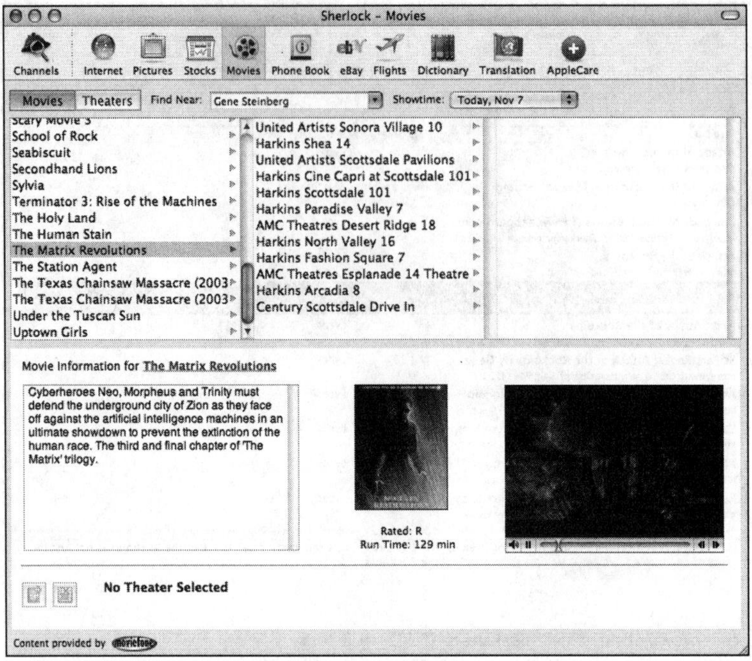

Figure 7.4   If you're not sure what to see, check the trailer first. This one is for the final episode of the Matrix trilogy.

- *Dictionary*—Check spelling and definitions, and consult Roget's Thesaurus to find the right word. No, I don't use it for every paragraph, but I've been known to turn to it from time to time.

- *Translation*—Use this handy tool to do a rough translation in a number of major languages, including Chinese to English. To use, just write the text, or copy and paste it from its source into the top or Original Text pane, select the language from the pop-up menu, and, in seconds, you'll see the result in the bottom pane.

NOTE: *Please understand that these translations are strictly fast and dirty, and aren't perfect, as you'll see soon enough when you try one. For example, if you try to translate English to Chinese, don't be surprised if the recipient of your message is either confused at the result, or just smiles in silent amusement over your inability to use the language properly.*

- *AppleCare*—Need more help with your Mac? Or, do you just want to check out the latest models? This channel has direct links to several of Apple Computer's Web sites, where you can bring up the latest Knowledge Base documents.

You can launch the Sherlock application, choose a category or channel, and then enter your search request in normal, everyday English. Sherlock will go to work finding the information you want. Whether you are searching for information already stored on your Mac or you want to check out the Internet, you'll learn how to tailor Panther's search tools for your needs in the next section.

NOTE: *What doesn't the AppleCare channel do? It won't let you print the information. Oh well, at least you can read it. Apple must have been in a tree saving mode when it made that component of Sherlock.*

Immediate Solutions

Searching for Files on Your Mac

In seconds, you can easily locate a file on any drive connected to your Mac or accessed across a network. Whether you're looking for a document, application, or folder, the finder's convenient Search feature can handle the job for you. There are two ways to seek information, depending on the scope of your search:

1. If you want to search for something within a folder or drive, open up a Finder window.

2. Click on the Search field and enter the name of the file or folder you want.

NOTE: *The little arrow in the search field lets you choose exactly what areas to search: Local Disks, Home, Selection (selected folder), and Everywhere. Pick your poison and search away.*

---

3. Press Return or Enter. Within seconds a list of files or folders matching your request will appear in the same Finder window in list view, sorted by title (see Figure 7.5).

TIP: *If you want to sort your search results differently, click on a title such as Date Modified and the results will be resorted. If there's an arrow in a title field, clicking on it will reverse the sorting order.*

NOTE: *No search field? If you've collapsed the toolbar, click the little rectangle at the upper right of a Finder window to bring it back. If you don't see the Search field in a toolbar, choose Customize Toolbar from the Finder's View menu, and add the icons you like, or just drag the Default Set to the toolbar window to bring it back to factory condition. Click Done when you've finished your setup.*

---

4. To actually use the file or folder, double click on it from the search window.

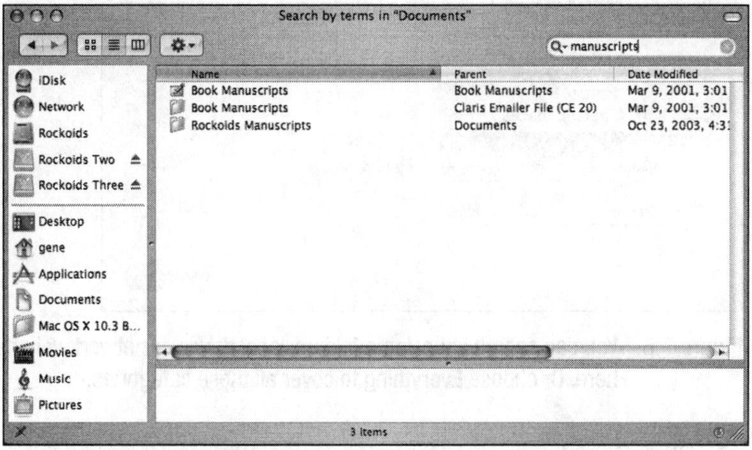

Figure 7.5 All the information the Finder locates appears in this convenient window.

TIP: *To actually see the location of a selected item, look at the bottom pane of the search window. If the window is too small, click on the bar above the bottom pane and drag it upward to expand its size.*

Speeding Up Your Searches

The Finder's built-in search field is strictly limited to the name of the file in the folder or disk you've selected. However, Panther has more powerful weapons in the Finder's search arsenal, including the ability to actually locate the text in a file.

Here's how to harness these powerful features:

1. Return to the Finder by clicking on the desktop, clicking on the Dock's Finder icon, or any visible Finder window.

2. Press Command+F to bring up the search window. Click the Search in the pop-up menu to indicate where you want to search (see Figure 7.6).

3. Click on the Search field and enter the name of the file or folder you want.

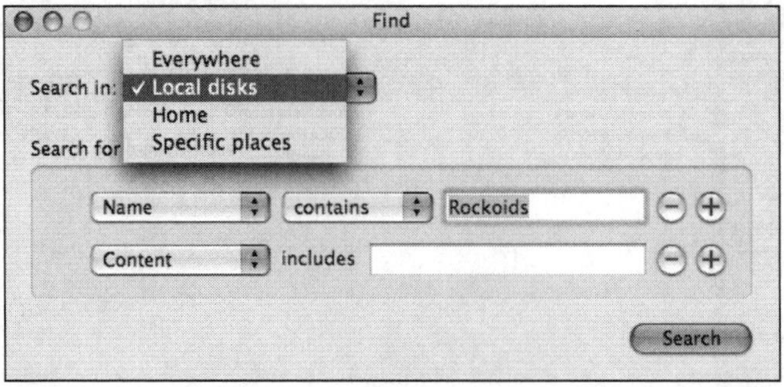

Figure 7.6 You can search your Home folders, local drives or network volumes here. Or choose Everything to cover all these categories.

4. Click Search or press Return or Enter. Within seconds a list of files or folders matching your request will appear in the same Finder window in list view, sorted by date to your search request. The bottom pane will reveal the file's location.

5. To actually view the file, double-click on it to launch its creator application and the file itself.

TIP: *To delete selected items from the Finder's Find window, press Command+Del. This action moves the selected item to the Trash but the Trash won't be emptied until you either perform that action in the Finder's application menu or click and hold the Trash icon in the Dock and select Empty Trash from the menu.*

Searching Files for Content

It's not enough to simply find a file by its name. Sometimes, you need to find files that contain a specific word or phrase. Fortunately, the Finder's search utility can handle that chore just about as easily as any other search routine. But first you have to index the folder or disk so the words can be found. When a drive is indexed, keywords to locate the text strings are all placed in a special file so Sherlock can access the information quickly. Here's how to perform the indexing process:

1. Select the folder or disk you want to index.

2. Go to the Finder's File menu and choose Get Info or press Command+I.

3. Click the Content Index disclosure triangle and then the Index Now button. With the progress indicated by a progress bar and

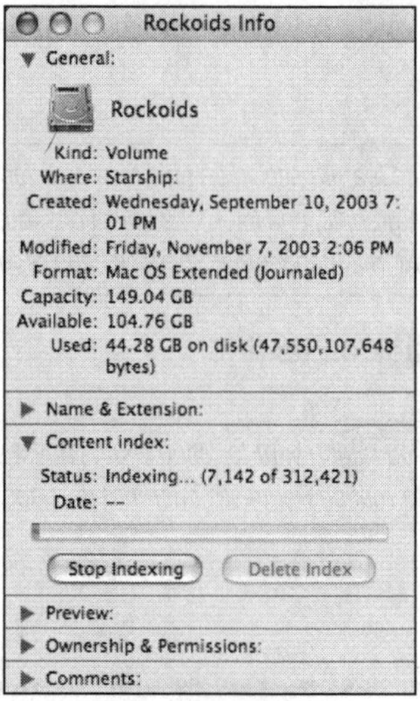

Figure 7.7 In this example, an entire drive with a ton of files is being indexed.

numeric display, the contents of the selected item will be indexed (see Figure 7.7).

4. Repeat the process for each drive or folder you want to index.

WARNING! Because a new index procedure can take a long time, as will an index of a drive on which lots of changes have been made, you might want to schedule the process for times when you're not using your Mac. Even though Mac OS X's preemptive multitasking feature can handle multiple tasks at the same time (more so if you have a dual-processor Power Mac), you should do the indexing when you're not apt to be changing the files that are being indexed.

Once you've indexed the item to be searched for content, here's what to do next:

1. Press Command+F to bring up the Find window.

2. Under the Content includes category, enter the word or phrase for which you want to search.

NOTE: No field for content? Just click the Add criteria menu at the bottom of the Find screen, and choose Content to add that field.

---

3. Click Search to start the process. Your search results will appear in a new Finder window, sorted by relevance. The bottom pane will show the folder hierarchy, displaying where a selected file actually resides.

7. Mac OS X's Search Feature

4. To change the sort order, you can click on a title field, such as Name or Date modified.

NOTE: *The text-parsing process isn't perfect. Panther's find feature should be able to search for the text in most documents from word processor, page layout, graphic, and Internet applications, but the possibility always exists that a program will encode text in a manner that Sherlock can't read.*

---

5. To actually read the file, double click on its title.

NOTE: *If your file and text search doesn't yield results, you might want to refine your request still further. Read the section "Customizing Your Sherlock Information Request," later in this chapter.*

Using Advanced Criteria

Still unable to find the information you want? You can add criteria to the Finder's search field to customize the process. Just click on the Add criteria button to bring up a pop-up menu where you can add additional search options (see Figure 7.8).

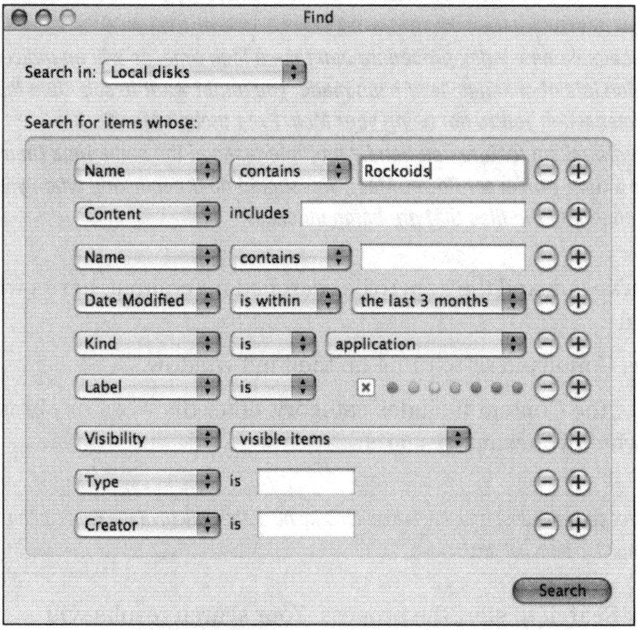

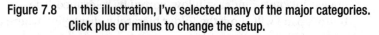

**Figure 7.8   In this illustration, I've selected many of the major categories.
Click plus or minus to change the setup.**

Here are most of the search options available, but each can be customized still further by clicking on the pop-up menus at the right of a specific category.

- *Name*—Click the pop-up menu to decide whether the file name begins or ends with the word or phrase.

NOTE: *You can add more File Name categories by clicking the Plus symbol at the right of the field, and remove a field by clicking on the Minus icon.*

- *Content*—Refine your file search by making sure that a certain bit of text (a word or phrase) is included. This topic is covered in more detail in the previous section.

- *Date Modified*—When was the file last changed? You can specify whether the date is "Today," or choose another option and specify a specific date.

- *Date Created*—Decide how closely the search will look at file creation dates in making your request.

- *Kind*—Is the file an alias, a document, or a font, or does it fit into a wide range of categories? Choose the one you want from the pop-up menu.

- *Size*—This option limits or includes files of a particular size. It's especially helpful for content searches—particularly if you want to look at text in a small document but don't want to wait until large documents are also searched.

- *Extension is*—Panther supports the same file naming conventions as windows, which means a Word document has a .doc extension, for example. You can search documents this way if you're just trying to find the ones made in a specific program.

- *Visibility*—Is the file invisible? Some files are declared invisible by the Finder because they are system-related and not intended for general access. You can specify whether a file is visible, invisible or both.

WARNING! *A number of system-related files under Mac OS X are set in a specific way or located in a specific place because they are required for your Mac to run properly. Don't attempt to seek them out and manipulate them with Sherlock, or you might find that your Mac fails to run properly or will not even boot when you try to restart.*

After you've fine-tuned your information request, click Search to make your request. The modification you make to the Find screen remains in place until you change it.

Setting Sherlock Preferences

The Sherlock Preferences dialog box, available from the application's menu, gives you a single choice, which is whether or not to set cookies, as you'll see in Figure 7.9.

Once you've changed or viewed Sherlock's preferences, close in the close box to dismiss the dialog box.

Enhancing Internet Searches

The first, core, feature of Sherlock is Internet searching. Sherlock uses a number of popular search tools to locate the information you want.

Here's how to use Sherlock for this function:

1. Log on to your ISP. (See Chapter 8 for information on how to configure Mac OS X to make your Internet connection).

2. Launch Sherlock, and then click the Internet channel icon (see Figure 7.10).

3. Make your search request. Enter the word or phrase that best describes what you're searching for in the Topic or Description field. For example, if you are interested in buying a new Ford, enter "Ford" or, more specifically, the model, such as "Ford Taurus."

4. Click the magnifying glass to start the process.

5. Sherlock produces a list of items that match your search request. Depending on the number of sites you've activated and the speed of the connection to your ISP, this process may take anywhere from a few seconds to several minutes. A progress bar indicates the status of your search. By default, items are listed in order of relevance (how closely they match your

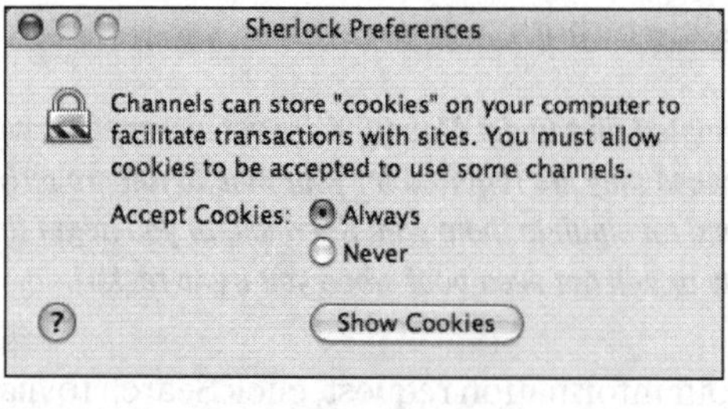

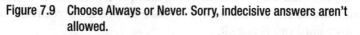

Figure 7.9   Choose Always or Never. Sorry, indecisive answers aren't allowed.

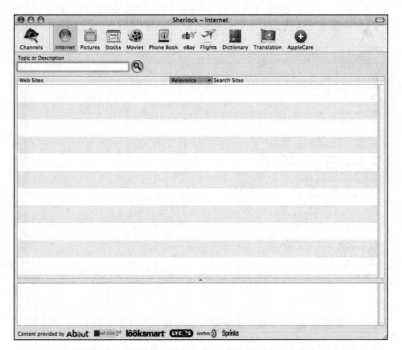

Figure 7.10 Enter your search request in the Topic or Description field.

search query). When Sherlock is done, click any item in the search list to see more information in the results pane at the bottom of the Sherlock application window (see Figure 7.11). This information will only appear if the selected Web page has meta tags that provide a description of its content.

NOTE: *Not all search requests will bring a response. If you don't receive any matches to your request, try refining the request a bit, perhaps by using a more descriptive phrase. I'll get to the process of customizing your search requests later in this chapter.*

---

6. If you've found an item you want to know more about, double click on the item. Your default Web browser will be launched and you'll be taken directly to the page you've selected (see Figure 7.12).

NOTE: *Even if a Web site is shown in Sherlock, it doesn't mean it's still available. Search engines don't always remove obsolete links.*

---

7. Repeat the process to search for additional information.

8. Quit Sherlock when you're done using it.

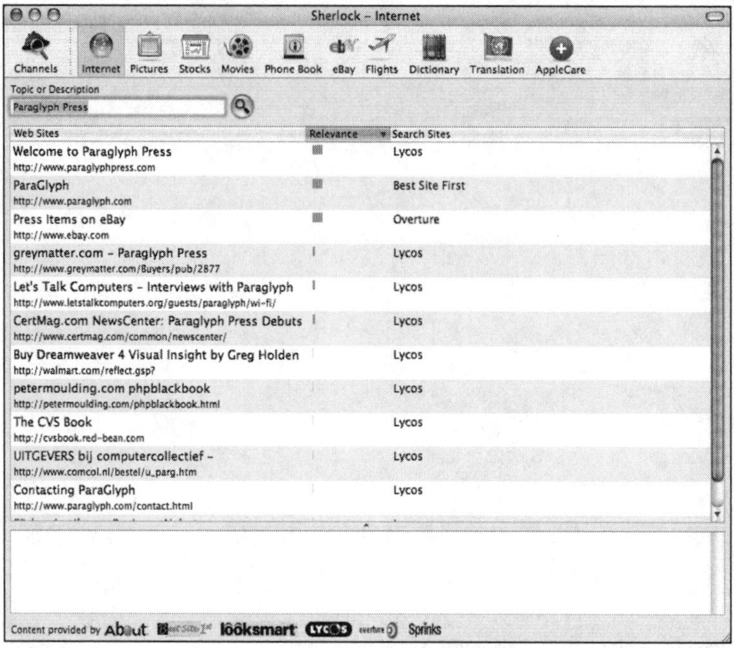

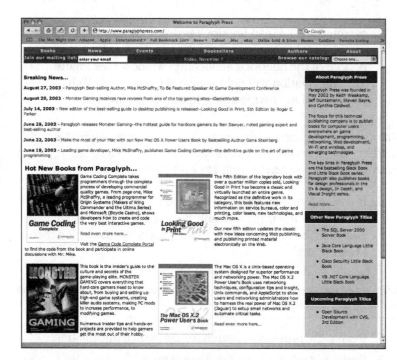

Figure 7.11 Select from the list of items to get more information.

Figure 7.12 Your browser opens and the page you've selected appears.

Related solution:	Found on page:
Using Internet Connect for Dial-Up Networking	185

Customizing Your Sherlock Internet Search Request

Not every request you make for Internet information in Sherlock's request will be successful, and it's not always because you've done something wrong. There is so much information available that sometimes you must fine-tune your request or try a few different ways of asking.

As mentioned, Sherlock works with plain English to send your requests, whether they're made locally, on a network, or on the Internet. However, you can narrow the information so you get what you need. Here are some suggestions:

- If you want your search request to include all the words of a phrase, type a plus (+) character between each word. So, if you're looking for a Ford Taurus, try "Ford+Taurus" if the original request isn't specific enough.

- To exclude a word, you'd think you'd type a minus sign, right? Well, no; you need to use an exclamation point (!). To refine that request on Ford products to exclude the Taurus from the search, use "Ford!Taurus."

- Now we get a bit more complicated. If you'd like to search for a group of items, use parentheses. You can even group items, yet exclude specific categories in this fashion: "(cars|Ford)! Taurus." Again, this request excludes the Taurus.

NOTE: That vertical bar character, described above as a means to group items (which looks like a slash in some typefaces), is accessed by pressing Option+Shift+1.

In the old days, if you wanted to find out someone's physical address, you had to check a phone directory or call the telephone company for the information. Now, there's a new way to let your fingers do the walking, with the help of Sherlock—and you don't have to go hunting for the right phone directory or pay your phone company a fee to look it up for you. You don't even have to call your roadside assistance company for directions, because, in most cases, Sherlock will give you driving directions. To find businesses on the Internet, just follow these steps:

1. Log on to your ISP in the usual fashion.

2. Launch Sherlock, and then click the Phone Book channel icon and select the business option, the tiny "i" icon at the left.

7. Mac OS X's Search Feature

3. Enter the business's name, as exactly as you can recall it, and the city, state and/or zip code.

4. Click the magnifying glass. Sherlock goes to work searching the Internet phone book for the business you want to contact. A progress wheel indicates the search is still in progress.

5. After you see a list of likely candidates, if any, click the item to bring up a map in the results pane of the Sherlock application window (see Figure 7.13). If the location is within reasonable driving distance, directions from the selected location will appear.

6. If you don't find the right company the first time, continue to select likely candidates from the list.

7. Should your initial request not be successful, recheck the spelling of the name. Try without the "Inc." if necessary.

NOTE: Don't expect miracles with Internet-based mapping services. In many cases, recently built roads won't be reflected, and sometimes directions will be more convoluted than necessary to reach a specific location. In one case, I found myself driving in circle, literally, after following one

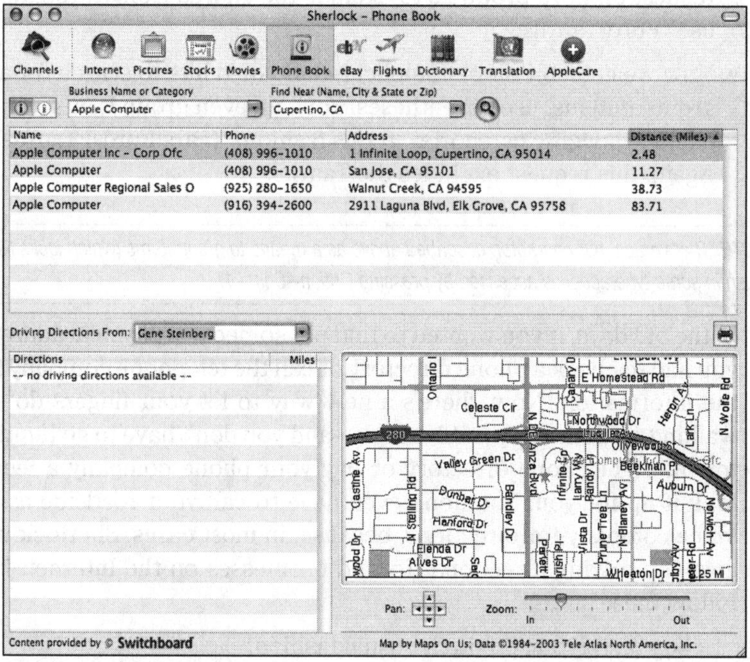

Figure 7.13   All right, I don't plan on driving from Arizona to California to visit Apple, but here's the road map anyway.

of these maps to the letter. I learned a hard lesson that day. And once, when I wanted the best route from Phoenix to Las Vegas, I went to three separate mapping services, and, while they all led me to the same destination, many of the choices made for the trip were different. Sigh!

8. If you want a hard copy of the address, map and directions, click the Print button.

9. If you want to search for a home listing, click the other "i" icon and follow similar steps. Just bear in mind that you will absolutely not be able to locate unlisted numbers.

10. When you're finished with the search request, make another or quit Sherlock.

NOTE: *The above directions give you information on how to use two of the popular channels of Sherlock. All the rest have a similar range of text entry and information fields that make them easy to follow. Over time Apple will be adding different changes to expand your range of options.*

Installing Additional Search Modules

As Apple signs new partnerships with content providers, it will automatically send you the channel updates, so you don't have to do anything to configure Sherlock to receive them.

Other Web sites also supply their own search components for Sherlock that can be downloaded, automatically, in the same fashion. When they show up, you'll simply have to click a link at the Web site to start the install process.

TIP: *You already have a bunch of third-party channels included with Sherlock. Just click on the Channels icon in Sherlock, and then Other Channels to see the listing. You'll need to double click a channel to bring it up, but then you can drag its icon to the toolbar for faster access.*

Another Solution for Web Services

Before Apple's Sherlock 3 appeared back when Mac OS X 10.2 came out, a shareware application, inspired by the original Sherlock, offered a wide range of Web services. Known, appropriately, as Watson, Dan Wood's highly acclaimed application (see Figure 7.14) offered, in the release shown in this book, a larger and more expansive range of channels.

7. Mac OS X's Search Feature

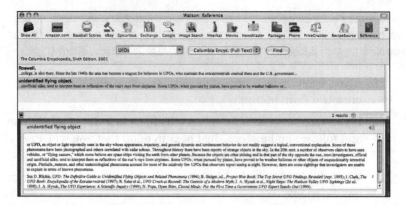

Figure 7.14   Some say Watson inspired Sherlock 3 and later versions, but they continue to exist as separate programs.

Fortunately, you can use both, and benefit by the different selection of services. To get a copy of Watson for evaluation, visit the publisher's Web site at: **www.karelia.com/watson/**. Watson is simple to install. It comes on a disk image file, and once the disk image is mounted, you drag it to your applications folder, and double click to get it going. The "Unregistered" version lets you sample all the features to give you an idea if it's worth the modest purchase price (I vote "Yes"). My favorite Watson features are the TV listing and package tracking components. While I have little doubt Apple will add such things eventually, I prefer to support Watson.

Chapter 8

Networking Overview

In Brief

PC users consider networking to be an alien world full of confusion and frustration. In the Mac universe, however, you don't have to contend with setup wizards or complex configurations to join a network. Although the Macintosh was originally designed as a computer that empowered the individual, easy networking was always a part of the picture. The first example of simple networking was the ability to easily set up a network-capable laser printer by plugging it in, turning it on, and selecting the driver that worked with the output device in the Chooser. The same easy networking extended to more powerful printers. Even an imagesetter used in the printing industry for high-quality output could be hooked up to a Mac just as easily as the cheapest laser printer. If you wanted to network Macs with each other, however, you needed special software.

Apple's personal file sharing feature was first introduced in System 7.0 back in 1991. It allowed Mac users on a small network to activate peer-to-peer file transfers without special software by attaching cables among the computers and turning on file sharing. In minutes, the shared Mac's drive appeared in the Chooser as an AppleShare volume available on your network (see Figure 8.1).

For more sophisticated setups, it was easy to use the Get Info window to set user access privileges for file sharing. Using this limited

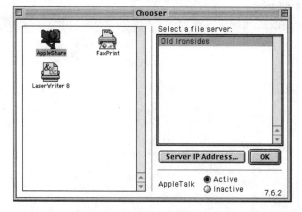

Figure 8.1   The late Mac Chooser is still required to configure printers from the Classic environment.

set of user controls, you could restrict the ability of users connected to a Mac to see or modify files. As file sharing matured, Apple also added the capability of sharing a Mac across the Internet with almost the same ease as connecting to a Mac on a local network.

Apple has advanced its networking architecture tremendously. It now employs industry-standard technologies to provide faster performance, greater reliability, and better cross-platform compatibility. For example, the operating system's Darwin core includes the BSD networking stack, which includes TCP/IP, the protocol used to power the Internet. You don't have to abandon your existing techniques for getting connected, either. Panther provides native support for Point-to-Point Protocol (PPP) connections, so you can access your ISP as easily as before—perhaps more easily. (I'll cover the subject of Panther's Internet features in Chapter 20.) AppleTalk is also supported, so you don't have to do anything extra to access your older Macs and printers. In all, Panther now includes built-in network support for such file services as AFP (AppleShare), Server Message Block / Common Internet File System (SMB/CIFS), WebDAV, and Network File System (NFS), which means you can mate not only with a Mac, but also with computers running Linux and other Unix operating systems, Novell NetWare, Windows 98, Windows Me, Windows NT, Windows 2000, Windows XP, and Windows Server 2003. All of this is accomplished under Panther without your having to learn special skills or trip through a complicated series of dialog boxes and interpret arcane commands.

Panther also provides flexible features to help support cross-platform networks. With a few simple settings on your Mac, your computer will appear as just another member of a "network neighborhood" on a Windows PC. That means that file transfers can work in both directions. The very same thing applies to shared network printers, which greatly increases deployment of your output devices.

NOTE: *Rendezvous is Apple's open source automatic network technology that is based on standard Internet protocols. It supports automatic discovery of network devices. Although Macs running Panther have this capability out of the box, other products, such as printers and handheld computers, will have to add support of their own to allow those products to be automatically recognized. Some Brother laser printers, for example, allow for this sort of automatic setup routine. By the way, iTunes for Windows actually brings Rendezvous to the Windows platform.*

Connecting to Networked Computers

If it's so easy to network under Panther, where do you start? Just take a look at your Finder's Sidebar, where a simple click of the Network icon will let you browse network servers (see Figure 8.2).

Figure 8.2   Click Network to browse file shares.

The second method used for browsing servers more or less works in concert with the first method. The Connect To Server feature (see Figure 8.3), available from the Panther Finder's Go menu, will both point back to the items displayed when you click the Network globe. It doesn't just duplicate the functions, though. It adds the ability to contact other computers by entering their IP address, URL, or FTP address.

A Different Way to Share Files

With older versions of the Mac OS, you'd normally share an entire disk or folder. For Panther, the safest routine is to place items you want to make available to others on your network in your Shared folder. That way, everyone who uses your computer can have access to the files by connecting as guests, without having to log in via any of your user accounts. That folder can also be used as a repository for the files you want to share or to receive across your network. In the "Immediate Solutions" section of this chapter, I'll explain how to establish access privileges so that only the users you specify can connect to your Mac without going through a login process.

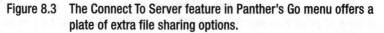

Figure 8.3   The Connect To Server feature in Panther's Go menu offers a plate of extra file sharing options.

TIP: To share a large number of files in other parts of your Mac's drive and see other files on your Mac's drive without having to provide access to the rest of the volume, create an alias for each of those items and place them in your Shared folder. Doing so will provide easy access to these items for users who connect to your Mac directly or across a network.

A Look at Panther's Networking Components

The tools to network your Mac require settings in two System Preferences panels and a dialog box. I'll describe them here and I'll discuss how they're used in the "Immediate Solutions" section:

* *Network*—This settings pane (see Figure 8.4) is used to configure your AirPort, Ethernet, and modem connections, all from a single set of screens. It replaces several control panels in the Classic Mac OS. This tool helps ease the setup process. Moreover, most of the setups are essentially the same as the ones you used in the Classic Mac OS. There's even a Location feature, which can automatically switch network settings when you move your Mac to different locales.

NOTE: If you are working in an organization where a systems administrator handles network-related issues, you should consult with that person before you attempt to change any of the existing network settings on your Mac.

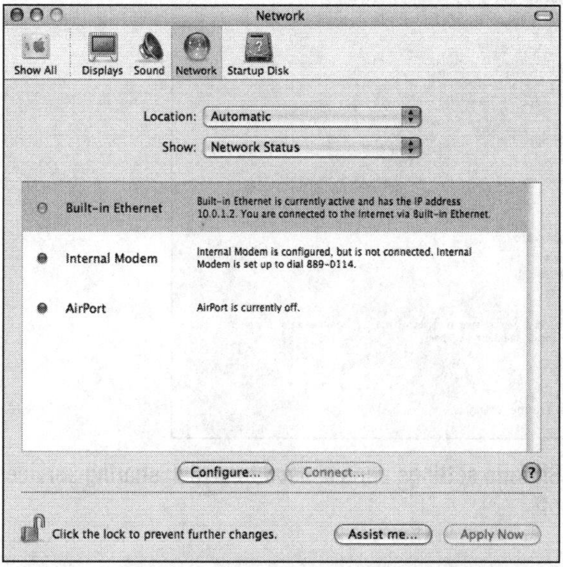

Figure 8.4   This screen gives you a clear indication of your Mac's network status. Double click on a network port label to configure that port.

- *Sharing*—You'll use this settings pane (see Figure 8.5) to activate Mac and Windows file sharing and other services. Personal Web Sharing uses the features of the Apache Web server software to let you run an Internet site from your Mac. You can also allow others to access your Mac via FTP or Telnet (remote login)—an option that adds to the flexibility of the new networking features. The Firewall button activates built-in protection for your Mac, and the Internet button is used to share your online connection across your network. When you choose the option to share the connection with others on your network, your Mac will distribute IP addresses across the network, and all the other computers have to do is use the DHCP option to receive the signal.

NOTE: Sharing a connection this way has its disadvantages. You need to keep your Mac on while the connections are being shared, and performance may take a hit as the Mac is doling out the shared hookup. In addition, I would not recommend trying to share a dial-up connection because the connection will be too slow. Imagine if two or more computers tried to share the same amount of limited bandwidth.

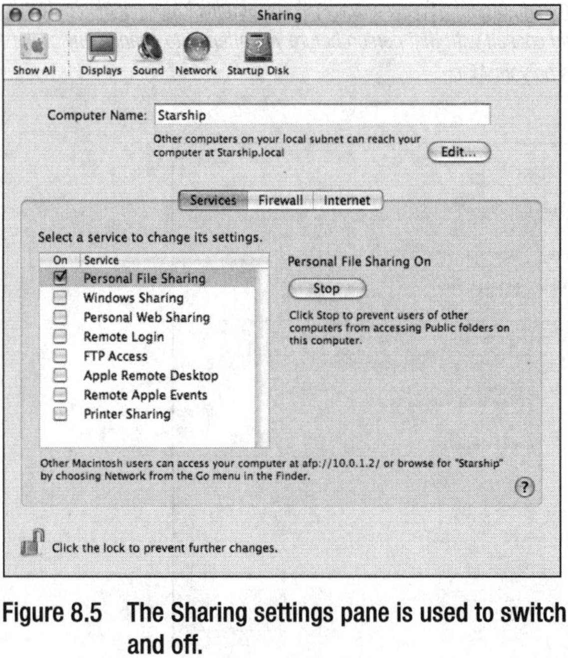

Figure 8.5   The Sharing settings pane is used to switch sharing services on and off.

Selecting Printers without a Chooser

In every version of the Mac operating system prior to Mac OS X, users relied on a somewhat clumsy little application—the Chooser (see Figure 8.6)—to both select a printer and connect to a Mac or PC with the proper networking software installed across a network.

For Panther, Apple uses a more conventional solution called Printer Setup. Even better, you can access this handy tool direct from the Print & Fax panel in System Preferences. As you will learn later in this chapter, this application can ferret out the printers on your network or the ones directly connected to your Mac. You can then select the ones you want to use and configure custom features. Panther also puts up an icon in the Dock that you can open to monitor and adjust your print queue while printing is in progress. You can even create a desktop printer icon.

One big advantage over the older Chooser is that Printer Setup can search for any available printer, even if it's on a USB port or accessible via TCP/IP across the Internet. You don't have to fiddle with multiple network adjustments other than turning to AppleTalk (for a network printer that requires it). What's more, if you have a USB printer connected to your Mac and the correct drivers installed, Panther automatically recognizes the device—no extra setup is needed. Once all your printers are configured, you can use the regular Page Setup and Print dialog boxes to switch among the available printers.

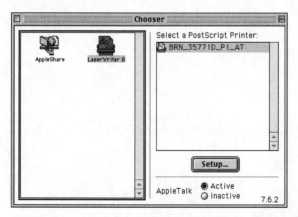

Figure 8.6   The venerable (and clunky) Apple Chooser is mostly history. Long live the Chooser.

8. Networking Overview

173

No more awkward visits to the Chooser, at least for Panther applications. If you're using a Classic application, however, you'll still have to select your printer the old-fashioned way, in the Chooser. When a document is being printed, PrintMonitor (or the print driver's custom print window) will appear to show its progress.

NOTE: You will also have to install the Classic version of the driver software for your printer if you intend to use a Classic application. The Panther printer drivers don't function in the Classic user environment, with the exception of networked laser printers, where the PPD (the file that customizes the system to the printer) is recognized by both Panther and Classic.

Immediate Solutions

Sharing Files with Panther

To share files with a Mac running Panther, you'll find the setup process familiar, even though you have to use a different set of dialog boxes to set things up and access your shares. The really sophisticated stuff happens behind the scenes, as Panther's highly flexible network services are activated to do your bidding.

Here are the basic steps to follow to activate file exchanges using Panther:

1. On the Mac running Panther, open the System Preferences application, click the Network pane, and double-click on Built-in Ethernet (see Figure 8.7) or AirPort from the Network Status display. I'll discuss the modem option in the section entitled "Using Internet Connect for Dial-Up," later in this chapter.

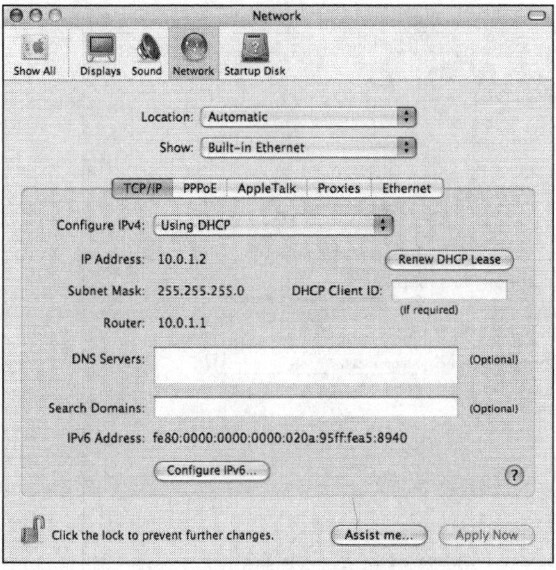

Figure 8.7   Change your network settings here.

2. If the padlock is locked, click its icon, and then enter your administrator's username and password. If the login window shakes (nervous little devil), it just means that you entered the wrong username and/or password—try again.

NOTE: If you do not have the username and password handy, please consult with your network administrator, if applicable. There's no way to access the protected features of Panther without entering this information. The padlock remains open whenever you log in with an account that has administrator access.

3. If you're going to share files with an older Mac running a Mac OS version prior to 8.5, you'll need to network via AppleTalk. (AppleTalk is also required for many network printers.) In this case, click the AppleTalk button and click the Make AppleTalk Active checkbox (see Figure 8.8). To change the name of your Mac for network access, you'll need to move on to the Sharing pane.

NOTE: If you need to split up your AppleTalk connection to specific nodes, click on the Automatically pop-up menu, choose Manually and enter the appropriate network information required in your installation.

4. Click the Apply Now button to store your settings. If you forget when you close the Network pane, you'll see a reminder prompt in which you can click the Save button.

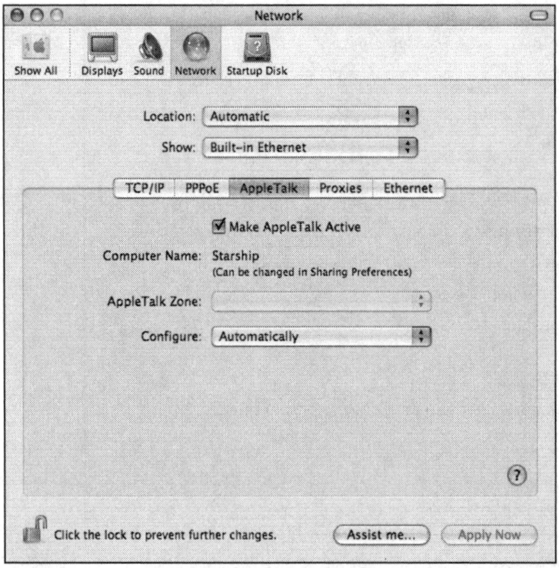

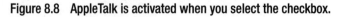

Figure 8.8   AppleTalk is activated when you select the checkbox.

5. Click Show All at the top left of the System Preferences application window to display the other settings panes in System Preferences.

6. Go to the Sharing pane and select the service you wish to share, which in this case would be Personal File Sharing. (I'll get to the other options, such as Windows File Sharing, later in this chapter.) This is the equivalent of selecting a service and clicking the Start button, but you save a keystroke. You can change the name of your Mac before sharing is activated, by the way. Once sharing is activated, it may take a few minutes to start up.

NOTE: Panther will use a computer's IP address in addition to its name to configure sharing. If you have five Macs at hand all named something like "Gene Steinberg's Computer," it would make sense to give each a unique identity so you know which is which without having to remember which IP address is correct.

---

7. Only the administrator can change access privileges for an entire drive. A regular user without those privileges can only change the access for his or her Users folder. To set custom access privileges for that folder or another disk volume on your Mac, return to the Finder or desktop, click on the icon, and then click on the name of the item you want to share.

8. Choose Get Info from the Finder's File menu.

9. Next click the Ownership & Permissions disclosure triangle to display your personal settings.

10. To see all the settings, click the Details triangle (see Figure 8.9). If necessary, click the lock and enter your user name and password to gain access.

NOTE: If your Mac is accessed by a user who has administrator privileges (and that includes you working from another computer), the entire drive will be available for sharing, with the exception of another user, unless privileges for that user are changed.

---

11. The full Ownership & Privileges window offers three sets of access privileges, in a fashion very much like previous versions of the Mac OS. These are:

- *Owner*—This is the name of the owner or administrator of the files on this Mac. The normal access setting is Read & Write, which gives the owner the ability to access and modify files. By design, you can restrict your own access to files, but I'm not sure why you'd want to do that.

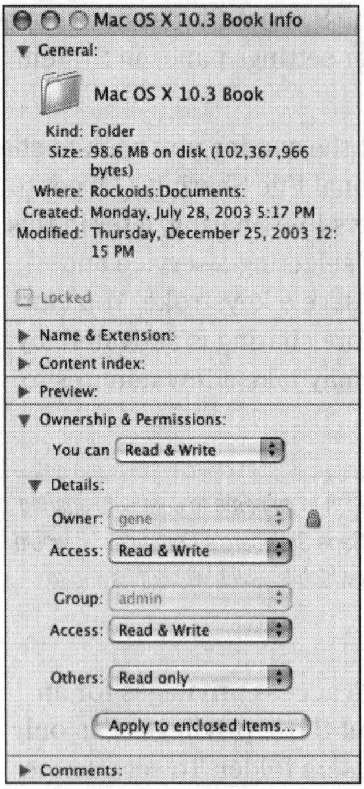

Figure 8.9 Set file access and sharing privileges in this window.

- *Group*—Each selected user of your Mac can be given a specific set of access instructions. Click the pop-up menu to change privileges, choosing Read & Write, Read Only, or Write Only. The Write Only setting lets the user place files in the Shared folder but not see any other files. Files or folders "admin" group, such as your Mac's hard drive, are accessible by anyone with administrator's privileges.

- *Others*—These settings are identical to those for a group, except that when you set them here, anyone who connects to your Mac as a guest can have that level of access—even if they haven't been given specific user privileges.

Set your access privilege settings. They are activated as soon as they are changed. To keep the same settings for all the files and folders within a folder, click Apply To Enclosed Items to incorporate the settings.

NOTE: *Depending on your needs, you may prefer to establish separate settings for individual files and folders. You should use the Apply function with caution because it will only duplicate the permissions you've set for the main folder or file. In addition, copying privileges to a folder with lots of files (or en entire drive) can take several minutes.*

---

12. If you have Macs on your network that are not using Panther and you want them available for file sharing, the users of those Macs need to launch the File Sharing Control Panel (see Figure 8.10) or, as it's known on older Macs, Sharing Setup.

13. With File Sharing open, make sure the Network Identity fields are filled in with Owner Name, Owner Password, and Computer Name.

14. Click Start to activate file sharing.

NOTE: The Network Identity is automatically configured when you use the Mac OS Setup Assistant to configure Panther. If your new Mac was pretested before delivery (perhaps to install a RAM upgrade due to those prevalent free RAM offers), you may find that the Assistant doesn't launch when you boot your Mac and thus no computer name was selected.

15. Once sharing has been activated (it can take a few minutes, particularly on a Mac with several large drives attached to it), click the Close box to dismiss the File Sharing Control Panel.

NOTE: If your Mac supports TCP/IP-based file sharing and you have an always-on Internet connection, you'll see the IP address of your computer displayed. If you are using an AirPort or compatible wireless network, you should use TCP/IP file sharing, where possible, for maximum performance in file transfers. AppleTalk file sharing with a wireless network can be mighty slow,

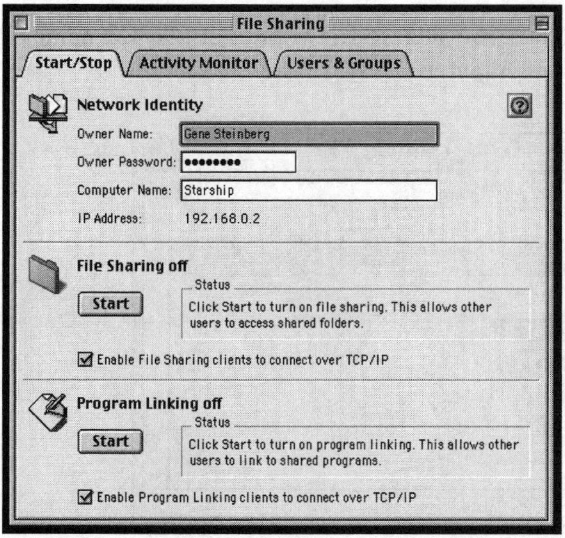

Figure 8.10 Make sure File Sharing is set up for your Classic Mac OS computers.

8. Networking Overview

and that's an understatement. In addition, for security reasons, you'll want to enable the maximum level of encryption supported by your wireless network. Otherwise, even folks driving past your home or office will be able to connect; a practice some call "drive-by hacking."

Accessing Shared Volumes with Network Browser

Depending on the Classic Mac OS version you're using, you can access shared volumes two ways: with Network Browser or the Chooser. These techniques are described in this section and the next.

Follow these steps to use Network Browser to access a shared volume:

NOTE: These file-sharing tools work only when you boot under a Classic Mac OS. If you are accessing shares under Panther, you'll need to use the Connect To Server feature from the Finder's Go menu, described in the next section.

1. To access the Panther computer from the other Mac (if it's running Mac OS 8.5 or later), launch the Network Browser application (it should be in the Apple menu), as shown in Figure 8.11. For earlier Mac OS versions (or as an alternative), you can also use the Chooser to access shares (see the next section).

NOTE: Be patient here. Each step might take up to a minute to complete, because the Mac takes a while to find that other computer with Network Browser.

2. Click the right arrow next to Network to display the name of your Panther computer.

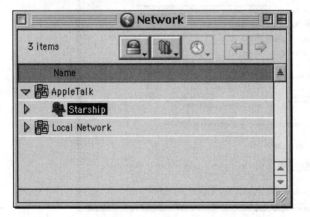

Figure 8.11 You'll see your shared Mac listed here.

3. Double-click the other Mac's name in the list to display the standard file-sharing login dialog. After you enter the proper user name and password and click Connect, you'll see a list of shared volumes that are just a double-click away from access.

4. When you've mounted the share volumes, you can quit Network Browser.

Accessing Shared Volumes with the Chooser

The other way to access a shared volume with the Classic Mac OS is with the famous (or infamous) Chooser. Follow these steps to use that feature:

1. Launch the Chooser from the Apple menu.

2. Click AppleShare to bring up the list of available file shares (see Figure 8.12).

3. Click the name of the share, and click OK.

NOTE: To access the shared volume via TCP/IP (which is available only for Macs running Mac OS X or Mac OS 8.5 through Mac OS 9.x on which the option to enable file sharing via TCP/IP is checked), click the Server IP Address button and enter the IP address of the computer you want to access in the text field.

---

4. Enter the user name and password in the login dialog box, and click Connect. You'll see a list of available shared volumes. Choose one or more to mount on your Mac's desktop. If you want to have those shares mount automatically at startup, check the appropriate boxes at the right of the volume's name.

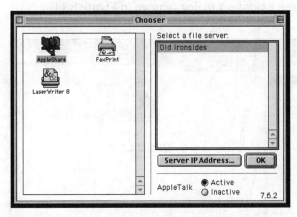

Figure 8.12 Select a networked computer from the list.

8. Networking Overview

5. Click the close box on the Chooser when you've finished mounting file shares.

Connecting to Networked Computers Under Panther

Panther provides a few different methods for connecting to a networked computer. You can use the Finder to connect to a network or you can use the Connect To Server feature. I'll show you how to use both methods in this section.

Networking with the Panther Finder

The Network globe in your Finder's side becomes a neat substitute for the Chooser and the Network Browser application. To access other shared computers, follow these steps:

NOTE: *Panther doesn't care if the shared computer runs Mac OS, Windows, or a flavor of Unix. The file listings will be essentially the same, except for the fact that the name of a Windows PC may appear within a WORKGROUP icon or similar listing. The connection process, believe it or not, is precisely the same.*

---

1. Click the Finder and select the Network globe (see Figure 8.13). You'll see a Servers icon representing your local Mac and networked servers, plus separate listings of available computers.

2. Click on the name of the computer you want to access and you'll see a Connect dialog (shown in Figure 8.14).

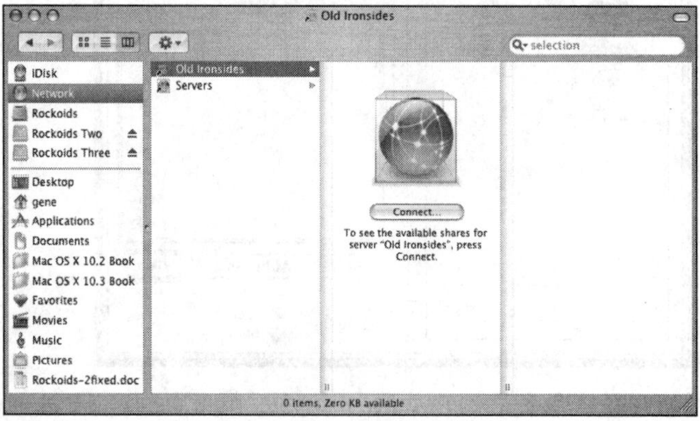

Figure 8.13 Pick a computer to share.

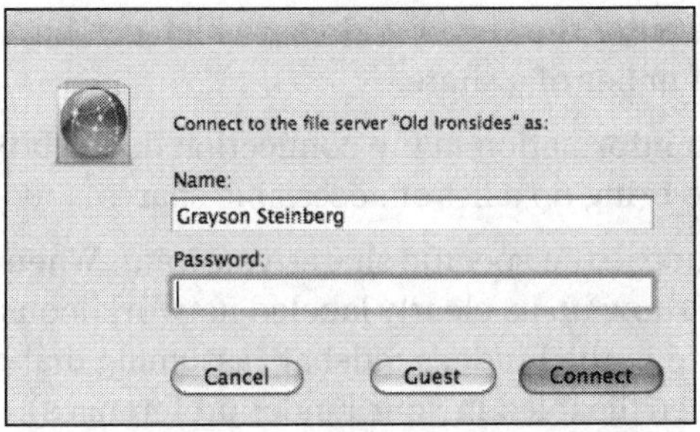

Figure 8.14 Enter login information please.

3. Once you enter the user name and password for the share, click Connect to access all the available drives connected to that computer. They'll be neatly displayed in the Finder window.

NOTE: If you click Guest instead, access will be strictly limited to the items in your Shared folder. This may be your preferred and most secure method of networking in an office environment where you need to place extra controls on who can get what and when.

Networking Via Connect To Server

There's a second way to access a network share, which is useful if you want to move beyond basic network shares to FTP sites, as an example.

To access that alternate networking feature, follow these steps:

1. Click on your Mac's desktop and choose Connect To Server from the Go menu to open the dialog box shown in Figure 8.15. You can also simply press Command+K.

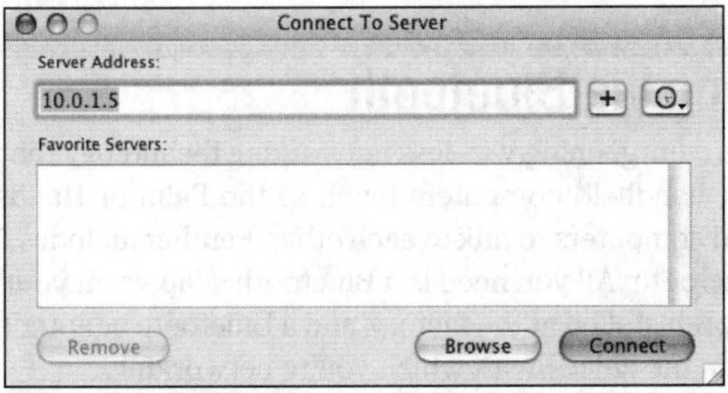

Figure 8.15 You can browse a network or enter a number or URL for direct access to an FTP site.

2. On the top pane enter the server address, which can be a URL or the local IP number of a share.

3. Enter your login information in the connection dialog box and click Connect to bring up a list of accessible shares.

4. Here you can choose the specific shares you want. When you connect, they'll show up as clearly labeled network icons on your desktop and in the Finder's Sidebar (assuming that display option hasn't been disabled in your Finder preferences).

TIP: *If you plan to log into a network frequently, click the plus button to make a selected share a Favorite. You can also click on the Recent Server icon at the left of the plus button to see the ones you've recently accessed.*

The shared volumes can be handled just like local volumes on your Mac's desktop, and can be accessed by Panther's Finder in the same fashion. The only significant difference is when you trash a file from the shared volume. If you drag the item to the trash, you'll see a prompt notifying you that the file must be deleted immediately (you can't leave it in the trash and decide later whether to zap it from your computer).

NOTE: *If the shared volume is no longer accessible because either sharing has been turned off on the other Mac or there has been a system crash or restart, you'll see a prompt saying the file server has closed and when it happened. Here you can click Disconnect or try to login again.*

Related solution:	Found on page:
Configuring Keychain Access	140

Networking Via Bluetooth

Bluetooth is a burgeoning wireless networking technology that allows cell phones, handheld computers (such as the Palm or Handspring), printers, and computers to talk to each other. Panther includes full support for Bluetooth. All you need is a Bluetooth adapter on your Mac, if one wasn't preinstalled at the factory, and a Bluetooth adapter or built-in support on the device with which you're networking.

Once connected, a new Bluetooth preference panel will appear in the System Preferences application, which allows you to customize how your Mac communicates with other devices. By default, your Mac is "Discoverable," which means it'll be recognized automatically.

Once Bluetooth is enabled, if a device that supports the technology is brought in range, and it's within 33 feet of the Bluetooth adapter, it will be discovered automatically. This allows you to share files with that device. It's here that Apple's iSync technology, described in Chapter 22, comes in handy. You can also print to an output device equipped with Bluetooth support.

Although the technology operates like Plug-&-Play, it has its limits. For one thing, file transfers are limited to a maximum of 723Kbps, which is quite a bit less than that of 802.11b, the technology used for AirPort and substantially less than what you receive with 802.11g, used by AirPort Extreme and similar products. In addition, it is possible for a Bluetooth network to interfere with a Wi-Fi connection or even a portable phone, so you may need to reposition your AirPort or similar device if problems occur with network transfers. But it's an ideal solution if you're sending small print jobs or exchanging address books and calendars with your phone or handheld.

TIP: If you want to keep your Mac's desktop free of wires, you might pick up a set of Bluetooth input devices, such as the Apple Wireless Keyboard and Wireless Mouse. These two products mirror the regular Pro versions. They provide the same basic feel and they will give you newfound freedoms, within Bluetooth's range of course.

Using Internet Connect for Dial-Up Networking

Although more and more Net surfers have opted for broadband, it may not be available in your city. It may be too expensive if it is available, or you may just not feel the need for extra bandwidth. So how do you get online? With Panther, you make your connection with the Internet Connect application, with more than a little help with the settings you make in the Network pane of the System Preferences application.

8. Networking Overview

NOTE: Depending on your ISP, these settings might be made courtesy of an installer, such as the one used by EarthLink Total Access. You had the chance to install them when you ran the Setup Assistant right after you installed Mac OS X. I'm covering the process here in case you didn't enter the settings then or you want to change them now.

WARNING! *If you have AOL, CompuServe, MSN, or the various United Online services, such as Juno, you will not be using Internet Connect to get online. All these services provide their own access or dialing applications to make your hookup. Just check their setup programs or Help menus to learn how they're configured.*

Here's how it's done:

1. Launch System Preferences from the Dock or from the Applications folder.

2. Click the Network pane and double-click on Internal Modem or choose it from the Show pop-up menu, which brings you the setup window shown in Figure 8.16.

NOTE: *One of the reasons for being able to enter separate settings for your AirPort, Ethernet, and dial-up TCP/IP access is to allow you to access any available network via Panther's multihoming feature. Working with the built-in Location software, you can automatically switch from AirPort to Ethernet to dial-up, depending on which port is available and which provides the speediest access.*

---

3. As I did in Figure 8.16, enter the telephone number, account name, and password for your account. When you click the Save Password checkbox, the password will be stored, but you can skip this process and enter it manually if others may have access to your Mac.

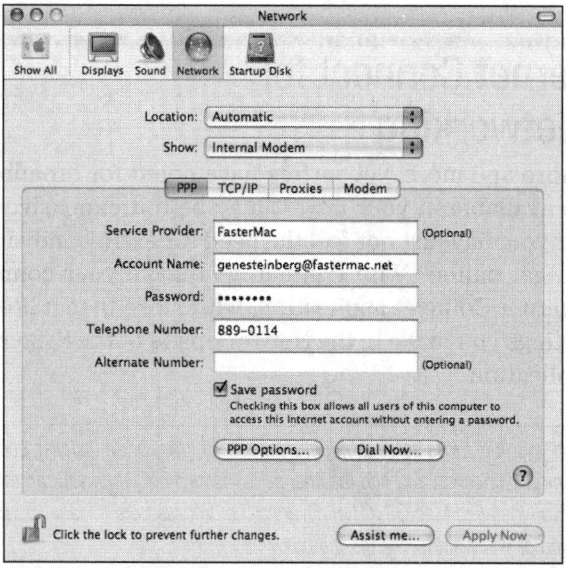

Figure 8.16 Enter your ISP's settings here. My entry is for FasterMac, a low-cost service that's designed strictly for Mac users.

NOTE: You don't have to enter an alternate number, but it's a good idea to because then you have a choice if the first number is busy. You should put the name in the Service Provider field for identification in the event you use more than one, or to help you choose the proper option if you've created multiple Location setups. (I'll cover multiple Location setups in the next section.)

4. To fine-tune your online session, click the PPP Options button and enter the appropriate information in the dialog box (see Figure 8.17). All the items shown are defaults, except Connect Automatically When Starting TCP/IP Applications, which you may want to activate. This option will log you into your ISP whenever you launch applications such as your browser or e-mail client. Here are the options from which to select:

NOTE: If you have both cable modem and dial-up access to an ISP at your location, don't enter the option to connect automatically because it will result in an attempt to dial up your ISP rather than use your network-based Internet access.

- *Session Options*—In addition to making your connection when you launch your Internet application, you can also get a warning prompt if you've been idle for a while, or automatically disconnect after a selected interval. This is especially helpful if you have a basic ISP account, which is billed by the hour when you exceed the monthly allocation. Another option, which is checked by default, redials your ISP in the event of a busy signal.

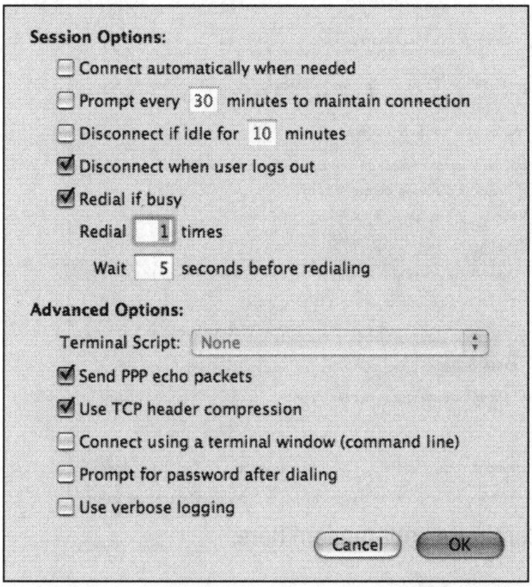

Figure 8.17 Choose your special connection options here.

- *Advanced Options*—Depending on the needs of your ISP, you may have to select one or more of the options beyond those already checked. Your ISP or network administrator can give you this information.

5. When your settings are made, click the OK button.

6. To double-check your modem setup, or if you're not using a standard Apple Internal Modem, click the Modem button (see Figure 8.18). You can select from a wide variety of modem scripts (connection profiles) by clicking the Modem pop-up menu.

TIP: *Although Panther has built-in support for most popular modems, if you don't find any from the manufacturer of the one you own, try a Hayes or Apple model and see which one provides the best connection. You can ask the company that makes your modem for a modem script, which would be installed under Panther via the following folder path: Library>Modem Scripts.*

---

7. If required by your ISP, click on the TCP/IP button and enter the correct numbers in the Domain Name Servers field.

8. Under Search Domains, input the proper information. Again, your ISP may not need this setting so don't guess unless you know for sure.

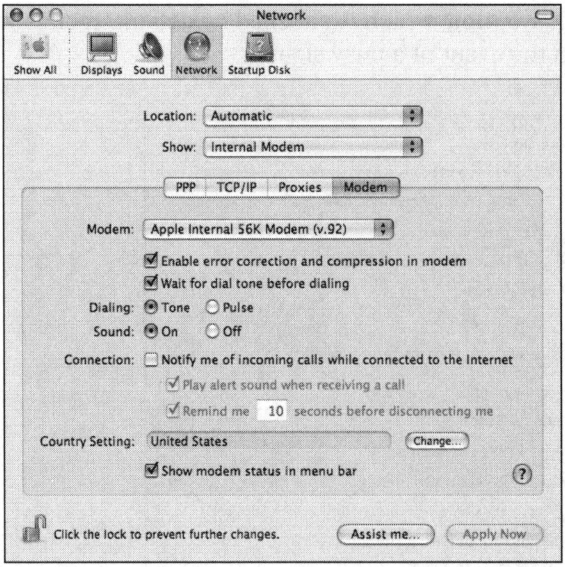

Figure 8.18 Configure your modem here.

NOTE: *Where did these settings come from? In Chapter 2 I suggested that you obtain your setup from the Remote Access and TCP/IP Control Panels or Network pane of your previous Mac OS installation, if there was one. If you don't have the information, contact your ISP directly.*

---

9. When you're done, click Apply Now to store your setup. Now you're ready to get connected.

TIP: *If you want to gain fast access to Internet Connect and your ISP, click Show Modem Status in the menu bar from the Modem pane. To get online, click on the Modem Status menu and select Connect. The status of your online connection will be displayed in the menu bar. Once you're online, you can disconnect in the exact same fashion. I should mention, though, that services such as Juno offer their own dialer applications, so you may not need to follow this step or use Internet Connect at all.*

Related solution:	Found on page:
Preparing for Panther	20

Verifying Connectivity

Once you've established your dial-up settings, you should try logging on to your ISP to make sure everything works properly. Here's where you'll see Apple's replacement for the Remote Access Control Panel. To get connected, follow these steps:

1. If you opted to display Modem Status in the menu bar, click Connect and watch the status messages. Otherwise, go to step 2 if you never enabled that function or prefer a cleaner modem bar.

2. Locate the Internet Connect application, which you'll find in your Applications folder.

3. Launch Internet Connect (see Figure 8.19) and, if it's not selected, click the Modem icon in the toolbar. The application displays the name of your modem, along with the settings you made for your ISP. If you didn't enter a password, the Password field will be blank for you to type that information.

NOTE: *You can redo the settings from the Internet Connect application by returning to the Network preference panel where you made your original settings. If you want to send or receive a configuration (useful for accessing the same ISP on other Macs you might use), you can Import Configurations or Export Configurations from Internet Connect's File menu.*

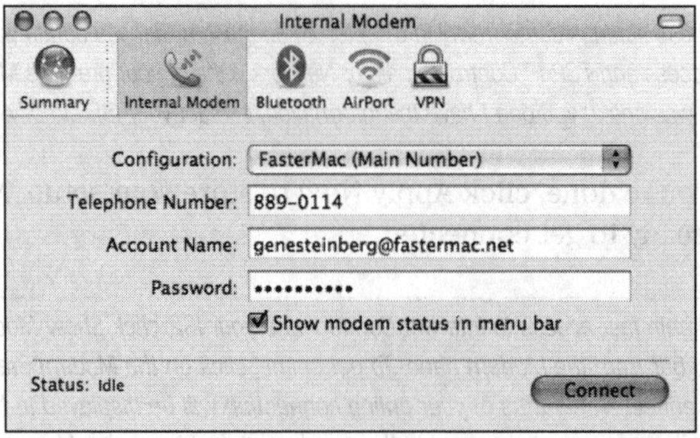

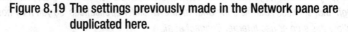

Figure 8.19 The settings previously made in the Network pane are duplicated here.

4. Click the Connect button to make your connection. A status window will appear, indicating when your connection is established.

5. When your online session is over, click the Disconnect button (which toggles to Connect). The process is no different from the way it was done under the Classic Mac OS.

NOTE: Internet Connect will work even if your Internet application runs from the Classic environment, but it doesn't support the ability to connect with an application that uses its own dialing method, such as AOL or CompuServe.

Connecting Via a Virtual Private Network

Are you away from the office but need to hook up to the corporate network to check e-mail or access your files? Panther includes support for connecting to a Virtual Private Network (VPN). Such a network can be accessed over your online connection as easily as connecting to a local network. You don't need special software or a complicated configuration to stay in touch.

Here's how to make that connection:

1. Locate the Internet Connect application, which you'll find in your Applications folder.

2. Launch Internet Connect and click the VPN window (see Figure 8.20). You can use the L2TP over IPSec or PPTP protocols to access the network. You'll need to check with your company's network administrator to be certain which option to select.

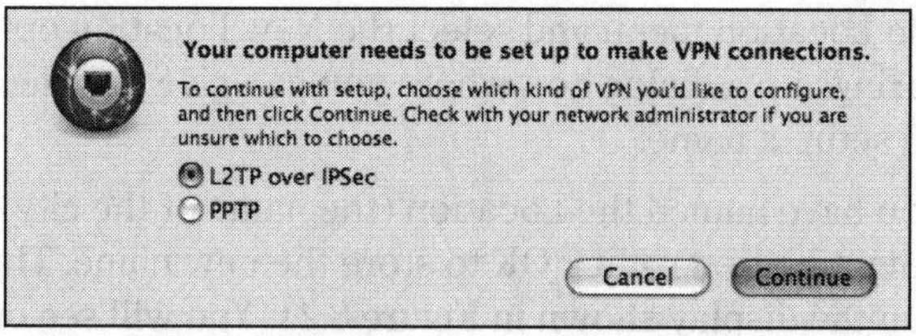

Your computer needs to be set up to make VPN connections.

To continue with setup, choose which kind of VPN you'd like to configure, and then click Continue. Check with your network administrator if you are unsure which to choose.

◉ L2TP over IPSec
○ PPTP

Cancel   Continue

Figure 8.20 Enter your corporate hookup information here and continue.

3. On the next setup screen, enter the name of your corporate server and your login information. A VPN icon will automatically appear in your menu bar for fast access.

4. Click Connect and your connection will be made. You should be able to access your files from the Finder, just as if they were on your Mac or a local network.

NOTE: Unless you have a high-speed connection to the Internet, however, don't expect blazing speeds when trying to retrieve files. It is, however, useful for simple documents.

Using Apple's Location Feature to Create Custom Setups

On occasion, or even on a regular basis, you may need to move your Mac to different places, particularly if it's an iBook or a PowerBook. Apple's Location feature lets you create custom AirPort, modem, and network setups for each place. That way, you can easily connect to the right local network and access the proper ISP without having to redo everything. As you move from one place to another, just choose the correct location from the Network pane in the System Preferences application. Frequent travelers will treasure these features. Here's how it's done:

NOTE: The most common changes you'd make would be to your Internal Modem, for accessing your dial-up ISP in another city. For some networks, you may have to set up special Ethernet configurations to allow for manual IP settings and network zones. Your network manager (if it's not you) would have to provide you with the relevant information.

1. Launch the System Preferences application and click the Network pane.

8. Networking Overview

2. Click the Location menu and select the New Location option, which brings up a dialog box where you can give your new location setup a name.

3. Once you have named the Location (the name of the city or office might be best), click OK to store the new name. This step brings up the display shown in Figure 8.21. You will see one of your Mac's network setups.

4. Make the Ethernet, modem, and connection settings needed for that location, and click the Apply Now button to store them.

5. Repeat this process for each location you want to create.

6. To switch locations, choose Location from the Apple menu and select the name of the location you want to use from the submenu. The default is Automatic, which simply accesses whatever available network service is required for a particular purpose.

NOTE: If your network in another city doesn't require any special setup, you may not have to deal with a new Location. For example, if your network at your main office requires DHCP to receive its IP numbers from a server or router, and the same situation holds true in another location, nothing has to be changed. Panther is also smart enough to sort between Ethernet, AirPort, and other connection needs.

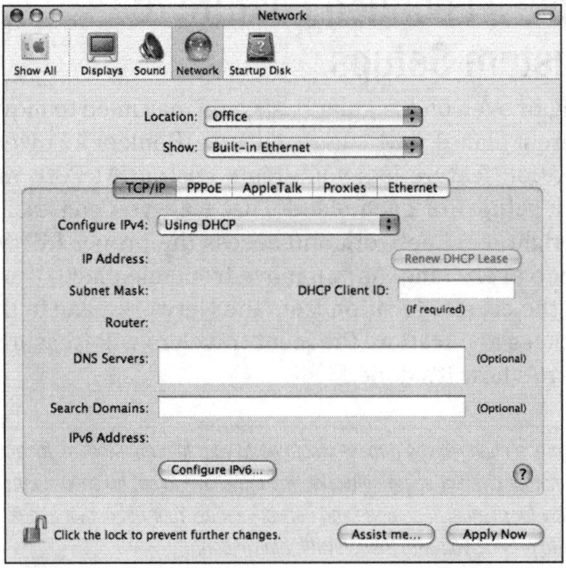

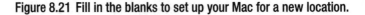

Figure 8.21 Fill in the blanks to set up your Mac for a new location.

Setting Up a Web or FTP Server on Your Mac

One of the extra networking features afforded by Panther is the ability to run your Mac as a Web server or to allow others to access files via FTP, which greatly expands your ability to make files available to others—with proper security precautions, of course (such as having a strong password).

Here's how to turn on Web sharing:

1. Launch System Preferences from the Apple menu, Dock, or Applications folder.
2. Click the Sharing panel.
3. Under Select a Service or Change Its Settings, click Personal Web Sharing.

NOTE: To allow FTP access to your Mac, click the Allow FTP Access button located just below the Web Sharing access control.

4. Check the bottom of the Sharing panel to see your Mac's IP number. Once activated, other users can connect to your Mac via this URL: **http://[computerIPaddress]/~[shortusername]/**. An example, to use a typical IP number, might be **http:/ 192.168.123.254/~gene/** to access a site I might make available under Web sharing (the IP number is actually the default number of an Asante cable/DSL sharing router).

NOTE: When you turn on Web sharing, the files placed in the Sites folder in your Home or Users folder will be available for Web access. The default index.html file that's already present in that folder includes more information about using the Web Sharing feature. You might want to print this file or save under a different name if you want to refer to it later on.

WARNING! Some ISPs prohibit Web sharing as part of the end-user agreement, and they will cancel your account if you violate their terms. Before setting up your Mac for full-time duty as a Web server, you may want to contact the ISP first. Just making your Mac available for a short time to share files or information with another user probably will be all right. If you want full-time access, consider one of the free Web spaces provided by your ISP or consider subscribing to Apple's .Mac service. For business use, you may want to contact your ISP or a third-party hosting service to set up a Web server.

5. If you want to allow other users to access your Mac and transfer files via an FTP client, such as Fetch or Interarchy,

8. Networking Overview

click Allow FTP Access. This setting is helpful if those with non-Apple operating systems are going to be connecting to your Mac.

6. To allow remote login to your Mac via a terminal application, click the Remote Login option in the Sharing preference panel. To send Apple events to your Mac (required for using AppleScript across the network), click the checkbox labeled Remote Apple Events.

WARNING! I mention this feature for your information only. You should use this feature with extreme caution, as it allows your user name and password to be clearly transmitted over the Internet, and thus make your Mac vulnerable to access by hackers. If you want to set up this sort of tool, you might consider downloading an SSH program instead. Check versiontracker.com for some choices for Panther users. In the meantime, you'll also want to click on the Firewall button and enable the feature for ports that are not being activated for sharing. This will provide an added measure of safety until better tools are secured.

7. Quit the System Preferences application after you've set your Web and FTP sharing options.

Fixing Network Access Problems

One of the hallmarks of the Mac operating system is easy networking. You plug one Mac into another, or into a printer, network hub or switch, and so on, and with a few simple setups, you are sharing files and printing without any great difficulty. Should your network installation not work, however, you should look into these possible solutions to the problem:

*   *Recheck your settings.* Your first troubleshooting step should be to verify your setups in the Network pane of the System Preferences application. Remember that you will need to click the Apply Now button for changes to become effective (fortunately you'll be reminded by a Save prompt if settings are changed and not stored). One common problem is the failure to turn on AppleTalk, which means that standard network printers may not be available.

NOTE: Don't assume Panther is at fault. You should also recheck the settings on the other computers involved in the network connection. If the setup is good, see if your Panther computer can work with a different computer or printer. By checking this, you will be able to isolate a probable source for your problem.

- *Examine your networking hardware.* Consider rechecking the network cables and your hubs or switches. Whenever there's a complete connection to the network hub or switch, one or more green lights will appear on that jack on a hub to indicate a proper connection is being made. If there's no activity or connection light, consider swapping cables to see if the problem transfers itself to the other computer or printer to which the cable was connected. If the problem travels, replace the cable. If networking still doesn't work, consider whether your hub itself might be defective.

- *Use the Network Utility application.* Panther supplies a handy tool that can help you examine the condition of your network in a more sophisticated fashion. You'll find the application in the Utilities folder, inside Panther's Applications folder. After you launch the application, click a button to access your network scouring features. Ping is the most common utility to check whether a network connection is being made; it sends a signal to the target Mac and then records whether the signal has been returned to you. Just enter the IP number of the Mac, click Ping, and see if you get a result on repeated probes. Click the Stop button when you're finished. Another useful feature is Traceroute, which displays the path packets take during their travels. It's useful in locating the source of a possible network problem. If these probes don't yield successful results, you should return to your network hardware and configuration to be sure you didn't miss anything.

- *Be careful about naming files copied to a Windows PC.* If you try to copy files to a PC on your network and keep getting error messages, make sure the file names are "legal." Under Windows, a file name cannot contain any of following characters: \ / : * ? " < >. You may also run into trouble using extended characters. Visually inspect and change the names as needed, or just take a few precautions when you first name the files.

- *What if Windows File Sharing Doesn't Work?* Be careful about doing custom installs when you upgrade to Panther. If you are having a problem getting Windows File Sharing to work, it could be because you did a custom installation and deselected BSD Subsystem. This is the danger of being too creative. The only solution is to reinstall Panther and keep this option selected. Fortunately, a simple "Upgrade" installation should not damage your settings or your Mac's reliability, but it's the only solution.

Protecting Your Network from the Internet

More and more folks these days have high-speed Internet connections. From cable to DSL, homes and businesses are joining the fast lane. (I'll discuss these and other fast access options in Chapter 20.) However, an always-on connection doesn't just deliver convenience; it also means your Macs are vulnerable to attack from Internet vandals who might want to play pranks with your computers, or attempt to retrieve passwords and other personal information. Nobody is immune from such intruders. As you know, Microsoft has been victimized by highly publicized network attacks on the secured servers that contain the source code for some of the company's software. Here are some ways to protect your network:

- *Use a hardware router to share connections*—Several companies manufacture Internet router products that will feed your Net connection across an Ethernet network to other computers (Macs and PCs). They include Apple's AirPort and AirPort Extreme Base Stations, plus products from Asante, Proxim (formerly Farallon), Linksys, and MacSense, to name just a few. These products are all designed to distribute the connection, and some include a hub or network switch. Most of these products also offer a built-in firewall, which sets up a secured barrier to prevent outsiders from entering your network. The common form of security employs a network address translation (NAT) feature that, in effect, manages requests to and from the network and hides the true IP numbers of your workstations. As a result, network intruders will find it far more difficult to invade your systems.

- *Set up software firewalls*—Apple's built-in firewall will provide a good level of protection, but if you have a lot of critical data to secure, you may want to get something more full-featured. Current commercial entrants in the Mac marketplace include Symantec's Norton Personal Firewall and Intego's NetBarrier X. Both programs will help to block unauthorized traffic from reaching your Macs and can be adjusted to selectively allow certain traffic, as needed.

NOTE: *Symantec has also bundled Norton Personal Firewall with Norton AntiVirus and Aladdin's iClean (which deletes old cache files and other items) and several privacy-related applications to form an integrated package called Norton Internet Security. A shareware alternative, FireWalk X, also offers a high level of protection.*

- *Restrict distribution of administrator passwords*—Many of you have heard horror stories about vengeful former employees of a company stealing confidential files and other proprietary information. Although you may have legal remedies to get this material back, the cost in manpower and legal action can be tremendous, with no guarantee of success. The best approach is to be careful who gets access to passwords in your company, and perhaps to consider a non-disclosure agreement if employees have access to company secrets that could give a competing company an advantage. You should also follow through with my suggestion to use strong passwords when setting user accounts to further protect your network.

Related solution:	*Found on page:*
Choosing Personal Firewall Software	400

Configuring Printing and Faxing

Apple has simplified printer setup for Panther to the nth degree, which is why this immediate solution is so short. If your Mac is using USB printers for which drivers are already available you may not need this solution at all. To find out, just click Print from the file menu of any application and see if your printer or printers show up in the Printer pop-up menu.

If they do, you're done with this chapter, unless you also want to use your Mac as a fax machine. If you see a prompt that shows no printers have been added, you'll have the choice of going direct to Printer Setup to configure one or more output devices.

If you want to add another printer, or start from scratch, just follow these steps:

1. Launch System Preferences and click on the Print & Fax preference pane.
2. Click the Printing button if it's not already selected (see Figure 8.22).
3. Click on the Setup Printers button, which launches Printer Setup as you see in Figure 8.23. (Printer Setup is also located in the Utilities folder if you want to get to it directly.)

WARNING! *What happened to your networked printers? Before you can check an AppleTalk network, you need to make sure AppleTalk is turned on. You turn on AppleTalk using the setting in the Network pane of the System Preferences application.*

8. Networking Overview

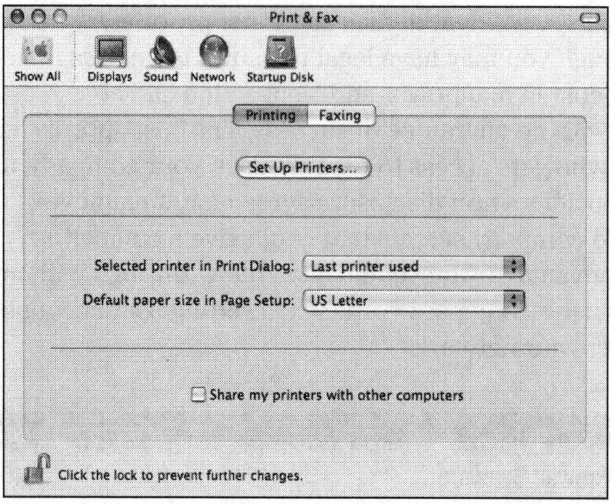

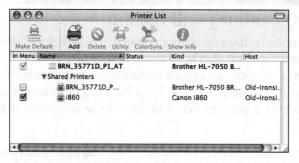

Figure 8.22 From here, you can setup your printer or even configure your Mac to receive faxes.

Figure 8.23 This is the list of printers on my Mac, plus the ones available for sharing on another Mac.

NOTE: If you have to wait an inordinate period of time for something to show up, don't be alarmed. It can take up to a minute for the next window to appear, even on a fast Mac.

4. Click the Add button. On the next screen, click the pop-up menu at the top and select the network or peripheral connection on which you want to check for printers. Depending on the kind of Mac you have, you can choose from AppleTalk, LPR Printers Using IP, or USB. Additional ports that support specific makes and models, such as network models from Epson and Lexmark, are also available. The Directory Services option can locate an enterprise printer located on your network. In the example shown in Figure 8.24, I chose AppleTalk to locate a printer on my Ethernet network.

8. Networking Overview

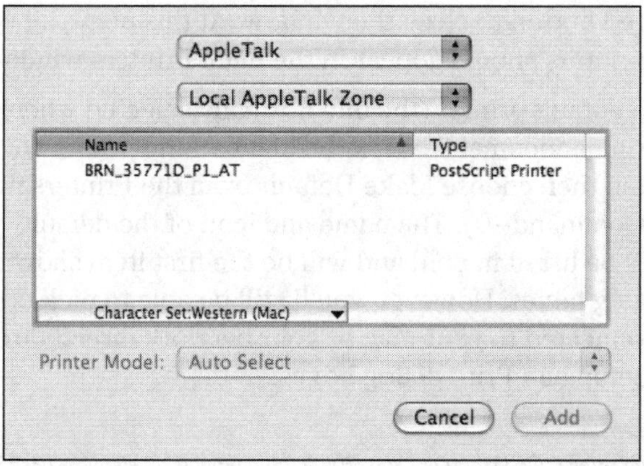

Figure 8.24 Just one network printer is presently available for my home office.

NOTE: Not all printers are clearly identified. The strange jargon in Figure 8.24, for example, lists a Brother HL-7050N network printer. So you may have to check the manufacturer's configuration page, which is usually generated by the printer's setup menu, to figure out what printer name should be selected.

---

5. If your printer is located in another AppleTalk zone, click the second pop-up menu to pick that zone.

6. Continue browsing for printers until they are all displayed.

7. Under Printer Model, leave the Auto Select option selected, or pick a printer from the list of PostScript Printer Description (PPD) files to provide maximum support for your output device. A PPD file will recognize the custom features of your network printer, such as extra paper sizes, extra trays, custom resolutions, and, if available, the ability to duplex or print on both sides of the paper. If you don't have the right PPD file available, your selections will be limited to the standard paper tray and a limited range of paper sizes.

NOTE: Panther shipped with files for a number of printers, including those from Apple, Hewlett-Packard, Lexmark, Tektronix, and Xerox. To install a PPD file, just drag it to the proper folder. You'll find it via the following hierarchy: Library>Printers>PPDs>Contents>Resources> en.lproj (for the English language version). You can obtain PPD files from the manufacturer, sometimes using a special installer provided by the manufacturer. There are also PPD files at Adobe's Web site but they are to be avoided ,because they are often way out of date, having not been updated in several years.

8. Networking Overview

199

8. Click the red button to close the window. At this point, all your available printers should appear in the main Printers window.

9. To select a default printer (the one normally selected when you want to print a document), click the name of the printer to select it, and then choose Make Default from the Printers menu (or press Command+D). The name and icon of the default printer will be listed in bold and will be the first item shown in printer dialog boxes. However, you'll still be able to pick other printers connected to your Mac or your network directly from the Page Setup and Print dialog boxes.

NOTE: Panther will always make the last printer you selected the default, so you may have to switch the settings if you prefer another to be your default. To change that setting, return to the Print & Fax preference pane and click on the Selected Printer in the Print Dialog pop-up menu to make a specific printer the default. While you're there, you can choose Share My Printer with Other Computers to allow other Macs and Windows PCs on your network to use a printer connected to your USB port.

---

10. You can remove a printer from the Printers window at any time by selecting the printer's name from the list of available printers in Printer Setup and clicking Delete.

11. Depending on the make of your printer, you may be able to configure other options by selecting it and choosing Show from the Print Center toolbar, or Printer Info from the Printers menu. In the case of a PostScript laser printer where several versions of a particular model are available, you can tell Mac OS X whether your unit has such things as extra paper trays, the ability to duplex or print on both sides of the page, or a built-in hard drive on which to store fonts.

NOTE: For ink jet printers, click Utility to launch the setup application, if available, which is used to check ink levels, clean print heads, and perform other maintenance functions. This application may not be available for all newly installed printers, so check your Applications folder too if nothing happens when you click this button.

---

12. Should you want to see the status of all your printers on the desktop, just like you did in the Classic Mac OS, select a printer, and choose Create Desktop Printer from Printer Setup's Printers menu. This step might sound redundant, but that's how it is.

13. After you've completed setting your preferences, click the close box or choose Quit from the application menu to close the program.

If you have no more printers to add, you will not see Printer Setup again until you print a document. Then, its icon will show up in the Dock. Click the Dock to bring up a status display of your printer queue, where you can monitor your print jobs and remove or stop processing of specific documents.

NOTE: When a job is being printed from a Panther application, the printer's Dock icon will appear with a document icon while processing continues. Then it will disappear. If there's a problem with a job, you'll see an onscreen prompt and an exclamation point within the Printer Center icon.

TIP: You can also schedule long print job, to print when you're at lunch or otherwise unoccupied. This way you don't have to tie up printers when other work has to get done. To schedule a job, choose Print from the File menu, choose Scheduler from the Copies & Pages pop-up menu, and set the time and priority for the document. Then set whatever printer options you need, such as the number of copies, page range, or, if available, the printer quality setting and layout (used for printers that can print on both sides of the page). At the appointed time, your output will be generated in the precise way you configured.

Turning Your Mac into a Fax Machine

The process of sending and receiving faxes is so simply you might wonder why I even write about it at all. For the sake of being complete, here's the basic setup:

1. To send faxes you don't need to configure anything special, except to make sure your Mac's modem is plugged into a working line. Next just choose Print from the file menu, and click the Fax button at the bottom of the Print dialog (see Figure 8.25).

2. Enter your recipient's fax number. If the number is already in your Address Book, when you start typing the name or number, the software will offer to complete the setup for you.

3. If you want to send a brief cover page, click the Subject line and enter the subject of your fax, and then click Cover Page, to enter a short text message.

NOTE: Please don't click Return until you're done. Doing this will immediately send the Fax.

---

4. Click Fax to start the process. A modem icon will appear in the Dock. When you click on it, you'll see a progress message showing when the modem is connecting to the recipient's fax

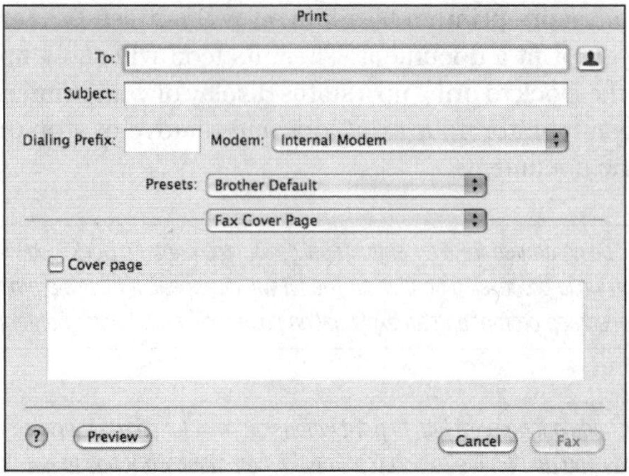

Figure 8.25 Prepare your document for faxing.

device, and when the fax is being sent. The icon disappears when the process is complete.

That's all there is too it. For receiving faxes automatically, here is a short setup process you need to follow, after which you'll be good to go:

1. Open System Printers and click Print & Fax.

2. Click the Faxing button to produce the setup screen (see Figure 8.26).

3. Click Receive Faxes on This Computer to start the process.

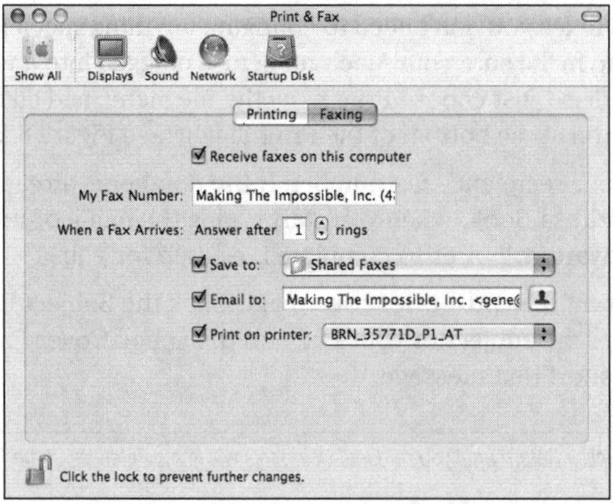

Figure 8.26 A few clicks and text entries and you're ready to receive faxes.

4. Under My Fax Number you can enter both the name of your fax station and its number. Yes, I realize it only mentions a number, but there's space for both, and this information will be displayed on all the faxes you send.

5. Now you need to tell your Mac how to handle a received fax. Under When a Fax Arrives, enter the number of rings under Answer After __ Rings.

6. Next check the Save To box and indicate where faxes need to go. The normal location is Shared Faxes in your Shared folder but you can specify another location for added privacy. The additional options let you e-mail your fax, which is sent as a PDF file, as soon as it's received, and automatically print it to the specified printer.

TIP: *If you've turned on Printer Sharing in the Printing preference panel or under Sharing, other Panther users on your network can use your Mac's modem to send faxes.*

NOTE: *Don't expect miracles from Panther's fax feature. It's all right for occasional use, for home or business. But if faxing is an important part of your business, you may want to consider a commercial program, such as Smith Micro's FAXstf X Pro or Page Sender, a shareware program that I've found especially useful. Check with www.versiontracker.com for the latest information on fax software available for Panther.*

8. Networking
Overview

Chapter 9

AppleScript for Panther

In Brief

Even though the G5 processor used in recent Power Macs has formed the basis of a real supercomputer, lots of you no doubt do lots of manual labor on your computers. You keep your keyboard and mouse working overtime. You locate a document in a specific folder with the Finder and double-click on the document to open it in the appropriate application. You then examine or edit the document. As necessary, you save it, print it, and proceed to the next task and do it all over again.

When you navigate the Web, you might enter a site's address or select one from your list of Bookmarks. During the course of a day, you carry out a number of repetitive steps. Maybe you'll wear out your input devices, or your wrists. Is there no easier way?

What if you could make your Mac perform a complex set of repetitive steps just by running a single application or by accessing a simple command within a program? What if the tools to provide all that functionality didn't cost an extra cent and didn't require installing additional software? A dream? Something only a skilled computer programmer can do? Read on.

For years, the solution to this dilemma was part and parcel of the Mac OS. That feature, AppleScript, is regularly used for creating print publications, editing videos, producing Web content, and automating everyday tasks such as copying and printing files.

The Things You Can Do with AppleScript

AppleScript, although not quite a plain English scripting language, is close enough to make it possible for folks like you and me to create scripts without a lot of training. Even better, you can get started simply by working on the prebuilt scripts that come with Panther and the ones you'll learn about at Apple's Web site.

AppleScript lets Mac programs communicate instructions with one another and with the operating system. You can create scripts to perform useful operations such as automatically copy a file from one disk to another, batch-process a series of images and apply certain

Photoshop filters to them, and save and print documents. Many popular Macintosh productivity programs depend on AppleScript to exploit some of their most useful features.

NOTE: *To learn what sort of support an application has for AppleScript, check the application's documentation. AppleScript's applications range from the simple to the complex and all variations in between.*

In the "Immediate Solutions" section of this chapter, you'll discover some of the tools Apple has already provided to let you exercise AppleScript. For now, here's a brief idea of what you can do with AppleScript:

* *Automate the Panther Finder*—Many common Finder functions can be scripted. That means you can harness complex file-management features by launching a single script.

* *Automate Panther system functions*—AppleScript can handle operations that require repeating steps. Here are some examples: searching the Internet, querying and directing XML-aware applications, and automatically adjusting a specific set of settings.

* *Automate workflow*—This is where AppleScript comes into its own in a working environment. Users of the popular desktop publishing application QuarkXPress, for example, can create scripts that access specific templates for pages, flow in text, import images, and scale and crop the images. In Adobe Photoshop, a script can be used to open all the images placed in a single folder, apply a specific set of program filters, and save the images in a specific file format. Deneba's Canvas Mac OS X can perform such functions as activating any of its extraordinary range of tools and functions, or preparing Web graphics without direct user intervention. Imagine if you had to do all this work manually, one step at a time, every time you needed to handle these chores.

* *Folder Actions*—This powerful feature allows you to apply a script to be connected or attached to a folder. The script is activated whenever a folder is opened, closed, moved, or items are placed within or removed from the folder. Even better, a combination of these actions can be configured to make for some pretty complicated operations with these folders, which one might call "drop boxes" or "hot folders."

* *Record your actions*—You don't have to write all your scripts from scratch. Many programs let you record a series of actions, using Apple's Script Editor application. After the steps have been

recorded, you can save them as a script, and then have them run the same as any other AppleScript.

- *Scripting unsupported applications*—A fair amount of what AppleScript does truly depends on if a program has support for the feature. Panther, however, brings just a bit more to the table, including the ability to script system-related functions, courtesy of its Graphic User Interface scripting capability (GUI Scripting). This allows you to query and direct the menus, windows, and dialog boxes used by those programs. This can be useful in automating some tasks, and may be useful at least until a program's publishers get around to actually delivering authentic AppleScript support.

- *Scheduling scripts*—Another new feature of AppleScript is the ability to have an AppleScript run at a scheduled time. You can use your Mac to wake you up by playing your favorite songs via iTunes or use iCal to run a series of scripts when a calendar event has been created. You can, if you wish, set a document to open at a specified time so you can begin to work on it. That will help you meet schedules.

AppleScript, however, is not the only desktop automation feature. CE Software's QuicKeys, for example, can perform similar functions but it has the added advantage of working with all Mac software, not just programs that can be specifically scripted. QuicKeys for Panther (see Figure 9.1) includes the ability to record mouse actions and multi-step actions (formerly called sequences), so that you can script complicated procedures.

NOTE: Name just about any application that comes with Panther and you'll find support for AppleScript. These include such standard applications as the Address Book, Finder, DVD Player, iCal, Image Capture, Internet Connect, iPhoto, iTunes, Mail, QuickTime Player, Terminal, and TextEdit. Add to the roster AppleWorks 6.2x, and lots of third-party programs such as Microsoft Entourage X and Stone Studio (a powerful set of graphic applications and tools), and lots more.

The Tools for Using Scripts in Panther

Aside from the built-in functions of some programs that use AppleScript behind the scenes, an AppleScript can come in several forms—applet, fully compiled script, or a text file containing the script commands. Which form to use depends on the program you're running, but the most common form of script is the applet. An *applet* is a

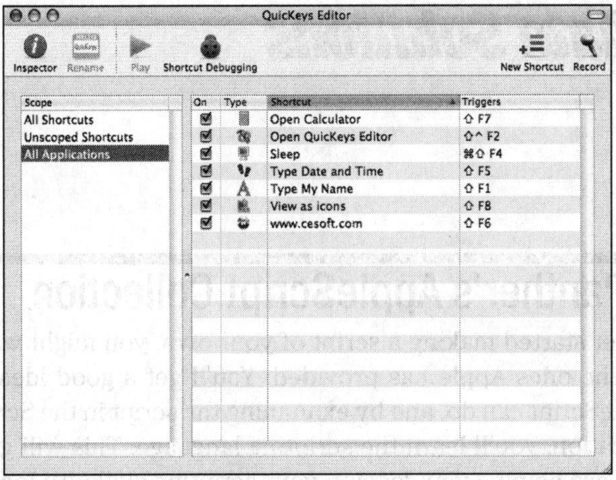

Figure 9.1   A long-time favorite of many Mac users, QuicKeys is available for Panther.

small application; you can double-click it to start it or you can drag and drop onto it an item that is subjected to the scripting action.

NOTE: In addition to double-clicking and dragging and dropping, you can use a handy utility Apple has placed in the AppleScript folder, in your Applications folder. The utility, Script Menu, installs a menu bar icon to access your scripts. To activate Script Menu, drag the little application to the menu bar and it will show up automatically. I'll tell you how to set it up in the "Immediate Solutions" section of this chapter.

AppleScript: The Future

The future of AppleScript is virtually unlimited. Scripts are available for both the graphical layer of Panther and the Unix core. More and more applications support the feature and, over the years, new versions of Mac OS X will take AppleScript to even wider boundaries, without sacrificing the relative ease of use. So stay tuned.

Immediate Solutions

Locating Panther's AppleScript Collection

Before you get started making a script of your own, you might want to try using the ones Apple has provided. You'll get a good idea of what an AppleScript can do, and by examining the script in the Script Editor application, you'll learn the scripting language. This will go a long way toward helping you develop your scripting skills. To locate the scripts, follow these steps:

1. Open the Applications folder.

2. Double-click on the AppleScript folder.

3. Open the Example Scripts folder, and then open the folder that contains scripts in the category you want to try.

After you've located the scripts you want, you can open them and see how they strut their stuff. You'll find that the lingo is clear enough for you to understand how they actually work.

Choosing Panther's Sample Scripts

As explained in the previous section, Apple has assembled a small collection of useful scripts that you can use to learn how AppleScript works. Here's a list of the script folders and some of the scripts provided:

• *Address Book Script*—These scripts provide a speedy way to import addresses from other programs and incorporate them into Address Book.

NOTE: *Many programs sport an AppleScript menu icon, and thus might offer a similar range of scripts. Address Book and Mail are examples of this breed.*

• *Basics*—These scripts are designed to help you discover the fundamentals of preparing your own AppleScripts. The scripts provided will transport you to the AppleScript pages at Apple's Web site, launch the Script Editor application, and give you a tour through the handy Help menus on the subject.

- *ColorSync*—Apple's built-in ColorSync technology allows for superior color calibration and the ability to match up the colors you see on your monitor with the colors from a scanner or other input device and a printer or proofing device. This folder contains a number of scripts that allow you to handle color profiles including one that will mimic a PC monitor. This particular script is useful if you work in a cross-platform environment.

- *Finder Scripts*—These scripts are designed to direct the Finder to perform various functions. They can alter file and folder names in various ways, from changing case to searching and replacing the names of files in a folder. In addition, file and folder names can be trimmed to look more readable in a Finder window.

- *Folder Action Scripts*—Actually Panther has two folders devoted to scripts that turn this nifty scripting feature on and off and add to its functionality. The first, Folder Actions, contains the scripts that turn the feature on or off or allow you to add or remove an action from a selected folder. The second, Folder Actions, is only usable once you run the script to Attach a Folder action.

- *FontSync Scripts*—These scripts are a boon for those with huge font libraries. The two scripts available with Panther let you create and match up your FontSync profiles.

- *Info Scripts*—One lets you change your Date & Time setting and another produces a font sample sheet in TextEdit with all your installed fonts.

- *Internet Services*—These scripts exploit AppleScript's XML capability to query Web sites. They provide the current temperature in any USA location and retrieve stock quotes (assuming you want to know if your favorite stock has gone up or down).

- *Mail Scripts*—One entrant in this folder can be used to set an address and a subject line for an e-mail message. Once you enter these values (you have to set a default address first), the script will automatically open the Mail application and then populate a new message window with the information. Other scripts include such features as enhanced import from other e-mail programs and address book import.

- *Navigation Scripts*—These scripts are designed strictly to work with the Finder. They will activate a new Finder window pointing directly to a specific folder. You'll find scripts for the Applications, Documents, Favorites, and Home folders.

- *Printing Scripts*—There are scripts here that you can use to convert files to PDF and PostScript and to print Finder windows.

- *Script Editor Scripts*—These all have a single purpose—to help you write a script that runs properly. Each is designed to test a particular script function, such as checking for syntax errors. They are all useful if you want to hone your AppleScript skills.

- *Sherlock Scripts*—The sole entrant when this book was being written allowed you to use Sherlock's handy Internet searching features. You'll learn more about Apple's search application in Chapter 7.

- *UI Element Scripts*—These scripts are worth a look. They allow you to explore some of the Aqua interface components.

- *URLs*—These scripts in this folder are designed to access specific Web sites.

Related solution:	Found on page:
Searching the Internet	160

Using Script Menu

To get started with AppleScript in Panther, you'll want to set up Apple's Script Menu, a useful system menu add-on. You can use this program to both organize and run your scripts (see Figure 9.2). Here's how to work and add scripts with Script Runner:

NOTE: *By default, Apple installs its sample collection of scripts for you. So, when you click the Script Menu, it's ready to roll with a decent number of scripts to try.*

---

1. Locate your copy of Script Menu. Script Menu is in the Applications folder.

2. Drag Script Menu to the left side of the menu bar, where an AppleScript icon will suddenly appear.

3. To access a script, click on the icon, which will bring up a list of available scripts, all neatly sorted into categories.

4. If you want to add some scripts of your own, click on Choose Scripts folder and place the scripts inside.

5. Removing a script is a simple matter of dragging it from the Scripts folder or whatever folder it's located in. The next time you invoke Script Menu, the script will no longer be available.

Figure 9.2 Script Menu is a convenient way to access all your scripts from a single, simple interface.

Creating Your Own AppleScripts

Although AppleScript is a plain-English language, you need to use some fundamental, rigid commands to make your scripts work. In this section, I'll show you how to create your first script just to give you an idea of how it's done. Using these techniques, after you learn the syntax, you'll be able to make scripts as easy or complex as you want.

NOTE: *I am not trying to minimize the learning curve for AppleScript. It takes time, study, and some practice to become flexible in writing reliable scripts. To learn more about the subject, visit the AppleScript Web site at **www.apple.com/applescript**. There, you'll discover sample scripts and online tutorials that will help you learn both simple and complex scripting skills.*

For this section, I'll take you through the basics of making some sample scripts. They are deliberately simple, designed strictly to get you interested in the possibilities of what scripts can do. If you like what you can do, I recommend you visit Apple's AppleScript Web site or sit down with a big book on the subject to discover more.

Dumping the Trash

In this script, you will automate one of your Mac's most basic tasks, and that is to empty your Mac's trashcan. Here's how you can create your first script:

1. Locate the Script Editor application, which is in the Utilities folder inside the Applications folder.

2. Double-click the program to launch it (see Figure 9.3).

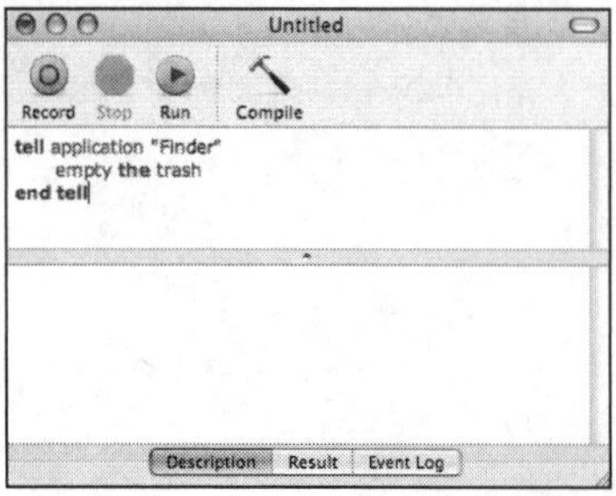

Figure 9.3   Creating an AppleScript starts here.

3. When the program is running, a blank script window should be on your screen. If it's not, choose New Script from the program's File menu.

4. In the Description field, enter a sentence or two that describes the purpose and function of your script.

5. The first element in your script is a **tell** command. This command is designed to talk to a program on your Mac, in this case the Finder. To make the following script consisting of three lines, simply type the text and follow it by the Return key (don't worry about writing commands in bold as you see them in a completed script; it's not necessary):

```
tell application "Finder"
        empty the trash
    end tell
```

6. You are almost at the finish line. The next step is to make sure the script was written properly. Click the Compile button. The script you just wrote will be checked for errors. AppleScript is very literal-minded, so if a single letter in a command is wrong, you'll see what it is and what you need to do to fix it.

NOTE: *When a script is examined for syntax, it will take on text formatting with bold commands. Before you check the syntax, the script is all straight text; you don't need to format any of it manually.*

---

7. If the script has an error, now's the time to recheck the script and fix the problem. If the script checks out, choose Save As from the File menu.

8. Type a name for your new script that corresponds to its purpose. Choose Compiled Script as the format and specify the

location where the script will be saved. The best place to save the script is in the URLs folder, under Example Scripts, so that it will be recognized by Script Menu.

9. Click the Save button.

10. To make sure your script truly does what you want, go ahead and run it via Script Menu.

Mapping an Address Book Contact

This particular script is somewhat more complicated, but still understandable. Assume you want to find out how to get to the home or office of a contact in Apple's Address Book. The next script, which is long but not difficult, will let you retrieve a map of that contact's location direct from MapQuest, the popular online mapping center. Here's what you need to do:

1. Launch Script Editor.

2. Enter the following commands, with the line breaks exactly as shown:

```
tell application "Address Book"
activate
set theSelection to the selection
if (count of selection) = 0 then display dialog "You must
have one person selected for this script to work" buttons
{"Cancel"} default button 1
if (count of selection) > 1 then display dialog ""You can
only select one person for this script to work" buttons
{"Cancel"} default button 1
set thePerson to item 1 of theSelection
try
set theAddress to item 1 of address of thePerson
on error
display dialog "No address information was found" buttons
{"Cancel"} default button 1
end try
set theStreet to the street of theAddress
set theCity to the city of theAddress
set theState to the state of theAddress
set theZip to the zip of theAddress
if theStreet is missing value then set theStreet to ""
if theCity is missing value then set theCity to ""
if theState is missing value then set theState to ""
if theZip is missing value then set theZip to ""
set theStreet to my replace(theStreet, " ", "+")
set theCity to my replace(theCity, " ", "+")
```

```
set toGo to "http://www.mapquest.com/maps/
map.adp?country=US&countryid=250&addtohistory=&address=" &
theStreet & "&city=" & theCity & "&state=" & theState &
"&zipcode=" & theZip & "&submit=Get+Map"
tell application "Safari" to open location toGo
end tell

on replace(localText, localSearchFor, localReplaceWith)
set oldDelimiters to AppleScript's text item delimiters
set AppleScript's text item delimiters to localSearchFor
set textList to every text item of localText
\set AppleScript's text item delimiters to localReplaceWith
set localText to textList as string
set AppleScript's text item delimiters to oldDelimiters
return localText
end replace
```

3. Once the script is entered, click Complile to make sure the script language was entered correctly and to clean up text formatting. If not, recheck the scripting language shown here to make sure that you did it properly.

4. Follow steps 7 and 8 in the previous section to save and compile your finished script.

5. Open Address Book.

6. Select the name of your contact and then run the script. It will retrieve the first address listed and launch MapQuest to create a map (see Figure 9.4). From here you can use MapQuest to give you driving directions from your home or office.

TIP: How can you tell if a program can be scripted? Here's a simple way: Drag the application's icon to Script Editor. If it is scriptable, you'll see a window with the dictionary of commands. If it's not scriptable, you'll get a message that it can't be scripted because the application has no dictionary. When you try AOL's software this way, you'll find a neat set of AppleScript capabilities for you to try (although this feature is not documented).

Unix Command Line Basics

Here are the steps to follow to run an AppleScript from Panther's Unix command line:

1. Locate the Terminal application in the Utilities folder, within the Applications folder.

Figure 9.4   Here's a genuine map of Apple Computer's headquarters.

2. Double-click the Terminal application to launch it.

3. In the command line, type "osascript" and then type the name of the script.

4. Press Enter to activate the script. If you enter the correct file name, the script should run precisely the same as if it were accessed from Script Menu.

A Sample Command Line Script

Now that you have the sense of how this is done, here's a sample script that incorporates what is called a *Shell Script*, another way to issue a command via Terminal.

In this script, you will simply make a screen shot.

1. Open Terminal.

2. To make a screen shot of something called capture.pdf on your desktop type the following command:

```
do shell script "screencapture ~/Desktop/capture.pdf"
```

NOTE: You could do the same thing by opening the document and using the normal keyboard shortcuts for screenshots, but this is one way to discover the body of your system. Chapter 19 has more information on the Panther's Unix command line.

A Quick Primer on Folder Actions

Once you have a chance to give Folder Actions a try, you'll wonder how you lived without them. From backing up critical files, to performing batch processing actions, this can be a powerful tool.

Here's how you use Folder Actions:

1. First you'll want to make sure Script Menu is installed. Click on Script Menu and choose Enable Folder Actions from the Folder Actions sub-menu.

NOTE: If you're adept at AppleScript, you can select from one of five Folder Action "handlers" that are located in the Standard Additions dictionary. You'll find a few examples of cool Folder Actions at Apple's Web site at **www.apple.com/applescript/folder_actions/**.

2. Return to the Script Menu, and this time choose Attach Folder Action from the Folder Actions sub-menu.

3. In the dialog box that appears, select a Folder Action and click OK.

4. Once a folder is selected, you'll see a standard Open dialog box to select the folder where the script is attached. After the folder is selected, click Choose. From here on, performing the specified action on the folder, such as adding or removing an item, or just opening or closing the folder, will trigger the script.

5. If you no longer want to use the script, return to Script Menu and choose Remove Folder Actions. In the next dialog box, choose the folder from which you want to deactivate the Folder Actions.

6. You can turn off Folder Actions entirely, if you feel the need to, simply by selecting Disable Folder actions from Script Menu's Folder Actions sub-menu.

Installing Programs Under Panther

In Brief

In 2004, the Mac reached the ripe old age of 20. That's pretty old in the computer business. Yet some things simply never change. Back in the 1980's, you would normally install an application on your Macintosh simply by dragging the application's icon from a floppy disk to your hard-drive icon. In a few moments, the program would be on your Mac, a double-click away from launching into action.

Over time, however, things became a lot more complicated for the Classic Mac OS as applications grew more sophisticated and delivered extra features. For various reasons not important here, some files had to be placed in a location other than the application's own folder. Some would go into disparate locations inside the System Folder. More often than not, it wasn't even readily apparent which file belonged to what program. So, the installation had to be handled by an installer that was designed to sort out this mess for you. In many cases, the installation would end with a Restart button and you wouldn't be able to use the program until your Mac had gone through the process.

Even under Panther, some programs still require a restart, although this is extremely rare.

Removing an application that sprays lots of files in various parts of your Mac's hard drive can be totally frustrating unless the installer has an Uninstall option. There's even a third-party program—Spring Cleaning, from Aladdin Systems—that is designed to remove all vestiges of a program. I'm reminded of the Add/Remove feature of Windows (which persists even in Windows XP) as an example of how complicated a program installation can get; some Windows software installations require multiple restarts.

NOTE: *Spring Cleaning does more than just uninstall files. It can also delete Internet cache files and other junk filling up your Mac. You can learn more about it from the publisher's site at* **www.aladdinsys.com/mac/springcleaning/index.html**.

A Fast and Dirty Package Overview

Beginning with Mac OS 9, Apple came up with a better idea for Mac users (although it's not unique to the Mac)—the *Package*. A Package is simply a folder that contains an application and all its support files, whether 1 or 1,000. But all these elements are hidden from the end-user—shades of the Invisible Man! The Package appears on your Mac as a single icon that you can double-click to launch the application located within the Package folder.

Installing is a dream—a throwback to the earliest days of the Macintosh. Just drag the application's package icon to the appropriate folder (usually the Applications folder) and launch it.

Removing an application involves the same process. You drag it to the trash, empty the trash, and all elements of that program (except for preferences and maybe some application support files) are removed. It's remarkable that the best way to install and remove a program was the way it was done back in 1984 when the first Mac appeared on the scene.

The Microsoft Way

If you're one of those anti-Microsoft people, maybe it's hard to imagine them doing anything good for our favorite computing platform. But when it comes to installing Office software, Microsoft has been doing right by the Mac. Beginning with Office 98, you only needed to drag and drop the application folder to your Mac's hard drive. However, you still have a visible folder containing loads of separate files, and you still must open that folder to run any of the applications you've installed. In addition, when you first run those programs, a few things are placed in other folders on your Mac, but nothing that endangers stability, or at least nothing that I could see.

NOTE: *To be perfectly fair, there is an installer on the Office v. X CD. But it's designed for optional installs of fewer or extra components, and isn't needed just to install the software in its standard form.*

Exploring Mac OS X's Application Features

As I explain throughout this book, any application written to support Mac OS X inherits a bevy of beautiful interface features and Unix-based reliability. In addition to preemptive multitasking and protected memory, you'll see visible differences to enhance your computing experience. These differences include:

NOTE: *Although older, Classic Mac applications can run under Mac OS X, they do not inherit any of the features I'm about to discuss. These are all the province of programs developed for the Carbon or Cocoa programming environments.*

- *Services*—Available in the Applications menu, the Services command produces a submenu that makes it possible for you to directly access the features of another application. This feature allows you to select text or a picture in your document and then go to the Services menu, choose a command from another application, and have that command executed in that program. In effect, you can send the text from one program to another without having to launch the second application, drag text between them, or use Export and Import features.

NOTE: *In theory, the Services menu ought to be available in all native Mac OS X applications. On the other hand, some of the earlier applications might not include it, although the ones I've examined seem to be okay in this regard. You won't find this feature in Classic software.*

- *Finder-like Open dialog box*—The venerable Mac Open dialog box has been one of the most confusing features of the operating system. It can be difficult for folks to navigate through large collections of nested folders and various disks to find a file. Although the Open dialog box was updated in Mac OS 8.5 with a new scheme, called *navigation services*, this was only part of what needed to be done. For Panther, Apple has redesigned this dialog box yet again, and the new version (see Figure 10.1), simplifies navigation tremendously because it, in great part, mimics the look of the Finder. In addition, it's non-modal, which means that it doesn't prevent you from doing something else on your Mac until it's dismissed. You can bring up the Open dialog box and then switch to another application, and the Open dialog box will still be there when you return; the operation of your Mac is not affected.

TIP: *Users often overlook the Open dialog box. A prime example is the common practice of many Mac users that head to the Finder and double-click a file's icon to open it, even if the application used to make the file is already open. Apple has had to do its homework here, and it has made things somewhat better for Mac OS X.*

- *Save As dialog box*—Another bugaboo of the older versions of the Mac OS was the Save As dialog box. When you wanted to save your document, where did you place it? How often did you waste time figuring out the correct place (if there was one) to put a file?

222

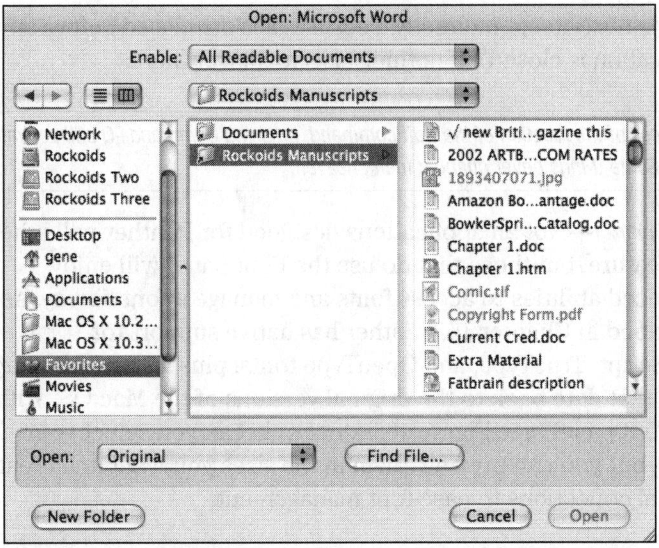

Figure 10.1   Panther's Open dialog box makes it easier for you to locate
the file you want to use.

The Mac OS X version of the Save As dialog box opens as a sheet
in the document window in which you're working (see Figure
10.2). There's no question about what you're saving, and the
simple elegance of its interface makes it easy for you to specify
precisely where your document is going so you can easily locate
it later—without a headache or constant use of the Finder's file-
search utility. Think of all the money you save on painkillers.

• *New location for the Quit command*—This is a logical issue rather
than a critical one. Instead of putting the Quit command in the
customary place in the File menu, Apple deposited it in the application menu. The logic is that the command affects the application,

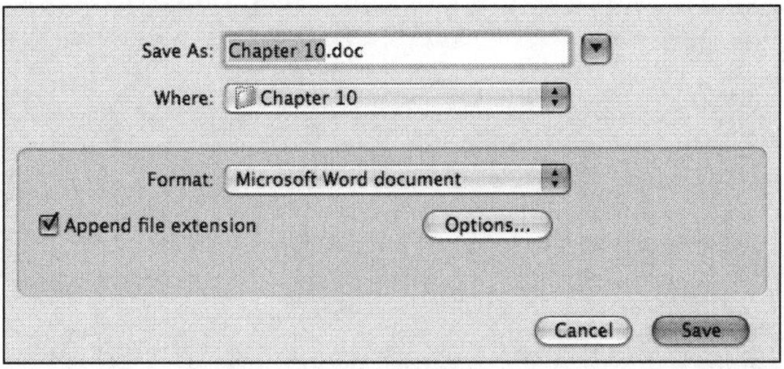

Figure 10.2   A better way to simplify the process of saving your document;
this is the version you see in Word for Mac OS X.

not the file (except indirectly, because files are closed before an application is closed). If nothing else, logic wins here.

TIP: *Regardless of the location of the Quit command, pressing Command+Q still activates this feature. Some things never change; thank heaven.*

- *Font panel*—Not all applications designed for Panther will inherit this feature, but those that do use the Font panel will enjoy enhanced abilities to access fonts and manage a font library. As described in Chapter 15, Panther has native support for PostScript, TrueType, and OpenType fonts, plus all those bitmap fonts that date back to the original versions of the Mac OS. With the Font panel (see Figure 10.3), not only can you select your fonts, but you can preview them in the sizes you want and create special collections to ease font management.

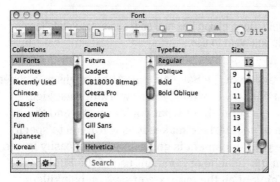

Figure 10.3   The Panther Font panel, when available in your application (at least the ones developed via Apple's Cocoa API), eases font handling.

Immediate Solutions

Handling Complicated Installations

Mac OS X's Package feature greatly simplifies the installation and removal of applications, but some programs, such as those from Adobe and Symantec, require more complex installation processes. This can also happen when you're trying to install a Classic application. The following sections describe some of the installation options.

Using an Installer

The normal way to install an application—when you're not using Mac OS X's drag and drop technique—is to load a CD and double-click an installer application. After an installer is launched, read the prompts and other onscreen instructions. Should the installer application ask for a location for the application, specify the Applications folder for ease of organization.

At the end of the installation, you should see a Quit button. But in some cases, you might, instead, encounter the Restart prompt. Click it to restart your Mac. After the restart, you'll be able to use the application normally.

NOTE: *Restart prompts are quite rare in Mac OS X installations. You usually see them only if the installer needs to install certain system-related software (or one of Apple's own Mac OS X updates), such as Norton SystemWorks or Norton Utilities. An example is Kensington MouseWorks, which is used to provide custom scrolling, mouse movement, and direct access features for Kensington's line of input devices.*

Using a Disk Image

Another way to distribute software is to use the disk image. The disk image has the virtue of being a carbon copy of the original distribution file or disk for the software, so you can use it without needing to have the disk media present. A disk image can consist of just the installation files or the full installation CD.

NOTE: *Just about all of Apple's software files are distributed in disk image form for convenience. Many other publishers (and even shareware developers) are using a similar technique for efficient transfer of their products.*

To use a disk image, follow these steps:

1. Locate the disk image file. It will usually be identified by a file name with the extension .img or .smi and an icon that looks like a small hard drive embedded into a document. Double-click the file's name. Over the next few seconds, the file will be checked to make sure it isn't damaged. If it turns out to be damaged, you will have to get another copy (download it again, for example).

TIP: *If a file was compressed for distribution to save download time from the Internet, the file may come as a compressed archive, which sports a .sit or .hqx extension. If you have a file of this sort, double-clicking it ought to be sufficient to activate the decompression software (StuffIt Expander, which comes with Mac OS X).*

2. When the file opens, a disk image icon will be placed on your Mac's desktop. Double-click the icon to reveal its contents (see Figure 10.4).

3. If the file contains an installer, double-click the installer to proceed.

NOTE: *When you open the contents of a disk image file, you'll want to see if they include any ReadMe files. If there are ReadMe files, open them to see if you need to follow any special instructions to install the application or prepare for the installation.*

4. Should the disk image contain the actual file or files to be installed, look for instructions on how to proceed. Microsoft's Office v. X (see Figure 10.5) and some Internet applications

Figure 10.4   A disk image's contents appear in the Finder window and sometimes it will have custom backgrounds or icons tailored to a specific software product.

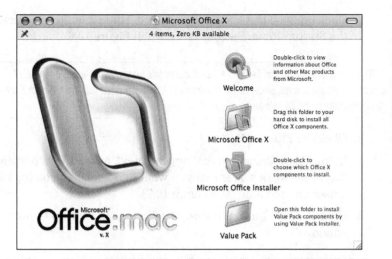

Figure 10.5   As you see from this Microsoft software disk, the installation file consists of a single installation folder, a Welcome message, a custom installer, and a folder of extras.

might even include a text description on the disk image or on the CD itself explaining what to do (usually just drag the installation folder to your Mac's hard drive).

5. When the installation is done, you can proceed with using the new software.

Adding a Startup Application

To have your application launch as soon as you boot your Mac, follow these steps:

NOTE: Panther uses no system extensions in the traditional sense (although there are kernel extensions that run at the core of the operating system). The alternative is to run your program as an application that starts up with your Mac. Some installers might set this up for you behind the scenes. These instructions tell you how to do it yourself.

1. Locate the System Preferences application icon in the Dock and click it, or double-click its icon in the Applications folder.

TIP: Startup applications apply strictly to a single user's account. Each user of your Mac can select from a different range of startup applications. If you want to make a system-wide startup application, place an alias to it in the StartupItems folder inside the Library folder at the root level of your hard drive. If such a folder isn't there already, just create one.

2. Click once on the Accounts pane and, when it launches, click the Startup Items Button, as shown in Figure 10.6.

NOTE: In previous versions of Mac OS X, Apple called this feature Login Items, which is, of course technically correct, since the applications or files launch when you login. But for Panther, Apple returned to the Classic terminology.

---

3. Click the Plus (+) button.

4. In the Open dialog box that appears next, select the application, file, or network server that you want to open when you log in as a user on your Mac (see Figure 10.7).

5. Click the Add button to store the file in your Startup Items window.

TIP: Another way to add a startup item is to simply drag and drop the item into the Startup Items window.

---

6. To hide the application (so its window is available only from the Dock), click the Hide checkbox.

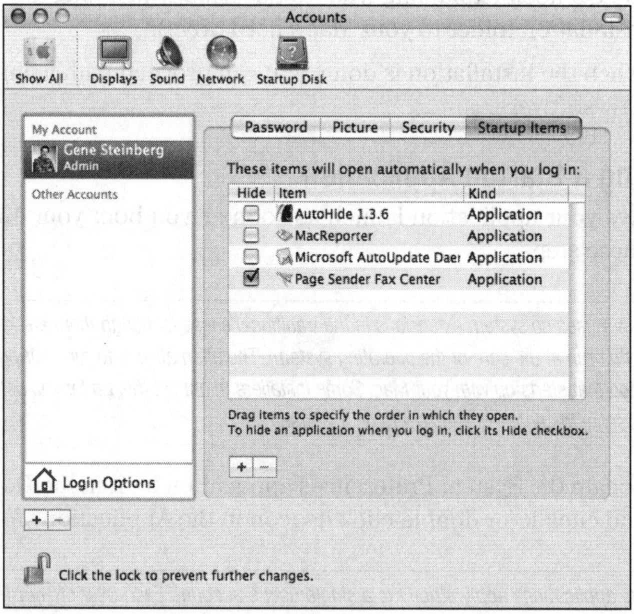

Figure 10.6   Add startup applications in this window.

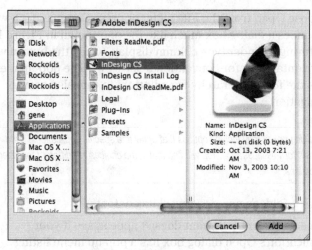

Figure 10.7   Select your startup item in this dialog box.

TIP: *Some applications, particularly those providing system-wide enhancements may include a preference to automatically make the program a startup application. That can be a time-saver.*

---

7. Choose Quit from the application menu or press Command+Q to quit System Preferences (or click the close button). The next time you boot your Mac and log in under that username, the selected application will launch. If the item is a network share, you'll have to respond to a separate login dialog for each server.

TIP: *If you decide you don't want to have your startup applications launch during a work session, you can use a shortcut that's reminiscent of how you avoided Startup Items under Mac OS 9. As soon as you see a startup progress bar on restart or login, hold down the Shift key. Release the key when the Finder appears and the startup process is finished. This process will prevent the startup applications from launching.*

Using the Panther Open Dialog Box

If you're used to double-clicking a document to open it, rather than going through the Open dialog box, here's Panther's better way:

1. Launch the application from which you want to open the document.

2. Choose Open from the File menu or press Command+O, which produces a dialog box much like the one shown in Figure 10.8, featuring a Finder-type column display. (Click the button with horizontal lines for conventional list view.) The pop-up menu lists the folder hierarchy from bottom to top, also easing navigation.

NOTE: *Open dialog boxes may include options that apply to a specific application. I used Microsoft Word X for this illustration. You will find that some choices are different for other Panther applications.*

---

3. Click a folder's name to reveal its contents.

4. If the document you want doesn't appear, see if your application's Open dialog box has a pop-up menu listing alternate file formats supported. Use them to see if the document appears.

TIP: *If a document's name is grayed out, the program you're using cannot open it.*

---

5. When you locate the document you want to open, either select it and click the Open button, or double-click the document's name.

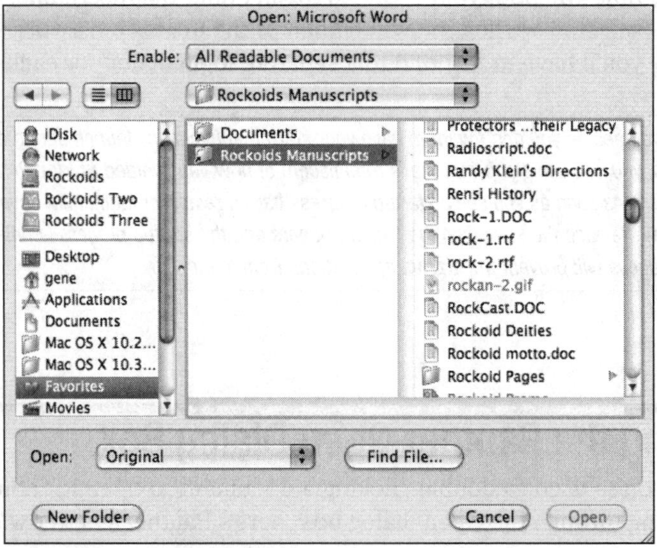

Figure 10.8   Easily locate the document you want to open.

TIP: *If a document you open is a template or was created in an older version of a program, you might see a new, untitled document on your screen, rather than the name of the document you selected. If this is the case, you can simply save the document with the original name to replace it, or give it a new name and store it in a new location, if necessary.*

6. If the document you wanted to locate isn't shown, click the Cancel button or press Command+. (period) or the Esc key to dismiss the Open dialog box. Then, use Apple's Sherlock search application to find the document. You'll find more information about Sherlock in Chapter 7.

Related solution:	*Found on page:*
Searching Files for Content	156

Using the Panther Save As Dialog Box

On the surface, saving a new document ought to be easy, but it hasn't always been thus in the Mac OS. Panther's Save As dialog box offers both basic and advanced options to help you quickly find a place to put your document so you can easily locate it later. Here is how to use this feature to its best advantage:

1. When you're ready to save your new document for the first time, choose Save As from the File menu. On some applications, a virtual sheet will drop down from the document's title bar (see Figure 10.9). With others, it'll appear as a separate dialog box but will function in essentially the same fashion.

NOTE: *When the Save As dialog box is displayed, you can move on to another document in the active application or to another application on your Mac. The dialog box will stay put, anchored to the original document's title bar, so you can return to it later without storing the wrong document by mistake.*

2. Type a name for your document in the Save As text field. It's always a good idea to be as clear as possible when creating a name so you can easily recognize the document when you need to open it again.

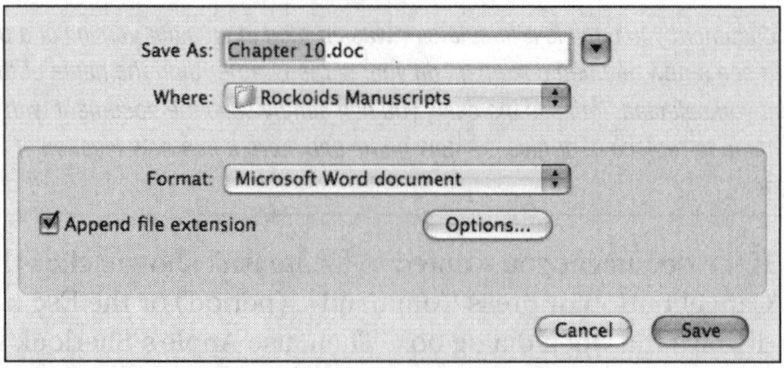

Figure 10.9   Where do you want to put your document?

NOTE: Although, in theory, Panther supports file names with a total of 256 characters, you should keep a file name to a reasonable length. Some applications, such as Word X (or 10), did not, at the time this book was written, support the expanded character set. But there is hope for the next version of Word, which may be out by the time you read this book.

3. To select a location for your document, click the pop-up menu to the right of the Where field. The default location is your Documents folder, inside your personal user's folder. You can also click the menu and specify another location.

TIP: The most logical place to put your file is in the Documents folder, which is where the Save As dialog box will usually point by default. If you plan to generate lots of documents for a single category or a single business contact or friend, you should consider making a separate folder within the Documents folder to avoid having to comb through long lists of files to find the ones that apply.

4. To see more locations and additional choices, click the down arrow at the right of the Where pop-up menu. You'll see the expanded view reminiscent of the Finder's column view (see Figure 10.10).

NOTE: When you choose an expanded Save As dialog view, the selection will usually stick for that particular application until you switch to the standard, simplified display by clicking on the up arrow to the right of the Where field.

5. Click a folder in the left column to see the contents in the right column.

6. To put your file in a new folder, choose the location for the folder from the column display, and then click the New Folder button to open the New Folder dialog box (see Figure 10.11).

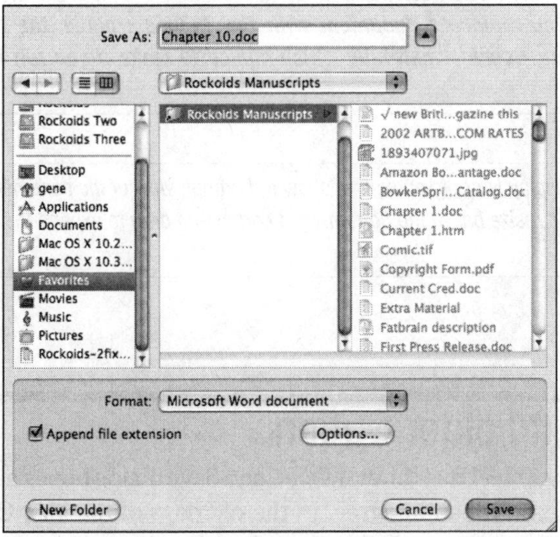

Figure 10.10 You have additional choices as to how to handle your new document.

Figure 10.11 Name your new folder.

7. Type a name for the new folder.

8. Click the Create button. The new folder will be placed in the location selected in the Save As dialog box.

9. After your save options are selected, click the Save button to store the file. If the document name you selected is already in use, you can either replace the document with the duplicate name or give your new document a different name; the document you are replacing must be closed for this to work.

NOTE: Depending on the application you're using, you may also see an Options button, which gives you access to program-specific features related to the Save As function.

WARNING! *Once you replace a document with the duplicate name, the replaced document is history. Consider carefully which choice to make if you run into this situation.*

TIP: *If the column display isn't big enough to show a thorough view of the contents of your Mac's drive, click the resize bar at the bottom-right corner and drag to expand the Save As window.*

The Default Folder Option

Most users might feel the Panther Open and Save dialog boxes are lacking in some features, and I agree. In the old days of the Mac OS, two popular programs were available for enhancing these dialog boxes to make them easier to navigate and add extra features to manage files.

One of my favorites was Now Super Boomerang, and a successor program called Action Files. A shareware alternative, Default Folder, is also available in Mac OS X form (see Figure 10.12).

Quite a few pages would be needed to cover all the features, so I'll deliver the highlights:

• *Recently used and favorite folders*—Panther no longer has a readily accessible Favorites feature (although one can be found, as you'll discover in Chapter 4). But Default Folder X does provide one, along with a list of recently used files for fast navigation.

• *Finder level functions*—You can rename, delete, and get information about files without returning to the Finder.

• *Rebound feature*—This feature is one of my favorites. Default Folder X returns to the last used file, which is already selected for you.

• *Dock and menu bar icons*—Provides fast access to Default Folder's features directly from the Finder.

If you want to try out a fully functional copy before paying the user license fee, check out St. Clair Software's Web site at **www.stclairsw.com/DefaultFolderX/index.html**.

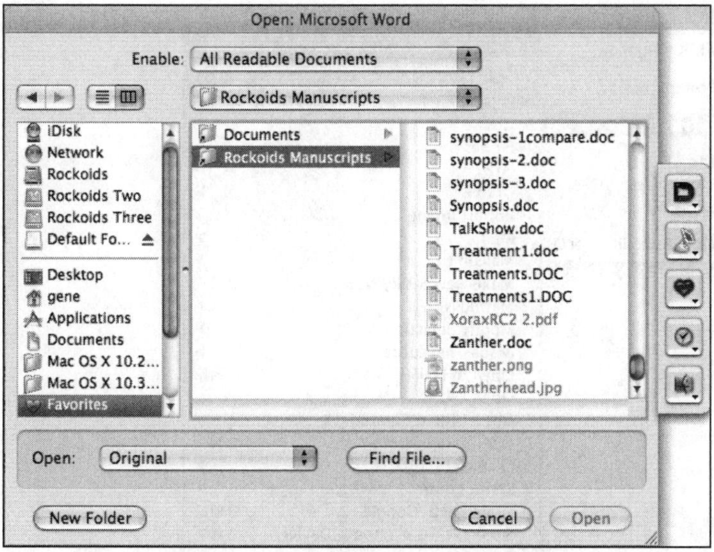

Figure 10.12 Default Folder X puts up five buttons at the edge of the Open and Save dialog boxes with enhanced functions.

Using the Services Menu

Wouldn't it be nice if applications could communicate with one another easily without your having to go through the confusing processes of cutting and pasting and dragging and dropping? The Services menu for Panther helps to minimize this problem. Here's an example of how it can be used to make two programs work together:

NOTE: This example is for demonstration purposes only. I used TextEdit and OmniWeb, a Web browser described in Chapter 21, but any Web browser that accesses the Services feature can accomplish the same task. You can download a copy of the latest version of OmniWeb from www.omnigroup.com.

---

1. Open a word-processing or text-editing program. For the sake of this exercise, I'm using TextEdit, the replacement for Apple's SimpleText.

2. Type the URL for your favorite Web site.

3. Select the URL.

4. Go to the application menu, choose Services, and scroll to OmniWeb, where the submenu will read Open URL (see Figure 10.13).

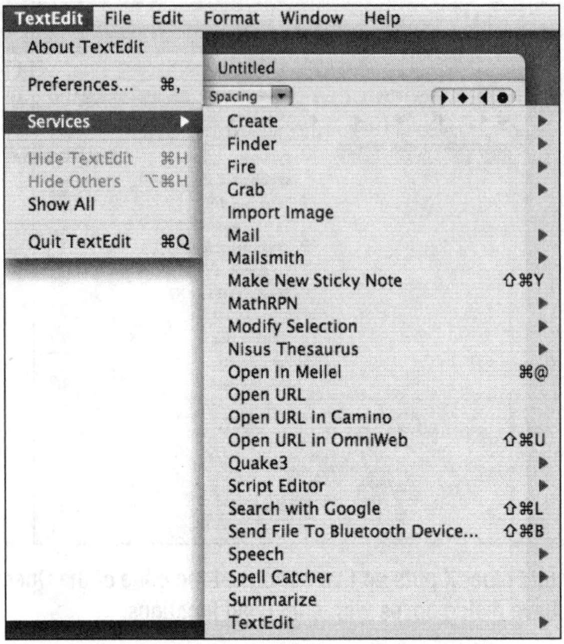

Figure 10.13 This feature takes longer to describe than to show.

When you select this option, the selected URL will open in OmniWeb (see Figure 10.14). Depending on the program you're using and the kind of text or picture objects you've selected, the Services menu will display different choices, and different commands will be available to apply to the selected material.

Troubleshooting Software Installation Problems

Mac OS X makes software installation easy, but sometimes things simply won't work. Here are some common problems and solutions:

- *The application won't launch.* Is it a Mac OS X application? If the program is Mac OS X–savvy, consider restarting your Mac to see if doing so makes a difference. If it doesn't, look for the application's preference files, in the Preferences folder within the Library folder of your Users directory and remove the appropriate ones, after quitting the application of course. As with previous versions of the Mac OS, a corrupted settings file can definitely cause performance problems or the failure to run. If it still doesn't work, reinstall the application. If this final step fails, contact the publisher about possible compatibility problems.

Figure 10.14 OmniWeb displays a Web site whose URL was selected in TextEdit.

NOTE: Although some Mac OS X programs have preference files clearly named, others use the native Mac OS X structure, which puts the maker's URL in reverse. For example, the preference file for Apple's Mail application is com.apple.mail.plist. Once you get used to the format, you should be able to locate such files without difficulty.

WARNING! *Before removing a preference file, bear in mind that for some programs such as Mail, you might have to spend a little extra time redoing various settings. In the case of Mail, all your mail account setups are stored in that file.*

- *The application keeps quitting.* Usually, this is an installation or compatibility problem. Your first line of attack is to try launching the application again. Mac OS X's protected memory will close down the memory space with the application (unless it runs in the Classic environment). If that doesn't work, restart your Mac. You might also want to consider following the remedies in the previous paragraph, by deleting the preference files and reinstalling the program. Otherwise, consult the documentation or the publisher's support department or Web site for information about possible bugs.

WARNING! *Some applications, such as Apple's Mail and Microsoft's Entourage, store saved messages in a database file. If you remove the file, the material is gone (unless you have a backup copy, of course). So it's best to stick with an actual application preference file when looking for the cause of a performance problem.*

NOTE: In the scheme of things, Mac OS X is quite new, even though Panther is the fourth major release. So, don't be surprised to find applications failing from time to time. You should check with the publishers about possible updates. In particular, you'll find that the Classic environment sometimes won't quit or will quit very slowly.

- *The application is installed in the wrong place.* Drag the application icon or folder to the Applications folder. Although this shouldn't make a difference, there may be other support files in a separate folder in the Applications folder that the program needs to run. It never hurts to try. When it comes to Apple's own software, there's really no choice. Apple's update installers are pretty strict about file location and the update won't work if the file is placed elsewhere.

Some Notes on Removing an Application

Sometimes reinstalling isn't enough. You actually have to remove most or all vestiges of a program before the program is really gone. Otherwise, the installer may not replace everything. Sad but true. You might also need to remove an application because you don't use it anymore.

Here's a quick checklist for removing Mac OS X software:

- *Trash the application folder*—This may do the job, particularly with Microsoft Office and other applications installed by a drag and drop process. If you had to use an installer, however, first launch the installer, and see if an Uninstall command is available. That's your first line of defense. Otherwise, you should begin, as I said, with the application folder.

- *Trash the application's preferences*—These files are, as stated before, located in the Preferences folder inside your personal users folder.

- *Trash Application Support files for that application*—Since not all programs require this sort of thing, you may not find one. But you should check both the Library folder at the root level of your hard drive and in your personal or Users directory. Just trash the ones specifically named for that application, or, if you are deleting all software from a particular company, trash all the files or folders with that company's name. If you reinstall later on, these files will be restored.

WARNING! *Please be very careful about deleting a folder named for the manufacturer if you have other software from that company. Otherwise, critical support files may be missing and you'll have to reinstall. And, of course, leave the actual Application Support folder alone, even if you think you pulled everything out of it. Some application installs may think it's supposed to be there and they won't setup a program properly.*

If you continue to run into problems with an application, whether newly installed or not, check Chapter 18 for more information about troubleshooting Panther.

Related solution:	*Found on page:*
Solving System Crashes and Freezes	417

Chapter 11

Setting Up New Hardware and Peripherals

In Brief

Panther may be a blessing when it comes to handling your Mac's system and application software. The hallmarks of the new operating system and the programs that come with it include ease of installation, simplified file management, and improved performance and reliability.

Most of the other chapters in this book deal primarily with the software, except for this chapter and the following one. Dealing properly with the Mac hardware itself is just as important on the road to setting up and maintaining a Mac system as the software. In this chapter, I'll cover the basics of surviving a new Mac hardware installation, some of the special features Panther provides to support that hardware, and some of the problems you may encounter and their solutions.

You'll also get some solid tips on installing Wi-Fi hardware and new peripherals, such as extra drives, scanners, printers, or whatever suits your needs.

Panther's Special Hardware Features

The system software is not the only component that provides the performance advantages and reliability for Panther. Panther includes special support to harness powerful features you might already have on your Mac.

Here are some of the main capabilities that can make your Mac more powerful and productive:

NOTE: To fully exploit these powerful technologies, you need to run Panther–savvy applications. Your older programs will run with fairly good performance in the Classic compatibility environment. But they won't run faster (except in a few rare circumstances) and they won't be more reliable than they were before. If any of these applications crashes, it will bring down the entire Classic environment. Fortunately, the crash won't affect the rest of the system. In some cases, you could experience a performance hit particularly if you're using programs heavily dependent on 3D graphics.

- *Advanced graphics management*—The Quartz imaging layer has built-in support for technologies such as PDF, OpenGL, and QuickTime. The superlative visual display of the Aqua interface is one of the features that maximizes the potential of the graphics chips in your Mac. Even the first-generation iMac with a 233Mhz processor (the original model) and the entry-level graphics chip from ATI Technologies can provide acceptable performance in most respects. The only exception is 3D games, but these still work best in the thousands-of-colors mode. Of course, if you have a top-of-the-line Power Macintosh computer with an NVIDIA GeForce4 Titanium or ATI Radeon 9800 graphics card, you will realize the maximum possible benefit from the new features, regardless of resolution settings. Apple's enhanced imaging technology, Quartz Extreme, will work with an AGP graphics card and 16MB of video RAM or greater, and supports any NVIDIA card or the ATI Radeon family.

WARNING! *If you do not have a Mac with a graphics chip from ATI, IX Micro, or NVIDIA, you will have to contact the manufacturer about driver updates to address Panther compatibility. This problem could be doubly difficult if you have a graphics card from a defunct maker, such as 3dfx Interactive (although a third party has been trying to build Mac OS X–compatible drivers for these cards). Check such software information sites as VersionTracker.com to see if any outside parties will provide updates.*

- *Symmetric multiprocessing*—Some Macs come with more than a single processor chip. Although previous versions of the Mac OS and a very few applications (such as Adobe Photoshop) offer limited support for multiprocessing, the extra brainpower doesn't do much good. However, it does help Apple's marketing department sell new Macs. This situation changed with Mac OS X because it has built-in support for multiprocessing and can efficiently parcel out tasks between processors to speed up performance. Any multi-threading application can also take advantage of multiprocessing. This allows you to get the maximum level of performance from the extra processors.

NOTE: *Multiple threading means simply that a program can handle more than a single chore at the same time.*

- *Preemptive multitasking*—The original Mac version of multitasking was cooperative, which meant that the programs themselves were designed to play nicely with one another. Under Mac OS X, the operating system is the traffic cop, parceling out tasks at a system level. This provides for better management of multiple applications.

- *64-bit support*—The Power Mac G5 and other Macs forthcoming with G5 processors can deliver extra performance if a program is specifically compiled to support the 64-bit capability of the newest Mac processors. Applications such as Adobe Photoshop CS and Apple's own Final Cut Pro multimedia software have been updated to deliver superior performance with a G5.

Taken together, these features can make your old Mac behave almost as if you bought a new computer. Your Mac will start faster, launch applications quicker, and it won't bog down at inopportune times when you're trying to make it do two things at once.

NOTE: *Multiprocessing isn't a panacea. Other systems on your Mac, such as your graphics card and hard drive, can conspire to put limits on overall performance.*

A Review of Mac Peripheral Ports

In the old days of the Macintosh, you attached your input devices to an ADB port, a printer to the printer port, a modem to the modem port, and an external storage device to the SCSI port. This approach changed with the 1998 arrival of the computer credited with Apple's resurgence—the iMac. Since that time, peripheral ports have continued to change so I'll give you this fast and dirty (or dirty and fast, depending on your point of view) look at the old and the new:

- *Apple Desktop Bus (ADB)*—This was an early standard input port for input devices, such as the keyboard and mouse, trackball, and joystick. It also includes extras such as digital cameras and scanners. Even some modems use this port. However, it can only support a very few devices. Performance tends to be slow for demanding accessories, and the plug-and-play aspect is a little murky. You have to shut down your Mac to remove and add devices, or you risk damage to the computer's logic board. The ADB port vanished with the arrival of the iMac and later new models, both desktop and laptop; it was replaced with Universal Serial Bus (USB), a much more flexible standard.

TIP: *If you have an older device you need hooked up to a newer Mac, consider an ADB to USB adapter, such as the Griffin Technologies iMate. It is compatible with Mac OS X, and, in fact, with Windows.*

- *Serial port*—Some Macs had two serial ports, and some PowerBooks had just one. A regular desktop Mac had one port for printers (it doubled as a LocalTalk port) and another for modems. PowerBooks combined the two and added built-in modems so that there was no conflict or need for a switch to allow you to use an extra device. Apple has replaced them with Ethernet, which is much faster and more reliable.

NOTE: *The original Mac serial ports simply are not supported for Mac OS X. If you have a LocalTalk printer, then the iPrint from Proxim (formerly Farallon) or the AsanteTalk will convert to Ethernet. But serial printers, such as the Apple StyleWriter, should be replaced with USB versions, even if you must use a USB adapter on your Mac. This is because driver support is not likely to be offered; a simple serial-to-USB converter isn't enough.*

- *SCSI port*—Except for the very first Mac (which used the floppy drive port to add a hard drive), the SCSI port was the original standard for adding storage devices, scanners, and some specialty printers to your Mac. This is the closest thing to plug and "pray" on your Mac. This is because SCSI can be problematic, especially when the SCSI chain is large. For regular SCSI, you can connect up to seven daisy-chained devices. Each device has a unique ID number, from 0 through 6 (up to 15 for some high-speed SCSI cards). The last physical device on the chain (regardless of ID number) must be terminated. With large SCSI chains, sometimes devices won't work properly or your Mac will crash frequently. The diagnostics include reordering devices (observing proper ID numbering and termination), swapping cables, taking two aspirins, and trying again. With millions of SCSI devices available, Mac users still need to employ this peripheral standard, although better ones are available.

- *Ethernet*—This high-speed networking standard is in use in homes and both large and small offices. The standard Ethernet protocols in use on Macs are 10Base-T and 100Base-T, and recent generations of desktop Power Mac G4s and PowerBooks feature Gigabit Ethernet. At its maximum speed, Ethernet can deliver networking throughput nearly as fast as a big hard drive. This is a true plug-and-play standard. You can connect multiple devices to a central connecting point, such as a hub or switch, and remove and reconnect as needed. Ethernet devices aren't limited to computers and printers. You can also add network routers and special modems for broadband Internet, such as cable and DSL.

- *Universal Serial Bus (USB)*—This peripheral protocol is available in two forms. The original 1.1 was a low- to medium-speed serial port that is standard issue on all Apple computers officially supported by Panther. Most Macs, except the iBook, have two

USB ports (the iBook has just one). To add more devices, you need hubs. In theory, you can connect up to 127 devices with full plug and play, but to do so you must install driver software for many products and unmount a storage device first before removal. The older standard claims performance of up to 12 megabits per second. USB 2.0, which is included on the Power Mac G5 and other Macs introduced beginning in 2003, claims a top speed of 480 mbps. This is slightly higher than regular FireWire, which makes it useful for high performance external drives and scanners.

- *FireWire*—This Apple invention is a high-speed peripheral port that puts the kibosh on SCSI for all practical purposes. It delivers either up to 400 megabits or 800 megabits performance, the latter of which pushes drive speeds to extremely high levels. Devices can be daisy chained, and there's a high level of plug-and-play compatibility, including hot-plugging. Drivers are needed on some devices, and storage devices must be dismounted from the desktop, but that covers most exceptions. FireWire devices include digital camcorders, which makes all recent Macs ideal desktop video-editing computers. FireWire storage devices and scanners are available. Apple's stylish music player, the iPod, uses the FireWire port to update the music on its internal drive or to serve duty as a regular storage device.

NOTE: *The speedier FireWire format, FireWire 800, is available in Apple's professional line, which includes the Power Mac and PowerBook. When this book was written, FireWire 800 hadn't spread to the consumer products.*

Adding a Missing Port

What do you do if you want a peripheral, but your Mac doesn't have the correct port? For desktop Macs with expansion slots, you can get relief in the form of PCI-based peripheral adapter cards. They come in many shapes and sizes, offering the following:

- *FireWire*—Two or more FireWire ports can be found on a single expansion card. Best of all, such cards usually don't need any special software and can cost less than $50 for FireWire 400 and a little more for FireWire 800.

- *USB 2.0*—You don't need a new Mac to take advantage of the speedier USB format. Panther supports third-party USB 2.0 expansion cards out of the box. And, no, I won't get involved in the argument of USB 2.0 versus FireWire 400, except to say that manufacturers often support both formats, so you can try the jacks you like.

NOTE: *When you're buying a FireWire or USB adapter, check the documentation that comes with the product closely. Some companies bury the Mac OS compatibility information on the back of the box. I ran across a $20 Belkin USB adapter at Wal-Mart that was labeled in this rather confusing fashion. If it doesn't say anything about Mac OS compatibility, be cautious. Although Panther has native support for numerous third-party products, don't expect perfection.*

- *High-speed Ethernet*—Although recent Mac desktops offer Gigabit Ethernet, you don't have to feel abandoned with an older Mac. Expansion cards fill this gap as well, but they're somewhat costly. Although fairly cheap models are available, for some strange reason Macs aren't always supported, so double check about Mac drivers before you pull out your credit card.

- *Combo cards*—If you don't have enough slots, take heart. Combination cards offer both FireWire and USB—you don't have to choose just one.

- *SCSI cards*—If you need to find a home for your existing SCSI devices, a ready collection of SCSI cards are available with various price points and speeds. The cheapest cards, at roughly $50, are up to twice as fast as the built-in SCSI on older Macs, and they get much faster as the price increases.

NOTE: *Before buying a SCSI card, make sure it supports the devices you already have and, just as important, Mac OS X. This may leave out a number of products from the used parts bin or a garage sale. If in doubt, contact the manufacturer about compatibility issues, particularly with the new PCI-X slots on the Power Mac G5, which do not work with some older cards. For a scanner, removable drive, and a regular SCSI hard drive, the cheaper cards are fine. But some external drives and even backup drives require cards with "wide" SCSI ports.*

- *SCSI-to-FireWire converter*—This is another way to have the best of both worlds. Several brands of such converters are available that allow a single SCSI device to connect to the FireWire ports on your Mac. Because they're single devices, you don't have to consider issues of termination and ID. On the other hand, my experiences with such products has been, in all fairness, a little mixed, and they don't always work as they should. Maybe it's time to just give up SCSI for good. I did that long ago, and it didn't hurt a bit.

- *Serial-to-USB converters*—These modules let you attach products that work on regular Mac serial ports, such as older ink jet printers and modems, to a newer Mac's USB port. The major limitation is the occasional software conflict and the inability to work with LocalTalk devices, such as AppleTalk printers that attach to a standard Mac printer port.

- *SCSI-to-USB converters*—This type of product would appear to be a blessing because it lets you continue to use those old SCSI products on a Mac that has only USB, such as the iMac. However, because the older USB standard is slower than SCSI, the conversion works best for a scanner or low-speed storage device (such as a Zip drive or tape drive). When this book was written, I did not see any SCSI-to-USB 2.0 adapters, which should, in theory be plenty fast. If the product isn't available, the speed doesn't matter.

- *LocalTalk-to-Ethernet bridge*—If you have an older Mac where Ethernet is an option or a network printer that only has a LocalTalk port, this device allows you to continue to use these products on your Ethernet network. You won't get any faster speed, but you won't have to buy a new printer or spend extra money on a peripheral card for an old Mac that is near the end of its useful life.

NOTE: You can share files on a Mac running Panther with a Mac running an older version of the operating system. If the older Mac is using Mac OS 8.5 or earlier, just remember to turn on AppleTalk in the Network preference panel of Mac OS X's System Preferences application. Don't forget that AppleTalk can only work on one port at a time. If you also have an AirPort system, you'll have to pick one or the other. I won't tell you why; that's just the way it is.

- *ADB-to-USB adapter*—Do you cherish that old keyboard, mouse, trackball, or similar input device? You can still use it on your new Mac with this type of adapter. On the other hand, many terrific input devices are available for Macs these days—particularly Apple's Pro Keyboard and Pro Mouse. (I love these and use them all the time.) These devices ship standard on new Macs and are available from the Apple Store for older models. You may find the money better spent acquiring something new.

WARNING! Not all peripheral cards work seamlessly with Mac OS X. Before you purchase one of these products, contact the manufacturer or check its Web site directly to see its plans. For example, older SCSI cards and none of the DOS cards that put an AMD or Intel inside your Mac will ever run with Mac OS X. You also shouldn't hold out much hope for driver updates. Ditto for PCI cards that do not work in 3.3V slots, such as the PCI-X slots on the Power Mac G5. If you have an older product, other than these two categories, I still recommend you double-check about compatibility.

NOTE: Unfortunately, the iBook, eMac, and the iMac were conceived as inexpensive consumer computers and thus lack extra expansion slots and the ability to add them (except for FireWire and USB 2.0 on some models). You must live with the ports you have, should you be using one of these models.

Peripherals Available for Macs

Although some folks decry the limited availability of products for Macs, they aren't really paying attention. Literally thousands of Mac products are available from Apple's own retail outlets, the Mac departments in other stores, and at mail order dealers. Many, in fact, are cross-platform—the same product is available for both Mac and Windows users, with the sole difference being the driver software or the label on the box.

NOTE: *Some companies with cross-platform products will, for some unaccountable reason, put their Mac software drivers only on their Web sites, rather than on the CD that comes with the product. If a product seems to work only under Windows, check the box and the manufacturer's Web site, in case you get lucky.*

Here's a short list of the kinds of products you can add to your Mac to help harness the power of Panther:

NOTE: *This list is meant only to give a sampling of the sort of products you can connect to your Mac. Check with a particular manufacturer to find out whether a special upgrade is needed for Panther. Some of these products will plug in and run, regardless of whether you have Panther or Mac OS 9.x.*

- *Scanners*—Desktop scanners were once the province of professional graphic artists. They were expensive, with color models of reasonable quality running from one to two grand. Although products are still available in that price range, literally dozens of models are available from less than $100 to around $200. Scanners are available in FireWire, SCSI, and USB form; some of the more expensive models support both FireWire and USB.

TIP: *Is the manufacturer of your scanner late to the party in developing Mac OS X drivers? Try VueScan, a clever third-party solution. I used this demoware scanning application until Microtek was able to deliver drivers for my scanner. (To use it you need to buy a user license to get it to scan without a watermark on your image.) Available as a download from the publisher's Web site at **www.hamrick.com**, VueScan supports a huge number of flatbed and slide scanners. It's also updated almost weekly. If your scanner isn't working with it when you try the program, just be patient or write to the publisher and see if support is coming. If you want something more sophisticated, and are willing to pay the price of admission, I heartily recommend SilverFast from LaserSoft Imaging. SilverFast supports dozens of scanners and offers powerful editing features that allow you to get the most from your artwork before the final scan is performed.*

- *Digital cameras*—Film may not be obsolete but it's getting there for all but professional photographers. Today's digital cameras are cheaper, and offer quality that rivals film in most any size you'd use. Some of the more expensive models even match film cameras with special features, such as single-lens reflex viewfinders (where you see the same image picked up by the camera's lens), and even the ability to do limited motion videos. Most of these products store data on small memory cards. Best of all, Apple's Image Capture and iPhoto applications provide built-in support for most available digital cameras. Just plug the camera into your Mac, and either of these programs will launch to download your pictures.

- *Hard drives*—Today's external hard drives come in FireWire, SCSI, and USB formats (both 1.1 and 2.0, but the latter requires an adapter on many Macs); the first two and USB 2.0 provide the highest degree of performance. In terms of speed, there should be no difference between external and internal drives. The Power Macs, except for the Cube, sport extra drive bays for additional internal storage devices, in case you want to put everything on one case.

- *Removable drives*—As I'll explain in Chapter 16, backing up your data is critically important. Even though Panther is a superbly stable, industrial-strength operating system, problems can happen to a drive's directory, and individual applications can still fail. That, plus the possibility of external hazards, such as a burglary, natural disaster, or weather-related problems, makes it imperative that you keep regular backups of your most valuable material. A removable drive is a convenient backup tool and just as handy for moving files to another location—particularly files that are too large to send online. The venerable Zip drive and, if your Mac doesn't have one, a CD or CD/DVD burner, are welcome additions if you want an easy way to store your critical data.

NOTE: *The issue of which backup device is the most robust one is a complicated issue. While optical media are supposed to survive for years, I've heard of some difficulties with older CD media, though I've not had the problem myself.*

- *Graphic cards*—Is your desktop Mac's bundled graphics card a little slow in rendering 3D games? Do you have a first generation Power Mac G4 with AGP and a card from the ATI Rage family that doesn't support the ultra-fast Quartz Extreme? Or do you have a blue and white Power Mac G3 with an early-generation ATI card?

Either way, you have options. ATI offers several products in its Radeon series that will provide better graphics acceleration in almost all respects. If you have a recent G4, you might also be able to get a high performance NVIDIA graphic card from Apple's own retail outlets or its Web site. All of these products will also support two displays, which is a boon for graphic artists and other content creators who need extra desktop space.

- *Wireless networking*—Apple's AirPort wireless networking modules are available for all new Macs. They allow Macs to network with each other at near standard Ethernet speeds at distances of up to 150 feet. The AirPort Base Station, known in its current iteration as AirPort Extreme, lets you share an Internet connection. With a growing number of Wi-Fi access points around the country, which include both McDonald's and Starbucks, you can really get work done and enjoy refreshments and perhaps lunch at the same time. Just keep your laptop keyboard clean.

NOTE: *If you have an older Mac without AirPort capability, other choices are available for wireless networking. Among these choices are the SkyLINE from Proxim and Asante's AeroLAN, both of which use the same industry standard protocols as AirPort (802.11b or 802.11g, commonly known as Wi-Fi) and can function as part of the same network. Both firms also offer Wi-Fi base stations that work on both Macs and Windows-based PCs.*

- *Loudspeakers*—Most loudspeaker systems you add to a computer plug in to your audio output or earphone jack, but some speakers connect directly to your USB port. These include the Harman Kardon iSub and SoundSticks. They take advantage of the Mac OS's sound control features to adjust volume, balance, and tone.

NOTE: *Apple's Pro speakers are neat and compact, but they require a Mac with a special connector that provides built-in amplification. If your Mac doesn't have this feature, consider the iFire, from Griffin Technology, which lets you run these speakers from any Mac with a FireWire port. You can even use these speakers with the iPod.*

- *Handheld computers*—These devices include the popular Palm OS products from Handspring and Sony. They aren't designed to be attached to your Mac all the time, but they need to interface with your computer for installing and removing software, or for just synchronizing information. You'll need special software to allow this connection to work.

NOTE: *Apple's iSync software does support both handhelds and some mobile phones, but you may need extra software and connection cables to make it operate.*

---

11. Setting Up New Hardware and Peripherals

- *Digital music players*—Apple's own iPod, that tiny, steel-clad player the size of a deck of cards, is the biggest and most trendy player in this arena. It is the modern day equivalent of the Sony Walkman. Huge numbers of Mac and Windows users own them. Add to the mix the iTunes Music Store, where you can legally download hundreds of thousands of tracks and full albums by most of your favorite artists, and you've got a real winner.

Although installing an accessory on your Mac is fairly easy, you should always take a few extra precautions to make sure everything is set up properly. This is particularly important if you are setting up a complicated peripheral device, such as a scanner, and some extra steps might be necessary. In addition, because many products come with very sparse documentation, these steps will help you get things working without extra fuss or confusion.

In the next section, I'll cover some of the basics of hooking up new Mac hardware and peripherals under Panther.

Immediate Solutions

Installing New Hardware

The arrival of a new Mac in your home or office can be a special event.
It may be your first Mac or your tenth, but you'll want to get it up and
running right away. The promise of getting on the Internet in 10 or 15
minutes flat is tempting. But here are some things to consider before
you deploy that new computer in a production setup:

1. Check your Mac for obvious damage. Macs are packed
   carefully by Apple and its dealers but sometimes they don't
   survive the trip to your home or office. If the box has
   severe visible signs of damage, let the shipper or dealer
   know right away. Then, open the box carefully and see if
   the computer also seems damaged. If so, don't use it. Wait
   for a thorough diagnosis or replacement.

*NOTE: I've had just one experience with a damaged Mac, the result of someone from an
overnight delivery service (withheld to protect the guilty) dropping the product off the truck by
mistake. Since it was a review product from Apple Computer, I just had it fixed, but it was a
jarring experience nonetheless. Apple wasn't fazed a bit, which means this must happen more
times than you'd expect.*

2. Assuming your computer looks fine, carefully follow the instructions to hook it up. If you intend to connect it to a network and/
   or hook up a bunch of peripherals, it's a good idea to first run the
   new Mac system all by itself, with just mouse, display, keyboard,
   and a modem or other Net connection to handle registration.

*NOTE: On a rare occasion, a Mac with no visible damage will be dead on arrival. If the Mac
refuses to boot properly or crashes constantly even before you can perform simple functions, you
should stop using it and contact your Apple dealer or Apple Computer about repair or replacement. Although Mac dealers usually will not exchange a Mac for another unit or give you a
refund, most (even The Apple Store) will replace a DOA unit.*

3. Turn on the Mac and follow the setup prompts to store your user settings and register the product. Registering from the Mac requires that you connect to Apple's Web site to send the information.

NOTE: *If you don't have ready Net access, check the documentation with the new Mac for a registration card that can accomplish the same task via the post office.*

4. Once the Mac is registered, try running a few programs and see if everything works.

5. If the Mac is running all right, connect your peripherals and/or network connections and see if everything functions normally.

6. If the computer seems to work, but you run into problems with one accessory or another, be sure you have installed the latest drivers for those products.

If your Mac comes through like a champ, you're ready to deploy it for production purposes.

NOTE: *The Power Mac G5 is a complicated computer, with multiple cooling fans and sensors to provide proper temperature control. Before you turn on your G5, you should pop open the side panel (the latch is at the rear), and remove the covering from the inside. Also make sure the plastic cover that fits on top of the chassis is snugly positioned. If you don't do this properly, your G5 may run with reduced processor performance. I have to admit that I ran my G5 for a couple of weeks before I removed that covering. It didn't harm anything, but I cursed myself for forgetting this critical step.*

Related solution:	Found on page:
Determining What to Do If an Accessory Doesn't Work	266

Maintaining Your Mac on a Daily Basis

If your Mac runs fine, you may be tempted to use it day in and day out and never concern yourself about proper hardware maintenance. Although a personal computer is nowhere near as sensitive to lack of proper care as the family car (where a missed oil change or two, or the failure to change worn brakes or tires, can be catastrophic), you should periodically give your Mac a once-over (or two or three) to keep it purring. Here's a simplified maintenance schedule:

- *Check the hard drive regularly*—Every week or so, use the First Aid component of Apple's Disk Utility or your favorite hard-drive diagnostic program to check all the drives connected to your Mac. Directory damage has a habit of creeping up on you: You'll receive reports of simple problems, and then they'll grow worse, until finally you lose files or the drive can't mount. But if you perform regular diagnostics, you'll be able to fix problems before they become too serious.

11. Setting Up New Hardware and Peripherals

NOTE: You cannot use Disk Utility to repair your startup drive, but you can run Disk Utility after booting from another drive, or you can access it from the Mac OS X Installer CD, in the Installer application menu, once you boot from that CD. Another way is to access the Single User mode, which gives you a command line at startup. I'll tell you how to use this feature to check your drive in Chapter 18.

TIP: Drives are scanned at each startup; so, even if your Mac has been running fine for days or weeks without a restart, it wouldn't hurt to restart occasionally to allow the disk scans to run.

WARNING! Many older hard-drive diagnostic programs are not designed to work with Mac OS X, even if you restart your Mac from the Mac OS 9 environment. You should check with the publisher directly about compatibility issues. The file structure under Mac OS X is different enough to cause bogus reports of disk problems, and attempts to fix those problems could create real ones. There are, however, Mac OS X-savvy versions of such disk diagnostic programs as Alsoft's DiskWarrior, Norton Utilities, and TechTool Pro.

- *Keep it clean*—I live in a Southwest desert state, so I have a chronic problem with dust buildup. In just a few weeks, the surface of the Macs in my home office can become dusty, and don't ask about the interior of the computers. I recommend you dust the case with a soft cloth (not abrasive) on a regular basis. Stay away from caustic cleaning solutions, but sometimes a light dose of a window-cleaning solution on a soft cloth is useful. If your display has become dusty, check the manufacturer's instructions about cleaning. Be especially careful with the soft surface of an LCD display—damage can be mighty expensive. Every few months, you might want to open your Mac (powered off, of course) and blow out the dust with one of those spray canisters (unless you have super-strong lungs of course). Excessive dust buildup could affect the integrity of the items, such as RAM, connected to the logic board or the expansion bus (PCI or AGP).

It can also hurt the performance of a cooling fan, or block the convection cooling vents on the iMac and PowerMac G4 Cube.

NOTE: *Excessive dust inside your Mac can cause performance anomalies. I once visited a client who had chronic crash problems. His software seemed up-to-date, and he had recently reformatted the drive, yet the problems persisted. Before sending him to the repair shop, I opened the Mac. A cloud of dust filled the room (and I suppressed a cough, with difficulty). A dose from a compressed air canister, placed just close enough to do some good, cleared out the Mac in short order. After removing and reseating the RAM and expansion cards, I closed the Mac. It ran perfectly; no more chronic crashes.*

- *Optimize sparingly*—The process of optimizing (or *defragging*) a hard drive rewrites all the files and puts them adjacent to each other, rather than spread across the drive as they are normally. In theory, sufficient file fragmentation might cause performance to suffer. In practice, it takes a lot to make a difference. Besides, Panther's improved file handling can reduce the problem because it automatically defrags files of up to 20MB in size when they are opened. However, if you remove and reinstall huge numbers of files, which is common in the graphic arts industry, you might experience a slight speed boost if you optimize. Video capture performance can be especially affected by such problems.

NOTE: *The ultra-efficient nature of the Unix File System (UFS) option means you shouldn't have to optimize your drive if it's formatted that way. The downside is that you can't run Classic from a UFS volume, nor can the UFS volume be seen if you restart from your Classic Mac OS.*

- *Check for driver/software updates*—Software and device drivers are all in a constant process of evolution and change. This is perhaps the biggest cause of problems with peripheral products, so you should stay in contact with the manufacturers about needed updates for better support of Panther. A good resource for such information is the **VersionTracker.com** Web site (see **www.versiontracker.com**).

- *Check your Mac after a power failure*—If a weather or power company problem has resulted in loss of power at your home or office, you should check your computers carefully when power is restored. Normally, when you restart or shut down your Mac, a "housecleaning" process writes cached files to the drive and updates the drive's directory. If the process is interrupted, files could be damaged, and drive directory problems might occur. Your hard drives will be scanned when you restart your Mac, but you may also want to use your favorite commercial hard-drive program to make sure everything is all right before you get back to work.

---

11. Setting Up New Hardware and Peripherals

NOTE: *As part of the normal installation process, Panther's Journaling feature is automatically engaged for the target drive. This feature puts hard drive file information in a database, which aids recovery in the event of a power failure or forced restart. But nothing is perfect.*

- *Shut down everything before you install something inside your Mac*—The delicate electronic components in your Mac, from the logic board to the processor, can easily be damaged by static electricity or a short circuit. If you need to add or remove a peripheral card or RAM, touch the power supply (with the plug in) to get rid of any static charge you might have and then pull the plug. Some of the better memory and peripheral card dealers will supply a wrist strap to help with the process. You may feel like a surgeon beginning an operation while thus equipped, but the benefit is that your installation can be done with the maximum degree of safety and the maximum protection to the delicate internal workings of your computer.

NOTE: *If you remove RAM or a peripheral card from your Mac, try to store it in a static-resistant bag. You may want to keep them around for warranty service or for storing old hardware.*

Should You Buy a New Mac?

You've probably been to someone's home or office and seen an original compact Mac still purring away in the corner, looking almost as good as new. Although it's possible to keep a Mac for many years without encountering more than the customary range of system crashes and reinstallations, sometimes you might just want to give the old computer to the kids, or donate it to your favorite charitable institution.

Here's what to consider when you're deciding if you should retire your computer:

- *Your Mac is too expensive to fix*—If you've encountered problems that are clearly hardware related, it is probably time to purchase a new machine. Although there are dealers who can supply used or reconditioned logic boards, RAM, graphics cards, and hard drives, consider the costs before you take this route.

- *Your Mac is too slow and won't run the latest software*—Do you really need to use AppleWorks 6 if ClarisWorks 5 still gets the job done? That's just one example, and it's significant. You may find that you're perfectly happy with the older version of a program and you don't want to learn new tricks. Although most older software still functions in Classic mode, if you're happy with your old computer and applications, don't let this book or the neat ads about new Macs from Apple deter you.

Looking at Extended Warranties

Whether you buy a new Mac from a local store or via phone from a mail-order house, before you complete the order, the salesperson probably will ask you to consider purchasing an extended warranty. Apple's computers, as of the time this book was written, had a one-year limited warranty on parts and labor, with just 90 days of free telephone support. If you plan to keep your new Mac for a while, the prospect of extended support might be tempting.

Consider this, though: Dealers often rely on the sale of extended warranties to shore up their profit margins, particularly in these troubled times. More often than not, a hardware failure will occur early in an electronic component's life, well within the warranty period. As with any insurance policy, you need to weigh the possible expense of an out-of-warranty repair against the certain expense of the extended warranty.

If you are using an Apple iBook or PowerBook, however, such a warranty might be a good idea. Laptop computers are potentially subject to far greater abuse than desktop computers, because they are dragged around so frequently. Having that extra protection might be worth the expense, but don't forget that no protection plan will cover the damage if you drop your PowerBook and crack the display.

WARNING! *If you opt to buy an extended warranty, double-check with the dealer to find out whether the warranty is Apple's (known as AppleCare) or comes from another company. I have seen instances where customers ordered AppleCare and got something else. When checking into such a program, compare the cost and benefits before signing on the dotted line—and look at the actual policy information. Don't just depend on what the salesperson tells you.*

Solving Hardware and Software Problems

Your worst nightmare is when your Mac crashes constantly, and you've gone through all the possible software troubleshooting you can, following the steps outlined in Chapter 18. But still your Mac misbehaves. Here are some additional choices to consider, along with cases when you might want to have the Mac's hardware serviced:

- *Chronic hard-drive errors*—Every time you check your hard drive with the First Aid component of Disk Utility or one of the commercial hard-drive programs, it comes back with reports of directory damage that needs to be fixed. Sometimes, you'll even see a message that the repairs can't be performed. Should this happen, first try restarting your Mac with a System CD or one of the CDs provided with the commercial drive repair utility. If you continue to run into problems that recur or can't be fixed, back up your data and reformat the drive. Leaving directory damage unfixed can eventually result in a loss of files or the inability of your Mac to recognize your drive.

TIP: *You should back up your important data regularly, not just in response to a report of a drive directory problem. Not all drive problems announce themselves in advance; sometimes the drive just fails.*

WARNING! *If you see a prompt on your Mac's display offering to initialize your hard drive, don't do it! This destructive act will erase the data. Although it sometimes may be possible to restore a drive with a program such as Norton Utilities or with an expensive trip to a drive recovery service, you should try other diagnostic methods before going this route.*

- *Hard drive doesn't work properly after it's reformatted*—You bit the bullet and reformatted your hard drive, but problems still occur. You continue to get reports of hard-drive directory errors, or the worst happens and the drive doesn't appear on your Computer directory in the Finder or the desktop. You should have both the drive and your Mac checked by a technician. It's possible one or the other has failed.

- *Mac makes a startup sound, but the screen is dark*—If you just installed Panther and you're using a graphics card that isn't from ATI, IX Micro, or NVIDIA, you should consult the manufacturer about Mac OS X support. You may need to restart with an Apple-approved graphics card to install updated software.

> **NOTE:** In recent years, some programmers attempted to develop Mac OS X drivers for the Voodoo graphic cards produced by the now-defunct 3dfx Interactive. But don't expect much progress. The more realistic approach is to spring for a new graphics card. Frankly, those old Voodoo cards delivered more in hype than in performance.

- *Mac with an upgrade card fails to boot*—Panther requires a Mac that shipped with built-in USB and a G3, G4 or G5 processor. If you have an older Mac and upgraded the processor or USB card, don't expect it to work or to receive support from Apple. However, you may want to check with the manufacturer of the upgrade card to see if it has a way to make it run.

> **NOTE:** Ryan Rempel's shareware utility, XPostFacto does allow many older Power Macs to run Mac OS X. The installation process isn't even all that difficult, but you are apt to encounter strange problems, particularly with sound and other basic features. If you really have no alternative, it might be worth your while, but take a little extra caution if you opt to go this route.

- *Mac fails to boot and doesn't make a startup sound*—Recheck the power cord, the power strip, and the devices attached to your Mac. If you recently installed a new peripheral card or RAM upgrade, remove each item in turn (closing the Mac each time) and see if you can get the Mac to run. If removing one fixes the problem, reinstall the item and try again. If you have a Mac older than one year, consider replacing the lithium backup battery, which, when spent, can affect the startup process. Should the problem persist, contact the manufacturer of the peripheral product for repair or replacement. If you cannot get the Mac to run, it's time for a trip to the dealer's service department.

> **NOTE:** Another potential cause of a Mac's failing to boot is a defective peripheral card, particularly the graphics card. Shut down, and then remove and reseat the video card, and see if doing so brings your Mac back to life.

- *Mac fails to boot with peripheral device attached*—The blame should be placed on the device. If it's a SCSI device, make sure it's powered on before you boot your Mac. One key test is to remove the device (after powering down); if your Mac then works, you have a good idea as to the culprit.

> **NOTE:** If your Mac has a SCSI adapter card, you should check with the manufacturer about Mac OS X support for its products. Unfortunately, a number of older SCSI cards aren't compatible with Mac OS X and, frankly, won't be. You'll need either a replacement card, or new peripheral devices that work under FireWire or USB 2.0.

• *Mac crashes constantly early in the startup process or right
after restart*—Follow the software diagnostics covered in Chapter 18. If a reinstallation of Mac OS X fails to fix the problem,
consider bad RAM as a possible culprit. Panther is more sensitive
to such ills than the Classic Mac OS. If the RAM doesn't appear to
be at fault, consider backing up and reformatting your drive. Or, if
the process seems daunting (as it truly is), have your dealer look
at your Mac and see what's going on. If you're computer is still
under warranty, this may actually be the best course.

*NOTE: Can you do your own hardware diagnostics? Possibly. MicroMat's TechTool Pro (and the
TechTool Deluxe application that comes with Apple's AppleCare service warranty) can test the
various systems on your Mac. Recent Macs come with the Apple Hardware Test CD that can be
used to perform a basic set of hardware tests. However, if you see a report of a potential
problem, let a technician make the final call. In general, some motherboard and RAM defects
would result in a Sad Mac, but sometimes they'll just result in more system crashes or the failure
to complete a startup process.*

• *You smell smoke or see a spark from your Mac*—What can I tell
you? Although laser printer toner can sometimes smell a little
smoky, if you see symptoms of this sort, don't try to use your Mac.
Unplug it immediately and move away from any flammable material. Let a dealer's service representative do a diagnostic first.

*NOTE: A slight spark could just be static electricity. If you have thick carpeting or you're in a
particularly dry climate, walking around may build up static electricity. If you touch a metal object,
you may see a slight spark.*

Related solution:	*Found on page:*
Solving Other Common Mac OS X Problems	423

Adding Wi-Fi Hardware

Installing Wi-Fi hardware should be a no-brainer. Unfortunately, Apple
has made the issue more complicated by giving its AirPort Extreme
cards a totally different form factor, which means they won't work on
Macs that do not specifically support the faster Wi-Fi standard. Here
are some basic guidelines to help you go wireless:

• *Tips for installing Apple Wi-Fi products*—You won't need to
install any software. Your Wi-Fi configuration applications are in

11. Setting Up New Hardware and Peripherals

the Utilities folder under Panther. The AirPort Admin Utility will
handle any Apple base station, and the AirPort Setup Assistant
can be used for basic configuration. When it comes to an AirPort
or AirPort Extreme card, just restarting with the card installed
should be sufficient to make Panther recognize its existence. You
can confirm this in the Network preference panel.

- *Unofficial support for third-party Wi-Fi cards*—Other makers
  offer Wi-Fi products such as PCI cards for Power Macs and PC
  cards for laptops. Before installing the maker's drivers, check to
  see that the card runs out of the box. If you don't succeed, try the
  company's own drivers; you may have to check their Web site for
  the latest driver versions.

TIP: *Another solution to your dilemma is IOXperts 802.11b driver X, a shareware product that supports dozens of third-party Wi-Fi cards, from such companies as Asante, Compaq, D-Link, HP, IBM, Linksys, Lucent, and others.*

- *Engage security*—I'll show you how to setup a secure configuration for AirPort in Chapter 12. Regardless of which type of Wi-Fi
  card or access point (the official name for a third-party base
  station) you choose, be sure to consult the documentation or
  configuration screens about turning on security. Without security,
  anyone within range can log into your network and steal Internet
  access with impunity. Even worse, they have a chance to crack
  your Mac's passwords, and possibly get your critical data. The
  more secure the encryption, the better, even if you're forced into
  a complicated password scheme, with arcane text strings.

NOTE: *Does that mean that AirPort is the best solution? For transparent setup (and there is an AirPort Admin Utility for Windows also), Apple's product is best. But the third-party access points are often cheaper, and have extra Ethernet ports and other features that might make them more suited to your needs. Don't be afraid to do careful comparisons before you choose your Wi-Fi solution.*

Installing a New Scanner

After unpacking the device, check the manual or installer card for
basic setups and follow these basic guidelines:

1. Locate the lock on the scanner. It might be identified by a
   padlock icon. Unlocking can be done with a screwdriver or just
   by turning a latch. This is critical, because you risk damaging a

scanner if you attempt to run it while the optical mechanism is locked. Some scanners, however, especially lower cost products, don't come with locking mechanisms. If in doubt, check the installation instructions.

NOTE: *If you plan to move your scanner to a new location outside your workplace, remember to lock the optical mechanism first to protect the unit. Also, not all scanners have locks. If there's no indication of one on the unit, check the setup documentation. If it's not there, you may be lucky (although only really cheap scanners seem to lack those locks).*

---

2. If another user has logged in to your Mac, you'll need to use your administrator's account. Installing anything that requires system-wide access can be done only in this fashion. If the installer requires a login, you'll see a prompt at the beginning of the installation process.

WARNING! *Before you install any software for new hardware, be sure to consult the documentation or contact the publisher about Mac OS X compatibility. Even if you bought the product long after Panther was released, don't assume the unit is compatible unless the package or the product's label provides specific information about the subject such as a "Built for Mac OS X" label. If you can't find this information, check with the publisher.*

3. Install the software. You should have a CD that shipped with the scanner. Some scanners include an integrated installation process, which handles the scanner drivers, image-editing software, and other extras. Others offer each element as a separate, clickable install. Follow the prompts about selecting installation options. Depending on the installer, you may have to restart your Mac (usually you don't).

TIP: *Be proactive about peripheral drivers. A product may be sitting around for weeks or months in a warehouse before it gets to your dealer, so don't be surprised if the software is out of date. Take a look at the maker's Web site or versiontracker.com for possible updates. Also remember that whenever Apple releases a major system upgrade, it may take a few weeks for companies to get with the program and release needed software updates.*

---

4. Connect the scanner to your Mac. If the scanner is a SCSI product, shut down your Mac and attach SCSI devices first, then restart after the hookup. For FireWire and USB, shutting down isn't necessary, because of the plug-and-play nature of these two peripheral standards.

NOTE: *If you are installing a SCSI device, make sure there are no duplicate ID numbers and that termination switches on the product are turned on or off as needed for your installation. If you're using a third-party SCSI card, verify its compatibility with Mac OS X before attempting to install devices on it.*

5. Launch your scanning software and run the scanner through its paces for scanning and processing images. If you have problems, consult the documentation (it might be on the CD) for further assistance.

NOTE: *Some scanner drivers don't work separately from a photo-editing program. So, you'll need to see if a copy of Adobe Photoshop or a similar program is on your Mac and use that program's Acquire feature to activate the scanning driver.*

Installing New Storage Devices

Depending on the sort of storage device you have, you may not need to add any extra software. Here are the basic steps to follow:

1. Consult the documentation or look for a CD to see if special software needs to be installed.

NOTE: *Mac OS X has built-in support for most popular storage devices. You should not need to install any software. So it never hurts just to hook up the device, and see if it runs. If not, move on to step 2.*

2. If software is required, make sure it's Mac OS X compatible. You will see a login prompt for your administrator's password if required for the installation.

3. Launch the installer application and follow the prompts.

4. If necessary, restart your Mac. (This step is necessary only for devices that load as part of the Mac's startup process.)

5. Connect the drive to your Mac. If you're hooking up a SCSI device, make sure that your Mac and attached SCSI devices are turned off first; you can safely restart after hookup.

NOTE: *Don't forget to check for SCSI ID and termination settings before powering up.*

6. Verify that the drive works properly. If it's a hard drive, copy files to and from it. For a removable device, insert the removable media and run it through its paces.

WARNING! *On a CD burner, it's worth trying one CD-RW disk just to be sure that you can copy data satisfactorily; the benefit of using a CD-RW disk is that you can reuse it after determining the drive is all right. You do not want to back up critical data and then find out, too late, that there was a problem reading the CD.*

Installing Digital Cameras, Palm OS Handhelds, and Other Products

The process of setting up a device that's not connected full time to your Mac is essentially the same as connecting a device that's always hooked up. Here are the steps to follow:

1. Unpack the device and check for interface plugs. If the device does not have a USB or FireWire cable, check to see if a serial cable is available. Depending on the kind of Mac you have, you might need an interface adapter, such as a serial-to-USB converter, to make it run.

2. After verifying Mac OS X compatibility, locate the installer CD and install the software. In many cases, you'll have to enter your administrator's password in the login prompt.

3. Check the device for proper operation, and then attach the unit to your Mac as instructed.

4. Consult the instructions about synching or interfacing with your Mac.

5. If the product doesn't run as expected, check manuals or the manufacturer's support Web site or telephone support line for further advice.

NOTE: *Most digital cameras work perfectly with Apple's iPhoto right out of the box. So before you actually bother with the software, see if just connecting it and putting it in playback mode is sufficient to activate iPhoto and begin the process of downloading your photos to your Mac.*

Determining What to Do If an Accessory Doesn't Work

Despite some of the concessions to mass production and competition to keep prices low, rarely will a hardware accessory product fail out of the box. Usually, when something doesn't work, you can take steps to address the problem.

Here are some items to check in case the accessory you've bought for your Mac isn't working as you expected:

- *Is the device compatible with Mac OS X?* Even if the box or documentation says it is, don't expect seamless compatibility in every case. You may need to double-check with the manufacturer to see if additional updates are required. If the box or documentation doesn't specifically address the issue, assume the product won't run unless there's built-in support under Mac OS X. Except for a limited number of products, the answer is probably no.

NOTE: Sometimes all you need is that driver update, so keep tabs on the company's Web site. Strangely enough, when I set up a brand new laser printer, I found it wouldn't print after installing the printer file (PPD) on my Mac. I later learned that the version that shipped with Panther was more current than even the one on the company's Web site. Fortunately, I had a copy on another Mac and didn't need to reinstall any system-related software to make it function.

- *Have you installed the wrong software?* New products are apt to have different installers for Mac OS X and for the Classic Mac OS. Double-check to make sure that you ran the correct installation. You might want to do it again and see.

- *Did you forget to restart?* It may or may not be necessary, but if a product won't work, this step is worth taking just to make sure the proper drivers load. In theory, restarts should rarely be required, but I don't always believe in theories.

- *Are you experiencing peripheral application crashes?* Even though the Darwin core of Mac OS X is highly robust and crash resistant, individual programs still may crash from time to time. Fortunately, protected memory means that even if an application quits, you can continue to use your Mac. Should the program continue to quit or freeze, contact the manufacturer about needed updates.

- *Is the device plugged in?* Even if the AC adapter is connected to the wall socket or a power strip, you may have to tear through a spaghetti-like maze of cables to see if everything is hooked up properly. Cables sometimes separate during spring cleaning.

NOTE: *This issue isn't as obvious as it seems. I once got a frantic call from a client who wondered why her printer had stopped working. I asked her to double-check her cables, and she assured me everything was plugged in. But when I visited her office to check, I discovered the loose printer cable lost behind a mass of similar-colored wiring that was extremely difficult to sort out. Apparently, a cleaning person had mistakenly pulled the cable from a USB hub in a futile attempt to make the wiring mess look neat.*

- *Is a cable bad or broken?* It's not always easy to see such a problem, because of the sometimes thick shielding on a cable. Try another cable, if you have one, as a test. Frayed or otherwise damaged cables should be replaced right away. Naked wires could cause a short circuit, which would fry the delicate electronic circuitry in the component.

- *Is the device faulty?* Perhaps the problem isn't your Mac or something you did. Sometimes, new products just fail out of the box or shortly after they're placed in service. That's the purpose of the new product warranty, and don't hesitate to read the fine print and find out what you need to do to get the unit repaired or replaced. Some companies will replace a product that's dead on arrival, by the way.

Chapter 12

Taking Panther on the Road

In Brief

2003 was considered the year of the laptop, at least according to Apple. Sure enough, sales of its iBooks and PowerBooks soared nearly to the level of its desktop Macs. The driving force behind this growth in mobile computing is Wi-Fi (short for Wireless Fidelity), the ability to connect up to the Internet and Web without needing wires and cables. Apple's AirPort technology was the first popular implementation of this feature, and it has really opened up doors for Mac users who need to connect to the Internet while they are on the road.

With mobile computing you can join your fellow road warriors and sit on the beach and finish that business proposal, or write your great American novel while on a Caribbean cruise. Apple Computer even ships its latest iBooks and PowerBooks with DVD drives, so you can catch your favorite flick on that cross-country or cross-continent flight and not have to depend on the often-mediocre fare the airline selects for you.

With the arrival of Panther, Apple Computer has made your portable computing experience even more pleasant, with clever touches that will make your iBook or PowerBook run faster and more efficiently.

Exploring Panther Tools for Laptops

Laptop computers nowadays are extremely powerful, in many respects on par with desktop computers. A notable example is the striking 17-inch PowerBook G4, which offers a brilliant LCD display and enough power (for many Mac users) to actually replace the big, bulky desktop versions. In addition, using the built-in peripheral ports, you can easily attach a regular keyboard and mouse and, on recent iBooks and the PowerBook, an external display, and put aside your desktop computer. If you need to take your work on the road, disconnect the laptop, pack it in a case, and you're ready to roll.

NOTE: *Recent PowerBook G4's also include a DVI port for a digital flat panel display. With an external adapter, they can also support Apple's own line of monitors, including the 23-inch Apple HD Cinema Display.*

Superior Power Management

Year after year, as computer processors get more powerful, they also require less power. Today's iBook and PowerBook can crunch numbers with the best of them, yet the low power requirements of their microprocessors and Panther's power-management features allow you to maximize the amount of time your computer can run without requiring a battery recharge or a nearby AC outlet.

Laptop as Desktop Replacement

The arrival of the 15-inch and 17-inch PowerBooks has made using a laptop as a genuine replacement for a desktop computer far more compelling. That way you don't have to worry about synchronizing files or just adjusting your mindset to a different system. The advantages of the latest PowerBooks include speedy processors and reasonably fast hard drives with plenty of capacity to store your stuff. In fact, even movie studios use the big PowerBooks to handle such location chores as sound mixing.

NOTE: *I am not overlooking the iBook, which now ships with a G4 processor. The 14-inch models are indeed suitable as desktop replacements, too. However, the PowerBooks have faster networking, higher memory capacities, speedier subsystems, and more expansion ports for peripheral devices.*

The desktop replacement solution introduces both positives and negatives as listed here:

- **Cost:** Although the cost of the laptop is higher, not having to buy two computers can offer you real savings.

- **Convenience:** You don't have to get files in sync between two or more computers, and your desktop and system organization only has to be setup once.

- **Space savings:** When you're finished working on your PowerBook, simply close the cover and pop it into a drawer. This is a great way to keep a neat desk.

NOTE: *I'm not overlooking the fact that many Mac users keep a separate monitor, keyboard, and mouse at their home or office to attach to the PowerBook, so using the laptop is not always a space saver.*

- **Reliability:** Even though a well-designed laptop is designed for a higher level of abuse than a desktop, problems do arise. You should really consider getting an extended warranty in case something goes wrong.

- **Hard drive performance:** The hard drives in an Apple laptop can hold almost as much data as the ones in desktop systems, but they are usually slower. If you perform disk intensive work, such as image and video editing, you may want to consider carefully whether this approach will suit your needs.

- **Theft magnets:** The road warrior has to always be on the alert for thieves. Someone bumps into you at an airport, and, while you put yourself together, that person's accomplice grabs your PowerBook before you have a chance to stop it. At the very least, you'll want to consider getting a special rider on your insurance policy to cover the loss of a laptop computer. Also make sure that you are diligent about making a backup at your home or office in case you lose or damage your laptop.

AirPort and the Wireless Revolution

More and more retailers, including McDonald's and Starbucks, are providing Wi-Fi "Hot Spots," places where you can sit, enjoy coffee and a burger, and stay connected. Although Wi-Fi access has become an important force in the PC industry and is available for both Macs and Windows PCs, there are a few security issues you should know about before you get hooked on this terrific feature. I'll let you know more in the Immediate Solutions section.

Apple didn't invent Wi-Fi, but it was the first computer company to make it popular, and the Windows platform quickly picked up on the trend. Today, there are dozens and dozens of Wi-Fi compatible products consisting of the access point, or base station, which beams the signal into the airwaves, and receivers, as exemplified by Apple's AirPort and AirPort Extreme products.

Wi-Fi is based on several industry standards, the most popular of which is 802.11b. This standard is rated at up to 11 megabits per second throughput. The newer 802.11g standard is backwards compatible with the older standard, but capable of speeds of up to 55 megabits per second with compatible devices.

NOTE: The real world speeds of Wi-Fi, which indicates how fast you can actually share files, is usually less than half the top rated speed. The rest is, roughly speaking, network overhead. Also, as the distance between the base station and your Mac increases, your system will default to lower connection speeds to maintain reliability.

Because Wi-Fi is a cross-platform standard, numerous third-party Wi-Fi cards are available that can work on both Macs and PCs. However,

Apple's AirPort cards, which support 802.11b, and AirPort Extreme, which supports that standard and 802.11g, work only in the proprietary slots on specific Apple computers. Apple's AirPort and AirPort Extreme base stations beam signals to any personal computer with a compatible receiver.

NOTE: I should also point out that you need the right software drivers to make a third-party Wi-Fi adapter function on your Mac. If you are trying to upgrade an older Mac, or seeking a solution less expensive than Apple's offerings, you should make sure software is available; otherwise, you'll be stuck. Fortunately, the major manufacturers of networking products, such as Asante, do have pretty good support for the Mac platform.

Automatic Location Configuration

One of the neat things about Panther is the fact that it is multihoming, and can automatically adjust to the fastest available network. This means that when you connect to an Ethernet network, your Mac will sense it, and when you move to a Wi-Fi system, it will configure itself for Wi-Fi without missing a beat.

As I'll explain in Chapter 8, you can even store separate Location setups for each place you visit. If you require custom network access or a dial-up setting, you can move to a different location by simply clicking on Location from the Apple menu and choosing the proper connection scheme from a sub-menu.

Integrated Keyboard and Mouse Preference Panel

When you launch the System Preferences application and click the Keyboard & Mouse settings pane (see Figure 12.1), you'll be able to adjust trackpad speed and double-click speed directly. This feature is identical to the desktop version, except the Mouse button is relabeled Trackpad and incorporates a few extra settings.

NOTE: Our test Apple laptop, a 17-inch PowerBook G4, had a built-in Bluetooth wireless module, which is why it has a Bluetooth option in the preference panel. If you don't have Bluetooth hardware installed, you won't see it. No sense letting an unusable feature go to waste!

Superfast Sleep and Awake Features

When you put your PowerBook to sleep in the old days (before Mac OS X) your Mac would take a few seconds to do its disk drive and

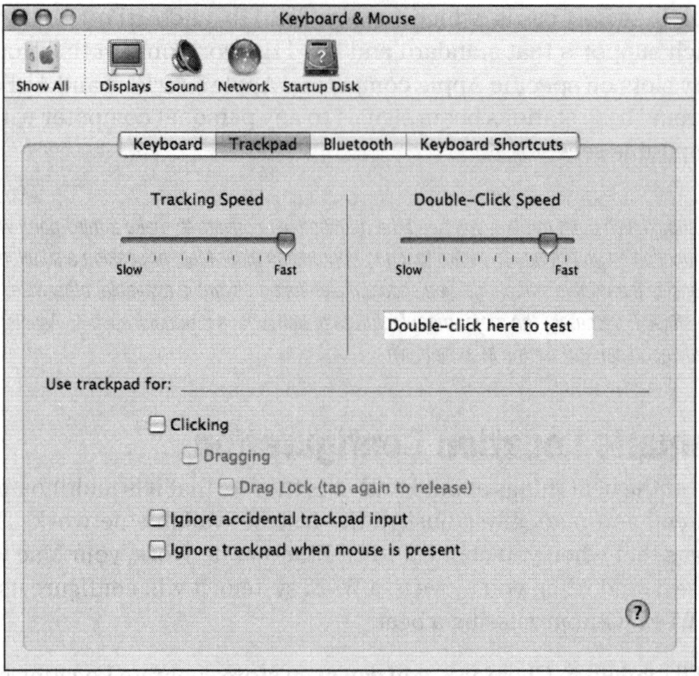

Figure 12.1   This settings pane handles trackpad adjustments for your Apple laptop.

network housecleaning chores before going into idle mode. The reverse process could take even longer; it might take up to a minute for your Mac to return to normal operating mode after being brought back to life.

NOTE: *The process of awakening from sleep mode is quicker for Mac OS 9 and later, but it's still not as fast as in Mac OS X.*

If you're new to Mac OS X, you'll be pleased to find both processes ultra-efficient and super-quick. Just choose Sleep from the Apple menu, and your iBook or PowerBook will close almost immediately. Best of all, you can bring it back to life almost instantaneously by pressing any key on the keyboard or, with most models (check your documentation to be sure), opening the case. It almost seems as if it was never placed in sleep mode to begin with. This side effect can help speed your passage through airport security when they ask to see the computer's desktop to confirm it's really a laptop.

NOTE: *If this seems a bit much, consider that airport security is far more stringent in the post 9/11 era. Most security check-ins I've visited require that you put your laptop computer into the scanning device separately, and many of the guards insist that you pop them up and prove they are actually computers and not some sort of secret weapon.*

Editing Vacation Videos on the Road

If your iBook or PowerBook has FireWire capability (and all but the oldest supported models do), you'll be able to edit videos of the family vacation or presentation on the road, using Apple's iMovie software (see Figure 12.2) or any video-editing tool you prefer.

NOTE: *It's not just videos. When the sound editors for the last Star Wars movie, Attack of the Clones, wanted to capture sound at remote locales, they used a PowerBook G4 running Panther.*

After you have shot your videos, you can easily copy them to your iBook's or PowerBook's hard drive and then edit the footage the way you like, adding special effects and sound effects. Then, after the movie has been prepared, you can save it in a variety of formats, including QuickTime, which allows for easy online distribution.

12. Taking Panther on the Road

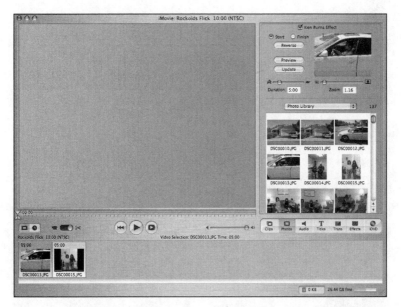

Figure 12.2   iMovie is the flexible yet super-simple desktop video-editing software that's included with Panther.

In addition to making and editing videos, you can also use programs such as AppleWorks 6 and Keynote to make slide shows. After you're finished, you can attach your Apple laptop to a TV or projector and use it for a portable presentation.

TIP: Apple iBooks equipped with FireWire have an AV output port that you can use to attach these cute laptops to a regular TV with composite video or camcorder ports. The PowerBook's output capabilities include S-video.

NOTE: Because video fills a large amount of drive storage space, consider bringing an extra drive with you if you intend to capture a large video. Remember that USB-based drives can be very slow and absolutely unsuitable except for lower-resolution video capture and playback. (If you have a newer Apple laptop supporting the much speedier USB 2.0 you don't need to be concerned about this.) FireWire drives in almost all cases are fast enough for good video speed.

Immediate Solutions

Computing on the Road

If Apple's dream is realized in the next few years, most computers will be mobile devices, designed to work efficiently on the road, yet ready to plug into a desktop docking system at a moment's notice. Apple flirted with this sort of setup some years back with the Duo system, but the product never caught on as expected. In the meantime, you can enjoy a flexible Mac computing experience with the iBook, the PowerBook, and, of course, Panther.

An Apple laptop comes complete with all the ingredients for performing the computing tasks you need when you're not at your home or office. The latest models include a built-in modem and Ethernet networking ports, and most models have a reasonable array of expansion ports so you can add extra devices to fill the gaps.

NOTE: *Remember the expansion bay that used to lurk inside PowerBooks? Why must Apple laptops make do with less expansion? In the drive to make them ultra thin, a few compromises were necessary, so you are left with an appendage if you want to connect an additional drive, even if it's the cool little iPod, which does double duty as a FireWire hard drive.*

Before you take your iBook or PowerBook on a trip, however, you'll want to be prepared for the worst and for the most effective computing experience, whether you're visiting someone's home, staying in a hotel, or camping out. With a little advance preparation, you can get the most value from your Mac computing experience regardless of your destination.

Setting Up Secure Wi-Fi Access

I'd like to say that Wi-Fi is a free ride. Hook up your network, and ditch the wires. But it's not that easy. You must consider security issues involved and you'll need to take precautions; otherwise, you might make yourself vulnerable for a new category of Internet mischief called "war driving."

Those words mean precisely what they imply. Net vandals drive around from neighborhood to neighborhood and from business to business looking for unsecured Wi-Fi access points. Then they simply connect and access the network, freely, stealing your Internet access and, sometimes, if the protections on your computer aren't sufficient, your files too.

Fortunately, you can apply a few simple methods to get around this, including password-protecting your computer. For this chapter, I'll focus on Apple's own AirPort management tools, but all other Wi-Fi components offer various security levels and techniques, so you'll want to check out the documentation for guidance on what to do.

If you are, for example, using an Apple AirPort Extreme base station, you'll want to use the AirPort Admin Utility (in the Utilities of course), to put the dead bolt locks on your system.

Here's what to do:

1. Launch the AirPort Admin Utility (see Figure 12.3). If everything is working properly, your base station's network name and default IP address will appear.

2. Double-click on the network name, or select and choose Configure from the program's toolbar. You'll see a status or Summary screen showing your AirPort system's present configuration, including your ISP's address.

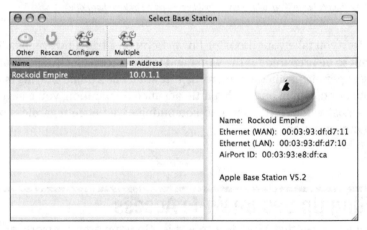

Figure 12.3   The default IP is always the same unless you change it (and that won't hurt your security).

NOTE: *If you've previously set an access password, you'll see a password prompt (unless it's already stored in the Keychain).*

3. Click Name and Password, which brings up a screen where you can make several settings to enhance security.

4. If you want to adjust your Base Station Name, enter it in the text field.

5. To add or alter your password, click the Change password button and enter a "strong" password, one consisting of mixed upper and lower case letters and numbers. You'll have to repeat the password before clicking OK.

NOTE: *Be careful about typing your password the second time because you will only see dots on the screen to represent the characters you're typing. You will also want to write down the password and put it in a safe place because you won't be able to access your base station or network without it. If you lose the password, you'll have to reset your base station to factory default (as explained in the unit's documentation).*

6. This takes us to the most important part of your setup, and that is the level of security. Click Change Wireless Security to bring up a setup screen where you can make your choices (see Figure 12.4). The choices are as follows:

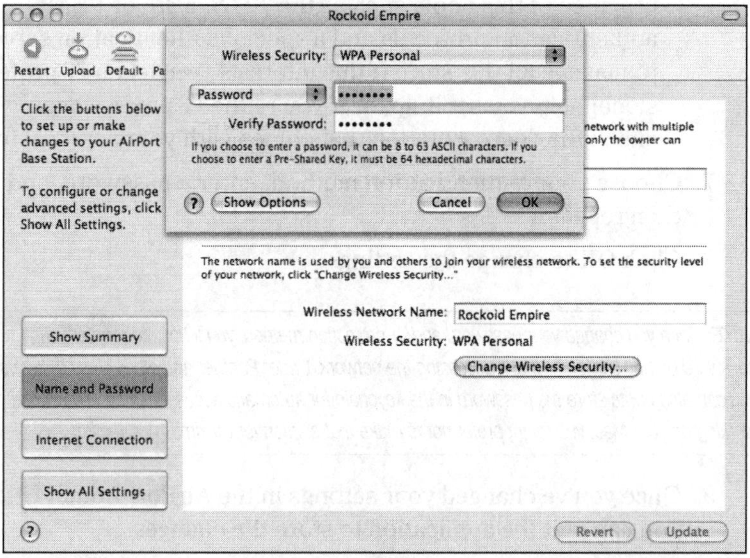

Figure 12.4 Use the Change Wireless Security window to change your Wi-Fi security levels.

- *40-bit WEP*—Apple's AirPort system offers two levels of Wireless Equivalent Protection (WEP) security. The lower level of encryption is fairly secure, but an experienced hacker can break through, so I'd only recommend this one if any of the Wi-Fi devices on your system do not support the more robust encryption methods.

NOTE: If you have an original edition AirPort card and base station, or an older third-party product, this may be the best you can get. My best suggestion is that you either upgrade your Wi-Fi apparatus or limit file sharing on your Macs to the times you actually need to exchange files, to make it harder for outsiders to invade your system.

- *128-bit WEP*—If you have equipment that supports this technique, this is a far more secure setup. However, make sure that all your Wi-Fi network cards can also support 128-bit WEB; otherwise, you won't be able to login.

- *WPA Personal*—For those with the latest AirPort Extreme equipment and compatible third-party cards, the WPA modes encrypt your passwords via the Temporal Key Integrity Protocol (TKIP) method, which is said to be far more immune to drive-by hackers.

- *WPA Enterprise*—This mode is the province of a larger network, and requires a lot of extras that are a little out of the province of this book, such as the TTLS, LEA, or PEAP authentication protocols and a special authentication server to manage all this stuff. If this interests you, let an IT professional help you set it up, or if you're the IT professional, check the documentation that comes with your server setup.

7. Choose your authentication method, enter a password, and then repeat it.

8. Click OK to change the settings.

NOTE: Once you change your password and/or protection method, you'll have to reenter your password on any computer that's accessing the network. Under Panther and other Mac OS X versions, you can also opt to store the password in the keychain for automatic access, but if you have others working on your Mac, you might prefer not to make that section for maximum protection.

9. Once you've changed your settings in the AirPort Admin Utility, you can quit the application to store the changes.

TIP: Whenever you make such a fundamental change as improving security on your AirPort or AirPort Extreme Base Station, it's a good idea to restart the unit to make sure previous settings are removed from memory. You'll find a Restart button at the top left of the toolbar of the Show Summary page of the AirPort Admin Utility. Once you click Restart, expect it to take a minute or two for your base station to restart and become fully active. Be sure to warn other users in your network before making any such changes.

Checking Battery Life

With older versions of the Mac OS, you could check the state of your laptop's battery courtesy of a Control Strip module or an optional icon on the menu bar clock. For Panther, Apple's new solution is a menu bar status display.

Where is it? You can enable this feature (if it doesn't already appear by default) in the Energy Saver preference panel (see Figure 12.5).

Once you check the Show Battery Status In Menu Bar item, you'll see a graphical display of estimated battery life. You can use it to keep tabs on how much juice your battery has left.

12. Taking Panther on the Road

Getting the Maximum Amount of Battery Life

Whatever you do, your iBook or PowerBook won't run forever before the battery is spent. If you have an AC outlet and your power supply nearby, this may be a minor inconvenience at most. But if you're in a plane or power is otherwise unavailable, you'll want to stretch your battery as far as you can.

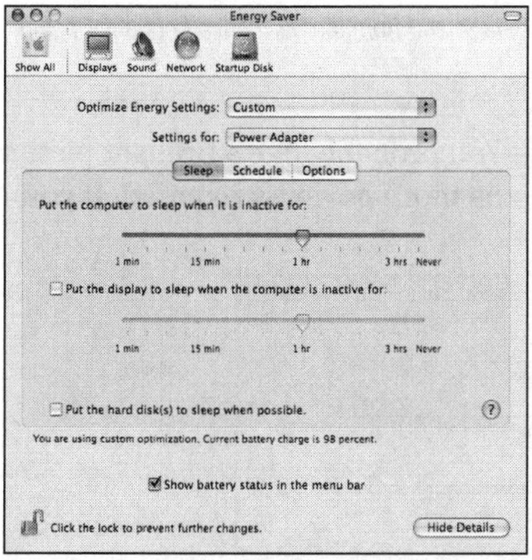

Figure 12.5   Activate the battery status display from this settings panel, which is collapsed unless you click Show details.

Here are some suggestions to get the most from your Apple laptop's battery power:

- *Let it sleep*—When you're not using your laptop, let it drift into sleep mode. Mac OS X will bring it to life in just a second when you're ready to use it again. While in sleep mode, all your applications remain open with your settings intact. Only your online or network connections will be deactivated.

WARNING! *Sleep mode doesn't last forever if you're not near AC current. Over time, possibly a week or two, or maybe a bit more, battery power will be spent and when you fire up your Apple laptop, you'll have to recharge the battery. So it's worthwhile hooking up your baby to its power adapter from time to time during a long period of sleep, or just turn it off altogether if you're not going to use it for a while.*

- *Use the Energy Saver preference panel*—Launch System Preferences and open Energy Saver. Choose Automatic to let it sort it out for itself, or just click the Show Details button to see the entire display (see Figure 12.6). You'll be able to adjust the intervals for system, display, and hard drive sleep. Because the hard drive can use a lot of extra juice, letting it go to sleep after a brief period of inactivity might conserve battery life far beyond the normal level. If you want to sacrifice a little power, click Options (see Figure 12.7), and click on the Processor Performance pop-up menu. The Automatic mode will cut processor power slightly on supported models when the battery is in use. But you can choose your performance option manually if you prefer.

NOTE: *Some applications cause a lot of hard-drive activity when running, so a sleep setting won't save battery life. In addition, if your laptop doesn't have a large amount of RAM, Panther's advanced virtual memory feature will swap data to and from the hard drive frequently, again limiting the effectiveness of this setting.*

- *Turn down the brightness*—You probably like a brilliant picture, but the brighter the setting, the more power is required. If you

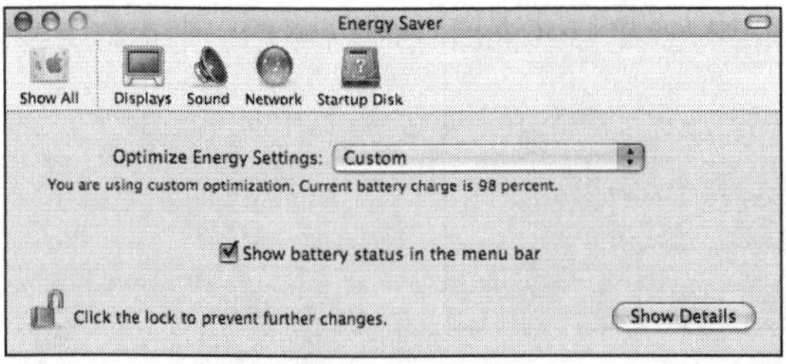

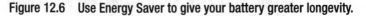

Figure 12.6 Use Energy Saver to give your battery greater longevity.

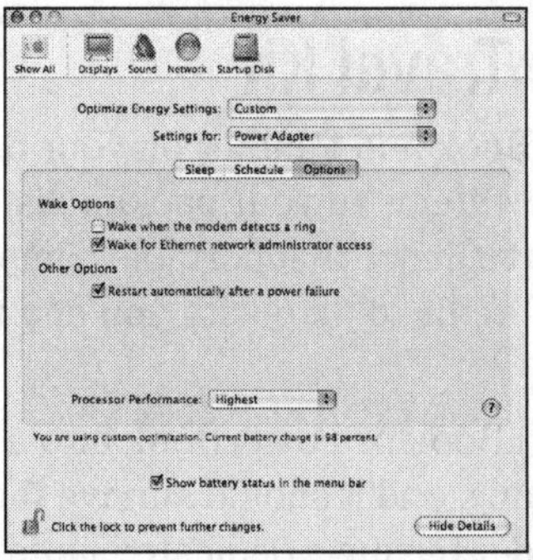

Figure 12.7 The Options panel has addition choices to optimize battery performance.

can reduce brightness and not suffer too much from the dimmer screen, you might buy some extra time from your battery power.

- *Don't use the modem*—If you don't have to surf, your iBook or PowerBook won't need to draw as much current from the battery. Hence, you'll get longer life.

- *Remove expansion bay devices*—If you have a PowerBook G3, remember that these devices are powered by your computer's battery and thus will reduce battery life. Just remember, if it's a storage device, you need to eject the disk icon first by dragging it to the trash before you disconnect the device itself.

- *Remove FireWire and USB devices*—Some FireWire devices, including Apple's ultra-cool iPod jukebox player, draw current from your Apple laptop to run. Others, such as USB devices, just get trickle current. Regardless, unplug these devices if you don't need them and want to get maximum battery life.

- *Avoid PC Cards*—Don't use a PC Card expansion module if you can help it, because it will require additional juice. Obviously this is not an issue with the iBook—no PC card slot!

- *Use headphones for audio*—Headphones draw less power, and you can turn the volume lower and save on precious battery life. The side benefit is that bystanders won't be annoyed if your sound, game, or musical preferences differ from theirs.

- *Forget the DVD*—If you have a model with a DVD player that's supported under Mac OS X, it's nice to be able to watch your favorite flick on the road, but doing so can sharply reduce battery life. It's a trade-off, but you might find the entertainment value to be worth the sacrifice.

Creating an Apple Laptop Travel Kit

When you take your iBook or PowerBook and Panther on your next trip, you should consider adding a few items to your packing list so you can get the maximum level of convenience that portable computing has to offer. Here's a short list of items to take with you and the preparations to make:

- *Traveling bag*—You can pack your iBook or PowerBook into a suitcase, well cushioned with clothing, and it should survive the trip just fine. But you should consider buying a dedicated laptop travel bag. Such products usually have extra pouches and specially insulated storage compartments for removable media, extra drives, batteries, cables, software, and other items you might need for your work. There's also usually a shoulder strap in case the entire package gets a little heavy for you. When buying such a bag, consider a product that has a well-cushioned area to protect your laptop from the rigors of such things as airline turbulence and driving on rocky terrain in a sport utility vehicle.

WARNING! *Some older laptop cases aren't large enough to contain the first-generation or clamshell iBooks or PowerBook G4s comfortably (especially the 17-inch version). Although the new Apple laptops tend to be lighter than many older models, they may be physically wider or deeper. I ran into this problem when trying to fit an original iBook into my favorite carrying case, although my 17-inch PowerBook G4 fit just perfectly (with not an inch to spare).*

- *Protection from the elements*—As rugged as laptops are in normal use, if you're going to be outside in a damp environment or you're at sea, make sure your computer is well protected. Check with your dealer about getting a case that can protect your laptop, particularly in a damp environment. You might want to check into some moisture-absorbing gel packs, like the ones that sometimes ship with consumer electronics, as they can help keep your computer dry in humid climates.

NOTE: *This may seem at odds with a book about Panther and Apple computers, but if you do travel to extreme environments, you may want to consider a notebook computer that's designed to withstand the elements. Called* ruggedized *notebooks, such products as the Itronix GoBook (a Windows-based notebook that can cost upward of five grand) and similar notebooks from such makers as Panasonic, are designed to withstand treatment that would cause any normal notebook computer to break or at least fail to run.*

WARNING! *Don't expect your iBook or PowerBook to run perfectly on your favorite ski slope or in the midst of a blizzard. According to Apple's spec sheets, the normal operating temperature is 50 to 95 degrees Fahrenheit. If you bring your laptop in from the cold, be sure to give it enough time to warm up before you use it.*

- *Backups for key files*—You plan to get some work done on the road, but your laptop's hard drive fails. Although these little computers are built to survive a reasonable amount of abuse, the fact is that storage devices fail at unexpected moments. It's easy for a repair shop to replace the drive, but recovering data from a defective drive can be costly, with no guarantee of total success. In addition to taking backup media for your most important files, you may want to include a copy of your laptop's system installer and restore disks in case you have to replace everything on a new hard drive.

TIP: *You might also want to take with you a backup for your home or office system. That way, should something happen at either location during your trip, you'll still be able to get up and running again upon your return.*

NOTE: *Having a hard drive fail on a notebook computer isn't as unusual as you might think. Just before I left to attend the Macworld Expo in San Francisco back in January 2001, the drive on my nearly new iBook Special Edition began to make a frightening clicking sound and quickly failed. Fortunately, I made a CD of the files I needed to continue working, and I was able to borrow another laptop from a colleague and continue working with minimal delay.*

- *Extra storage devices*—Whether your Apple laptop has a built-in expansion bay port or not, plenty of convenient storage devices are small enough to pack in a PowerBook case. A number of external FireWire and USB storage devices, from such companies as Iomega, LaCie, and SmartDisk, are *bus powered* (meaning they are powered by your Mac's ports). As a result, you don't have to deal with power bricks and finding extra AC outlets in your hotel room. If you can put up with the little appendage, you can even use these devices during airline travel.

TIP: *If you have an iPod, you can also use its built-in FireWire drive for backups.*

- *Diagnostic or repair CDs*—In addition to a Mac OS system disk, you might want to bring along an emergency CD for such programs as Alsoft's DiskWarrior, Symantec's Norton Utilities, or MicroMat's TechTool Pro or Drive 10. These programs offer an extra measure of protection against drive directory problems and, in the case of TechTool Pro, potential hardware issues.

WARNING! *Some disk diagnostic programs won't work properly under Panther, but they will function properly when you boot under Mac OS 9.1 or later, assuming you have an Apple laptop that can still boot under the older OS. Before using any of these programs to diagnose a possible disk-related problem, check the compatibility information from the publisher.*

- *Extra input devices*—Not everyone loves the feel of a laptop's keyboard; I have been hot and cold about the PowerBook G4 (the 17-inch model has a more solid keyboard, and feels much better), although the iBook seems nice for my purposes. Such a keyboard might be fine for occasional use, but if you have to pound a keyboard or do lots of mousing around during your trip, you might want to pack a full-sized keyboard and mouse in your carrying bag. If you're into computer games, or the kids are part of the trip, consider buying a trackball or joystick, both of which are recommended for superior computer gaming.

- *Patch cables*—Need to hook up to a network, a phone jack, or an external drive or scanner? Don't forget to bring the proper cables, along with your laptop's AC power supply. Even if you're not 100-percent certain you'll need a specific cable setup for a specific purpose, having an extra cable isn't likely to weigh down your carrying bag much.

TIP: *Don't assume that the phone in your hotel room is in a convenient location. It might be next to the bed, but you want to work on a table. It's a good idea to get a long telephone cable for just this purpose. Another good addition to your packing list is an Ethernet crossover cable, in case you need a direct connection (without a hub or switch present) to another Mac, network printer, or cable/DSL modem.*

- *Consider a wireless connection*—Apple makes it possible to network or explore the Internet with the iBook and recent PowerBooks without a direct connection cable using its AirPort wireless networking system. You can install the AirPort or AirPort Extreme module in your laptop and attach a base station to a phone. Then, you can stay connected for a distance of up to 150 feet (sometimes more). You can lounge on a patio or a beach, and surf the Net with your Apple laptop without having to run a long cable.

- *Special connection cables*—For trips overseas or when you are staying in a hotel or other locale where a convenient modem data port isn't available, you'll have to be creative to find a way to get connected. One useful resource is a company called TeleAdapt (**www.teleadapt.com**), which makes connection cables and power adapters for a variety of installations around the world. You'll be able to cope with foreign power connections, portable power supplies, and various forms of telephone hookups with the right connection kit. Although nothing is perfect, if you need to stay in touch, this is an option to consider.

- *Portable printer*—The major manufacturers of ink jet printers, such as Canon, Epson, and HP, all have smaller models that are designed for travel. What they lack in terms of print quality and speed is more than made up for in size and convenience.

TIP: My personal favorite right now is the Canon i70. It's twice as expensive as a comparable desktop printer, but it weighs maybe two pounds and matches its big brothers page for page in terms of print quality and output speed. I seldom leave home without one.

- *Insurance*—Laptop computers are theft magnets. The convenient carrying handle of the first-generation "clamshell" iBook, for example, may tempt you to just carry it in your hand and leave the rest of the accessories in your suitcase or laptop accessory bag. But it can also attract thieves who'd love to separate you from your computer. Be wary of tight crowds at the airport and deliberate distractions—especially in light of the increased security since the September 11, 2001 terrorist attacks—and definitely don't put down your computer, even for a moment. Professional thieves know all the tricks. The best preparation you can consider, however, is simply to get a good insurance policy so you can replace the computer in case the worst happens. A number of major insurance companies offer computer coverage, including units taken on the road, as part of homeowner's and small-business policies.

TIP: If your insurance agent can't cover your computers, consider Safeware (see **www.safeware.com**). It has been in business for years, it's listed favorably with the Better Business Bureau, and many PC and Mac laptop owners swear by it. Remember, however, that insurance will cover only the cost of replacement hardware and software, but not your data. So have a backup ready in another location (at home or a bank vault, or both) if something goes wrong.

- *Airport X-rays*—Through the years, I've dutifully put my iBooks and PowerBooks under the airport security X-ray machines and haven't suffered any losses of data or computing power. Just let them do their job; the enhanced security at airports often requires a personal inspection of your computer. Just remember to put your laptop in sleep mode rather than shut it down, to speed up the inspection process. The security personnel primarily want to see the computer's desktop display so they know it's really a computer. Imagine their surprise when they see how quickly Mac OS X starts up.

- *Games for the kids*—If you are taking your clan on a long trip, you may want to bring along some of their favorite computer games for relaxation. Games can keep them from getting into your hair, plus they can help you get the most value out of your iBook or PowerBook. The latest generations of both products are, in fact, decent game machines, with fairly good performance on high-action 3D games.

TIP: If games are your "bag," or your children are picky, consider that present-day iBooks and PowerBooks have ATI or NVIDIA graphics chips that deliver superior 3D graphics and improved frame rates for more fluid gameplay.

Related solution:	Found on page:
The No-Frills Daily Backup Plan	379
MicroMat's TechTool Pro	383

Getting the Most Efficient Online Performance

Today, it's getting increasingly difficult to stay away from your email, unless you can afford to let the mail sit unopened until your return. Fortunately, if you must keep up with the messages, there are ways to stay in touch even if your ISP isn't available in the area you're visiting.

Here are some considerations to help you track your email in the event you need to surf the Net:

- *Check your ISP's access*—Such services as AOL, its sister service CompuServe, EarthLink (Apple's recommended ISP), and other large services have access numbers in many major cities around the world. Before leaving, you should retrieve and print out a listing of the phone numbers in the cities you plan to visit. If your itinerary changes along the way, you can usually go online and look for additional numbers. If you're using a local service, however, you may have to consider other options. One possible solution is the EarthLink Mobile Broadband service, which uses a special high-performance wireless model to deliver speeds of up to 128KBps. Many services, such as AOL and EarthLink, also offer Web-based email options to retrieve your messages, or you can sign up for a free email account from such services as Microsoft's Hotmail or Yahoo. That way, if you can get online from, say, a public library, you can still retrieve your email. If you intend to travel to an out-of-the-way locale without convenient online access, check with the hotel or airline or travel agent for suggestions. On the other hand, it was once possible to survive on a trip without cellular telephones or email, so you may find that you can live without the luxury.

TIP: *You may want to check whether your hotel offers high-speed Internet access. Some hotels offer DSL or Wi-Fi access for a daily surcharge in some rooms, but you must make sure you reserve a room that's prewired for the Internet. Although you may have to redo your ISP settings (usually outgoing, rather than incoming mail), this is a way to speed up your on-the-road computing experience and have more time for rest and relaxation. The hotel should have an instruction booklet from the broadband ISP about how to access its services and your existing email.*

- *Send messages to yourself for backup*—If you plan to get some work done on the road, consider sending copies of your documents via email so you can retrieve them at your home or office. That way, if something happens to your laptop during the trip, you'll still be able to get the files when you return.

NOTE: *Some ISPs have strict limits on the size of file attachments you can send with your messages. For AOL, it's 2MB outside the service and 16MB within the service. Other online services limit the size to 5MB or 10MB. If you need to handle larger files, consider compressing them, or bring along extra disks and a removable device for storage. Another possibility is to subscribe to Apple's .Mac service, which includes 100MB of storage space on your personal iDisk. Since you can password protect your iDisk, this may be an ideal spot for sending big files, so you don't overwhelm your ISP's limited storage space.*

- *Use a fax machine for a printer*—You can use your computer's fax modem to print a document by sending a fax to yourself. If you're using the hotel's fax machine, check the hotel's fees beforehand, because some charge several dollars per page. Or, perhaps you can find a local business or travel office that will lend a hand. Another way to get printed pages is to visit a print shop that can provide output for your files.

TIP: *Some upscale business-oriented hotels even place fax machines in some rooms, but check the price list to see if there's a daily or per-page charge. You may also find a small business center at the hotel, where you can plug in your iBook or PowerBook to a networked printer. Again you'll want to know the costs of this service before outputting those pages.*

Using FireWire Target Disk Mode

Once you return to your home or office, or you need to set up shop at another office, you'll be pleased to know that FireWire-equipped iBooks and PowerBooks offer a speedy way to retrieve files without having to concern yourself with a new network setting. The feature is called FireWire Target Disk Mode. Here's how to set it up:

TIP: *Target Disk Mode isn't reserved for late-model Apple laptops. The feature is also available on any PowerMac G4 with AGP graphics, the PowerMac Cube, and slot-load iMacs with FireWire ports.*

---

1. Shut down your Apple laptop.

WARNING! *Target Disk Mode is best used while your iBook or PowerBook is connected to AC current. Running out of juice during a copy operation may result in missing or damaged files.*

---

2. Take a regular FireWire cable and attach your iBook or PowerBook to the host computer (which can be a desktop Mac or another Apple laptop).

NOTE: *Because FireWire is a hot-pluggable technology, it's not necessary to turn off the other computer when you make the connection.*

---

3. Boot your Apple laptop and hold down the T key. Keep pressing the key until you see a FireWire icon on the laptop's display. Wait a few seconds, and the laptop's drive icon should show up as another FireWire device on the host computer.

4. When you're finished transferring files, you can remove or dismount the drive icon from the desktop by selecting it and pressing Command+E or by choosing Eject from the Finder's File menu.

Mac OS X-Savvy Applications

In Brief

Panther introduces many clever interface elements and features that can provide a more productive, enjoyable, and reliable computing experience. But to be able to use those features, you have to run software that is specifically compiled to run under Mac OS X.

Let's take a fast history lesson: Back in 1994 (has it really been that long?), Apple moved to PowerPC processors from the 680x0 processor family. An emulation mode let you run older software at reduced speed, but it took months and in some cases a few years for most Mac software companies to move their products over to the new architecture. Some applications never made the switch, but emulation was there to fill the gap.

The Two Forms of Mac OS X Applications

When Apple announced their original iteration of Mac OS X (it was then known as *Rhapsody*), the company, believe it or not, actually expected software publishers to totally rewrite their products in a new compatible programming language. This requirement, of course, fell on deaf ears to the major companies that didn't want to invest years and millions of dollars in the effort to rewrite tens of millions of lines of computer code (over 30 million in Microsoft Office alone). Thus, Apple had to go back to the drawing board.

Its answer was a smart mix of the old and the new—the Rosetta Stone that enabled Mac OS X to become a credible alternative. Here are the components that helped make this a reality:

- *Carbon*—This is Apple's trump card. Carbon is a special set of application programming interfaces (APIs) that can be used to modify an existing Mac program and make it support all or most of the features of Mac OS X. Rather than having to rebuild the program from scratch, only 10 to 20 percent (on average) of the program's code must be updated to support the updated system architecture. Even better, most of these same applications can run normally on Macs equipped with Mac OS 8.6 through the various versions of Mac OS 9, by virtue of a system extension called *CarbonLib*. Depending on the program, the update could take days or months, so check with specific publishers about their plans.

NOTE: *Unfortunately, not all Carbon applications are designed to also run in a Classic Mac OS. Adobe's CS graphic suite, Microsoft Office v. X, QuarkXPress 6, and AOL for Mac OS X are examples of such applications because they run strictly under Mac OS X. This has become a growing trend because it allows software publishers to optimize performance and not make compromises to support two operating systems.*

- *Cocoa*—A native Mac OS X application can also be developed using either Sun Microsystems' Java programming language or the one descended from the original NeXT-based Objective C. These programs will yield full support for all the core features of Mac OS X, but they won't run under the regular Mac OS. For new programs, it's a lot faster to build a program from scratch this way, but this isn't the best alternative for existing publishers that have to rewrite up to millions of lines of code. It's also not a good solution if you want to reuse your program code for a Windows version of your software.

The best thing about the way Mac OS X is set up is that you don't have to concern yourself with the choices publishers make to achieve product compatibility with Mac OS X. You can just install and use the program and take advantage of the features and improved performance and reliability.

Key Mac OS X Software Profiles and Previews

As of the time this book went to press, nearly 7,000 Mac OS X applications were available. Some were out, and others were promises of what was to come. Virtually every major Mac application is available in a version that runs native in Panther, and most of the remaining stragglers are moving in that direction on a fast track, or a fast run, depending on your point of view.

This section profiles some of the significant programs. In the "Immediate Solutions" section, I'll describe some useful features you'll want to try from three of the available Mac OS X-savvy programs—AppleWorks 6, Microsoft Word, and Stone Design's Create suite.

Microsoft

It may come as a surprise to some but one of the first publishers to declare support for Mac OS X was Apple's former adversary, Microsoft. The original Public Beta of Mac OS X, back in September of 2000, included a Carbonized version of Microsoft's Internet Explorer browser (see Chapter 20), and the final version was bundled with

Mac OS X. A Mac OS X version of Office 2001 for the Macintosh was announced in January 2001 and released in November of that year as Office v. X (see Figure 13.1).

The Mac OS X version of Office includes extensive revisions for Entourage, Microsoft's powerful e-mail client and personal information manager, in addition to support for Mac OS X's robust features. A handful of minor features are spread across the remainder of the suite (Excel, PowerPoint, and Word). Microsoft boasted in the product's rollout that over 700 icons and numerous dialog boxes were carefully redesigned to take best advantage of Aqua.

NOTE: *This book was written using Word X, and it was a joy to write and edit. A new version of Microsoft Office was announced as this book went to press.*

Apple Computer

The standard installation of Mac OS X includes a number of utilities for you to try. These include the Mail application described in Chapter 21 plus revised versions of old standbys such as the Calculator (now a nearly full-fledged scientific calculator with print capabilities), Disk Utility (a combination of Disk Copy, Disk First Aid, and Drive Setup), QuickTime Player, Script Editor, Sherlock, and Stickies. In addition, Aladdin's StuffIt Expander is along for the ride, so you can open compressed files created in a variety of formats (even those from the Windows and Unix environments).

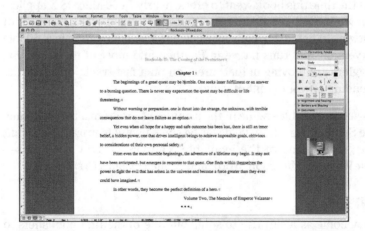
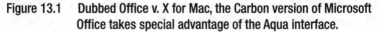

Figure 13.1   Dubbed Office v. X for Mac, the Carbon version of Microsoft Office takes special advantage of the Aqua interface.

The installation includes quite a few new contenders, as well as Apple's famous "iLife" applications, designed as centerpieces of its digital hub strategy. In the next section I'll provide a brief description of a number of the most interesting programs included with Mac OS X, in the Applications and Utilities folders.

NOTE: *I've made no effort to cover all the extras that come with Panther or with a new Mac, such as AppleWorks or Quicken, since the software bundles can change as models are updated. In addition, as you add software to your Mac, this list will enlarge many times. My Applications folder, for example, has 123 items in it. This is the price one pays for being a technology journalist!*

Panther's Applications Folder

When you open this folder, you'll see, in part, the following:

- *Acrobat Reader*—Adobe's popular application reads the many electronic documents that software publishers include in place of printed manuals these days. However, as you'll see shortly, it's not the only option available for viewing such files

- *Address Book*—This Rolodex-like application works with Apple's Mail application (described later in this list) to keep tabs on your personal and business address books.

NOTE: *Address Book is set up so other applications can hook up to it. iChat, Apple's instant messaging software, supports Address Book as do such third-party programs as Page Sender, a powerful shareware fax application.*

- *Chess*—Pit yourself against your Mac's G3, G4, or superpowered G5 processor and see how well you can do in an interactive chess game (see Figure 13.2) designed to exploit the ultra-crisp graphics of Mac OS X.

- *DVD Player*—If you have a Mac with DVD drive (and it's supported by Mac OS X), you can watch your favorite flick at home or on the road. DVD Player's controls mimic what you find in a home DVD player. New for Panther is the ability to playback your videos with true digital sound, assuming you have a Mac, such as the Power Mac G5, which offers digital outputs.

NOTE: *By default, DVD Player is installed only on Macs with supported DVD drives. The version shipping with Panther works with Macs that feature AGP graphics capability and a handful of other models. Check your Mac's spec sheet to see what sort of graphics system it has, although the presence of the DVD Player is usually the best clue.*

Figure 13.2   A grayscale picture doesn't really do justice to Mac OS X's interactive chess game.

- *iChat AV*—Tens and tens of millions of online visitors communicate via instant messaging. Apple's iChat (see Figure 13.3) takes the concept a step further. It not only supports AOL's sprawling instant messaging system with a spiffy new interface, but allows you to send messages to fellow Jaguar and Panther users on your local computer network, courtesy of Apple's Rendezvous technology. Even better, if you have Apple's iSight camera or a similar product, using the FireWire ports of your Mac, you can do audio and videoconferencing. Just make sure you comb your hair first.

NOTE: Another cool feature of iChat is the ability to put up an icon of your personal photo when sending a message to an iChat or AOL Instant Messenger user. That assumes, of course, that you feel comfortable displaying your photo.

- *Font Book*—Do you have lots of fonts and are you eternally confused about how to manage the whole mess? As you'll learn in Chapter 15, font management under Panther isn't as easy as it could be, but Font Book (see Figure 13.4) lets you view, organize, install, enable, and disable fonts with a click here and a click there. Maybe it's not as full-featured as the high-priced spread, such as Alsoft's MasterJuggler or Extensis Suitcase, but since it's free, it's a great starting point to bring order out of your font mess.

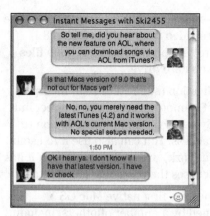

Figure 13.3 Your chat message can include your photo too. Here I took a calculated risk, as I didn't want to frighten away my friends.

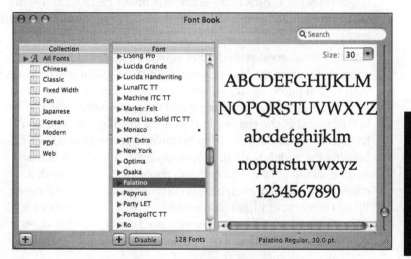

Figure 13.4 View, organize and install your fonts with Font Book.

- *Image Capture*—Found in the Applications folder, this application can be set to open automatically whenever you hook up a supported digital camera or need to use a scanner. It can then download files from the camera; you don't need any extra software to get pictures. You can even use it for a limited number of supported scanners from such companies as Epson.

- *iCal*—You can set up a personal or business calendar on your Mac, or on the Internet for sharing with your friends and business associates. When you need a reminder for that important event, iCal will be there to keep you from forgetting (as much as I'd like to when I'm recording a dental appointment).

13. Mac OS X-Savvy Applications

- *iMovie*—Apple's great video-editing application is standard issue with Mac OS X. It will capture video from a DV or Digital8 camcorder via your Mac's FireWire port, or edit the video files you already have on your Mac's hard drive.

- *Internet Connect*—This application (see Figure 13.5) incorporates some of the elements of Remote Access, with a direct link to the Network pane of the System Preferences application to help you set up your dial-up access. You can also use it to establish a VPN (Virtual Private Network) with your company, if it has such a system. Chapter 8 discusses the subject in more detail.

- *Internet Explorer*—This is the very first native Mac OS X browser. It has now been joined by a number of others, including Apple's own Safari. While it's true that Microsoft has given up on developing this program, except for necessary bug fixes, you still might prefer it. It runs more efficiently under Panther, and some Web sites still demand MSIE to produce accurate displays of their content.

- *iPhoto*—What good is the hub of your digital lifestyle, which is supposedly what the Mac represents, if there's no way to organize your digital photo library? iPhoto combines simple management of pictures from digital cameras and scanners with basic retouching. Removal of the red eye look is done in a flash, so you don't have to worry about your friends thinking you may have been burning the midnight oil the previous night, or perhaps had an extra cocktail or two. You can also enhance the image with a single click, or adjust brightness and contrast to suit your needs. What's more, your photo album can be posted directly to your .Mac Web site or you can order up a high-quality printed version that'll look just wonderful on the coffee table.

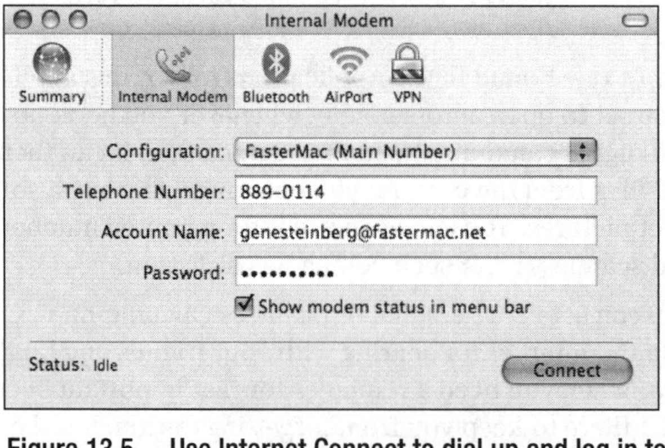

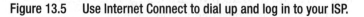

Figure 13.5   Use Internet Connect to dial up and log in to your ISP.

- *iSync*—If you have an address book on your mobile phone, your handheld, and your Mac how do you keep all this stuff synchronized? iSync comes to the rescue, and it works with a growing number of phones, so it's highly likely you already have one that's compatible. If you have a .Mac account, you an also synchronize such features as Safari bookmarks and other stuff with other Macs.

- *iTunes*—Apple's popular jukebox program is a place to import and organize music or listen to Internet radio. It is fully integrated with Apple's ultra-slick, best-selling music player, the iPod and some third- party players. And if you want to download music legally, the iTunes Music Store (see Figure 13.6) lets you do it cheaply and quickly. It also helps you get files that deliver surprisingly good sound.

NOTE: *A matching version of iTunes is available for the Windows platform, and your songs can be shared over a network, so folks in your home or office can enjoy your music. Just don't play it too loud!*

- *Mail*—Email is often the most-used feature on the Internet, and Apple has delivered a brand-new application for the purpose (see Figure 13.7). Mail will handle most of your email accounts. It provides a bevy of features, including the ability to import your messages from several other email programs, multiple signatures,

Figure 13.6   Hundreds of thousands of songs populate the iTunes Music Store.

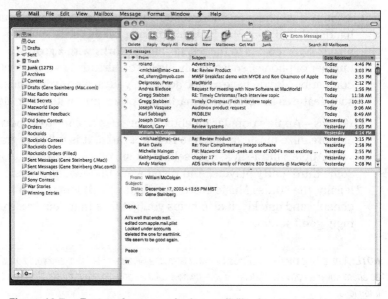

Figure 13.7   Fast performance, junk e-mail filtering, threading and lots more in Apple Mail.

email rules, scheduled retrieval of messages, and a Finder-like interface where you can change the toolbar icons to meet your needs. Even better, it has a powerful junk e-mail filter that, when activated, can catch the vast majority of those annoying unsolicited messages. Chapter 21 discusses the subject in more detail.

- *Preview*—This application can read both PDF files (and convert documents to that format as well) and pictures in such popular formats as GIF, JPET, PICT, and TIFF. For Panther, Apple claims that Preview actually performs basic rendering, scrolling, and searching faster than Adobe Acrobat.

- *QuickTime Player*—This is yet another program that inherits nothing more than a new look for Panther. It's used to play QuickTime movies from your Mac or from the Internet.

- *Stickies*—What's a Mac without Stickies, your personal post-it note system? For the Mac OS X version, Apple has taken the basic features of the famous Classic version, added some additional text formatting and import features, and put them into a familiar package. You can import all your Stickies from your Classic Mac System Folder, so you don't lose a thing in switching over.

NOTE: *Of course, nothing prevents you from running the Classic version of Stickies, but because the conversion is completely accurate, doing so shouldn't be necessary.*

- *System Preferences*—Apple's replacement for Control Panels, System Preferences is used to configure most of your system settings. This application is also extensible, so third-party software companies can put their own components in System Preferences (it will appear in a category labeled Other).

- *TextEdit*—The Classic Mac OS had TeachText and later SimpleText, to open and view short text files, such as the ReadMe files that come with new computer products. TextEdit can view ReadMe files, but it's also a simple word processor complete with spell checking and a basic level of document formatting capabilities. It can create and open documents in both Microsoft Word and Rich Text Format (RTF), so you can see files created in a wide variety of software.

NOTE: *TextEdit's Word translation feature is good for normal text documents, but as soon as you toss in added stuff such as tables, the track changes feature (used by publishers and editors to keep track of the editing process), and so on, things will get lost in the translation. To take advantage of these advanced features, you really want to buy Word, which is, by the way, quite a good program. I address that comment even to those Mac users who boast of having a Microsoft free computer.*

Utilities Folder

Where would Mac OS X be without a repository for seldom-used programs, diagnostic software, and other miscellaneous stuff? The Utilities folder is a toolbox containing an extremely powerful range of support applications. Some, such as Disk Utility and ColorSync, are useful to most of you. Others, such as Console and NetInfo Manager, are oriented towards the power user or system administrator who needs to check for problems or create custom network configurations.

Here's a brief overview of the contents of the typical Panther Utilities folder:

- *Activity Viewer*—Do you have a program that is hogging memory and CPU horsepower? What about hard drive activity and network actions? You can get a visual indication (see Figure 13.8) of what's really going on with Mac OS X by using Activity Viewer. You can use this handy tool for diagnosis or just to watch the display and satisfy your curiosity.

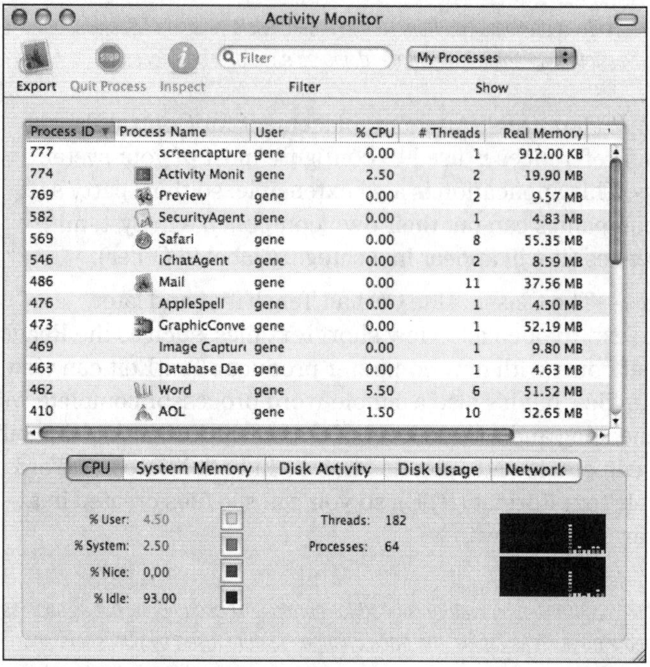

Figure 13.8 My Power Mac G5's twin processors were essentially loafing when I captured this screen shot.

NOTE: *I am not ignoring the Bluetooth applications. You can learn a bit more about configuring them in Chapter 3, where I detail the various components of System Preferences.*

- *ColorSync*—Panther comes with ColorSync, which offers automated support for color calibration between your Mac's display and an input or output device (such as a scanner or color printer). The ColorSync utility also includes a special First Aid feature that verifies a color profile against ICC specifications and repairs such problems to ensure the best possible color matching. In addition, if you're planning on using Panther's built-in PDF conversion feature, this application lets you fine-tune the settings for specific environments, such as a high-end printer.

- *Console*—As you use your Mac, you might, from time-to-time, see some strange error messages because of a printing problem or system-related issue. The Console application (see Figure 13.9) keeps a log of those messages. They may not be directly useful to the average Mac user but you can use the information to help a software publisher figure out what went wrong with its product; you don't have to remember the arcane messages or prompts. This utility resides in the Panther Utilities folder.

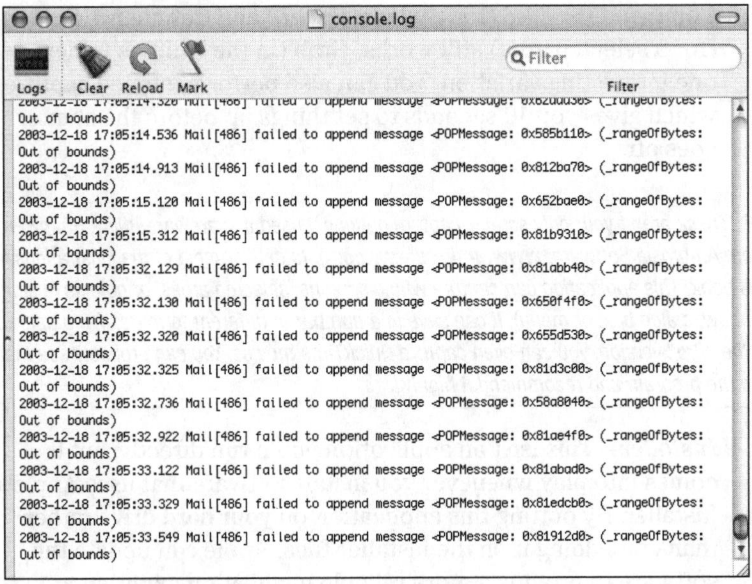

Figure 13.9 The log can display system-related error messages that might help you troubleshoot a problem on your Mac.

- *Digital Color Meter*—This application is used to measure the colors as you move the cursor to particular points on the screen. It's useful for color matching.

- *Disk Utility*—Take one part Disk Copy, one part Disk First Aid, and one part Drive Setup, and the result is an application that will check and format a drive, and also make disk images of files (and an entire hard drive for that matter). The sole limitation of the First Aid component of Disk Utility is its inability to check a startup drive for directory problems (but that's already done during the boot process). However, it does have the ability to repair permissions, which can help in situations where you find you don't have access to some of your files even though you have administrator's access. Permissions problems can also cause unstable or flaky behavior, so this is something you'll want to address occasionally.

NOTE: *Another useful feature of Disk Utility is its ability to format IDE and SCSI drives in Redundant Array of Independent Disks (RAID) format (FireWire isn't supported yet), for the highest possible performance for content creators.*

- *Grab*—This utility grabs a screenshot of your Mac. This is useful in providing illustrations for documentation. Although

Command+Shift+3 (for a whole screen) and Command+Shift+4 (for a selected area) still works, Grab (in the Utilities folder) adds one interesting variation. You can also perform a timed capture, which gives you 10 seconds to set things up before the shutter goes off.

TIP: *These aren't your only screen-capture options. I used a shareware utility, Snapz Pro X (from Ambrosia Software, **www.ambrosiasw.com**), to deliver most of the illustrations for this book. This application can capture whole screens, selected areas, or objects (a single window, dialog box, or menu). It can save in a number of different formats. If you upgrade to the "Pro" version, you can even capture QuickTime movies. You can probably see that I like the program and recommend it highly.*

- *Installer*—This isn't an application you'll run directly, but it comes into play whenever you install software that uses Apple's Installer. By putting this application on your hard drive rather than embedding it on the installer files, Apple can update the software to provide a more reliable installation experience without forcing software publishers (or itself for that matter) to have to update their products to be compatible.

- *Keychain Access*—Beginning with Mac OS 9, Apple incorporated a keychain feature that lets you manage all your user passwords from a single application. This application, in the Utilities folder, is used to configure keychains. You can also do so automatically via such features as the Finder's Connect To Server function for accessing network shares.

- *NetInfo Manager*—This application, in the Utilities folder, is a valuable tool for system administrators to manage Panther users and directories. You can use it to create root access to your Mac (a kind of super-user), which may be useful for some trouble-shooting purposes, but is otherwise the province of the advanced user. You can get a fairly extensive and technical explanation of how this powerful application is used from Apple's Web site at **www.apple.com/macosx/server/pdf/ UnderstandingUsingNetInfo.pdf**.

- *Network Utility*—What's happening on your network? Are you encountering a problem connecting to a shared computer or printer, or is your Internet access not functioning as you expect? This application (see Figure 13.10) can be used to perform such functions as *ping* (contact and return, like sonar) or *traceroute* to find the source.

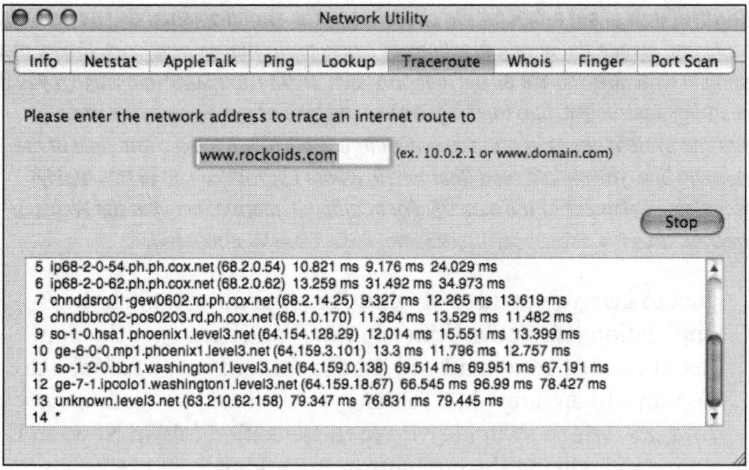

Figure 13.10 You can use this application to test the condition of your local network or Internet connection.

- *Terminal*—Apple has gone to great lengths to bury the native Unix command line for Mac OS X. As a result, Mac users can continue to use the new operating system without taking a gander at the core; but Terminal (see Figure 13.11) gives Unix mavens full access to the command line and a chance to explore the underpinnings.

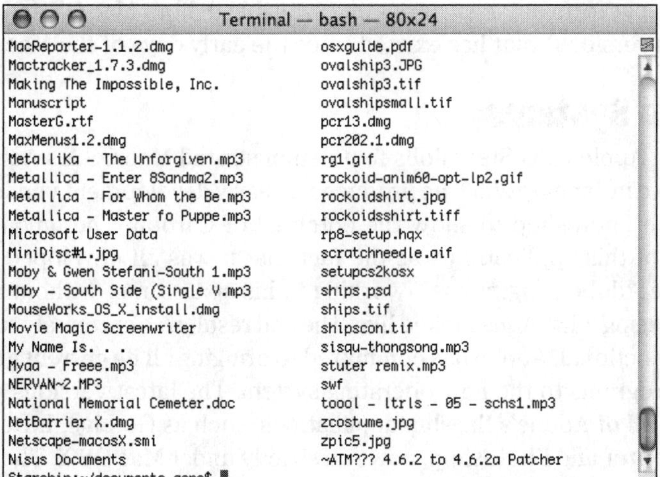

Figure 13.11 Experience the guts of Unix with this application.

WARNING! Unix is not a tool for the casual user. The wrong commands can get you in trouble and invoke the wrong functions or cause performance problems. Unlike most graphical software, there's no opt-out provision or "Are You Sure" message if you do something destructive, like trashing files by mistake or removing a directory the operating system needs in order to run. Before you explore the ins and outs of the command line, you should read Chapter 19, where I introduce you to this highly sophisticated element of the Mac OS. For additional information, visit the Web site http://public.sdsu.edu/Docs/unixf/basic_unix_f/basic_unix.html.

Just to give you an idea of what Terminal does, launch the application (it's in the Utilities folder) and then type the command **ls**. This command will list the contents of your Mac's drive. To move to an individual folder, type the command **cd** *<name of folder>*, which switches you to the specified folder. Now, an **ls** command will list the contents of the folder.

Mac OS X Applications Profiled

Here is a brief look at some of the more popular Mac OS X applications. There are plenty more where these came from. Check your favorite dealer for the specifics.

FileMaker

Apple's spin-off, which handles development of FileMaker Pro, was one of the early applications to move to Mac OS X. FileMaker Pro is a cross-platform database program (available in both Mac OS and Windows versions) that has existed since the early days of the Mac.

Adobe Systems

When Apple CEO Steve Jobs first demonstrated Mac OS X's Aqua interface in January 2000, he produced an early development version of Adobe Photoshop to show the potential of Carbon. The unique aspect of this application was the fact that it was all developed by a single Adobe programmer, working in his spare time, without actually seeing what Aqua looked like. The end result was extremely rough, but functional. Adobe has committed to bringing all its current graphics programs to the new operating system. The latest versions of almost all of Adobe's flagship applications, such as Go Live, InDesign, Illustrator and Photoshop, now run strictly under Mac OS X. The only notable exceptions are PageMaker and FrameMaker.

NOTE: Adobe PageMaker, one of the original desktop publishing applications, has been officially discontinued. FrameMaker, a powerful application that can be used to create long and complex technical publications, is still a treasure to many special publishers, but as of the time this book was written, there was no indication when or if a Mac OS X version would be produced.

Alias|Wavefront

One of the most significant developments for Mac OS X users is the arrival of powerful new programs on the Mac platform. The $1,999 Oscar-winning 3D animation program, Maya Complete is a prime example. Although the program isn't quite a household name, the work done with Maya has been prominent in a number of popular movies. Maya has been used to create spectacular effects for films such as *Star Wars Episode I and Episode II, Hollow Man,* and *The Perfect Storm.* A number of the major production houses have this application doing duty in their special effects labs.

NOTE: *If you are learning your craft and find paying nearly two grand for animation software to be a little bit much for your budget, you can use the free Maya Personal Learning Edition to perfect your skills. It's designed for non-commercial use, and your files will bear a watermark to identify the fact that you're using a student version. However, you'll have access to Maya's powerful content creation tools and when you know you're ready, you can buy the full blown version and do it for real.*

Corel

This Canadian software publisher, now run by Vector Capital, a San Francisco-based firm, is best known for CorelDRAW, which has always been more popular on the Windows than Mac platforms, but the beleaguered company is still trying. Version 11 of the Corel Graphics Suite came out pretty near the time of its Windows equivalent, and runs only in Mac OS X. In addition to CorelDRAW, a host of useful applications are provided for additional content creation capabilities, including Corel PHOTO-PAINT 11. The bundle also includes a Mac OS X version of DiamondSoft's Font Reserve for native font management, tons of clip art, and 1,000 PostScript and TrueType fonts. While critics maintain the program isn't quite up to the competition from Adobe and Macromedia, its economical price and bundled extras make it an attractive alternative.

Deneba

From sunny Florida comes Canvas 9, an application that combines superior graphics, page layout, and HTML tools in a single application. The feature-set is huge and not easily summarized, although Deneba claims it beats the competition and then some. Product reviewers say

Canvas excels at technical drawing tasks, since it handles extremely large documents (would you believe 2,000 miles by 2,000 miles?) and zooming up to 114,000 percent.

Macromedia

Program for program, a number of Macromedia's offerings are in direct competition with those from Adobe. It comes as no surprise, then, that Macromedia is also in the forefront of Mac OS X development, offering native versions of its flagship software, such as Dreamweaver, Fireworks and FreeHand.

Stone Design

This publisher has migrated from the NeXT world and has embraced Mac OS X. Among its most useful applications is Create (see Figure 13.12), an integrated illustration program that also incorporates HTML authoring and page layout. Create treats every element, from text to pictures, as an object, which can then be dragged and dropped onto other objects to create sophisticated illustrations.

NOTE: *The various Stone Design applications stand as evidence of the power of Apple's Cocoa development environment. One person, Andrew Stone, did considerable work on these programs. Using traditional developer tools, it would have taken a programming team to create software of this level of sophistication in a reasonable amount of time.*

AOL

The world's largest online service has committed itself to fully supporting Mac OS X. AOL version 10.3 includes many of the fancy broadband access features incorporated in the Windows version, including multimedia presentations. You can also add special backdrops and icons for your instant messages.

United Online

No, I am not talking about an airline. This company is a major ISP, and its low-cost BlueLight, Juno, and Net Zero services all support Mac OS X. Unlike other cheap services, they use a custom dialer program that puts up a small menu at the top of the screen that you can use for quick access to special content features and to end your session.

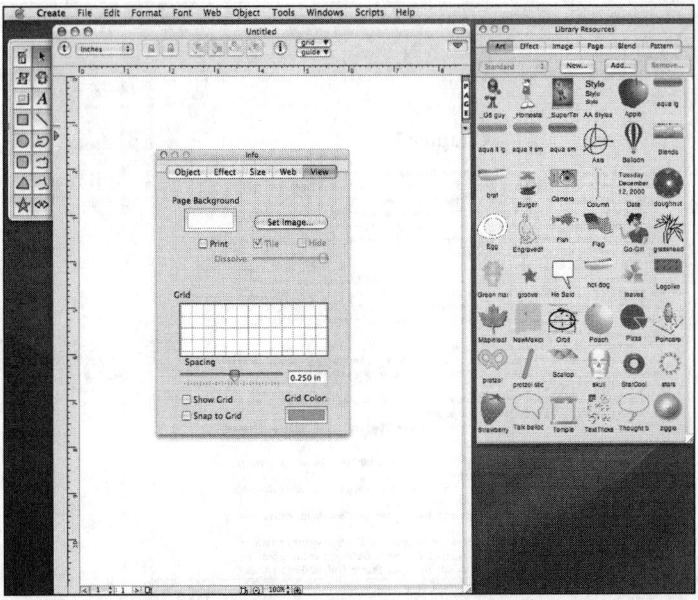

Figure 13.12   Create is the centerpiece of Stone Design's Mac OS X product line.

Low-Cost Word Processors

If Word is too rich for your blood and you still need a powerful word processor with at least limited file exchange capability with Microsoft's application, there are several spiffy alternatives to look at.

In addition to Mariner Write, which is a competitor to the word processor module of AppleWorks, there are two fascinating alternatives to consider. First is Nisus Writer Express, which is the Mac OS X version of the venerable multi-featured word processor. The second one is from Israel and it is called Mellel (see Figure 13.13). This program is a shareware application with a surprising number of features, including footnotes, endnotes, and tables.

NOTE: *The publishers of Mellel were boasting, as of the time this book was written, that they were going to give their little application more features than Word by some time in 2004. You can download the demo version yourself and see if they're right.*

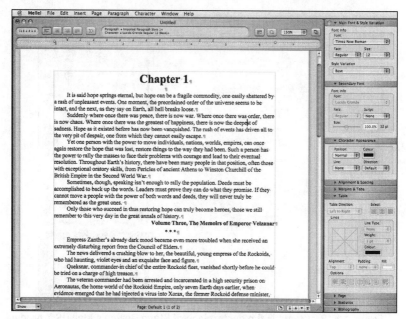

Figure 13.13 A pretty interface and a pretty large number of features highlight Mellel, a shareware word processor.

With over 7,000 Mac OS X applications out, I can't cover more than just the main ones. You can find the latest updates and new offerings listed at **www.versiontracker.com.** Just use its search tool to find software in any specific category. You can also search by name.

Immediate Solutions

An Overview of AppleWorks

What was the first real application for Mac OS X? AppleWorks 6, although it wasn't originally advertised as cross-platform compatible. Some Mac users don't take AppleWorks seriously but it is a perfectly capable application suite. It features word processing, drawing and painting, a spreadsheet, a database module, and a simple presentation component. AppleWorks is shipped free on Apple's consumer models, such as the iBook, eMac, and iMac. AppleWorks may not replace Microsoft Office but it does read many Office files and has a pretty good set of features for the home or small office user on a budget.

Here's a brief overview of this cleverly designed program—the first Carbon application from a major publisher (which is fitting).

Using AppleWorks Starting Points

When you first launch AppleWorks, you'll be greeted by the program's Starting Points (see Figure 13.14), a floating tabbed palette. From here you can create new documents or open recent ones. Here is a brief description of what you get when you click each tab:

NOTE: *Starting Points has had its influence in big places. The Project Gallery featured in Microsoft Office 2001 and Office v. X is highly reminiscent of this feature.*

- *Basic*—Access any of the six AppleWorks modules by clicking once on the kind of document you want to make. Depending on what you select, the user interface will vary in terms of menu bar commands, toolbars, and features.

Figure 13.14 Use Starting Points to originate or open documents in AppleWorks.

13. Mac OS X-Savvy Applications

TIP: Where's Starting Points? If you don't see it, choose Show Starting Points from the File menu.

- *Assistants*—AppleWorks is designed for users of all skill levels, from novices setting up their first Mac to power users. The Assistants palette provides step-by-step guidance in setting up a new document in several useful categories, from a business card to an envelope.

- *Templates*—To help get you started with a new document, you can choose from a collection of document templates. Click a preview icon to bring up a blank document with the template ready to roll.

- *Web*—Apple keeps an updated collection of clip art, templates, and tips about AppleWorks 6 at its Web site. When you click this tab, you can access a current list of what's available. If you're logged on to your ISP, a single click in the listing automatically downloads the templates to your Mac.

- *Recent Items*—This tab provides a fast way to open a document you've worked on previously. When you click here, you'll see a list of dozens of documents you've created in the program, sorted alphabetically.

- *+*—You can use this tab to make your own custom palette, and then drag and drop items to fill it in.

Using Tables in AppleWorks

One of the most important new features of AppleWorks 6, aside from the user interface and Panther support, is the Table tool. You can easily add tables to any AppleWorks document and resize the tables to fit your needs. To use this handy feature, follow these steps:

1. Launch AppleWorks 6.

2. Start a new document.

3. Make sure the program's toolbar is open. If it's not visible, go to the program's Window menu and select Show Tools (see Figure 13.15).

4. Locate the Table Frame tool and select it.

5. Place the cursor in the location in your document where you want to put a table, and then drag the mouse in a diagonal direction to set the approximate size of the table. The size can be changed easily.

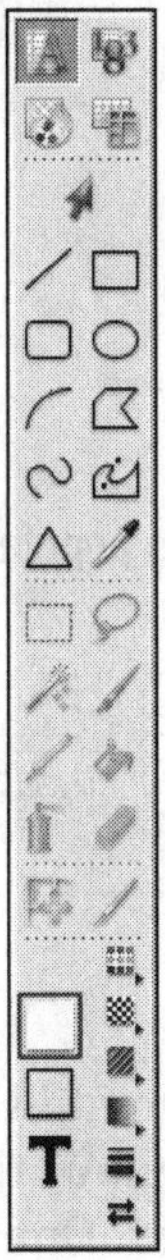

Figure 13.15   The toolbar you see in AppleWorks changes depending on the kind of document you're creating.

6. In the Insert Table dialog box that appears (see Figure 13.16), type how many rows and columns you want to put in the table. These values can also be changed easily.

7. Click OK to finish the table setup process.

After you have set up the raw essentials of your table, you can easily adjust the table as you see fit. The entire table or rows and columns can be resized by clicking and dragging. When you're working in a table, a new Table menu appears on the menu bar; you can use it to add or delete rows and columns.

An Overview of Office v. X

When you first take a gander at any of the Office v. X applications, it's hard to get beyond the luscious Aqua interface; but some new features are particularly useful. I'll cover three of the highlights here, features new to the Mac OS X version. It would take a large book to even scratch the surface of what's offered in this sprawling business application suite.

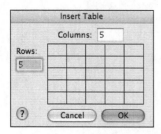

Figure 13.16   Choose how many rows and columns with which to populate your table.

NOTE: At the time this book was written, Microsoft was working on a new version of its Mac Office suite, which was expected to appear some time in 2004.

Profiling the Project Gallery

When Microsoft introduced the Project Gallery (see Figure 13.17), some people thought it was the company's answer to AppleWorks' Starting Points palette. But it does offer some neat features. One of them is the new Based On Recent feature, which is a super Save As capability that lets you automatically open a new document with all the formatting and content of the original.

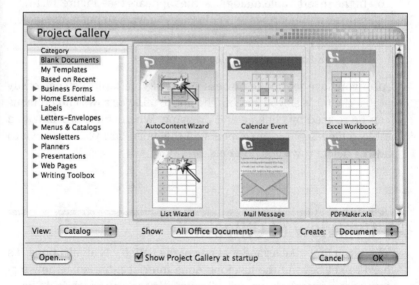

Figure 13.17   The Project Gallery is a flexible beginning for any Office v. X document.

Using Word X's Multiple Selection Feature

This isn't an original feature (such Mac word processors as Mariner Write and Nisus Writer Express already have it). But in practice, it's both simple and useful. When you want to select more than a single item in your Word document, hold down the Command key and click and select each item, in succession. Once you've done that, all you have to do is apply updated text formatting to these items. Or, just cut and paste or drag and drop into a new location.

Using Excel X's Auto Recover Feature

Suppose you are busy working on a long spreadsheet, and there's a power outage. (I won't dwell on the possibility of a system crash, but it can happen, even in Panther.) You restart your Mac and find that your Excel spreadsheet is damaged beyond recovery or doesn't reflect all the changes you made since the last time you saved. Mimicking a feature already present in Word, you don't have to change anything to use AutoRecover. It's already in your Excel Preferences box under the Save category. The default setting is to save every 10 minutes, but you can change that. So, even if your original document is damaged or not up to date, when you launch Excel, you'll see the version automatically recovered; you can save and use that version without missing a beat.

Introducing Create for Mac OS X

Stone Design's clever illustration suite, Create, is an all-purpose illustration program that provides elements of several applications rolled into one. In addition to being able to produce simple or highly complex drawings, you can create special effects, manage complex text stylings, and build your own Web site.

Using the Inspector

A lot of the work you do in Create is directed by the Inspector window. It's a mélange of buttons, checkboxes, sliders, and text entry points where you can originate the look and feel of your document.

NOTE: *The Inspector feature available with Create is not the same as the Finder's Inspector. It provides services strictly for the application, and not for the rest of the Mac OS.*

---

13. Mac OS X-Savvy Applications

To access the Inspector, follow these steps:

1. Launch Create.
2. Go to the Tools menu and choose Info (see Figure 13.18).
3. Click the tab that represents the type of project you are working on.

With the Inspector active, you'll find an easy way to manipulate your artwork, configure Web pages, and apply and change color selections.

TIP: *You can use another terrific feature of Create—the Resources palette—for clip art and document templates. If the Resources palette isn't present, choose Library Resources from the Tools menu to bring it up.*

Starting a Web Page in Create

In addition to being a flexible object-oriented illustration environment, Create lets you generate a fully professional Web page. Here's how to get started setting up a Web page in this program:

1. Launch Create. A new Untitled document window appears, along with, by default, the Resources and Inspector windows.
2. Type your text and place your pictures in the document.
3. When you're ready to enter URL links to other pages or sites, click the area of your document where you want to place the link.

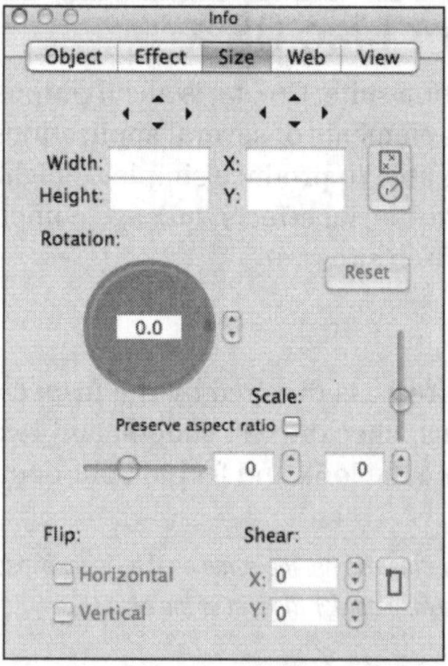

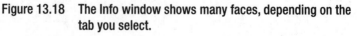

Figure 13.18   The Info window shows many faces, depending on the tab you select.

4. Click the Web tab of the Info window, as shown in Figure 13.19.

5. Enter the URL. To specify special options for this link, click the Use Custom HTML option.

6. When your Web page is finished, choose Create Web Pages from the Web menu and name your file. When you click Save, you'll see the page opened in the Web browser set as an Internet preference in the System Preferences panel, so you can check to see how it will look when it's published on the Web.

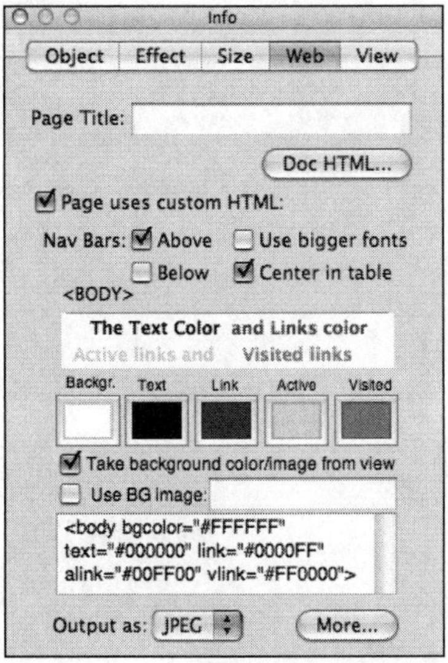

Figure 13.19 The multipurpose Info window or palette lets you configure your Web page It is shown here with the Use Custom HTML option selected.

Using Older Programs with Panther

In Brief

When Apple Computer released its first Macintosh computer with a PowerPC processor in early 1994, the landscape was quite lonely. Although these computers offered the promise of far greater levels of performance, the performance gains would only occur when programs were ported (or updated) to support the new chip architecture.

Thousands of Mac applications, however, were designed to run on the older 680x0 Motorola processors. With this in mind, Apple devised a (mostly) transparent method to allow Mac users to continue to use the vast majority of these programs with decent performance, and then gradually migrate to the PowerPC versions as they were released. The ROMs for PowerPC Macs came with an emulator (extensively updated via patches to the system software). The emulator would, on the fly, behave like a 680x0 processor. It would allow those programs to run with good compatibility—except for software that required a Mac with an FPU chip for special math-related functions. At first, the speed of the emulator barely kept up with 68030 processors, let alone the fastest 68040 processors that were produced before the PowerPC took over. But as the emulator got better and the new chips got faster, performance of the older programs was so good that it was sometimes hard to see a significant difference.

These days, with the newer Macs running many times faster than a decade ago, that old emulator actually runs applications much faster than any of their developers could have imagined.

Introducing the Classic Environment

For Mac OS X, the changes are far greater than the switch to the PowerPC's RISC code. The underlying structure of the operating system would seem, in comparison, to originate on an alien world. It's Unix-based—the same operating system that powers some of the most powerful Internet servers—and thus the situation is rather more complex.

However, Apple has an inventive solution: the Classic Compatibility environment (see Figure 14.1). This environment is not an emulator, such as the one used for PowerPC Macs, nor is it in the tradition of software that emulates Windows on a Mac, such as the Microsoft Virtual PC.

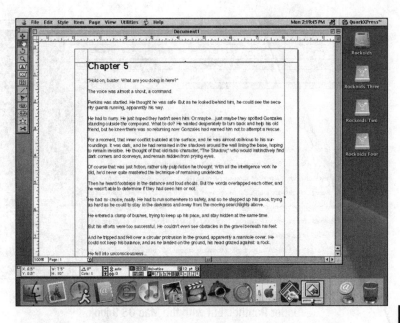

Figure 14.1   Yes, this is truly Mac OS 9.2.2, but it's running within Panther.

NOTE: *If you're into Mac history, the original name for Classic was actually the Blue Box and some long-time Mac users still refer to it that way. This was a cool name but wasn't particularly user friendly.*

The closest description would be that Classic runs as a sort of virtual machine in which Mac OS 9 runs as a separate process or application within Panther, but without inheriting the Aqua user interface or the robust operating system features of the Darwin core. Basically, when you run a Mac OS 9 program, the old menu bar, Apple menu, Control Strip, Launcher, and most features of the older operating system take over your screen (see Figure 14.2). However, when you switch out of a Classic application, you're back in Aqua.

NOTE: *The real version of Office v. X came out in November 2001. But if you haven't upgraded to that version yet, you can continue to use the Classic version with good performance and compatibility. Although the native version looks a lot better, it only offers a handful of new features.*

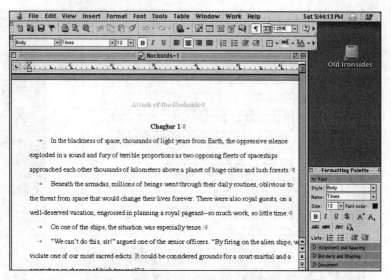

Figure 14.2   This is the Classic version of Microsoft Word 2001 running under Panther, but with the Mac OS 9 look.

Classic Environment Limitations

As seamless as switching to a Classic application may seem (and I'll explain the best ways to use the feature in the "Immediate Solutions" section of this chapter), there are limits to compatibility, more so than with the switch from 680x0 to PowerPC. Although you can run most of your applications with good performance, some programs just won't run until updated for the new operating system. Here's the short list of potential problems:

- *It still crashes a lot*—The Classic environment doesn't inherit the robust features of Panther, such as preemptive multitasking and protected memory. It has the same limitations as the original Mac OS, which means that if a single application crashes, you will need to restart Classic. However, because it operates in its own protected memory space, that memory is walled off from the rest of the system, so you can continue to use your Mac OS X applications without a problem. If Classic crashes, just run it again.

NOTE: *Before you send the cards and letters, I realize that it is possible to fine-tune Mac OS 9 to deliver pretty good performance and decent stability. But it usually takes a bit of work, whereas under Panther, problems are, or should be, the exception rather than the rule.*

- *Many system extensions don't run*—Mac OS system extensions that access hardware functions will probably fail, or will run only with limited compatibility. I'll explain ways to clean out your Mac OS 9 user environment for best performance in the "Immediate Solutions" section of this chapter.

- *CPU-intensive applications are slower*—Adobe Photoshop and other programs that tax the Mac's processor to the limit may run somewhat slower in the Classic environment. The amount that the performance suffers depends largely on the speed of your Mac's processor, hard drive, and graphics hardware. However, other functions, such as launching and screen refreshing, will seem not much different from a regular Mac OS 9 Mac.

- *Certain Mac peripherals fail*—Any product that requires special drivers to run will probably fail under Panther, even if run from the Classic environment. Although it's possible that some of these devices will work after a fashion, don't expect consistent compatibility. Among the affected products are CD burners, DVD-RAM burners, removable storage devices (except for Imation and Iomega products), scanners, tape backup drives, and peripheral cards that provide such features as extended audio editing or video capture. Even graphics cards that were not provided by Apple's graphics chip partner, ATI Technologies, IX Micro (which is now defunct), or NVIDIA won't function unless the company that makes the product has produced drivers for Panther. The best source of information about what works and what doesn't is the manufacturer of these products.

NOTE: *Formac, a German-based manufacturer of high-performance graphics cards for Macs, indicates that its ProFormance 3 products will run under Mac OS X (at least through Mac OS 10.2), but that 3D acceleration isn't supported. Formac is no longer manufacturing graphic cards, and further driver enhancement of its older products isn't likely. 3dfx Interactive, which went out of business in late 2000, never updated drivers for its Voodoo cards for Mac OS X, though some third parties are looking for a solution. Fortunately, most digital cameras work fine under Mac OS X and the Image Capture application without the need for special drivers.*

- *Some printers won't work*—You can continue to use most laser printers by using the Print Center application of Panther. But some special laser printers that do not have Adobe PostScript installed or that use the USB rather than Ethernet ports may not work without driver updates, except from the Classic environment. The same holds true for those ever-popular ink jet printers that have captured a large portion of the printer market.

A decent selection of printers from such companies as Canon, Epson, HP and Lexmark work just fine. But you'll need to check with the manufacturer directly (probably at its Web site) for drivers that aren't supported by Mac OS X out of the box.

NOTE: *One potential source of hope is the inclusion of the open source Gimp-Print drivers with Panther. This adds a number of previously unsupported printers to the mix, including the popular Epson Stylus Color 1520, a staple among graphic artists because of its excellent print quality and the ability to handle larger paper sizes.*

- *Third-party hard drive formatters won't work*—Any device that provides low-level support to storage devices probably won't work until a special Mac OS X version is delivered. Apple's own Disk Utility can handle most—probably all—ATA drives and many recent SCSI drives. Otherwise, you have to wait for the third-party manufacturer to come through for you.

NOTE: *As of the time this book was written, the only Mac OS X-savvy hard drive formatter was Apple's Disk Utility. Third-party formatting utilities, such as FWB's Hard Disk ToolKit, will probably never be updated for the new operating system, but I never mind being amazed.*

- *Some Windows emulators are not compatible*—Although Microsoft Virtual PC 6.1, which supports Mac OS X (except for the Power Mac G5), there's no solace for users of the rival product, SoftWindows. FWB has made it clear that it won't update the product, and the chances of the Classic Mac OS version running under Mac OS X aren't terribly high. Ditto for PC processor cards from such companies as Orange Micro.

- *Internet software compatibility is a mixed bag*—If you have a high-speed (broadband) Internet connection, you may be all right, but dial-up connections that require a custom dialing program (rather than just a straight PPP connection that can be configured via the Network preference panel), have problems of one sort or another. Although a shareware program, PortReflector, may help resolve some dial-up problems, programs with their own dialers, such as AOL and CompuServe, must be updated to the Mac OS X versions.

- *Some classic games won't work*—Although Mac OS X is designed to be a gamer's paradise, the realization of that promise won't happen until games are truly ported to the new operating system. In the meantime, you can run many older games in the Classic environment, but do not expect stellar performance. Frame rates, for example, will not be quite as high as you experienced under Mac OS 9, because of less complete support for graphics acceleration.

Immediate Solutions

Launching Older Mac Programs

You don't have to do anything special to run your Classic Mac applications within Panther. The operating system is clever enough to sort it all out for you and give you the proper environment for the program you run. To launch an older Mac program and have it work, just do the following:

1. Locate the document or program on your Mac's drive.

TIP: Do you have both a Classic and Mac OS X version of a program, such as Microsoft Word? In theory, the Mac OS X version should launch, but in practice, the Classic version may run instead. Should this happen, use the Finder's Show Info command on the document and use the Open with: option in the Finder's Get Info window to make the Mac OS X version the default (it won't affect how the document opens if you restart under Mac OS 9.x, when the available Classic application will launch).

---

2. Double-click the application icon or a document created with the application.

3. If the Classic environment isn't running, it will go through its regular boot process (see Figure 14.3).

4. The first time you launch Classic from Mac OS X, you'll see a dialog box notifying you that some resources (extensions) need to be added to the Classic System Folder to continue the startup process. You must click OK to accept the installation and continue running Classic. Otherwise, click Quit, and the process will stop.

Figure 14.3   This progress bar shows that the Classic environment is starting up.

> **NOTE:** Mac OS 9.2.2, the most recent version available when this book was written, included several Classic-related extensions to run under Mac OS X's Classic environment. However, the Panther upgrade generally uses later versions of these utilities, so don't be surprised if you see that message anyway and if it returns as more updates to Mac OS X arrive.

5. If you click the disclosure triangle in the Classic window, you'll see the standard Mac startup screen (see Figure 14.4), but it happens within an application window within Mac OS X. Clever! Once the Classic environment is running, the application you launched will be opened as well. Then your document will appear on the screen, surrounded by a user interface that is essentially the same as what you experienced under Mac OS 9.x.

> **NOTE:** When Classic is launching, its icon will appear in the Dock and will (assuming you haven't changed the option) bounce up and down rhythmically as the environment is loading. You'll also see an icon representing the Mac OS 9.x application you opened. However, once Classic is open, its icon will no longer be present, so do not get concerned. You can easily verify Classic's presence in the Classic preference pane of System Preferences. You can also control Classic access via a system menu icon, using the Show Classic Status in Menu Bar checkbox, which will give you a popup menu that lets you connect to the contents of your Mac OS 9 Apple menu.

Figure 14.4   If you click the disclosure triangle, you'll see the standard Mac OS 9 startup screen.

Running Classic as a Startup Application

It's highly likely that, if you haven't yet upgraded your applications to Mac OS X native versions, you'll have to spend plenty of time in the Classic environment to run your older programs. Therefore, it may be a good idea to have Classic as a startup application so that you don't have to wait for it later when you're running those programs. Here's how to make it a startup program:

1. Launch the System Preferences application (it's normally in the Dock).

2. Click the Classic icon. The Classic preference pane, shown in Figure 14.5, appears.

3. Choose the startup volume that contains the Mac OS 9.x System Folder you want to use from the scrolling list.

NOTE: Which to use if you have several? Well, you might want to have a backup System Folder on another partition or drive in case something happens to your Classic System Folder, or perhaps you have one with a lean set of system extensions for best Classic performance. So long as it's 9.1 or later (and the later the better), any of these will work, but later versions work faster and more reliably.

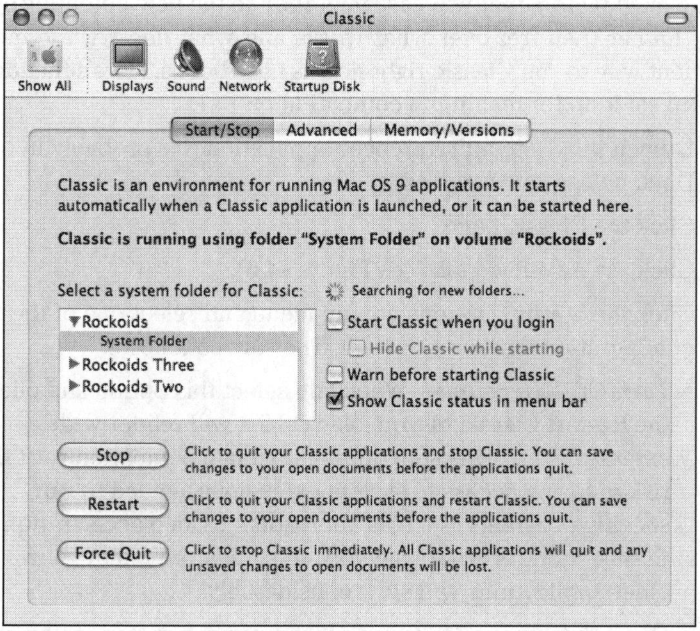

Figure 14.5   The Classic preference pane is used to set up the environment as a startup process.

4. Click the Start Classic when you log in checkbox. Whenever you log in to your Mac OS X user account, Classic will be launched. You can still quit the environment in the normal fashion later, but you'll be all set when you're ready to run your older software.

5. If you want to begin Classic right away, click the Start button.

6. Choose Quit from the application menu or type Command+Q to leave the System Preferences application.

NOTE: *The next section discusses the settings found in the Advanced Classic settings pane, which will help you tailor Classic performance and reduce potential system hang-ups or performance problems.*

Getting Reliable Performance from Classic Applications

Making it possible to run older Mac programs under Mac OS X is one of the main factors that will ease migration to the new operating system. Rather than fret over what works and what doesn't, the most efficient way to run Classic right now is bare bones. Here's the ideal way to set it up for maximum compatibility:

1. Launch the System Preferences application (it's probably in the Dock unless you removed it).

2. Click the Classic pane.

3. Click the Advanced tab (see Figure 14.6).

4. Click the Startup Options pop-up menu and select one of the configuration options you want. They are as follows:

   • *Turn Off Extensions*—When you select this option and click the Restart Classic button, Mac OS 9.x will reboot with extensions off. This step offers maximum compatibility at the risk of losing access to system extensions needed to run specific programs (such as Microsoft's). Video acceleration in Classic mode is also turned off, so screen refresh of your older applications will slow considerably.

   • *Open Extensions Manager*—When you select this option and click the Restart Classic button, the Extensions Manager application will open as Mac OS 9.x boots, giving you a way

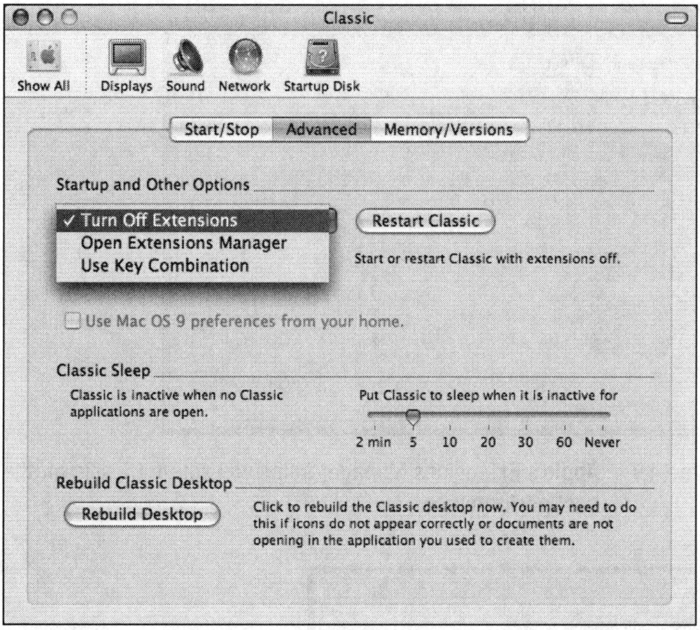

Figure 14.6   These Advanced settings help you tailor Classic performance and compatibility.

to fine-tune your extensions lineup to remove items that may cause performance hits or incompatibilities. I'll cover this in more detail shortly.

- *Use Key Combination*—When you select this option, you'll need to enter a keyboard combination in the data field that will appear below the pop-up menu to trigger Classic with System Preferences open.

5. The easiest management technique is to select the Open Extensions Manager option. When Classic starts, this option acts as the equivalent of holding down the spacebar at startup under Mac OS 9.x. The Extensions Manager window appears, as shown in Figure 14.7.

6. Choose the Mac OS 9.x Base set from the Selected Set pop-up menu.

7. Go to the File menu and select Duplicate Set. A window appears allowing you to name the set, as shown in Figure 14.8. This simply makes a copy of the Base set you've already selected.

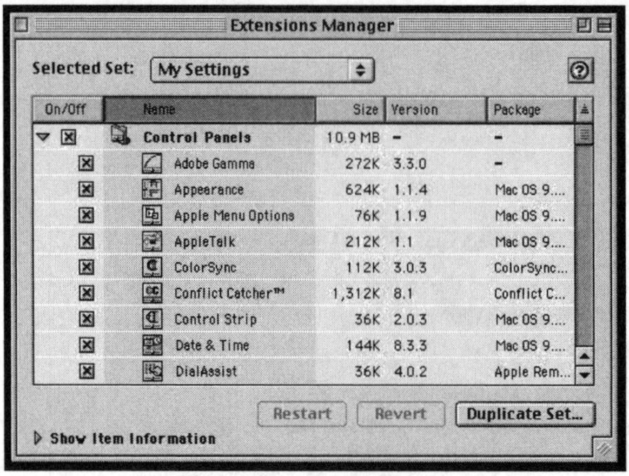

Figure 14.7   Apple's Extensions Manager helps you set up Classic for the best performance.

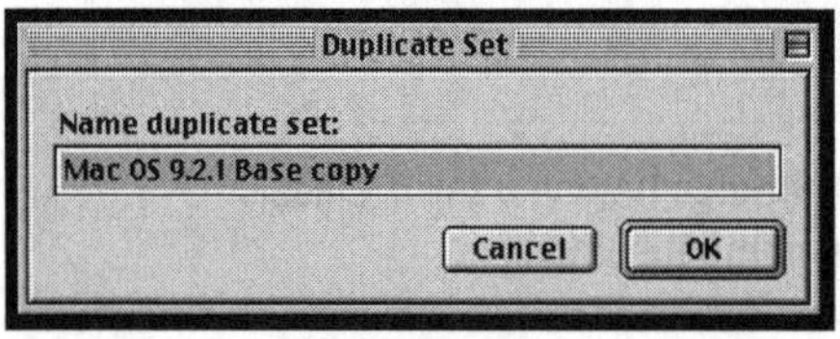

Figure 14.8   This is a duplicate of the extension set you selected.

8.   Name the copy of the Base set something that will identify it for the purpose, such as "Mac OS X Classic Set."

NOTE: *If you run any recent Classic version of Microsoft's Internet programs or any Microsoft Office application while using this Mac OS X set, a number of system extensions required by these programs will be installed the first time any of those programs are launched. There's no reason to be concerned; the installation is normal. This is why I am not recommending you run a Base set, because those sets cannot be modified; that is extensions such as those from Microsoft can't be added.*

9.   Close Extensions Manager to save your set. From here on, whenever you want to start your Mac under Mac OS X, make sure you activate this special "lean and mean" set for Mac OS X.

NOTE: *You can perform essentially the same operation if you use Casady & Greene's Conflict Catcher to manage your Mac OS 9.x System Folder. However, you should use version 8.0.9 or later. Earlier versions of Conflict Catcher had a peculiar bug when they interacted with the Classic environment, with recurring requests for the program's serial number. Unfortunately, the* *publisher is out of business, so getting any updates at this point is probably not going to happen. You may prefer to go back to Extensions Manager. This can be done by restoring the software from your Extensions (Disabled) and Control Panels (Disabled) folders to the regular folders, and then removing Conflict Catcher, after which you restart Classic.*

After this special set has been created, you might want to consider adding a few of your cherished extensions and see if Classic continues to run efficiently. There's no reason to abandon your normal extensions set; just switch over before you install or run Mac OS X.

In my experience, a lean and mean Classic environment is a good way to get the most out of Mac OS X without wasting a lot of time seeking out possible extension conflicts. If you need to return to Mac OS 9.x after restart (see "Returning to Mac OS 9.x" later in this chapter), hold down the spacebar until the Extensions Manager (or Conflict Catcher) window appears. Then switch back to your regular extension set (which will probably bring up a dialog from Conflict Catcher stating that it will restart your Mac yet again). That way, you can enjoy the best of both worlds.

TIP: *If your Classic application runs very sluggish, check the Memory/Versions tab of the Classic preference panel and see how much RAM the program is using. If the dark bar is close to the end, you'll want to quit the application and use the Finder's Get Info feature to increase application memory. Click the Memory disclosure triangle and increase the memory allocation in 1,000K increments. Launch the application and see if it runs better.*

NOTE: *If you switch extension sets with Conflict Catcher, on occasion you'll see a prompt indicating that you need to restart your Mac again. This happens if some of the extensions that were activated must boot before Conflict Catcher. It is normal behavior.*

Keeping Your Mac OS 9.x System Folder Safe and Sound

You can also protect your Mac OS 9.x System Folder by using another startup drive for your regular setup when you're not using the older operating system. This way, you don't have to fret over special startup sets, extra extensions in the System Folder from Mac OS X, or other possible problems that might result from the switching process (although it should, in theory, work all right). Here's how to get the most value out of this multiple System Folder scheme:

1. Before you install Panther, back up and reformat your Mac's hard drive into at least two partitions. After restarting with your first Panther installer CD, you can use Apple's Disk Utility, available from the Mac OS X Installer menu, to handle this task. Just click the Partition tab, select the drive, and bring up the Volume Scheme pop-up menu to choose from default partition methods.

WARNING! *If you have an early version iMac, you must put Panther on a partition occupying the first 8GB of space on the drive. When you use Disk Utility to reformat a drive on one of these models, make sure the first or top partition is no larger than 8GB. It doesn't matter how big the second partition is, so long as Panther isn't placed on it.*

2. Install the version of Mac OS 9.x you want to use with Panther on your first partition.

3. Install the System Folder you want to use for regular work on the second partition.

4. Proceed with your standard installation of Panther, as described in Chapter 2.

5. When the installer proceeds to the dialog box where you select a disk for installation, choose the one on your first boot partition. Be sure not to check the box to erase the partition; otherwise, you'll wipe out the data on that drive.

6. Continue with the Panther installation. For now, whenever you wish to use Classic, you'll choose the Mac OS 9.x System Folder on the first partition. When you want to work full-time in the older operating system, you'll simply select the System Folder in the second partition.

TIP: *If one or the other System Folder isn't recognized for startup or by the Startup Disk pane in the System Preferences application, open that folder and then close it again. This action has the effect of "blessing" the System Folder, making it possible to boot your Mac from it.*

NOTE: *Some folks feel that putting Mac OS X on a separate partition from the Classic Mac OS might improve performance and compatibility. Apple installs both operating systems on a single partition on all new Macs. My personal experience with a single partition and dual-partition setup yielded no significant differences. If you want to go through the trouble to back up your data and reformat your drives, it may be worth trying, at least as a measure of protection in case something goes wrong with the partition on which Mac OS X is present. Consider, however, that this might be best done on a new Mac, where you can partition the drive during the initial setup process and just restore all the standard files to one of the partitions.*

Related solution:	Found on page:
Installing Panther	28

Solving Classic Environment Problems

If you follow the steps in the previous sections, you should be able to continue to use your Classic Mac OS applications with decent performance and the maximum level of compatibility. However, if you choose to abandon the simple setup to add extra extensions, you may encounter some troubles along the way. Here are likely causes and solutions:

- *A slow startup of the Classic environment*—If it seems to take a long time to access a Classic application, consider this remedy: Pare down Mac OS 9.x system extensions to the Base set, and then create a new Mac OS X set from it. The startup process should be much faster, and your problems fewer.

- *Classic startup applications switch back and forth*—I have observed this phenomenon when the Launcher and the Mac OS 9 version of Spell Catcher played a game of dueling launches (but it can happen whenever there are multiple Classic startup programs). The immediate solution is to click the menu bar and quit the Spell Catcher application, but the long-term remedy is to disable one or the other.

> **14. Using Older Programs with Panther**

NOTE: *Spell Catcher is a terrific interactive spell-checking and thesaurus utility. It runs in virtually all programs and will flash warnings if you make an error. The Mac OS X version carries over the vast majority of its feature set, and it works in all Mac OS X applications that I've been able to test. Yes, Apple builds in a spell checker for its Cocoa applications, but Spell Catcher beats it hands down.*

- *A nasty startup crash when returning to Mac OS 9*—More than likely, you will need to restart under Mac OS 9.x for one reason or another, unless the Mac on which Mac OS X is installed is devoted to testing and nothing else. Shortly after the startup process begins, before extension icons appear, all or part of a blank bomb screen may bring the whole process to a halt. One of the causes could be a corrupted TCP/IP Preferences file. The solution is to restart with system extensions off (hold the Shift key down at startup), and then trash this file, which is located in the Preferences Folder inside the System Folder. Then it will be safe to restart normally. You'll need to re-create the settings (or keep a backup around, just in case).

TIP: *One way to avoid this annoying file corruption is to remove your standard TCP/IP Preferences file and keep it for safekeeping. Upon restart, a new, empty file will be created. With no data entered, it is less apt to become corrupted when you try to run your old Mac Internet software from the Classic environment. Another way is to lock your settings, so that they cannot be modified. You do so by changing the user mode to Administration (via the File menu). Once you're in Administration mode, you can lock down any setting.*

- *Launching Internet programs doesn't get you connected*—If you have dial-up access to the Internet, you need to launch the Internet Connect application first and then connect. You can then use any Carbon or Cocoa Internet application. If you're trying to use a program that does its own dialing, such as AOL or CompuServe, you'll need to check for Mac OS X updates to their client software.

Returning to Mac OS 9.x

There is no reason not to switch back to Mac OS 9.x to run programs and hardware that aren't ready to work under Mac OS X (that's why it's part of the Mac OS X package). To return to your former environment, do the following:

1. Launch the System Preferences application.
2. Double-click the Startup Disk pane (see Figure 14.9).

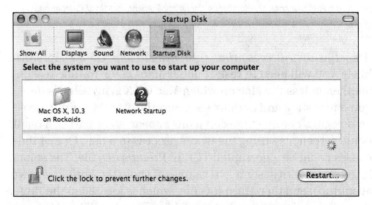

Figure 14.9   Choose your startup disk from this screen.

NOTE: *Beginning in 2003, more and more Macs lost the ability to reboot under Mac OS 9. If you have a model lacking this feature, you'll know pretty quickly by the lack of the listing of a Mac OS 9 System Folder in the Startup Disk preference pane.*

3. If you are not using an administrator's user account, click the padlock icon (if it's closed) and then type your username and password to get access to changing the startup disk.

4. Click your Mac OS 9.x startup disk.

5. Click the Restart button that appears at the bottom of the Startup pane in System Preferences and then in the confirming dialog box to save your settings (see Figure 14.10) and restart. In a few moments, your Mac will restart under Mac OS 9.x.

NOTE: *If you followed my recommendation to establish a special set in Extensions Manager or Conflict Catcher to use when running Mac OS 9.x in the Classic environment, be sure to hold down the spacebar when starting under Mac OS 9.x. Doing so will bring up your startup manager's screen, and you can then switch to your preferred Mac OS 9.x startup set for regular use and enjoy all your favorite system extensions. Apple calls your default extension setup My Settings unless you've renamed it.*

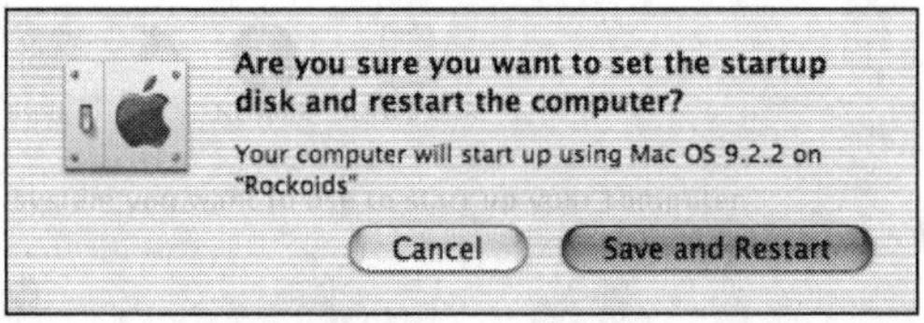

Are you sure you want to set the startup disk and restart the computer?

Your computer will start up using Mac OS 9.2.2 on "Rockoids"

Cancel   Save and Restart

Figure 14.10   Are you sure? Confirm your choice here.

14. Using Older Programs with Panther

Panther Font Management

In Brief

The Mac operating system became credible because of the desktop publishing revolution and the arrival of PostScript. Where you once had to use an artist's table, dedicated typesetting computers, and high-cost output devices to produce artwork for a brochure or publication, the Mac made it possible to do it all on your desktop at relatively low cost, even in your own home. Page layout applications, such as Adobe PageMaker and QuarkXPress, reasonably low-cost fonts, and relatively high-quality laser printers combined to bury much of the traditional typesetting industry, except for extremely specialized work.

However, the availability of tens of thousands of high quality fonts has proven to be the bane of the Mac user's experience, because it creates new concerns and sources of confusion.

There Are Fonts and There Are Fonts

It would be nice if fonts all came in just one format and were easy to install, but the situation has been otherwise. There are multiple font formats, and fonts of different types with the very same name. Where do you begin?

Font Formats Defined

Before you even select a font to use in your document, you are faced with choices of installation and organization. Here's a list of the types of fonts commonly used on Macs:

- *Bitmap fonts*—The original Mac font format, bitmap fonts are designed for printing and display in a single size. If they are scaled to one size or another, the quality of the image deteriorates in proportion to the size difference; the image can become an almost unreadable collection of pixel shapes when printed or viewed at a very large size.

- *PostScript fonts*—This scalable font format was developed by Adobe Systems in the 1980s and quickly came to dominate the printing and publishing industries. See the next item for a full description of how such fonts work.

- *Scalable fonts*—Whether PostScript or TrueType, these fonts can be printed in any available point size at the full resolution of the printer or other output device. However, the fonts come in a form that confuses many Mac users. The scalable fonts, called variously *outline fonts* or *printer fonts*, are separate from the fonts that generate images on your Mac's display, the *screen fonts*. This arrangement is a carryover from the way fonts were organized in the days of traditional typography, when font sets were divided into two parts for width or space values and for output. But it causes confusion because the lack of the screen font means your font won't show up in a Font menu, and the lack of a printer font means it won't print at full quality.

- *Multiple Master fonts*—This is a special font that can be modified to provide customized variations, such as having thicker letters, narrower and wider widths, and so on. Although the tools for making the various "instances" of multiple master fonts are not available for Panther, existing fonts can be used with full compatibility.

NOTE: *A likely downside to all this joy was the fact that it was one big headache for graphic artists to figure out the font that was being used by looking at a printout. Even those who prided themselves as true typographers, able to recognize fonts at a single bound, were confounded by the strange variations some would produce with multiple master fonts.*

- *TrueType fonts*—In 1990, to avoid having to pay license fees for use of PostScript fonts—there's always a reason—Apple, with a little help from Microsoft in the final stages, developed a new scalable font format. TrueType fonts include the screen font and outline font in a single file. For that reason alone, they are easier to handle. However, they have downsides. One is that you should not try to use a PostScript and TrueType font of the same typeface family. At worst, printing of the document will be inconsistent or output in the wrong font. Or, letterspacing may be distorted. The other problem with TrueType is that printers and service bureaus with high-resolution output devices may not fully support the format, particularly if they are using older hardware.

NOTE: *Although originally introduced on the Mac platform, TrueType fonts are the standard font format for Microsoft Windows. On the Mac platform, however, PostScript remains the font format of choice for the publishing industry because the high-resolution output devices used may not always support TrueType (a situation that has been largely fixed with newer devices). New Macs and the Mac OS ship with TrueType and .dfonts. (I'll get to this shortly.)*

- *OpenType fonts*—A recent entrant in the font arena, the OpenType font format can combine elements of PostScript and

TrueType fonts in a single file, along with more extensive character sets, including decorative characters and such. It's fully supported by Panther and more and more font makers, such as Adobe, are coming around to supporting the format. Someday maybe it'll replace those old fashioned PostScript fonts.

- *.dfont*—What, pray tell, is this? Well, rather than go into painful detail, it's simply an alternate way of building a font file. Mac files are traditionally built in two parts: the data fork and the resource fork. The .dfont format, used for system-related fonts in Panther, puts it all in the data fork. That's the beginning and end of it. This new font format was introduced with the original release of Mac OS X.

Font Organization under the Mac OS

Before Mac OS X arrived, Mac users had to rely on extra software for flexible font handling and, in fact, to use fonts with some printers. These programs would allow you to store fonts in places other than the Fonts folder and only activate them when needed. That and various degrees of font organizational capability made these programs essential for handling large font libraries. Even better, most of these applications, with only one notable exception, are available in native Mac OS X versions, and as you'll see Panther takes the world of font handling to a new level of complexity.

Here's a list of the font management options and what they offer:

- *Adobe Type Manager (ATM)*—Originally introduced in 1989, this program is designed to provide clear screen display of PostScript fonts in all available sizes. It also has the side effect of allowing non-PostScript printers, such as ink jet printers, to use PostScript fonts and deliver the maximum quality they were capable of. An enhanced version of ATM, ATM Deluxe (shown in Figure 15.1), also allows you to activate and deactivate fonts that are not installed in the System Folder, check for duplicates and damaged fonts, and print font samples.

NOTE: *Although a Mac OS X version of ATM will never be produced, according to Adobe, you should still keep it at hand for clean display of PostScript fonts used in the Classic environment. This is the only program in this list that will probably never be updated for the new operating system.*

- *Font Book*— Like the commercial alternatives, Apple's new font management application, which is now called *Font Book* (see Figure 15.2), can be used to install your fonts, put them into sets

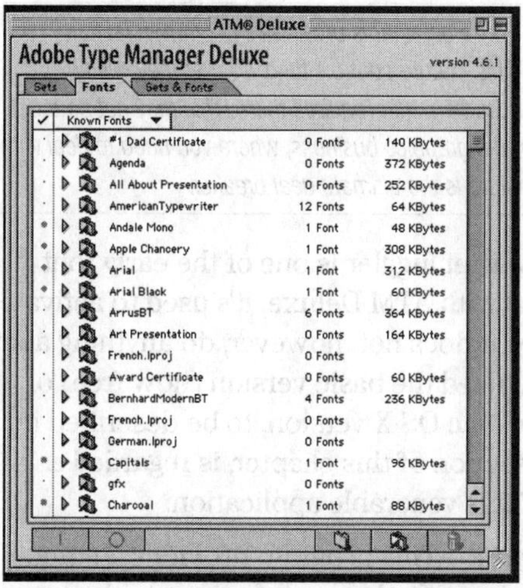

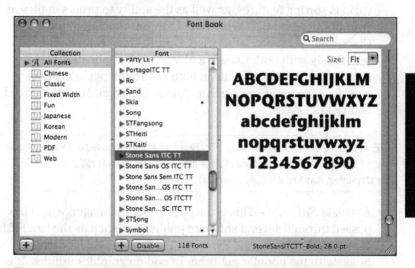

Figure 15.1   ATM Deluxe manages your font library and provides clear display of fonts, all in the same program.

Figure 15.2   Font Book is Apple's clever new answer to font confusion.

or collections, and activate and deactivate them as needed. Font Book integrates well into the Panther environment by building upon the interface of Font Panel, a feature used to select fonts and styles in many applications. Some Mac users suggest that Apple should have brought Font Book out years ago, or some variation thereof. As you'll learn in the Immediate Solutions section, however, Font Book isn't quite as flexible as the commercial alternatives, and its capabilities aren't quite so extensive.

> **NOTE:** One significant feature missing in Font Book that is provided by commercial font management programs is autoactivation. This feature controls fonts so that they will not automatically load whenever you open a document that requires them. This may not be a big deal for many Mac users, but if you are in the graphics business, where you need to deal with huge numbers of fonts, the lack of this feature is the ultimate deal breaker.

- *Alsoft's MasterJuggler*—MasterJuggler is one of the early font management programs. As with ATM Deluxe, it's used to activate and organize a font library. It does not, however, do anything about font rendering, so you still need the basic version (now free) of ATM for that purpose. The Mac OS X version, to be described in the Immediate Solutions section of this chapter, is regarded as a total rework or rewrite of this venerable application.

- *DiamondSoft's Font Reserve*—This program provides a unique way to store and manage fonts. It places all fonts outside the System Folder in a database file, so you don't have to concern yourself with placing them in any particular location. It offers various sorting features, as well as the ability to print samples of your library. Again, ATM is needed for font rendering in the Classic environment. Otherwise, Font Reserve can work seamlessly with both Classic and Mac OS X applications, and automatically activate fonts in both environments in many of your favorite programs, such as Adobe InDesign, Microsoft Word and QuarkXPress.

> **NOTE:** At the time this book went to press, Font Reserve had been acquired by Extensis, and was expected to be combined with Suitcase at some future time. Since it was still available as a separate product, however, it is being covered in this book.

- *Extensis Suitcase*—This is the original font manager, which has passed through several software publishers (such as the late Fifth Generation Systems and Symantec) before finding its current home with the popular publisher of add-on graphics utilities. It is somewhat similar to MasterJuggler in terms of its focus and features, but you still need ATM for clean display of PostScript fonts. The Mac OS X program, as described in the Immediate Solutions section of this chapter, provides an interface that closely resembles the Classic version.

Mac OS X's New Font-Handling Scheme

When developing Mac OS X, Apple Computer realized that font management was confusing for many Mac users and often the source of trouble in preparing and outputting documents. The response is the

Apple Type Solution (ATS). This mechanism, which works with the Quartz 2D imaging layer of the new operating system, delivers system-wide handling of all the major font formats—PostScript, TrueType, OpenType, and even the original Mac bitmap fonts.

ATS handles font rendering of all the formats using Mac OS X's Portable Document Format (PDF) mechanism (which uses Adobe's popular open standard for creating electronic documents), so you don't need ATM for PostScript font display. In addition, built-in tools organize font collections, display samples and enabling and disabling, which may reduce or eliminate the need for a font management program.

Mac OS X applications can use fonts stored in all the Mac OS X Fonts folders (yes, there are several), plus the Fonts folder in your Mac OS 9.x System Folder. Classic applications are restricted to the contents of the Classic Mac OS Fonts folder; that is, unless you install a font management program to manage your library (as described earlier).

NOTE: *As you'll see in the pages that follow, the ATS font system isn't a panacea, and it doesn't work with all programs; nor will its font-handling features appeal to everyone. This is apt to leave plenty of room for third-party publishers to update existing font managers or develop new programs to provide needed features lacking in the core operating system.*

Additionally, fonts are made available in several ways to users of Mac OS X:

- *System-wide*—Fonts can still be placed in a Fonts folder, but several Fonts folders are in use under Mac OS X. The one you'll be using most often for system-wide fonts is in a new location, but it is used in a fashion similar to the Fonts folder under the Classic Mac OS. You'll find it in a folder labeled Library, where a number of folders related to system settings and preferences are located. Fonts in this folder are available to all users of that computer. Changing fonts or anything else on a system basis, of course, requires that you log in using an administrator's account name and password, unless you log into that sort of account by default.

NOTE: *Is that all? Not quite. Within the Mac OS X System Folder, in a folder also labeled Library, is yet another Fonts folder, containing fonts required by the system for display of menu bar titles, Finder labels, and other purposes. However, you cannot normally add or remove files to this folder, because it's protected. Fonts may also be shared from a Mac running Mac OS X Server, and made available via the Network folder at the top or root level of your hard drive, under, of course, the Server category.*

- *User-specific*—Each user can have a separate library, stored in the Fonts folder, in his or her personal Library folder. The Library folder is located within the Home or Users folder, which bears the user's name. Those fonts are available only to that user, but they behave transparently to Mac OS X otherwise and look just the same when they appear in the Font menu. When you log off or another user connects via Fast User Switching, the fonts aren't available to that user.

- *Application specific*—Some applications have their own private Fonts folders in the application folder. Fonts installed in that location are only activate when that application is running, and are only usable in that application.

NOTE: *Another advantage of Mac OS X is the number of fonts you can use. Under Mac OS versions prior to 9, the limit was 128 font resources, meaning bitmap and suitcase files. Some users would drag and drop font suitcases atop one another to combine them and get around this limitation. The limit went to 512 fonts under Mac OS 9, but Mac OS X has no limit to how many fonts you can install, other than the size of your Mac's drive and the agony you want to experience in looking at an endless font display.*

Introducing the Font Book

In answer to the clamor for some way to deal with the chaotic font management situation on the Mac OS, Apple brought forth the Font Book. This application takes over the basic font handling functions in Panther, and is thoroughly integrated with the Finder for maximum performance.

For example, you can double-click on any font in a Finder window and Font Book will display a preview. Click Install and it'll be moved (or copied, depending on your preference) to the appropriate Fonts folder (system-wide, User, or Classic).

One of the benefits of Font Book is the fact that it doesn't need to be running for you to benefit from its font management features because the fonts are copied or moved physically to be activated, and moved to a Fonts (Disabled) folder to be turned off. In fact, the application does its thing pretty much the same way as Extensions Manager handled extensions in the Classic Mac OS.

Introducing the Font Panel

Apple has made a significant stride toward more efficient font management with Mac OS X's Font Panel (see Figure 15.3). This handy feature not only simplifies selection of fonts, but also allows you to organize your collection, regardless of size, according to your needs.

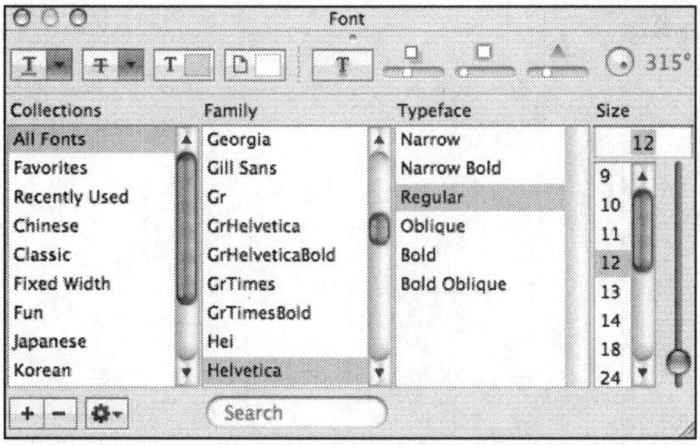

Figure 15.3   Choose, sample, and organize your font library here.

The Font Panel may even partially replace the need for a separate font management program—except that it has a serious limitation. When software publishers Carbonize their applications to work under Mac OS X, they must make a number of choices. One is to make the program run in the new environment and be compatible with the basic features, such as preemptive multitasking and protected memory. This option entails less work on the part of a publisher's programming team. Apple also provides tools to exploit the features of Carbon, should the publisher undertake the extra work. However, at least with the version of Mac OS X covered in this book (Panther), Font Panel support wasn't available. As a result, an application that otherwise fully supports Mac OS X will have a plain-Jane Font menu (see Figure 15.4). Unfortunate, but true.

NOTE: *Something else you may miss under Mac OS X is a font menu modifier, such as Adobe Type Reunion, Action WYSIWYG or Menu Fonts. Such programs would group fonts into families, to keep font menus shorter, and also provide WYSIWYG display of fonts, meaning they appear in the actual typeface. Some programs, such as AppleWorks and Word, do provide the option to display this way, but only Adobe, so far, groups fonts by family in its font menus. Perhaps someone will develop a Mac OS X variation of one of those font menu modifiers by the time you read this book.*

However, if the publisher has developed a Cocoa application, you'll find the Font Panel to be a flexible way in which to manage your font collection.

TIP: *One quick way to see whether a program was developed for the Carbon or Cocoa environment is to see whether it has a Font Panel. However, regardless of which environment was used for developing the application, it should work fine under Mac OS X, with full support for its industrial-strength operating system features.*

Font	Tools	Table	Window	Work

25 Helvetica UltraLight

26 Helvetica UltraLightItalic

35 Helvetica Thin

36 Helvetica ThinItalic

45 Helvetica Light

46 Helvetica LightItalic

55 Helvetica Roman

56 Helvetica Italic

65 Helvetica Medium

66 Helvetica MediumItalic

75 Helvetica Bold

76 Helvetica BoldItalic

85 Helvetica Heavy

86 Helvetica HeavyItalic

95 Helvetica Black

96 Helvetica BlackItalic

American Typewriter

American Typewriter Condensed

American Typewriter Light

Andale Mono

Apple Chancery

✓ Arial

Arial Black

Arial Narrow

Arial Rounded MT Bold

Baskerville SSF

B Univers 65 Bold

Baskerville

Baskerville Semibold

BERTRAM LET

Beckley Swipe LET

Big Caslon

BLAIRMDITC TT-MEDIUM

Blk Univers 75

BlkO Univers 75 BlackOblique

BO Univers 65 BoldOblique

꽃꽃꽃꽃 美美美美미 ᵝᵝᵝᵝ

Bodoni SvtyTwo ITC TT-Bold

Bodoni SvtyTwo ITC TT-Book

Bodoni SvtyTwo ITC TT-BookIta

Bodoni SvtyTwo OS ITC TT-Bold

Bodoni SvtyTwo OS ITC TT-Book

Bodoni SvtyTwo OS ITC TT-BookIt

Bordeaux Roman Bold LET

Bradley Hand ITC TT-Bold

Brush Script MT

C Univers 57 Condensed

CAPITALS

CB Univers 67 CondensedBold

▼

Figure 15.4   This particular application, although Carbonized for Mac OS X, yields only an old-fashioned Font menu.

Special Font Features of Mac OS X

If an application supports the Font Panel, it also inherits some additional system-wide font features that used to be available only in separate programs. When you call up a Font menu in a Mac OS X program that offers the expanded font capability, you'll see a number of those additional features (some will vary from program to program) in addition to the normal range of font formatting choices. They include the following:

- *Kern*—Used by graphic artists, *kerning* is the process of adjusting the spacing of letter combinations that would otherwise be wide apart visually. For example, in the word *To,* kerning tucks the lowercase *o* closer to the letter *T* for a more pleasing appearance and better readability. Mac OS X lets you use the kerning features of a font. You can also adjust the overall spacing between characters, which is sometimes called *tracking* or *range kerning.*

- *Ligature*—In high-quality books and ads, *ligatures* create single, integrated characters of such combinations as *fi* and *fl*, by joining the tops of the characters, such as fi and fl. The conversion is done automatically when you type a character.

NOTE: *Such programs as QuarkXPress and Adobe InDesign, two popular page-layout applications, can convert ligatures on the fly. Panther lets you do it with all programs that support its font-handling features. In addition, automatic kerning is also supported by the major desktop publishing applications, and, to some extent, in graphics software.*

With all the great font-handling features of Panther, you may begin to cherish the ease with which you are able to manage your library, whether it includes a few dozen or a few thousand fonts. In the "Immediate Solutions" section, I'll cover the ways you can install or use fonts under the new operating system.

Immediate Solutions

Installing Fonts Under Panther

As explained at the beginning of this chapter, fonts can be installed on a system-wide basis for everyone who uses your Mac or on an individual-user basis (so only that user can access them). Here's how to install a font on a system-wide basis:

1. Log in as the administrator of that Mac or a user with administrator's rights, if that's not your normal mode of operation. If another user has logged in, use the Log Out command in the Apple menu, confirm the logout and then enter your username and password in the Login prompt.

2. Locate your Mac's Library folder, which is located on the startup drive and locate the Fonts folder within it.

3. Copy the fonts directly to the Fonts folder. The fonts will be recognized by your newly opened applications. If they don't appear right away, restart your Mac (this shouldn't be necessary, however).

The other way to install fonts is for the individual user only. Here's how it's done:

1. Log in under the individual user's or an administrator's account.

2. Locate the Home or Users folder, and then the folder with that user's name.

3. Locate the Library folder and copy the fonts directly to the Fonts folder located within it. Fonts installed in this fashion should show up immediately in your Font menu. If they don't, follow the steps in the preceding list and restart your Mac.

WARNING! *Fonts installed under a user's account are available only to an individual user. If you expect more than one user will work with a font, it's better to install the font on a system-wide basis.*

NOTE: Am I missing something? I didn't mention the Panther System folder and its Fonts folder, located within the Library folder. You normally cannot copy or remove any files from this folder with a couple of exceptions. One is to gain root access or just restart under Mac OS 9, if you feel you want to touch those fonts. Best thing is to leave them be, since most are required for various system display functions.

Using Font Book

The nice thing about the Font Book application is that there's nothing to install. It's there when you put Panther on your Mac, right in the Applications folder.

Here's a fast guide on how it works and how you control your font library from this neat little program:

1. To start Font Book, simply double-click to launch it or double-click on a font (your choice).

2. If you double-click on a font that isn't installed yet, you can click Install to add it to your library (see Figure 15.5).

NOTE: Font Book's preferences can be used to specify where to put your newly installed fonts. By default, they are placed in the Fonts folder inside your personal or Users folder. You can change this too For All Users of This Computer, or For Classic Mac OS. The latter makes them available not only to everyone using your Mac, but to Classic applications too. The final preference gives you the option to copy rather than move the fonts to their new locales. You may prefer this option if you don't want to mess up your original font library.

Figure 15.5   Click a button and your new font will be ready to use.

3. Once your fonts are installed, you can use Font Book to organize your fonts in a way that makes sense to you. That means alphabetically (the simplest way), by the name of the project, or by the name of the client. The latter pair of choices are good if you need to set up your fonts for your business.

4. Once you've built your font collection, you can enable and disable fonts either individually or as a collection of a number of faces. To activate a font or collection, select the item and click Enable (see Figure 15.6). The font collection toggles to Disable in case you want to turn it off.

NOTE: *In each case, you'll get an acknowledgement prompt asking if you really want to do that. A little click on the checkbox on the lower left can be used to turn off the reminder if you grow tired of it.*

WARNING! *When you enable a font with an application running, there is no guarantee that the font menu will be updated. This depends on the program. If it doesn't update, you will have to quit the program and launch it again. Also, turning off a font you're using in a document will cause the document text to re-flow and will cause appearance problems as text using disabled fonts reverts to an application's default styles.*

5. If you simply want to see what a font looks like, select the font and you'll see a preview in the right pane. If it's not large

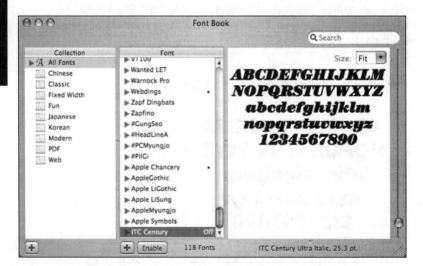

Figure 15.6   You can turn on this font or the entire font family with a single click.

enough, just move the slider up and down to change the size dynamically. Fixed sizes can also be saved on the Font pop-up menu.

Once you have mastered these simple techniques, you can quickly build a sizeable font library to meet your needs. You'll also be pleased to find out that the Font Book gives you the ability to search your fonts by family or name to quickly find the ones you need.

Fonts can be displayed at any size using Panther's Quartz rendering technology. And, as I said before, you can't print samples, at least not yet. If you need that feature and autoactivation, you will have to use one of the third party font managers.

Using the Font Panel

For many Mac OS X applications, including those developed in its Cocoa environment, or new Carbon programs updated for the feature, no standard font menu is provided. Instead, you have the Font Panel.

NOTE: Just so we're perfectly clear here, the Font Book is a Panther application used to install, activate, and deactivate fonts. It shares the Font Panel's capability of selecting fonts and organizing them into collections. The Font Panel, on the other hand, is simply a Panther replacement for the font menu and it even works with other font managers, such as MasterJuggler, FontAgent Pro, and Suitcase.

Panther's Font Panel provides a feature-laden way to organize and access the fonts in your library, regardless of its size. (You don't use this tool, however, to turn fonts on or off—that's a job for Font Book.) You can also use Font Panel to take advantage of the special typographic features of Panther including ligatures, characters such as *fi* that flow together, kerning, a wide variety of fractions, swashes, and special styling features such as colors, underlines, shadows, and others.

Here's how to use the Font Panel:

1. From within an application that supports the feature, go to the Format menu and choose Font. Select Font Panel from the submenu. The window in Figure 15.7 appears. To open it more quickly, press Command+T.

2. Under Family, select the font you want to use.

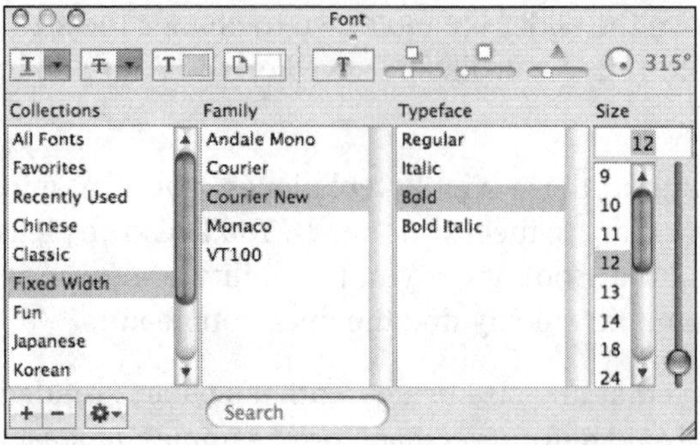

Figure 15.7   Many Mac OS X-savvy applications support the Font Panel.

3. If the font has several styles, choose the one you want from the Typeface column.

4. Pick the size you want from the Sizes column (or type the size in the text field at the top of the column to get a size not listed in the display).

TIP: *If the Font Panel is too large to fit comfortably on your Mac's screen as related to your document window, resize it by moving the resize bar. Fonts are also organized into collections. If you expand the width of the Font Panel, you'll see one more column, Collections, from which you can select a different group of fonts.*

---

5. Close the Font Panel screen and continue to work in your document.

TIP: *If you plan to switch fonts back and forth from among your font collection, feel free to keep the Font Panel window displayed so that you can return to it quickly from your document. Unfortunately, the Font Panel doesn't have an active minimize function, so you can't leave it on the Dock for quick access.*

NOTE: *Commonly available weights of a font, such as bold or italic, can be selected directly from the Font menu without invoking the Font Panel, although purists say you'll get better printing results if you choose the correct font weight from the panel itself.*

Adding Font Favorites

Another great feature of the Font Panel is the ability to store fonts as favorites for fast retrieval. Here's how to set them up:

1. From within an application that supports the feature, activate the Font Panel.

2. Select the font family, style, and size you want.

TIP: *The toolbar at the top of the Font Panel gives you speedy access to special font formatting and size features. Give it a workout and you'll find that your font selections go much faster than you ever imagined.*

---

3. Click the Actions pop-up menu (see Figure 15.8) and select Add To Favorites.

4. Repeat the process for each font you want to use as a favorite. Favorites will list not just the typeface, but also the exact size you specified.

Using Favorites

To access a font from your Favorites list, follow these steps:

1. Activate the Font Panel. Click the resize bar and extend it to the right, to expand the width of the Font Panel.

2. From the Collections column, click Favorites to see the display in Figure 15.9. The Favorites list will show the selected fonts in their actual size and style.

TIP: *If you want to check on how the font looks, click the Show Preview option in the Extras pop-up menu. The preview will display the actual face in the actual size you select. The Show Characters option will produce a convenient palette showing optional characters available in a font.*

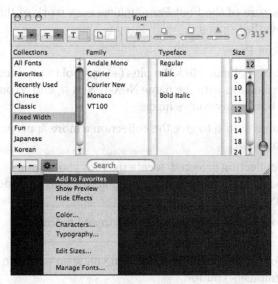

Figure 15.8 Additional commands are available for you to organize your font collection.

15. Panther Font Management

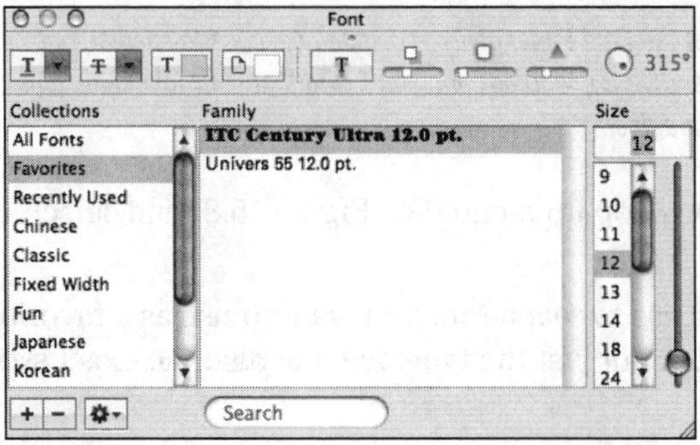

Figure 15.9   Choose your favorites from this list.

3. To remove a font from your Favorites list, select it and choose Remove From Favorites from the Actions pop-up menu.

Creating a Font Collection

One of the more useful features of Panther for managing a large font library is the ability to create a custom collection to match your specific needs. That way, you can have one font collection for personal use and another for business. If you're a business user, you can subdivide fonts by the name of your client, your document, or the type of fonts you're using, such as serif and sans serif, or title and text, to name a few.

The Collections feature of the Font Panel makes easy work of this process. Just follow these steps:

1. Activate the Font Panel.

2. In the Collections column, click the plus (+) symbol to produce a brand-new collection with the name New-1, New-2, and so on, depending on how many you've made.

3. Click the Rename button to give the collection a more appropriate name, if you wish.

4. With the new collection selected, locate the font you want in the All Families column and click the left-pointing arrow to add it to your collection.

5. Repeat the process for each font you want to add to that collection.

6. To remove a font collection, select the item you want to delete and click the minus (–) button.

WARNING! *There is no warning prompt if you click the minus button when selecting a font collection. So, be certain you want to remove that collection before clicking the button. This feature may or may not be fixed in the final release of Mac OS X.*

7. Click Done when you're finished making your collections.

8. To add that particular font collection as a favorite, choose Add To Favorites from the Font Panel's pop-up menu.

9. When you're finished creating font collections, close the Font Panel.

10. When you need to use a specific collection, access the Font Panel and click the collection's name in the Collections column.

11. Select your font in the same fashion described at the beginning of this section.

Choosing Custom Font Sizes

The Font Panel includes a standard set of popular display sizes, but if your needs require more fine-tuning, follow this process:

1. Activate the Font Panel from a program that supports the feature.

2. With the Font Panel on display, choose Edit Sizes from the pop-up menu to bring up the screen shown in Figure 15.10.

3. In the New Size box, enter the size you want to include in the Sizes list, and click the plus (+) button. Alternatively, you can choose the Adjustable Slider button and move a slider to select the various font sizes.

4. To remove a font size, select it and click the minus (–) button.

5. Click Done when you're finished. You'll be returned to the Font Panel.

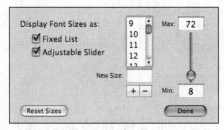

Figure 15.10   Add new font sizes here.

15. Panther Font Management

Checking the Characters in a Font

You probably remember Key Caps from the Classic Mac OS. This font management scheme persisted through Mac OS 10.2 Jaguar. With Panther, the Font Panel adds a more powerful action, a real character palette (see Figure 15.11). (And no puns about your humble author being a real character; I resemble that remark.)

To use the Character palette, follow these steps:

1. Open the Font Panel.

2. Choose Characters from the Actions menu.

3. The keyboard layout displays the characters available. Choose the character you want to use by its category.

4. Select the character and click Insert to place it at the insertion point in your document.

TIP: *If you want to use those special characters over and over again without going through multiple categories, select the character, click Add to Favorites, and then click on the Favorites button to see them quickly.*

Avoiding Too-Small Fonts in TextEdit

Apple's replacement for SimpleText, TextEdit (shown in Figure 15.12), can be used as a simple word processor, with full management of

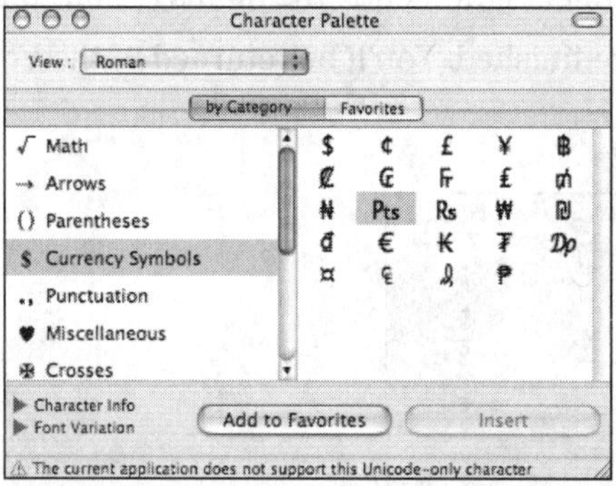

Figure 15.11   Use the Character palette to see all the characters of your fonts.

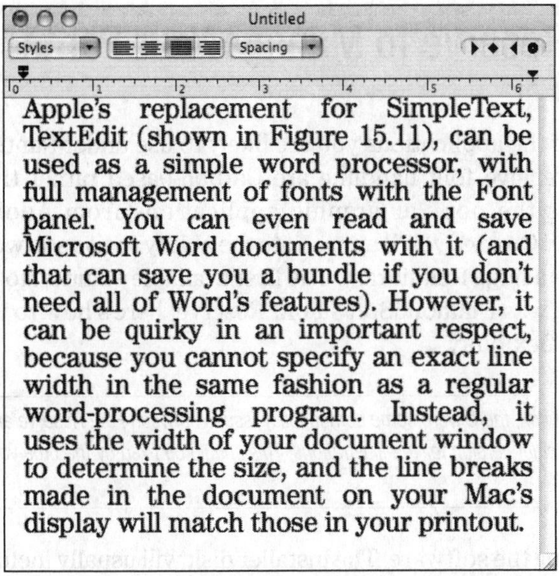

Apple's replacement for SimpleText, TextEdit (shown in Figure 15.11), can be used as a simple word processor, with full management of fonts with the Font panel. You can even read and save Microsoft Word documents with it (and that can save you a bundle if you don't need all of Word's features). However, it can be quirky in an important respect, because you cannot specify an exact line width in the same fashion as a regular word-processing program. Instead, it uses the width of your document window to determine the size, and the line breaks made in the document on your Mac's display will match those in your printout.

Figure 15.12   TextEdit is meant to be a less modestly featured replacement for the famous SimpleText application.

fonts with the Font Panel. You can even read and save Microsoft Word documents with it (and that can save you a bundle if you don't need all of Word's features). However, it can be quirky in an important respect, because you cannot specify an exact line width in the same fashion as a regular word-processing program. Instead, it uses the width of your document window to determine the size, and the line breaks made in the document on your Mac's display will match those in your printout.

However, if your printout uses a page width smaller than the screen, the font's size will be scaled down in proportion, and under some circumstances, it can get downright small. However, a simple solution to this dilemma exists:

1. Go to TextEdit's Format menu.

2. Select the Wrap To Page option. When this feature is active, lines will wrap on the basis of the page size selected in the Page Setup box. No more ultra-small (or ultra-large) letters, and the size that's printed will be the exact size you selected in the document itself.

Using Font Reserve to Manage Your Panther Font Library

Because most of the applications you are likely to use under Panther that require extensive font handling are Carbon-based rather than Cocoa (such as the popular graphic applications from Adobe, Macromedia, and Quark), you'll appreciate the ability to use software that can manage a huge font library. The first available solution to hit the marketplace was DiamondSoft's Font Reserve; here's how to use it for maximum flexibility.

NOTE: When I wrote this book, there were some compatibility issues between Font Reserve and Panther, so I'm using the older version for the illustrations. This should be fixed by the time you read this book.

Begin by installing the software. The installer disk will usually include both the Mac OS 9.x and Mac OS X versions and runs the same as any other installation program.

TIP: You can get a free limited-edition version of Font Reserve for Mac OS X as part of the Corel Graphics Suite 11 package. The sole limitation is the number of fonts you can use: 2,000. But that isn't an issue unless you expect to use more than that many fonts.

After performing the installation, here's how to set up the program to recognize your library. The first consideration, of course, is that for maximum efficiency, the program should manage all but your very basic operating system fonts:

1. Make sure none of your applications are running. Quit any that are still active (using the Dock as the guide to see which ones are open).

NOTE: What's a system-related font? Keep such fonts as Charcoal, Chicago, Courier, Geneva, Lucinda Grande, Monaco, Times, and Symbol where they are. You can safely move the rest.

2. Locate the Font Reserve application in your Panther Applications folder and launch the Font Reserve Settings application (see Figure 15.13).

3. Click the On button at the top of the application window to make Font Reserve active.

4. To avoid having to launch the application each time you log in

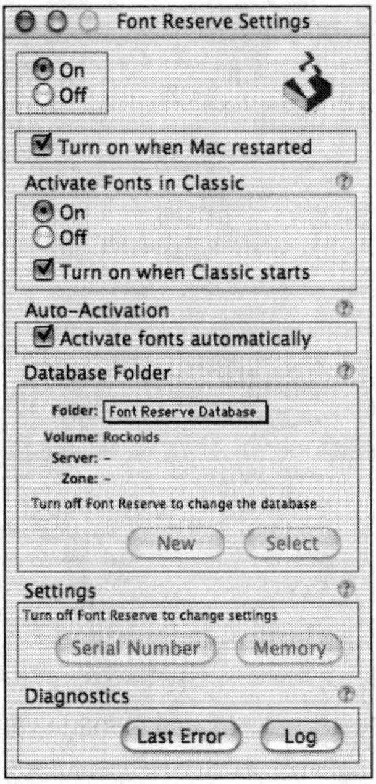

Figure 15.13   Activate Font Reserve from this application.

or restart your Mac, click the Turn On When Mac Restarted checkbox, which will make the program a login or startup application.

5. Quit the Font Reserve Settings application and then launch the Font Reserve Browser application (see Figure 15.14), which you'll use on a regular basis to manage your fonts.

6. To add fonts to Font Reserve, they need to be placed in the Font Reserve Database, the program's font storage area, located in the Font Reserve Browser application window. Drag and drop the Temp Fonts folder you made into the lower pane of the Font Reserve Browser window.

NOTE: *The first time you add a fonts folder or set of files to Font Reserve, you'll see a Preferences dialog box in which you tell the program how to handle the fonts. The best option, Copy Into Font Reserve Database, will simply make a copy rather than put the original fonts in the database. This option leaves the fonts intact and will consume extra storage space, but it's useful if you need to install and use both the Classic and Mac OS X versions of Font Reserve and want to make duplicate Font Reserve Database files.*

---

15. Panther Font Management

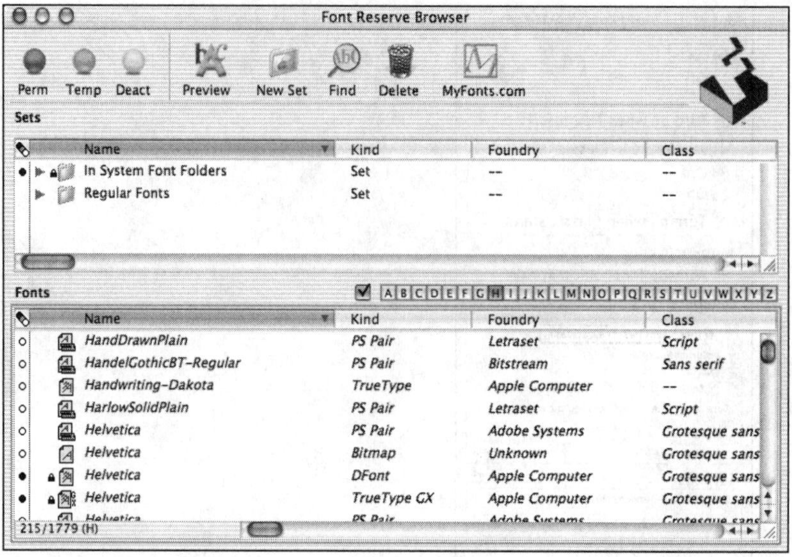

Figure 15.14 This application is used to locate, sample, and manage your Mac's font library.

After your font library has been compiled into Font Reserve, you can use the Font Reserve Browser application's toolbar to activate or deactivate fonts as needed. Font Reserve supplies plug-ins that can be used with such programs as QuarkXPress to provide automatic activation of fonts stored in an opened document, or when fonts are activated with Font Reserve.

Using Suitcase to Manage Your Panther Font Library

While it may not have been the first out of the starting gate, Suitcase XI (or 11) for Mac OS X was long-awaited and highly praised by folks looking for an easy font management solution. In this section, I'll give you a brief look at how you manage your fonts with Suitcase.

NOTE: It's interesting to note that some users of Extensis Suitcase actually began working with the program in the late 1980s, while using Mac System 6. A lot has changed since then, but the program continues to be an important tool for graphic artists who need to handle large numbers of fonts with relative simplicity.

Since it works in both the Classic and Mac OS X environments, there's an installer to sort things out. Once the program is installed, you'll find an Extensis Suitcase folder in your Mac OS X Applications folder and several system extensions in your Classic Mac OS System Folder. The latter are used to allow Suitcase to bridge both environments and let both Classic and Mac OS X folders access your entire font library.

When you first launch Suitcase (see Figure 15.15), you'll see a simple interface with intuitive controls. If you want to have the program recognize fonts stored outside of your Classic and Mac OS X Fonts folders, click on the Add Fonts button on the program's toolbar to locate and incorporate those fonts in its database.

Fonts can be organized as sets (see the top pane), which allows you to activate a group of fonts in a single operation, and, in the lower pane, you can display fonts in different categories, from the entire library, to just the fonts stored in individual Fonts folders. The pane at the right lets you easily preview a font before you use it.

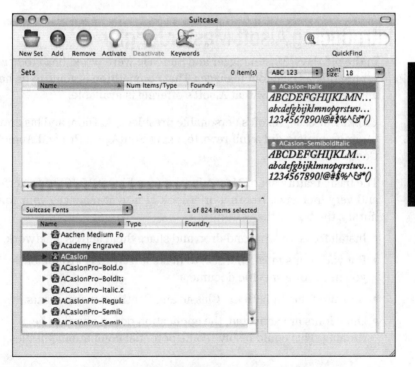

Figure 15.15 Suitcase for Mac OS X lets you do your font management from a single window.

15. Panther Font Management

> **TIP:** *Suitcase also lets you print a sample page for the fonts in your library, so you can keep a convenient font book at hand for personal reference or to help your clients select the right fonts for a particular job. To print the samples, first select the fonts in the Suitcase pane, and choose Print Sample Pages from the File menu and then select your printer's options in the Print dialog box.*

To activate a font, simply click at the left of its name. The font will be activated on a temporary basis, until the next restart. To keep a font activated all the time, hold down the Option key when you click the font to activate it.

Is that all? Mostly. Fonts can be autoactivated when you launch a number of Classic programs that contain those fonts. Autoactivate support under Mac OS X applies to the major graphics and publishing applications from Adobe and Quark, Inc. In addition, some Mac OS X applications allow autoactivation without any special setups.

Introducing Alsoft MasterJuggler

In the old days, MasterJugger and Suitcase were pitted head to head for the title as best font manager. That competition is going to be hot and heavy again, now that Alsoft's offering is available.

Unlike Suitcase, Alsoft's personable president, Al Dion, and his crew of programmers did a full rewrite, using FontAgent Pro and Apple's Cocoa environment.

The basic feature set of MasterJuggler (see Figure 15.16) is powerful and very inclusive. Here's a brief look at how it manages your font library, the bigger the better:

- Install fonts via drag-and-drop and share them across a network.

- Put your fonts in custom sets to make it easy to get to the ones you need for a specific document.

- Activate fonts in both the Classic and Panther environments.

- Once fonts are activated, the application doesn't have to be running. This could resolve some potential compatibility issues.

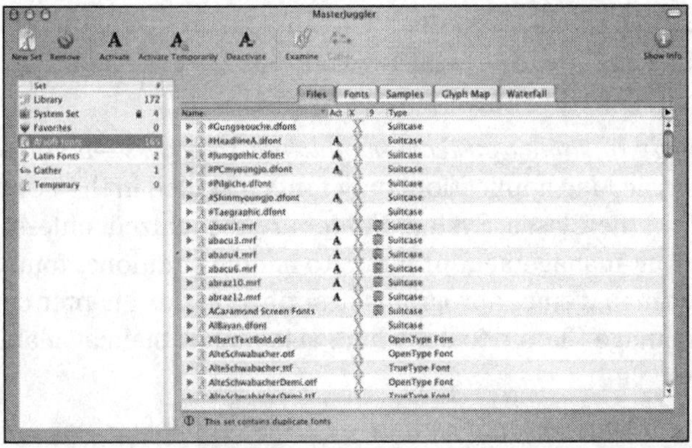

Figure 15.16   MasterJuggler goes its own way with two, rather than three, panes in its application window, but with buttons to select other features.

Introducing FontAgent Pro

Another variation on the font management theme is Insider Software's FontAgent Pro. This program's stock-in-trade is that it was developed in Panther's native Cocoa environment for fast performance, and that it automatically repairs and organizes your fonts when they are added to the program.

Another powerful feature is the ability to present a group of fonts in a slide show, using its Font Player feature. This allows you to sit back and watch the fonts you're planning to use, so you can get a good idea which ones suit for a specific project.

Handling Panther Font Problems

The new, more robust font-handling features of Panther usually make it far easier to handle a font library, whether small or large. But because of the interaction between Panther and the Classic environment, for example, you may still run into problems.

Here are some common Panther problems and the standard range of solutions:

- *Fonts not in the Font menu*—If a font was installed in a user's folder, it won't be available to any other user on your Mac. If you want more than a single user to access a font, install it under that user's account as well, or system-wide. If you did install the fonts in the proper fashion, try restarting your Mac just to make sure they are recognized by the operating system.

- *Fonts appear in some applications but not in others*—If you're using a Classic Mac application, only fonts installed in the Fonts folder within the Classic System Folder are recognized, unless you use a font-management program to handle additional fonts. All the font management programs described in this chapter can be set to manage Classic fonts, which also makes them available for Panther.

- *Garbled or bitmapped font output*—This is probably a font conflict, similar to those that afflicted earlier versions of the Mac OS. The best way to handle this problem is to make sure you have installed only one version of the font, and not both PostScript and TrueType versions. Another possible cause is installing two or more fonts of the same name from different sources. If you buy fonts from different collections, you may run into a problem of multiple versions of Futura and other typefaces. You'll want to recheck your fonts to make sure you have only activated the correct one. Font manager programs can help you by providing previews of a selected font before it's actually turned on. The operating system won't be able to sort them out.

- *Poor letterspacing*—Check the previous item to be sure you do not have fonts that are in conflict. Another possible problem is a damaged font suitcase or TrueType font, which may not provide the right letterspacing information.

- *Missing font collection*—Are you sure you didn't delete it by mistake? You get no acknowledgement if you click the minus button by accident. Otherwise, make sure the fonts added to a collection were not part of another user's account. That would explain why the collection isn't there when you try to access it.

- *Font menus too long?*—The reason font managers are useful is because they allow you to deactivate fonts you aren't using. The best way to control the symptom of the mile-long font menu is just to turn on the fonts you need, other than the standard ones used by Panther. Do not place the fonts you only use occasionally in the standard Fonts folders. Use the instructions provided with the font manager program for guidance on organizing a font library.

Chapter 16

Performing Backups

In Brief

One of the common comments I hear as I support Mac users is "What's a backup?" To many, this essential chore is drudgery and is considered a last resort activity. If you're too busy surfing the Net, writing a letter, or you really don't know which files to back up or where to put them, you are probably not backing up like you need to.

Unfortunately, there is no telling what might happen to your files during your day-to-day Mac computing experience. Although Panther offers a robust computing environment, about as free of potential system crashes as the state of the art allows, both the operating system and application software can still fail under normal use. When the software fails, such as unexpectedly quitting, it could conceivably harm the document you're working on. This is especially true if you're saving the document at the time the mishap occurs. In addition, hard drives, being mechanical devices, can fail unpredictably, even though they are supposed to have lengthy mean times between failures (sometimes 500,000 hours or more).

All sorts of potential issues beyond your Mac and computing environment could also conspire to cause data loss. They include weather-related problems such as hurricanes or tornadoes, natural disasters such as earthquakes and floods, and potential disasters like fire, theft and, heaven forbid, a terrorist act. In addition, any factor that might cause a power outage or power spike, even if caused by a problem at the power company, can result in a damaged file or hard drive directory damage if it occurs at the wrong time. Even if all your computing equipment is protected by insurance (and it should be, especially if used for business purposes), insurance reimbursements cannot re-create the files you lose. However, if you have recent backups of all your critical data, you will be able to resume operation without having to re-create the material.

A Survey of Backup Software

Depending on your setup and requirements, different methods are appropriate to perform backups. The easiest is just to copy your critical files to another drive by dragging the files or folders to that drive's icon or the appropriate folder on the drive. If you don't have a lot of files to handle, this may be the perfect and highly practical solution, as long as you remember to do so on a regular basis.

NOTE: *All Macs of recent vintage have one or more Software Restore CDs that allow you to return the Mac to its shipping condition (minus the files you've added, of course). In addition, the vast majority of software shipped nowadays comes on a CD. So, even if you only back up the documents you create, you can restore your Mac's hard drive without a full backup, although at the expense of losing your user settings, such as those required for Internet access, and any applications you've added.*

The other method is a lot more reliable, because you don't have to remember to make those backup copies. It's done for you on a more or less automatic basis, and it involves using dedicated backup software.

I'll list several of the popular backup applications in this chapter. No doubt, as Mac OS X continues to gain in popularity over the years, additional backup options will be available to suit a variety of needs.

An Overview of Retrospect

Most people regard Retrospect from Dantz Development as the most popular and feature rich backup program for the Mac (check **www.dantz.com** for more information). This program is bundled with a number of backup drives, which makes the choice automatic. It's also sold separately and is available at most Apple dealers. Besides its market share, the various forms of Retrospect routinely get top reviews from the Mac magazines.

Depending on your needs, there are three versions of Retrospect to consider:

- *Retrospect Express Backup*—Consider this the no-frills version of the program, although it doesn't scrimp on important features that you need for regular, robust backups. You can use its EasyScript feature to create a custom backup routine by simply answering a few basic questions about the sort of backups you plan to do and how often you want to do them. Based on this information, Retrospect Express will build an automated backup routine that suits your needs. Say, for example, you want to back up your Mac at 4:30 P.M. each afternoon, using your external Iomega Zip drive. You just place your backup disk in the drive and leave the drive and your Mac on. At the appointed hour, Express will launch itself, and then run your scripted backup precisely as you specified. You can backup a group of files or folders, or your entire hard drive, and the program has its own compression feature to reduce the size of backup sets. Hundreds of fixed and removable storage devices are supported, including CD-R/RW and DVD-RAM. Backups are stored in *sets*, which are special files containing all the data you've backed up. You can perform full backups and incremental backups (just the files that have changed). The Express version of the software only lacks support for networking backup and tape drives. It may be all the backup software you need, however, for a small home or business office setup.

NOTE: Dantz Development no longer sells the Express version of Retrospect as a separate retail product. These days you'll find it bundled in Norton SystemWorks and with a number of backup drives.

TIP: A particularly useful feature of Retrospect is multiple snapshots, which are, in effect, backups of your Mac taken at different points in time. Snapshots give you the power to restore your drive to the state it was in at a given point in time.

- *Retrospect Desktop Backup*—This version of Retrospect (see Figure 16.1) has all the features of Express, including EasyScript. It adds support for a large variety of tape drives (including support for the hardware compression offered by some of these drives) and the ability to expand support to networked Macs and Windows-based PCs via Retrospect Client. These programs allow the files on each Mac on a network to be backed up to the same set of storage devices, in a single or separate backup session. Because Retrospect is also available for the Windows platform, cross-platform backups are possible. This version of Retrospect can also be configured to send backup status reports to you via email.

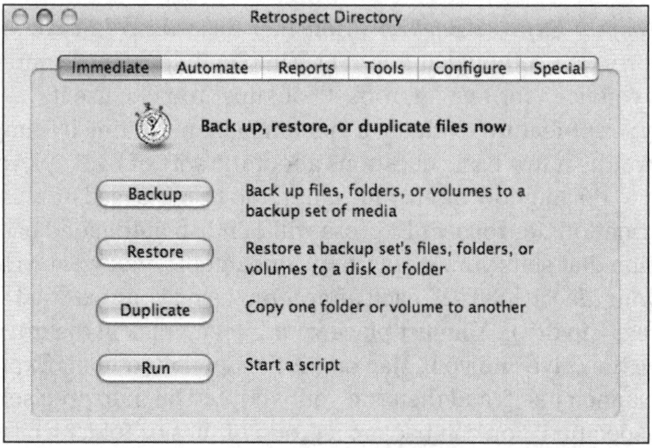

Figure 16.1   Retrospect Desktop Backup is bundled with a number of backup devices and is also sold separately.

NOTE: All versions of Retrospect include a robust security option. This allows the backup sets to be encrypted, so only those with the correct username and password can access and decrypt the backups or retrieve files from them. When I tested this feature with a security expert several years ago, efforts to crack the password encryption scheme proved unsuccessful. It doesn't mean it's perfect, but the results should deliver a greater feeling of confidence.

- *Retrospect Workgroup Backup*—This is a fully packaged solution for automatic backups. The program comes with the standard Retrospect application and thus supports the entire set of features. You also get client software (see Figure 16.2) for a number of networked computers.

An Overview of Intego Personal Backup X

Intego Software (see **www.intego.com**), publisher of several popular Mac security products, targets Personal Backup for single users or small offices (see Figure 16.3). The program supports standard removable media, but it doesn't work with tape drives. In addition, it has no network client option.

The following are Personal Backup's features:

- *Single window interface*—The program's features can be accessed from a single, simple application. Just drag and drop the drive icons to the Source and Destination locations in the application window, and click on a pop-up menu to select backups, clones, restores, or create scripts.

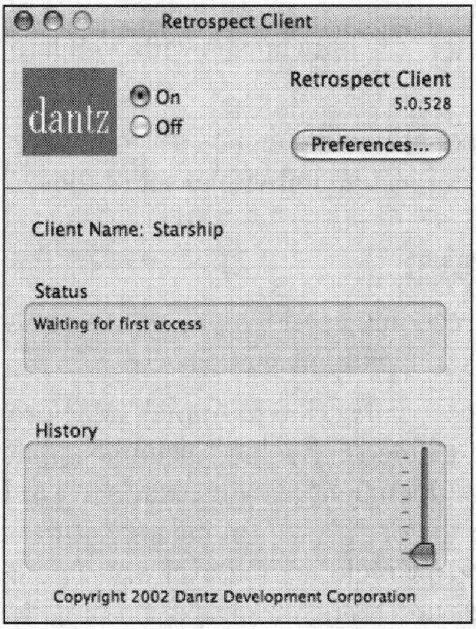

16. Performing Backups

Figure 16.2   The Client version of Retrospect offers a simple interface that displays backup status.

369

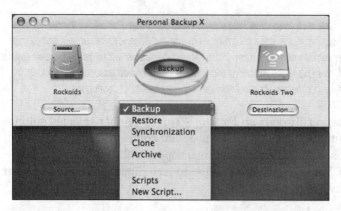

Figure 16.3   All of Personal Backup's features are available from a simple application window.

- *Easy scripting*—You can schedule multiple sets of automatic backups without scripting knowledge simply by clicking the dates, times, and options you want.

- *File synchronization*—You can compare the files you create on your desktop Mac with the ones you make on your iBook or PowerBook (or any other Mac you use to work at a different location), so that you always have the latest versions on both systems.

- *Finder format backups*—The files you back up are simply copied in regular Finder format for easy access without your having to use a special restore feature. This may be an advantage over Retrospect, which puts files in its own proprietary format, which means the application itself is the only means with which to restore the files.

- *Full Volume Clones*—Personal Backup can be set to backup and restore an entire volume, not just an individual set of files.

Other Backup Programs

The choices listed in the preceding sections are not the only ones available. Here are some other backup programs:

- *Apple's Backup*—If you opt to subscribe to Apple's .Mac program, one of the features that's included is Backup, a simple application that can be used to backup documents to your Mac's CD or DVD drive, an external drive or to your iDisk. Among its features are drag and drop backups and a QuickPick feature, which guides you through the sometimes confusing process of finding files you need from multiple locations.

16. Performing Backups

- *Iomega's QuikSync 3*—This program is easy to set up for on-demand or scheduled backups. The new version overcomes the limitation of the previous edition, by supporting storage devices not manufactured by Iomega. Among the features of QuikSync 3 are:

  - *Easy setup*—A convenient setup wizard guides you through the process of setting up an unattended backup without your needing to understand scripting or complicated setups.

  - *Automatic copying*—You can specify certain folders on your Mac's hard drive for automatic backup. Files that are copied or moved to those folders will be duplicated automatically in the "sync" location, which is usually an external storage device.

  - *Multiple revisions*—By being able to save more than a single revision of an individual file, you can view documents in progress at different stages and restore the ones you need to use.

  - *Enterprise implementation*—As with Retrospect, QuikSync 3 can be administered from a central location, making it easy for IT managers to set up the program on a network system.

NOTE: *QuikSync 3.1 and later will run native under Mac OS X. While it hasn't been updated since 2001, it appears to run under Panther as of the time this book was written.*

- *Data Backup X*—Prosoft, publisher of Data Rescue and other hard drive utilities, is the American publisher of this handy backup application. Data Backup X (see Figure 16.4) does all its work via a simple application interface. The Automatic Backup feature performs your backups at regular intervals. An Incremental Backup feature, like the one in Retrospect, backs up only the files that have changed. For road warriors, a Synchronization feature eases the task of making sure both your Mac and your iBook or PowerBook have the same sets of files. The notable missing feature is the ability to work with tape drives.

NOTE: *An earlier version of Data Backup X was distributed by FWB Software under the name Backup ToolKit. Since FWB's agreement with the original publisher of the software has long-since expired, you might want to upgrade to the Prosoft version to be current and fully compatible with Panther.*

In addition to the commercial programs, several freeware and shareware offerings promise many of the basic features of the commercial options. These include such entrants as FoldersSynchronizer, Gemini, Project Backer, Revival, SwitchBack, and Sync X. You'll want to check out the feature sets at VersionTracker.com

16. Performing Backups

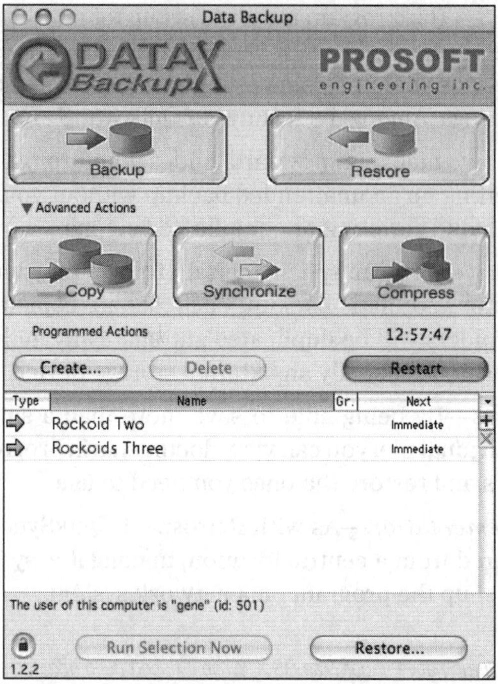

Figure 16.4   Data Backup X is a full-featured application that's easy to setup and use.

(**www.versiontracker.com**) and see which ones might be worth a second look.

When you decide which program to deploy in your environment, consider the features offered and how they fit your situation. A simple file synchronization utility may be all you need if you just need to back up document files.

WARNING! *Don't even think of trying to back up system files and applications with software that isn't Mac OS X compatible. The file system changes will conspire to give you nothing more than a set of damaged files. If you aren't ready to upgrade your backup software, consider copying your critical documents manually to backup media.*

An Overview of Internet Backups

Panther's user interface is designed to, more or less, blur the differences between the location of shared volumes, so it no longer makes a difference whether they're located at the other end of your room or at the other end of the world (except for file transfer speed, of course).

The ease of Internet networking and the lack of standard backup drives on some new Macs have resulted in a search for other backup methods. One of those methods harnesses the power of the Internet as a repository for your backed up files. Following are descriptions of two Internet-based backup resources. Both are extra cost services:

- *iDisk (www.mac.com)*—Apple's .Mac subscription service offers backup software and virus software, a custom mac.com email address, the ability to create a personal home page, and iDisk (see Figure 16.5), which sets aside 100MB of storage space for your files. iDisk is easily accessed as a disk icon, which you can use in the same fashion as a volume connected directly to your Mac or your local network. iDisk is useful as a limited, fairly robust backup solution. It allows you to store your files in a private area, free from public access.

NOTE: *When you install Panther or set up a new Mac, you get a 60-day trial membership to give .Mac a whirl. The trial iDisk storage space is limited to 20MB until you upgrade. You can also opt for up to 1GB of storage space, should you require it, but it may cost a bundle compared to local backup storage.*

16. Performing Backups

Figure 16.5   Apple's iDisk feature gives you online storage to use for backups or to make files available to your Internet contacts.

- *BackJack (www.backjack.com)*—This Canadian-based company claims top ratings from Mac support Web sites. It offers a dedicated program that will provide automatic, unattended backups to its 128-bit secured Web servers. It also uses StuffIt compression technology to maximize the number of files you can send in a given amount of storage space. Pricing plans depend on the amount of storage space you need.

Although Internet backups are a reliable method of backing up critical files, and they offer the added benefit of being offsite, they have some decided disadvantages. Chief among them is throughput and capacity. Transferring even a few megabytes of files via a standard 56Kbps modem connection can be a tedious process. Worse, if you are disconnected during the transfer process (a fairly common occurrence), you must go through all or most of the process again to make sure all your files were sent. Consider broadband access, such as a cable modem or DSL (if available in your area), should you choose this backup solution.

TIP: *Even if you have broadband Internet service, don't be surprised if your upload speed is throttled to a level far below that of download speed. Typically, cable modems limit uploads to 256Kbps (often less), even though they promise download speeds from 1 to 2Mbps or greater. The reason cited by some of these providers is to give maximum emphasis on downloads, and to limit use of their services by PC users who want to set up personal Web servers.*

The other shortcoming is capacity. If your Mac's hard drive is filled to the gills with data, and we're talking of standard drives as much as 160MB here, no commercial Internet resource could accommodate the space, even if you were willing to stay online long enough to send the files. It works better with fairly modest amounts of data. For example, BackJack offers 400MB for its standard setup and additional per-megabyte charges for larger storage capacities.

An Overview of Backup Media

A number of storage media are useful for backups—some more robust than others. When choosing a product, you should consider your specific needs, such as the amount of data you wish to back up and how robust the medium is for long-term storage, if that's one of your requirements. Here are your choices:

NOTE: *I have made no attempt to cover all of the older, discontinued removable devices, such as SyQuest drives. Any of these products can be judged compared to the products mentioned here in terms of speed, capacity, and reliability. You should consider, however, whether it's a good idea to trust your backups to an obsolete product without customer support.*

- *Floppy drive*—This was the original backup medium, not offered on Macs in several years. It isn't terribly robust; floppy disks are known to develop disk errors after being used just a few times. Worse, capacity is extremely limited. Even if you have an older Mac with a floppy drive, or you're using HD-style floppy disks on a SuperDisk drive or external floppy drive, you'll find this medium works best for small documents or pictures when transferring them from one location to another.

NOTE: *Worse, the standard floppy drive on older Macs isn't supported unless you're willing to install a third-party patch that recognizes those old devices. One such driver is available from this site: www.darwin-development.org/floppy/.*

- *SuperDisk drive*—This product was a would-be floppy drive replacement, but never managed to catch on (although some dealers still sell the product from such makers as QPS Inc.). It has the benefit of reading and writing to HD floppy disks at a speed greater than a standard floppy; it's most noticeable if you have the "2X" SuperDisk product. It allows support for legacy media (except for 800KB and 400KB floppies, of course). The SuperDisk medium is a 120MB disk that, at first glance, looks very much like a floppy (there's also a 250MB version). The media appears to be robust and relatively inexpensive. Such drives are not particularly fast, however, which makes them less efficient for larger files, and the user base is relatively small.

NOTE: *Let me emphasize that the SuperDisk drive isn't the same as the SuperDrive, the optical drive that is available in some Mac desktop computers, including Power Macs, PowerBooks, the eMac and the flat-panel iMac. The SuperDrive can play and record to both CD and DVD media.*

- *Zip drive*—This is Iomega's most popular product; Zip drives are found in many business environments. The medium resembles a fat floppy disk, and it uses a mixture of floppy- and hard-drive technologies to provide storage capacities of 100MB, 250MB, and 750MB. Zip drives have been standard issue on many of Apple's desktop models (but not anymore), and millions of drives are out there, so it's easy to find compatible drives at other locations. The drives and media are considered quite robust, standing the test of time beyond some early reliability concerns about the mechanisms.

> **NOTE**: One particularly vexing problem that still occurs sometimes is the so-called "click of death"—an annoying sound that emanates from the drive when you're using defective media or when the drive is poised for failure. Should you encounter this problem with a Zip drive, remove the disk and see if the sound persists when you insert another one. Should it still occur, have the drive serviced or replaced. It appears more recent Zip drives are far less vulnerable to such ills.

- *Castlewood ORB drive*—This product has superficial similarities to the long-departed SyQuest drives, perhaps because the founder of Castlewood was also the founder of SyQuest Technologies. The standard drive uses low-cost 2.2GB cartridges and employs a variation of standard hard drive technology called *magneto-resistive*, now standard on modern fixed drives. Its long-term robustness may be questioned, however. A review in *Macworld* magazine, suggested there might be some reliability concerns with the product. In any case, the product is compatible with Mac OS X without the need to install any extra software.

- *Portable hard drive*—Because this standard hard drive is in a small case, it is suitable for easy transportation. Such drives are available in all the popular storage technologies, including FireWire, SCSI, and USB. Some notable examples include a FireWire product line from SmartDisk (see ***www.smartdisk.com***), which uses the FireWire bus for power. That and its Hot Plug feature make such drives easy to set up and move from workstation to workstation.

- *CD-R/CD-RW*—These products use special CD-based media, offering a high degree of longevity. The standard recordable CD technology is write-once, meaning that you cannot erase or replace the data already recorded. However, the medium is very cheap, so this isn't a serious problem. The more expensive CD-RW products let you rewrite data up to 1,000 times, but the discs themselves do not work on some regular CD drives, particularly older models. The shortcoming is speed, although newer 24x and faster CD recorders promise to record a complete 650MB CD in just a few minutes. Optical media are great for archiving files for an extended period of time.

> **NOTE**: The figures 12x, 16x, and so on refer to multiples of the normal CD record speed, which takes approximately 74 minutes to write to a 650MB disc. In addition to the basic speed in recording data, you have to add the time it takes to read back the completed CD for verification (although that process is much faster, because standard CD readers on the Mac reach and exceed speeds of 32x, and third-party drives are even faster).

- *DVD-RAM*—This product uses a variant of the newer high-density DVD form to reach a storage capacity of up to 5.2GB. Recording speed is equivalent to the fastest regular CD recording devices, and thus this is a useful method for backing up large amounts of data for long-term storage.

NOTE: *Apple no longer ships the high-end PowerMac G4 with a DVD-RAM drive. In addition, a number of third-party peripheral companies, such as LaCie and QPS, offer drives using this format. However, the format is unfinished enough that the media recorded on one drive may not work on another brand.*

- *DVD-R/DVD-RW*—Still another variation of DVD technology is supported by Apple's SuperDrive, which comes on a number of Macs. In addition, a growing number of third-party products incorporate the same drives, which are sourced from Pioneer, Sony, and other firms. Under Mac OS X, you can create movie DVDs using Apple's iDVD software, or store your data files via the Finder's disc-burning feature.

NOTE: *As of the time this book was written, iDVD did not support third party external DVD writers. These products all include their own DVD authoring software, which may be, and usually is, not quite as flexible or as easy to use as iDVD. However, some folks report that iDVD will recognize third party internal drives of this sort, so long as the product carries the same model number is a device sourced by Apple.*

- *Tape drives*—Such drives come in several forms, using tapes that are roughly similar in setup to a cassette deck. Tape drives are not cheap, but the media are. You can buy DDS tapes for around $10 apiece or more, with storage capacities of up to 40GB (depending on the ability of the tape drive or software to compress data). Larger capacities are available for some tape drive formats, such as AIT. Tape drives tend to be slower than the other media, except for CDs, and the technology doesn't offer random access. Therefore, restoring files in different locations on a tape can take a while. In addition, although tapes are subject to wear and tear, the medium is easily and relatively cheaply replaced.

- *Network volume*—You can also back up your data to a drive on another computer (a Mac or a Unix- or Windows-based server), located on your local network. Such techniques are useful for each individual workstation, but the volume to which you are backing up should also receive a regular backup routine to ensure the highest amount of protection for the files. Consider the network backup, then, as just an intermediary to a full backup solution. At the other end of the equation, the system administrators should be using one of the previously described media for backup and archiving.

More Discontinued Drive Formats

- *Jaz drive*—The long-discontinued Iomega Jaz drive was essentially a portable drive using traditional hard drive technology. It came in 1GB and 2GB formats (the latter product was known as the Jaz 2), with media to match. It has the benefit of being relatively fast—about the equivalent of a slower hard drive. Long-term reliability of the media is something of a question, although the drive seems solid enough for part-time use and archiving.

- *Iomega Peerless drive*—This was an interesting variation of the removable drive scheme, brought up to date for the needs of twenty-first century PC users, although it never quite caught on. The Peerless Storage System, to use the official term, consisted of two parts: a Base Station, which worked with a Mac's FireWire or USB port (the former is best to access this product's performance potential) and an actual disk, which comes in a 10GB or 20GB format. The product was sold as a bundle, with Base Station and disk, and sold separately).

NOTE: *Even though the Jaz and Pioneer drives are no longer being produced, you can still obtain support and media for these products because Iomega is still around.*

Immediate Solutions

The No-Frills Daily Backup Plan

This plan doesn't require special backup software. All it requires is a commitment to a regular program so you don't face the loss of crucial files in an emergency.

Before you begin your backup, you need the following elements:

- *Backup media*—Use a separate drive or networked volume (local or Internet-based). The "In Brief" section covers a number of backup products you might want to consider. You should also make sure you have backup media with sufficient capacity to store all the files.

- *A plan*—Create a small word-processing document listing the files and folders you want to back up on a regular basis.

TIP: *To keep track of your backups, you might want to include a list of dates and times on your backup list, along with an underscore or checkbox where you can easily mark your backups as you complete them.*

- *Logically named folders*—Create folders on the backup drive to easily identify the files you are backing up. If you plan to keep separate copies of each generation of your backup files, consider putting a date on each folder or other identification information that will help you quickly locate the files you need at a later time.

- *Reminder device*—It will help to have an alarm clock, clock radio, reminder program, or other means to notify you of the time of the scheduled backup.

- *Easy access to your original system or application CDs*—As mentioned earlier in the chapter, new Macs come with a Restore CD (or set of Restore CDs for the latest models), which can put the computer back in the form in which it shipped (at the expense of losing application and system updates and preferences).

16. Performing Backups

379

> **TIP:** The standard user license for most every program allows you to make a single backup copy. It is a good idea to make a backup of your software CDs and store them off site, in the event of theft or damage at your original location. Remember that if you are backing up a bootable CD, follow the instructions in the CD software to make your copy bootable as well.

After you've got the raw materials set up, follow these steps:

1. Make sure you set your notification device to alert you of the appointed time for the backup.

2. Have your backup medium ready. If you're using a removable drive, such as a Zip drive, be sure that a disk is in the drive, ready to roll.

3. Refer to your backup list for the files and folders you need to copy.

4. Drag the files to the appropriate folders.

5. After the files are copied, put a note on your backup list confirming the day's backup is complete.

> **NOTE:** If your Mac is set up for multiple users, you may want to establish a single backup folder to which all users have access, such as a Shared folder. That way, each user does not have to run separate backup sessions (a potentially confusing, awkward process).

These steps allow you to easily keep track of your daily backups, to make sure that you or one of your employees has performed the task as scheduled.

> **TIP:** If you are working on a mission-critical document that will take you a long time to re-create in the event of loss or damage, you may also want to perform frequent backups of the files throughout the workday. I do this regularly when I'm writing a book, because re-creating even a single chapter or portion can be an annoying, time-consuming process. It only happened to me once, and that was quite enough.

The Special Software Backup Plan

The following steps are based on using one of the backup programs described in the earlier section, "A Survey of Backup Software." I'm assuming you will be installing the software according to the publisher's instructions and that you will be setting up your backup media as indicated.

First, take steps to prepare for your regular backup regimen:

- If you're using a removable device, be sure the disks or cartridges are inserted into the drive and ready to run at the appointed time.

NOTE: If you expect your backups to fill more than a single disk or tape, you should have spares available in case additional media are requested. You may, of course, recycle media if you want to discard older backups that are no longer useful. For tape-based media, however, you should replace the cartridges every year or two; they do wear out, just like with videotape.

- Make sure that the backup software is properly installed.

- Use the program's scheduling features to create a regular backup routine that meets your needs. You may schedule full backups once a week and incremental backups (which cover only the changed files) each day.

- If your backups are likely to consume more than a single disk or tape, be sure someone is available to insert extra media, if necessary.

- If your backup software includes automatic notification of problems via email, such as Retrospect offers, be sure the program is configured to contact you or your systems administrator at a location where they're likely to be at the time the backups occur. This may, for example, include the email address you use at home. If you have email service on your pager or mobile phone, that might be a convenient option to use for offsite notification.

WARNING! If your Macs are located in an office, take the time to explain your backup schedule to your staff. Advise them to try not to use their Macs while files are being backed up, or to leave them on at the end of the day for after-hours backup duty. Files created or left open during the backup process are often copied in an incomplete form or not at all. This is especially true of e-mail software, where your latest messages won't be included if the program is running.

After your backup program is in place, here are the steps you'll follow to make sure the process is done correctly:

1. Schedule your backups to occur at least once every workday, usually at a time when your Macs are not in use, so as not to interfere with your work schedule.

TIP: Although some firms run backups at the end of the day or during the early morning hours, backups can also be conveniently done during lunchtime (which is when I do mine) or any time when all or most employees aren't present, if the backups can be completed within that time frame.

16. Performing Backups

2. Before the scheduled backup is to begin, be sure the backup drive or drives and media are ready so that the process can occur (where possible) unattended.

3. Make sure that the backup drive and all the computers from which files will be retrieved are left on and ready to run at the appointed time.

4. If the backups are unattended, check your software to see if it produces a log of the backup (Retrospect offers this feature). If a log is available, consult it regularly for information about possible problems with your scheduled backup.

Tips and Tricks for Robust Backups

Once you get accustomed to a regular backup routine, you'll appreciate the added security it offers. Consider the following additional procedures to customize your backups:

• *Store additional backup disks off-site*—Financial institutions, ISPs, and other companies store backups at other locations. That way, if something damages or destroys equipment and media at the original location, the valuable files are still available to be copied onto replacement equipment. A bank vault is one possible location. Although it may not be convenient to store all your files off-site, those most valuable to you should be considered as candidates for such storage.

NOTE: Particularly tragic examples of lost data occurred during the bombing of the World Trade Center some years ago and the September 11, 2001 terrorist attack that destroyed the Twin Towers. Even if a firm managed to stay in business after this disaster, only an offsite backup would restore operations to a reasonable degree.

• *Test your backups*—Don't assume you will be able to restore your files, even if the software reports the backups were successful. From time to time, do a test run to make sure you can easily retrieve files if necessary.

WARNING! Tape drives need to be cleaned at regular intervals, because clogged read/write heads can result in premature wear of a drive or incomplete backups. Low-cost cleaning cartridges are available for such drives. The manufacturers of the mechanisms usually recommend cleaning them every 15 or 30 hours (check the documentation to determine the correct interval).

- *Use the automatic backup or autosave features from your software*—A number of Mac programs include the ability to save documents at a regular interval or make extra copies. Check a program's preference dialogs or documentation for information about these features. Among the programs that offer one or both of these features are AppleWorks 6, Microsoft Word, and QuarkXPress. Financial programs, such as Intuit's Quicken and QuickBooks, also can create backup files of your financial records.

- *Perform extra backups of work-in-progress*—Whether you are compiling a financial profile, writing a novel, or creating an illustration for an important ad, it's a good idea to create extra copies from time to time. You can simply drag a copy of your document to a backup location, so there's always an extra one in case the original is damaged.

WARNING! *Although using the Save As feature is a possible method of making an extra copy, the end result is that you will end up working with the new document rather than the old, which means the original won't be updated.*

- *Save often*—The best protection against loss of a document in case of a crash or power outage is to have a copy on disk. Consider saving the document each time you make an important change and certainly after you create a new document.

- *Get file recovery software*—Even if you take extra steps to make sure you do regular backups, it's always possible you will trash a necessary file by mistake. Programs such as MicroMat's TechTool Pro and Symantec's Norton Utilities are able to restore files you delete by mistake. They work best when you install them first, because they are able to track files as you trash them. Another option, Prosoft's Data Rescue, is designed strictly to resurrect trashed data or data lost because of a hard drive directory problem. Keep in mind that it doesn't actually fix a drive.

TIP: *If you delete a file by mistake, try to recover it right away with one of the programs mentioned. When a file is trashed, it is not actually erased. The portion of the drive on which the file is located is simply marked as available, meaning new data can be written there. If you don't create new files, there is a greater possibility you'll be able to recover the file.*

- *Use a program's incremental backup feature*—Backup software will handle a backup in two ways: a full backup, in which all of your files are copied; and an incremental backup, in which only the files that have changed are added to your backup. The most effective, time-saving routine is to use a mixture of both. The initial backup should include all the files that need to be backed up, and the subsequent backups should be limited to changed files until the backup medium is filled. Then you should begin from scratch. In either case, you will probably want to do a complete backup once a week if you have a steady flow of files, or once every two weeks otherwise.

WARNING! Backup programs that use tape-based media may restore files much more slowly if they have to check for a large number of new or changed versions of files when retrieving files. You should use this feature judiciously at best, particularly with tape media.

- *Double-check your network setups*—In order for a networked backup to work, you need to make sure that your networked volumes are accessible when the backup is being performed. Pay particular attention to such issues as access privileges and whether your backup software is properly installed. Also make sure that your media are large enough to handle the available files. If not, an unattended backup won't be a good idea. If you run into problems in getting a useful network backup, examine your network configuration from stem to stern and also look at the backup logs made by your software to see what errors are being reported. Basically, if a shared volume is available for exchanging files, it should work fine for a networked backup.

WARNING! If you want to back up an entire Mac OS X volume, including system files, you need software that's compatible with this operating system. Older backup software may work fine with application and document files, but it won't see the thousands of hidden or invisible files that are part of the Mac OS X installation, nor will such software work with volumes formatted in the Unix File System (UFS) format.

Doing a Folder Backup via the Command Line

You can also copy your files courtesy of Panther's Terminal application, which is located in the Utilities folder. If you're accustomed to dragging and dropping files in the Finder, you are used to some of its quirks and advantages. The Finder, for example, assumes that you want to move a file when you drag its icon from one location on the same disk to another and that you want to copy (not move) a file when you drag its icon to another disk.

On the other hand, when you use a command-line interface, you have to tell the operating system specifically what you want to do, and not make assumptions.

WARNING! *Do not attempt to copy a Classic application via the command line. Unix doesn't understand the traditional Mac way of separating the elements of an application into data and resource forks; thus the file will be corrupted. But document files can be easily copied this way.*

To copy your Documents folder to a backup drive, follow these steps:

1. Launch Terminal if it's not already open.

2. In the Terminal screen, type "sudo cp –R Documents /Volumes/Backup" and press the Return key. The first time you type a **sudo** command, you'll be asked for your administrator password, because the command grants you Super User access (a sort of temporary root access); it allows you to perform basically any system command via the terminal. Such access will remain in effect for five minutes, after which you'll have to authenticate again to perform more functions.

NOTE: In the previous command line, cp is the copy command. -R is a flag that stands for recursive, which means that you are copying a folder, not a file, named Documents. The name Backup in this case represents the name of your backup medium; you can use any name you want. Also bear in mind this command requires the presence of a folder or file named Documents. Chapter 19 covers the Unix command line in more detail.

3. To copy additional folders, use the same commands, substituting the name of the folder you want to copy.

NOTE: When you want to copy a file rather than a folder, do not use the recursive command. Specify the path or location of the file, such as Documents/filename for a file in your Documents folder.

Related solutions:	Found on page:
A Short List of Popular Command-Line Features	439
Using Mac OS X's Command-Line FTP Software	443

Security and Panther

In Brief

The news media has written part of this chapter. As I was writing this book, the media presented month after painful month of reports of rampant e-mail viruses affecting the Windows platform. It seemed as if nothing was safe except, perhaps, your Mac.

To be perfectly honest, Macs are not immune to computer viruses. Even if you use your computer at home or in a small business, the danger, while not as ever-present as on the Windows platform, still exists. It's often believed that the pranksters who create such viruses have no time to do their dirty work with Macs, simply because there are far fewer users. What's more, Panther is built upon a tried and tested Unix platform that is more resilient to such infections.

However, those of us who have worked on Macs for many years realize the conventional wisdom isn't necessarily so. There have been several dozen Mac viruses over the years, some just annoying, others causing crashes and possible loss of data.

NOTE: I have seen two serious instances of mass virus infections on Macs. In the early 1990s, a virus called WDEF infected the desktops of Macs running System 6. The arrival of System 7 pretty much did away with that program because desktop files were managed differently. More recently, in 1998 and 1999, many Macs were infected by the AutoStart virus, which even managed to turn up on a few commercial CDs—ones quickly withdrawn, I might add.

Worse, all those macro viruses that affect Microsoft's Office software can impact the Mac platform too. Although these viruses won't cause some of the dire effects that may be prevalent in the Windows variations, such things as damaged documents and problems with document templates have been legion.

NOTE: Some folks tend to be overconfident about Word macro viruses or cavalier about installing virus software in general. I have seen viruses in documents from software publishers that ought to know better (names omitted to protect the guilty).

In addition, the growth of high-speed or broadband Internet connections, such as cable modems and DSL, and support for Internet-based file sharing, have made Macs increasingly vulnerable to direct attacks from the Internet. Over the history of Mac OS X, Apple has periodically released security updates that address various vulnerabilities.

That means that there are occasional problems that can be exploited. Ignoring the potential threat is not a good idea.

WARNING!: Just because your Mac is immune from a particular viruses doesn't mean you shouldn't be a good citizen. If you forward a message or give a disk to someone that contains a PC virus, the Windows user is just as vulnerable as if he got it directly all by himself. This is a cross platform world and you don't want to be considered a Typhoid Mary and spread such things around, even if you don't care for another's choice of operating system.

An Overview of Mac Viruses

In the world of motion pictures, computer viruses are sometimes portrayed as a good thing—a clever scheme to beat the bad guys and win the day or even save the world, depending on the particular situation. From *Independence Day* to *The Net*, the underdog who is smart enough to write a virus manages to snatch victory from the jaws of defeat.

NOTE: Trivia buffs do not have to remind me that viruses flooding the world's systems are, in part, responsible for the "Judgment Day" scenario in Terminator 3: Rise of the Machines.

But in our real world, the author of a computer virus isn't the hero, and the victims of such viruses are not the villains. They are folks like you and me who just want to compute in comfort and safety, without having to concern ourselves with invasions of our privacy and of the sanctity of our personal computing experience.

Types of Computer Viruses

There are three basic types of computer viruses, but extensive variations exist in each group:

- *Virus*—The standard form of a computer virus is a piece of code that's attached to a program or other file. When the file is opened, the virus is activated. It can, in turn, be spread to other files as part of its function. Such a virus may be meant as a simple joke, putting up a silly message on the screen. Others may cause system crashes or damage files and perhaps the hard drive directory.

- *Trojan horse*—This is the worst sort of virus-related affliction because, on the surface, it appears to be a file or program that has a useful, productive function. However, like the Trojan horse of old, embedded within that file is a malicious application that's ready to wreak havoc on your Mac once the virus is unleashed. A recent example was the Graphics Accelerator or SevenDust virus. It was sent as a system extension called Graphics Accelerator, which supposedly was designed to enhance video performance. The virus would actually erase files on a Mac's drive. Complicating matters is that a Graphics Accelerator extension was indeed provided with older versions of the Mac OS to support models equipped with ATI graphics chips. Later, that extension and its associated files were renamed with ATI prefixes so they are easy to identify and there's less confusion.

- *Email virus*—In a sense, you could call this a Trojan horse as well. You receive a message from someone you know, claiming to contain the file you were expecting—except you weren't expecting any file. But, because you know the sender, you launch it anyway, and it does its dirty work. Usually the net effect is to copy an email address list and send similar files to other users. Most such viruses do their thing under the Windows platform. However, the infamous Mac.Simpsons@mm virus, a macro virus that exploited AppleScript under Mac OS 9, was indeed a Mac-only variation that affected Microsoft's Entourage and Outlook Express users. The best approach to take is never to assume that it's all right to open a file you didn't expect to receive. Write to the sender and confirm what the file is and why it was sent to you. Get the OK before launching. Whenever you send a file to someone it's a good idea to explain what kind of file is being sent and its purpose, so there is no room for error or suspicion.

NOTE: *The prevalence of email viruses has resulted in some companies setting up firewalls and mail servers to strip the .exe extension from an email attachment before delivery. Should you have a problem sending an executable file to a Windows user via email, ship it as a Zip file instead.*

Viruses and Panther

There's little doubt that someone, somewhere, will create a virus to exploit a vulnerability in Panther. You shouldn't ignore the fact that computer viruses were first produced under Unix, and that's an important incentive not to ignore such possibilities. In addition, because you may still spend some portion of your day running programs in the Classic environment, your older applications and files can be infected if you don't take precautions, in the form of an antivirus program. Fortunately, there are several Panther applications that can protect you in both environments.

You'll learn more about them in the "Immediate Solutions" section of this chapter. The watchword is this: If you are cautious in your personal computing habits, you should be able to get the maximum amount of protection with the least amount of interference. The author of a now-discontinued virus application once urged Mac users to practice "safe hex," and I'm sure you get the drift.

Broadband Internet and Invaders from Out There

No, I am not referring to a possible invasion by beings from another world, although I'm not one to dismiss the possibility that such a thing might happen someday. But a possible virus threat results from the fact that more Mac users have upgraded to high-speed Internet services. Whether it comes by way of a cable modem, DSL, or a wireless connection, the primary difference between this sort of connection and regular dial-up is that you spend far more time online. It's rare for someone to be connected via a modem 24/7, but with a broadband connection you're almost always connected to the Internet, in the same way that you may be connected to a printer or shared Macs or Windows-based computers on a local network.

NOTE: I have seen cable modems, such as one from the Motorola Surfboard line, which can be placed in a standby mode, in which you can deactivate the modem when your online session is over. That is one way to reduce the risk of being ever-present on the Internet, but it still leaves you vulnerable during the times you are online.

In addition, Macs can easily share files via the Internet, a feature of both Mac OS 9 and Mac OS X. Such networking, combined with a high-speed connection, can, in effect, minimize or eliminate the difference between a local and Internet-based network. As a result, your Mac may be more vulnerable to another form of attack, from outsiders who try to take control of your computer via your TCP/IP-based Internet connection.

To protect yourself from such invasions, consider using Panther's built-in firewall feature, or if you want a greater range of configuration options, a third-party application. A firewall monitors Internet traffic and block attempts to access your Mac from outside.

NOTE: A firewall program puts an armed guard on your Mac, monitoring traffic coming to and from your computer and preventing unauthorized access.

The "Immediate Solutions" section profiles three programs designed to protect your Mac against computer viruses and several software firewall solutions, including the one available in Panther.

Introducing FileVault

Perhaps the easiest solution is to encrypt all of your files so that they can't be opened by anyone else without the proper password. Apple's FileVault delivers 128-bit encryption, which is powerful enough that it's not likely to be cracked or broken by anyone in our lifetime, or at least that's what the security experts tell me.

In any case, once you establish a master password for your Mac, using the Security preference panel of System Preferences, you'll be able to turn on this feature, which works strictly with the files in your Home or Users folder.

During the encryption process, all these files are copied to a disk image file, which is read back as files are retrieved. But all this happens behind the scenes. You'll learn more in the final section of this chapter.

Immediate Solutions

Choosing a Mac Virus-Detection Program

In the early days of the Mac platform, a number of commercial and shareware virus-detection programs were available. Over time, many of these programs were acquired by other publishers or discontinued. Shareware antivirus offerings included VirusDetective, which was continued until the early 1990s when its author decided that payments were too small to continue. Here are the currently available commercial Mac virus-protection applications.

NOTE: One of the early Mac antivirus programs, Rival, went abroad and was developed strictly for the European market for several years. However, the publisher's Web site was down when I checked it for this book. In addition, the Mac OS X version of MicroMat's TechTool Pro, which did include a virus detection component in the Classic version, no longer sports that feature.

Intego's VirusBarrier

The most recent entrant to the antivirus application arena comes from the publishers of NetBarrier, a firewall program that will be discussed later in this chapter, and several security-based utilities. VirusBarrier has a particularly unique user interface that puts configuration panels in a drawer that can be opened and closed as needed, as shown in Figure 17.1.

Here are the features of VirusBarrier that will help provide the maximum degree of virus protection:

- *Simple interface*—As shown in Figure 17.1, VirusBarrier has a minimalist interface where all features are easily activated.

- *Automatic repairs*—You can opt to have infected files repaired automatically by the program, a feature that matches the capabilities of the other contenders. A system log will report on such episodes so you can see what was fixed and why and also if the file couldn't be fixed.

17. Security and Panther

393

Figure 17.1   Click a button to open a drawer that offers additional settings.

- *NetUpdate*—This feature allows the program to scan the Internet for program upgrades on a regular basis, or whenever you want to do a manual check. If an update is available, it'll be downloaded automatically. Unlike other programs of this type, when new virus-detection capabilities are added, the application will sometimes (but not always) be updated, too.

- *Doesn't intrude on software installations*—Although it's best to disable an antivirus program before performing a software installation, VirusBarrier is designed to allow such processes to run without interfering.

- *Doesn't affect boot or system performance*—Because virus scans may slow your Mac's performance, VirusBarrier promises fully transparent operation so you won't notice its presence unless a virus infection is found. My personal experience with version 10.1 of the application showed this claim to be largely realized on the G5 hardware on which I tried it.

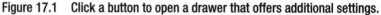

NOTE: Since I haven't tried VirusBarrier on a really slow Mac running Panther, I won't swear that there will be no discernible slowdown. However, a slight delay in application launching is largely compensated by your high level of immunity to virus infections.

Network Associates' Virex

One of the older Mac virus-detection programs, Virex (see Figure 17.2), has had a checkered history as far as having a steady manufacturer is concerned. It has gone through several software publishers, finally ending up in the hands of the McAfee division of Network Associates. This should not, of course, deter you from buying Virex; it continues to be developed and supported with regular program and detection string updaters. The version shipping at the time this book was printed was 7.2.1, fully native to Mac OS X, which is being bundled with Apple's .Mac subscription service.

Here are the basic features of Virex:

- *Drag-and-drop scanning and cleaning*—Just select a file, folder, or disk icon and drag it to the Virex application icon, and the scanning process will commence in short order. Depending on the preferences you set in the application, you'll be able to see which files might be infected, or automatically repair them to the limits of the technology.

- *Advanced cleaning*—This feature essentially tries to remove the infection from a file and restore it to its normal condition. Once again, it's not a feature that differs materially from the competition.

- *Checks for virus-like activities*—In addition to using detection strings to detect the presence of known virus strains, Virex can scan for what it considers to be virus-like activity. This way, Virex can help protect you against virus strains not already discovered.

NOTE: *Virex 7 was released without a big publicity flourish from its publisher and may be difficult to find at the company's Web site. The easiest way to acquire a copy appears to be as part of Apple's .Mac subscription program. I even wonder whether you could buy it elsewhere anymore unless you're very lucky.*

- *Frequent updates*—Virex is updated on a monthly basis, or more frequently if the need arises, to detect and repair the latest virus strains.

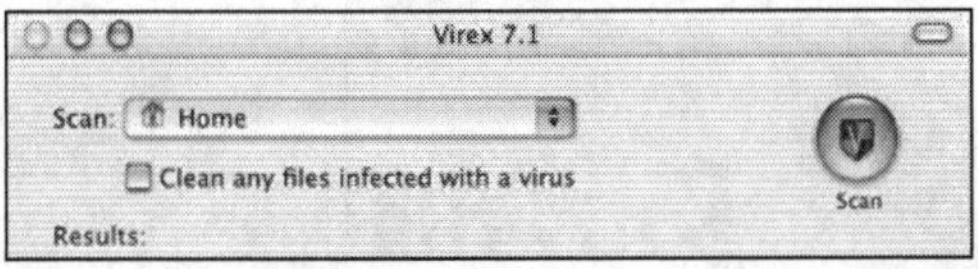

Figure 17.2   Virex continues to be updated to support newly discovered virus strains.

- *Command-line scanner*—If you want to get deeply involved with Unix command line of Panther's, you can use the Terminal application to run on-demand scans or configure scheduled scanning runs.

- *Missing features*—Unfortunately, some of the features present in the Classic version of Virex are not part of Virex 7. The most useful is background scanning, where the act of mounting a disk or launching a file causes Virex to check it for the presence of a virus. The scan-at-download feature, which checks files that you retrieve from the Internet or a network file share, also is not available, nor is a graphical interface for the scheduling operation. Background scanning can, if you're so inclined, be enabled via the Terminal application as a *chron* task but it's not a process for the faint of heart. The program's documentation explains how it's done.

Symantec's Norton AntiVirus

Perhaps today's most popular Mac antivirus program is Norton AntiVirus. The version shipping when this book was printed, 9.0 (see Figure 17.3), runs fully native under Mac OS X.

The following is a brief list of the major features of Norton AntiVirus from Symantec. If you're familiar with the Classic versions of this

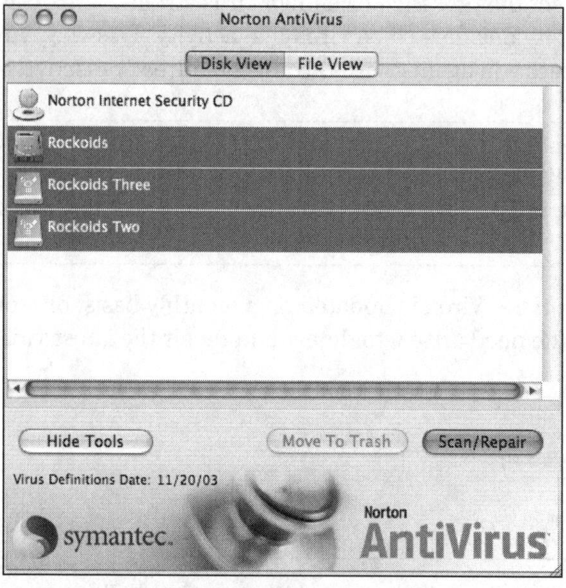

Figure 17.3   Norton AntiVirus in action, looking at my drive for potential virus infections.

application, you'll find that many, but not all, of the key features are intact with the Mac OS X native release available at the time this book was written.

- *Startup CD*—You can run Norton AntiVirus from its startup disk, which includes a bootable System Folder. This is the ultimate protection against a possible virus because an infection can't contaminate a CD.

NOTE: As Apple releases new hardware, you'll need to order updated startup CDs for Symantec's utility products so that they will start your Mac. Bear in mind that Symantec does charge a small fee for such CDs, even if you just bought the program from a dealer with an earlier CD.

- *Automatic repair of infected files*—This option is in the program's preferences dialog box and is turned on by default. The application will automatically attempt to repair any file that's infected. The downside to such a feature is that it's not always perfect, and the removal of the virus strain may also damage the file so that it's not usable. This is always a good argument for having recent backups of all your critical files.

- *Checks of suspicious files*—This feature allows the program to check for system activities that may indicate the presence of a computer virus. Several levels of protection can be configured in the program's preferences. Keep in mind, however, that if made too robust, this feature can cause a number of annoying error messages for tasks that really don't appear virus-like at all, such as expanding a compressed file that contains a system extension that is not infected.

- *Examine compressed files*—Even though a virus in a compressed file cannot infect your Mac unless the file is opened, Norton AntiVirus gives you the added ounce of protection to scan the files anyway.

- *Scans e-mail for potential virus infections*—Even though only one notable Mac e-mail virus has appeared as of the time this book was written, if you regularly communicate with Windows users, it's easy to accidentally transfer a virus that will infect their computers. This is your protection against that possibility.

- *LiveUpdate*—This feature is shared with other Symantec programs. LiveUpdate goes online to seek out revisions for most of your Symantec software in a single operation. You can configure it to access the Internet regularly in search of the updates or only when you want. This feature can be a godsend if you don't have the time to constantly monitor the Internet in search of the latest updates.

17. Security and Panther

- *Missing in action*—As with Virex, certain features that were part and parcel of the Classic Mac OS version of Norton AntiVirus were not available in the first Mac OS X release. The most important of these features is scheduled scans, the ability to run a scanning operation at the times you select. Whether you actually need such a feature is questionable, however, since automatic scanning ought to be sufficient to weed out potential virus infections.

Using Panther's Built-in Firewall

With so many folks getting always-on Internet services, it stands to reason that there is a far greater vulnerability to potential invasions from the Internet. Although this would seem a fairly unlikely source of trouble, there have been some well-publicized instances of so-called *denial of service* attacks, where personal computers are commandeered by Internet vandals and used to flood popular Web sites with meaningless data, which prevents real access by visitors to those sites.

Until now, those problems haven't affected Macs but that doesn't mean our preferred computing platform is immune. Although large companies often seek hardware solutions to such problems in the form of network routers or dedicated hardware-based firewalls, some relatively inexpensive Mac programs can offer good protection for homes and small-business users.

NOTE: How bad is the risk? Well, many cable systems support equipment (including cable modems) that support the Data Over Cable Service Interface Specification (DOCSIS). Not only does it allow these services to use conventional cable modems you can buy at a computer or consumer electronics store, but also it encrypts the data flow from customers. This doesn't mean you are totally safe from Internet vandals, but it does reduce and usually eliminate the possibility that those who share your cable ISP's node can see your shared printers and disks. Vulnerability to denial of service attacks or similar invasions, however, still exists. No protection scheme will ever be perfect.

Related solution:	Found on page:
Protecting Your Network from the Internet	196

Whether you use a cable or a DSL modem, you'll want to think seriously about enabling Panther's own firewall. Although this feature has always been available in Mac OS X, only with the 10.2 and 10.3

releases did Apple offer a readily accessible (not requiring the Terminal) on/off switch. To enable the feature, simply follow these steps:

1. Launch System Preferences, and click on the Sharing preference panel.

2. Click the Firewall button (see Figure 17.4).

3. If you want to allow a service to run despite the firewall, such as Mac or Windows file sharing and FTP access, click the appropriate On checkbox.

4. Once configured, click the Start button to activate the firewall.

5. If you want to allow additional network access, such as instant messaging, networked backups via Retrospect, or other functions, click the New button to configure the port to which you want to receive network traffic (see Figure 17.5).

6. Once a particular port name is chosen, the appropriate port will be selected. Click OK to store your settings.

7. If you want to turn off Panther's firewall, click the Stop button (it toggles to Start for the next activation).

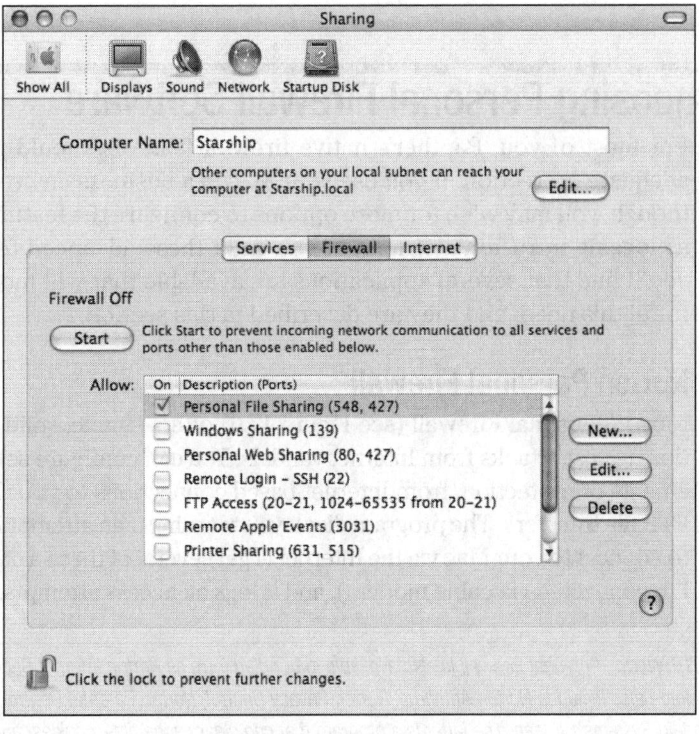

Figure 17.4   Configure Apple's firewall protection on your Mac.

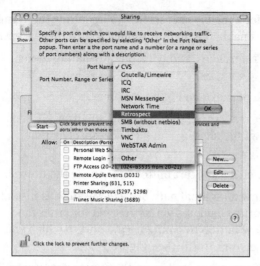

Figure 17.5   Choose the kind of network access you want to allow.

8. To leave the System Preferences application, choose Quit from the File menu.

Choosing Personal Firewall Software

For most of you, Panther's native firewall features should provide adequate protection. If you use your Mac in a business environment, though, you may wish for more options to configure the feature, such as logging intrusion attempts. If you want these advanced features, you'll find that several applications are available that will more than fulfill this need, and they are described in this section.

Norton Personal Firewall

Norton Personal Firewall (see Figure 17.6) offers simple, solid protection against attacks from Internet vandals. You can configure several elements of protection, from Internet-based connections to your Mac, to FTP file transfers. The program displays a warning if an attempt is made to connect to your Mac via the Internet (I get several of these a day when I'm connected via cable modem), and it logs all access attempts.

NOTE: Norton Personal Firewall is also available in bundled form as Norton Internet Security. The package also includes Norton AntiVirus, Norton Privacy Control, Norton Parental Control, and Aladdin Systems's iClean. The latter is a program that can clear cache files, cookies, and other files you may want to discard from your Mac's hard drive.

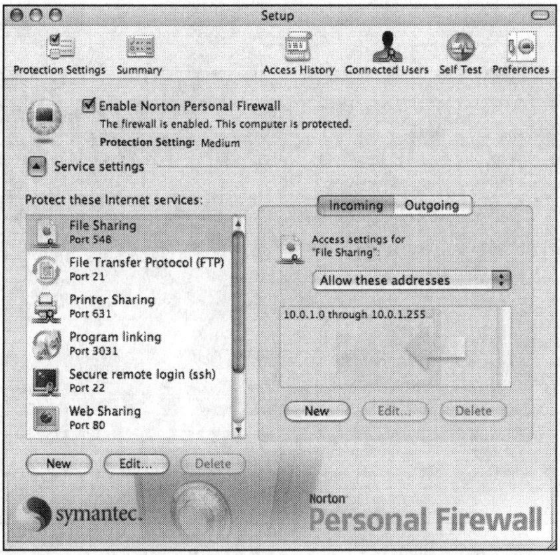

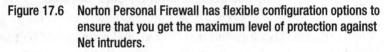

Figure 17.6 Norton Personal Firewall has flexible configuration options to ensure that you get the maximum level of protection against Net intruders.

Intego's NetBarrier X

This program made Intego's reputation. NetBarrier (see Figure 17.7) shares its uniquely different interface with VirusBarrier. It lets you set several levels of protection, depending on the level to which you want to limit access to and from your Mac via the Internet.

Among the program's powerful features is the ability to protect against browser plug-ins and Java applets that may house hostile code. It also provides built-in protections against access of personal information on your Mac, such as passwords and credit card information.

Intego's ContentBarrier

The programs described so far will protect your Mac against outside Internet-based invasions or virus infections. Intego's ContentBarrier, on the other hand, is designed to monitor Internet access. It works for both home users and businesses, by allowing you to filter content that might be unacceptable to those using your Mac. Additionally, you can block Internet access at specific times of the day so that children don't waste time surfing rather than doing their homework assignments and household chores. It also helps increase employee productivity because less time is wasted on unproductive pursuits.

17. Security and Panther

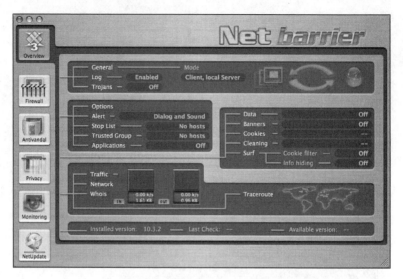

Figure 17.7   NetBarrier offers several levels of firewall protection.

ContentBarrier also logs Internet access, and settings can be password protected, so only those with access privileges can change program settings.

Firewalk X

Another option I'll mention, Firewalk X, a shareware application, is similar in concept to the other commercial programs because it doesn't use Mac OS X's internal firewall. Firewalk X offers a sophisticated range of configuration choices.

Like the commercial products, Firewalk X directs access to your Mac's ports and keep logs of attempts to penetrate your Mac's defenses. Setting up Firewalk X is quite easy because it works as a System Preferences pane, and has relatively easy setup screens that provide a lot of powerful configuration options.

As this book was written, the author, Mike Vannorsdel, assures us that the program will continue to be updated despite the presence of basic firewall access in Panther.

BrickHouse

Brian Hill's BrickHouse, also shareware, takes a somewhat more modest approach to firewall protection by harnessing the built-in protection features of Mac OS X. However, its ability to keep tracking logs and built-in support for Mac OS X's Network Locations feature, makes it far more flexible. The author informs use that he expects to continue to update the program.

Hardware Firewalls

Another route to firewall protection is hardware-based. Several Internet sharing hubs or switches work with your DSL or cable modem and distribute an ISP connection across your network. These products, from such companies as Asante, D-Link, MacSense, NetGear, and Proxim (formerly Farallon), and even the latest version of Apple's AirPort Base Station, include a feature called network address translation (NAT) firewall protection. With NAT activated, the IP numbers of the computers on your network are hidden, and thus outsiders cannot see them. This provides a high level of security.

Such routers offer other features, such as one or more ports for Ethernet hookups. (Asante and Proxim have models with four ports, sufficient for most home office networks.) Some even include a wireless capability, supporting the very same 802.11b and 802.11g protocols used by Apple's AirPort wireless networking system (which also includes NAT support in its latest software release).

TIP: *One way to test the resiliency of your firewall protection is to use a set of Web-based tools from Gibson Research called Shields Up. You can access the tools via www.grc.com. Although the company makes software primarily for the Windows platform, its Web-based firewall tests will function with the Classic Mac OS and Mac OS X, and you may be surprised at the results.*

Using FileVault

What if someone broke into your home and stole your computer while you were out for a short shopping trip to the supermarket? What if you went on a lunch break at work and returned to find that a co-worker with mischief on his or her mind was busy examining files that he or she was not supposed to see?

How do you avoid such things? Do you have to go out and buy security software or is there a simple way to avoid such problems? While burglar alarms and the security staff in a gated community can help reduce the possibility of theft, nothing is perfect, unfortunately.

17. Security and Panther

403

NOTE: *The so-called gated communities in my area, like others I know about, may be OK at blocking automotive traffic from strangers, but they are hardly likely to prevent someone from just walking in while the security guards are otherwise occupied.*

While Apple can't stop someone from stealing your Mac, there are things you can do to reduce the possibility of loss of data. In addition to protection from computer viruses and online predators, you can actually protect your files with a few simple precautions and without buying anything extra.

The quickest way to create protection is to set up your Security preference panel, and this is how it's done:

1. With System Preferences running, choose Security (see Figure 17.8).

2. Before getting started, you need to set a Master Password to allow you to use FileVault. After clicking the Set Master Password button, you'll be able to enter an appropriate password (see Figure 17.9).

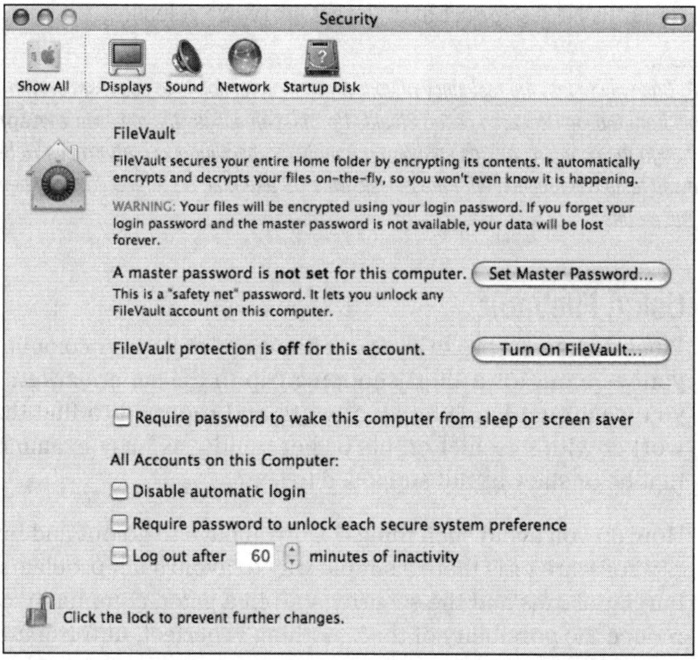

Figure 17.8   You can configure several security-related settings from here.

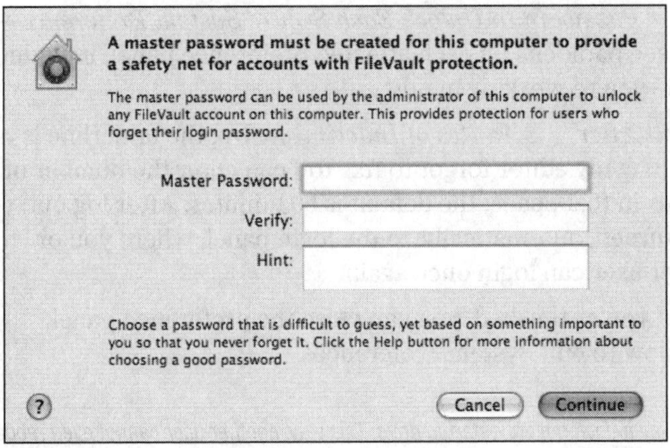

A master password must be created for this computer to provide a safety net for accounts with FileVault protection.

The master password can be used by the administrator of this computer to unlock any FileVault account on this computer. This provides protection for users who forget their login password.

Master Password: [   ]

Verify: [   ]

Hint: [   ]

Choose a password that is difficult to guess, yet based on something important to you so that you never forget it. Click the Help button for more information about choosing a good password.

Cancel   Continue

Figure 17.9   Set up your master password here.

WARNING! FileVault only impacts your Home directory or folder. This is a point I want to emphasize. Files on the rest of your hard drive, including your system-wide Documents folder at the root level of your hard drive, remain accessible, unless you set up one or more of the other security measures in the Security panel.

NOTE: Your master password doesn't have to be the same as your Panther user's password. In fact it is best to keep it different because that step provides an extra measure of security. Regardless, you'll want to use a strong password, which is, as I've said elsewhere in this book, a mixture of upper and lower case letters, interspersed with numbers.

---

3. Click Continue to conclude the FileVault setup process.

NOTE: Once FileVault is configured, be prepared to wait a short time for the initial encoding to proceed. The time it takes depends on several factors, including the speed of your hard drive and Mac, and the amount of data that needs to be processed. Once this is done, you can decide what security to add next.

---

4. The bottom portion of the Security preference panel has additional options, which I'll explain now:

- *Require Password to Wake This Computer From Sleep or Screen Saver*—Self-explanatory. By configuring the Energy Saver and Desktop & Screen Saver preference panels to activate these items after a brief idle interval, you can make it difficult for someone to get a hold of your files.

- *Disable Automatic Login*—This applies to all user accounts, and it overrides all automatic logins. Instead, you'll be confronted with the standard login panel at each startup or logout.

17. Security and Panther

- *Require Password to Unlock Each Secure System Preference—* You'll see padlocks on each affected preference panel, including the one you're working in now.

- *Log Out After __ Minutes of Inactivity*—No, the underline is not something my editor forgot to fix. You can enter the number of minutes in that space; the default is 60 minutes. After log out, you are returned, automatically, to the login panel, where you or another user can login once again.

5. Once you're finished, you can close the preference panel window to quit System Preferences.

TIP: *Here's a way to lock out your startup drive. This way, another user cannot even reboot your Mac without knowing your password. To enable this feature, download and install the Open Firmware Password utility from Apple. Before you set it up, make sure your Mac is running Panther. Then run the utility, which establishes a password that's stored in the Open Firmware or ROM of your Mac. The directions supplied with the utility explain which Macs it runs on, and that includes most recent models that can run Panther. Once the password is established, startup tricks, such as using the "C" key to reboot from a CD, the "T" key to engage FireWire Target Mode, or Command-S to set up Single User Mode, are blocked. You must use the password to make your Mac successfully go through the boot process.*

Chapter 18

Troubleshooting Panther

Personal computers are a far cry from appliances, despite what the manufactures may tell you. A normal part of the life of every personal computer owner is to have a program suddenly quit or to find the entire computer frozen, totally unable to function. Such problems are not restricted to users of either Macs or Windows-based PCs. Both platforms are quite capable of failing at unexpected moments, usually when you need to complete an important document and time is short. In fact, if your everyday automobile had the same reliability as your computer, you could barely make it to the supermarket without brakes failing or the car randomly stopping.

A more telling comment came from CBS News correspondent Andy Rooney, who is featured in *60 Minutes:* "I bought one typewriter for 50 years, but I've bought seven computers in six years. I suppose that's why Bill Gates is rich and Underwood is out of business."

Long-term experience on a personal computer is littered with system troubleshooting, reinstallations, and endless searches for program updates that address one problem or another. Beginning with Mac OS 9, Apple introduced a System Update control panel that was designed to periodically check the Apple's support Web site in search of necessary system updates. Even third-party publishers have gotten into the act. Programs from Intego, Network Associates, and Symantec have built-in features to seek out updates.

Panther comes with the promise to liberate Mac users from regular diets of system-related troubles. Like Unix servers, which can run for days, weeks, or months (and sometimes years) without suffering breakdowns, the revolutionary new version of the Mac operating system is designed to be as resilient as possible to the trials and tribulations of daily computing.

Panther's Crash-Resistant Features

Whether you surf the Internet, use heavy-duty graphics programs such as Adobe Photoshop or InDesign, or use database software that must perform a lot of sorting and organizing, sometimes your Mac will be susceptible to problems. Here's a look at what Panther has to offer to provide greater reliability:

- *Protected memory*—Every time you run a native application under Mac OS X, it gets its own memory partition, dynamically allocated by the operating system and walled off from other programs. Should that program quit or crash, the memory allocated to it is reallocated as part of the memory available to your Mac. You can continue to run your Mac safely without having to restart; don't try that under any previous version of the Mac OS without risking a serious crash. Although a Restart command is still available, now located in the Apple menu, you will find yourself using Force Quit more often. Apple doesn't expect you to have to restart except when installing a new program or leaving Panther to return to your Classic Mac OS.

NOTE: *As a matter of fact, shutdowns are seldom necessary with the newer Macs. You can use the Sleep command to have the Mac run in a super-low-power mode (using less power than a normal light bulb), ready to awaken in a second or two by a simple click of the mouse or by pressing any key on your keyboard.*

- *Advanced memory management*—Under previous versions of the Mac OS, an application received a specific portion of available memory. If this wasn't enough to run the program efficiently, you had to quit, open the Finder's Get Info window, and allocate more. In addition, if you didn't have enough free RAM to open a program, it would not run, or it would run so inefficiently that you risked poor performance, an out-of-memory error, or perhaps a system crash. Mac OS X dynamically allocates the memory a program needs and, if need be, provides virtual memory. Therefore, in theory, a program can never run out of memory.

NOTE: *Don't assume that a Unix-style virtual memory system is a panacea that has no downside. It's always better to have enough RAM to run a program—if the operating system has to use virtual memory instead, performance slows down and you'll see a spinning cursor when data has to be retrieved from your hard drive. Even though Apple recommends a minimum of 128MB of RAM for Mac OS X, having at least twice that amount delivers noticeably better performance and I recommend at least 512MB for graphic artists and other content creators. Even 2GB isn't a lot these days. There's no free ride.*

- *Preemptive multitasking*—Can a superior way to manage multiple applications improve reliability? Very possibly. Some applications hog available processor time, making it difficult for other programs to run efficiently. Too many programs competing with one another can create the potential for a system crash. With Mac OS X, the operating system is the task or traffic manager, making performance better—sometimes much better—when multiple programs are performing complex tasks, such as downloading files, rendering a multimedia presentation, and printing at the same time.

NOTE: *One of the clever demonstrations Apple sometimes uses to show how resilient Mac OS X is involves running a special application that repeatedly attempts to crash the operating system while a movie trailer continues to play flawlessly.*

Keep in mind, however, that although Mac OS X is resilient and reliable, this doesn't mean that your Mac will never crash, or that programs will never quit. As long as software is written by human beings, the potential for conflicts exists. In the Immediate Solutions section, I'll show you how to cope with common problems and how to get the most reliable performance from your Mac.

The Software Update Application

Beginning with Mac OS 9, Apple added a useful new feature, Software Update. Similar to some third-party applications that search for updates, such as the LiveUpdate utility that ships with Symantec's Mac utility programs, Norton AntiVirus, Norton Utilities, and Norton SystemWorks, Apple's utility checks the system-related files on your hard drive and seeks out updates at Apple's support sites on the Internet.

This utility continues in essentially the same form under Mac OS X (see Figure 18.1), but has migrated to the System Preferences application. When you activate this pane, just click the Update Now button to have Software Update check Apple's Web site for updates. If

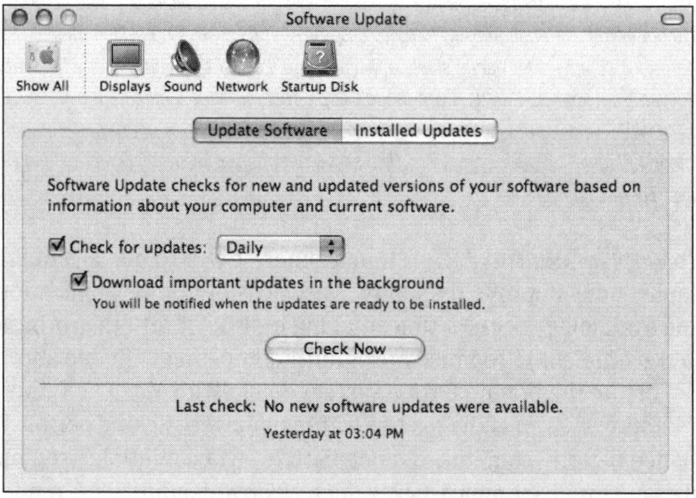

Figure 18.1   The Software Update pane from System Preferences will find needed Mac OS X updates for you.

they're available, they'll be listed in a dialog box. Check the ones you want, click the Install button, and the program takes care of the rest, from downloading to installing. Depending on whether an update is system related or application related, you may have to restart your Mac for the changes to take effect.

TIP: *You should save a copy of the update installer. Right after an update has been downloaded and installed, while the System Update application is on your screen, click the Update menu, choose Save As, and select a location in the Save As dialog box for a copy of the update. Another method is to use the option to save the file to the desktop before you install it. This can be done, via the appropriate preference, in the background. You can then continue to work normally, and you'll get an onscreen prompt when the software is ready to be installed. If that sounds like something "borrowed" from Windows, you can bet on it.*

---

18. Troubleshooting Panther

Immediate Solutions

Solving Panther Installation Problems

In Chapter 2, I covered the simple installation process for Panther. For most users, everything should proceed normally. In some situations, you will encounter problems, warnings, or errors that prevent the process from continuing.

The following is a list of potential problems and solutions:

- *The firmware isn't up-to-date*—Recent Macs have a small updatable boot ROM that's used to start your computer and perform small diagnostic checks (on older Macs, upgrading isn't possible). This firmware is updated from time to time to address hardware-related problems. If you receive a warning that the Panther installation cannot proceed until you install the update, visit Apple's support Web site and see which updates apply to your model. The update site is located at **www.info.apple.com/ support/downloads.html**.

WARNING! *Don't assume the Panther installer will always be smart enough to figure out the firmware you need. Attempting installation with older firmware has been known to black out the screens on some slot-load iMacs, for example. Although, it's fair to say that this problem largely occurred with the previous version of Mac OS X. If your Mac can boot under Mac OS 9, return there and run Software Update to see if a new firmware update is delivered. For Macs that only boot into Mac OS X, your current Software Update should deliver the proper update. If you're still not certain, go to Apple's support site and see if an update is available. Just remember that the firmware update won't install on your Mac if you are already using that version or a later one.*

- *The hard drive cannot be repaired*—At the very start of the installation process, the Installer examines the target volume (the one on which you're installing Panther). Minor directory damage will be fixed before the installation starts. If the damage cannot be fixed, you'll see a prompt on your screen about the problem. If this happens, the installation will stop dead in its tracks. At this point, you can try other options to repair the drive. After you restart in your Classic Mac OS environment, you can try using the version of Disk First Aid that came with the Classic Mac OS or one of the hard-drive diagnostic programs described in Chapter 2. Should none of these remedies succeed, your remaining choice is to consider backing up your files and formatting the drive. Unless the drive has a hardware problem, that final drastic step ought to take care of the trouble and allow you to install Panther.

NOTE: Is it possible to know for certain that you have a hardware problem? Well, there are drastic symptoms, such as a constant clicking and clacking, which indicates the drive's read/ write heads aren't able to locate data on the drive, but in this case you won't even be able to reformat the drive successfully. Lesser hardware problems may result in continuing directory damage even if you do manage to make installations succeed. But I wouldn't take chances. Backup your files and replace the drive.

TIP: Drives that support IBM's S.M.A.R.T. (Self-Monitoring Analysis, and Reporting Technology) keep tabs on performance, and can sometimes warn you if a failure is imminent. Disk Utility can monitor this information on many drives, except for FireWire devices. To check on your drive's health, simply launch Disk Utility, select the name of the drive, and take a look at the bottom of the window, which displays the S.M.A.R.T status of the device. If it says "verified," the drive is all right. If "About to Fail" appears there, back up the drive, and replace it pronto!

- *The hard drive cannot be updated*—During the installation process, the Installer attempts to update the hard disk device driver. If the drive is already formatted with Apple's Drive Setup utility, this step should not present a problem. Drive Setup works with any ATA-based drive and many SCSI drives. But if you have a hard drive that didn't come from Apple, it's highly likely that the drive was formatted with a different program, such as FWB's Hard Disk ToolKit or LaCie's Silverlining. You only need to make sure that the program used is compatible with Mac OS X. Otherwise, you should update the drive with the right version of your disk-formatting program. In these two cases, the message can be ignored.

WARNING! You shouldn't ignore messages about drive problems or allow installation on a drive not formatted with a Mac OS X–compatible utility. The consequences can be serious—damage to your hard drive's directory and possible loss of data.

- *Your drive is not formatted correctly*—As I explained in Chapter 2, on a number of older Macs, such as the early iMacs, you must put Panther on a partition that occupies the first 8GB of the drive. (It will appear first in your list of available volumes in the Mac OS X installer.) If you've purchased a larger hard drive and divided

18. Troubleshooting Panther

413

up differently, you'll have to back up your files and reformat with the proper partition scheme. This is a hardware limitation of the models in question, so you're stuck. You have to obey the rules; I don't make them, I just report them.

- *Your Mac can't be restarted after installation fails*—When you run the Mac OS X Installer, it changes the Startup Disk selection so that it will boot from the new operating system. Should something happen to abort the installation, you need to change the setup manually. You can do so by starting your Mac with your Mac OS X CD. Just restart and hold down the C key to boot from the CD. Once you're running from the CD, the first installation screen will appear. Go to the Installer's application menu and choose Open Disk Utility. With Disk Utility launched, click the name of your target volume, and then click the Repair button. Let Disk Utility examine your Mac's hard drive for disk-related problems. Next, run the Repair Disk Permissions feature, which can also confound upgrade installations. If you get a clean bill of health or any drive directory or permissions problems are fixed, go ahead and reinstall Mac OS X. Should that installation fail on a Mac with dual-booting capability (able to boot under Mac OS I), restart with your Mac OS 9.x CD, again holding down the C key. Locate the Startup Disk control panel (in the Utilities folder) and select your Classic Mac OS System Folder to restart your computer. At this point, you should consider backing up and reformatting your Mac's hard drive before attempting a new installation.

WARNING! *I am assuming that before you began the installation, you verified that your Mac is compatible with Panther and that it has the right amount of memory and storage space. Although it is possible to install Panther on a non-supported model, and many users manage to do it successfully using such applications as XpostFacto, Apple will not provide any help if you attempt this method.*

- *You encounter chronic kernel panics*—You see a warning message on the screen in several languages that you have to restart your Mac. A kernel panic is the Mac OS X equivalent of a system-related error, and you must follow the instructions to force a restart. Most times, that's enough to get things to run, but if it doesn't work, there are some possible answers. The first problem is a hard drive problem, but if you followed the information I gave you above, this should not be an issue. The next most common problem is defective RAM. Even if you ran under previous versions of Mac OS X or the Classic Mac OS without trouble, the fact is that Panther is more sensitive for such ills. The easiest way to diagnose this problem is to remove any RAM you added beyond the factory compliment. But even if everything came from Apple, it doesn't hurt to remove all but one of your RAM upgrades and see if the problem disappears. Since most RAM carries a lifetime warranty, contact the dealer or manufacturer about replacement.

TIP: *You can use your Mac's Hardware Test CD to run a limited RAM test and a somewhat more extended test. MicroMat's TechTool Pro is better capable of handling these chores, but even then the tests may not be sufficient to establish that your RAM is defective. The switch RAM gambit is usually the best way, and if you still run into trouble or don't want to tear your Mac apart to get at the memory chip, let your dealer do it for you. I would, for example, stay clear of trying to get at the inner RAM module in the flat panel iMac, which requires applying a sealant when reinstalling the internal workings. Yes, I know how to do it, but my patience has limits.*

- *You can't log in*—This is not as difficult as it may seem at first glance. Being a Unix-based operating system, Mac OS X expects you to enter the correct username and password unless the option to bypass the login panel is left selected in the Login pane of the System Preferences Application (this is the system default). If the problem affects an individual user of your Mac, you can log in as administrator, open the Accounts System Preferences panel, click the Password button, and change the user's password. Should you be unable to access the administrator's account, restart with your Mac OS X CD by holding down the C key. When the Installer launches, go to the Installer's application menu and choose Reset Password. In the Password Reset application window, click the drive for which you want to reset the password, and then choose the name of the user whose password you want to reset from the pop-up menu. Type the new password in the first text field, and then verify it in the second. Click Save to store the new password and then quit the application. You'll be returned to the Installer application, where you can restart by quitting Installer and clicking the Restart button in the "Are you sure?" prompt. When you reboot your Mac, the new password should be in effect.

NOTE: *It's not uncommon for someone to activate the Caps Lock key by error, which means that the password would be typed in all caps. Look at the Caps Lock light on the keyboard to be sure when you're typing or creating a password.*

Related solution:	*Found on page:*
Installing Panther	28

WARNING! *Since it is easy to restore a password with the installer disk, you should keep it locked and safe if you're in an office where security is important.*

- *Finder refuses to load at startup*—I ran into this situation after restoring files from a first-generation iMac to a flat-panel model. Even Apple's experts at the "Genius Bar" at one of their own stores were stumped, although I discovered a Knowledge Base note about the solution later on (after I solved the problem). Mac OS X loads not only the fonts in the various Mac OS X Fonts folders, but the ones in the Classic Fonts folder as well. One of the fonts transferred from the old iMac to the Classic Fonts folder was damaged, somehow (although it worked on the old computer). When I rebooted under Mac OS 9 and removed the non-Apple fonts from the Fonts folder inside the Classic System Folder, I was able to restart under Mac OS X without further incident. Of course, this requires a Mac that *does* restart under Mac OS 9. If you have a newer Mac without dual-booting capability, I've got a tip for you below. If the tip doesn't work, you may just have to reinstall Panther.

NOTE: *I've yet to run into this problem with Panther, which is supposedly more resilient to such ills. But I never say never, so keep it in mind if you run into a problem of this sort.*

TIP: *Another diagnostic tool that sometimes works whether or not you do have dual-booting capability is Mac OS X's Safe Mode. Like the Windows equivalent, it lets you start up with the minimum amount of software needed to make your Mac run. To activate this feature, restart with the Shift key held down and keep it down until you see the progress circle under the Apple logo on the startup screen. If all goes well, you'll see a "Safe Mode" label in the Welcome to Mac OS X progress screen. During this process, your Mac undergoes a test of your startup drive. If everything works correctly, check your Classic System Folder for non-Apple fonts and remove them, or just remove the fonts folder and place it on your desktop. Restart your Mac, and it'll go through the normal startup process and, one hopes, things will work normally from here on.*

- *Installer quits at startup*—Like constant kernel panics, this problem may be caused by RAM that's defective or out of spec. The solution is to remove third-party memory and restore the RAM that shipped with the computer. Once Mac OS X is installed, you can restore the additional RAM. If you run into a problem with frequent system crashes, consider contacting the dealer or manufacturer from whom you bought the RAM about replacements. Remember that high quality memory upgrades usually come with a lifetime warranty.

NOTE: *Do RAM problems mean you shouldn't buy the cheap stuff? Not necessarily, except that the companies who deal with more expensive products often subject their RAM modules to more severe testing, to reduce the possibility of such ills. Besides, you might indeed find that the cost of RAM from such mainstays as Crucial and Kingston actually don't cost much more than the bargain basement brand. The Power Mac G5 is said to be more sensitive to such issues, so if you spent all that money to buy a powerful Mac, don't shortchange yourself on memory. You'll lose a lot more in lost time and possible corrupted data than you might save by choosing the cheap route.*

Solving System Crashes and Freezes

You may have hoped that Panther would represent salvation from constant system crashes, but in the real world, it doesn't work that way. From time to time, you will encounter programs that behave as badly as they did under Classic system versions, but you'll be able to exit far more safely under Panther.

The following sections address some common problems and solutions.

An Application Refuses to Quit

Here's a problem you likely have seen: You can't, for the life of you, make an application stop running. It seems to be active, and you may even be able to open, edit, and save documents, but you cannot quit the program. The solution is the Force Quit feature, performed as follows:

1. Choose Force Quit from the Apple menu or press Command+Option+Escape.

2. On the Force Quit Applications dialog box that appears (see Figure 18.2), scroll to the application you want to quit. A nonresponsive application will sometimes be listed in red.

NOTE: *Mac OS X's Force Quit feature, with its ability to selectively choose any open application, is not unique to Mac OS X. Even Windows works this way, with its End Task feature.*

3. Click Force Quit. The selected application will proceed to quit (well, usually).

TIP: *Another way to force an application to quit is to hold down Option and click and hold the application's icon in the Dock. Choose Force quit from the popup menu. This is sometimes a useful last resort if the regular method fails to close the application. Besides, it looks cooler.*

18. Troubleshooting Panther

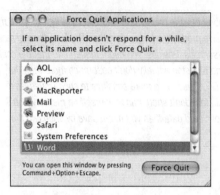

Figure 18.2   You can force quit one or more applications when this screen appears. Non-responsive programs carry a warning label to that effect.

After the application has been shut down, you can continue to use your Mac in the normal fashion. Panther's protected memory allows programs to crash or be forced to quit without affecting system stability. Now you can try running the application again and see if it works all right. If it still misbehaves, you should contact the publisher for technical assistance.

NOTE: On some rare occasions, you may need to force quit an application twice before the action "takes." Such are the vagaries of software bugs even with an industrial-strength operating system.

WARNING! If a Classic application freezes, it's best to force quit the Classic environment instead, because it is apt to become unstable otherwise. Classic applications do not take advantage of Mac OS X's robust system protection features. When you launch your next Classic application, Classic will come along for the ride. If you have open documents from a Classic application, however, you'll want to close those applications first before attempting to force quit Classic. Otherwise, you'll lose any unsaved changes to those documents.

Applications Refuse to Run

If the problem you encounter involves just a single application, try launching it again. If that doesn't work, you might need to reinstall the application.

If all your applications fail to run, however, restart your Mac and try again. Usually the restart will fix the problem. If the problems persist, contact the publisher of the software updates for Mac OS X.

NOTE: *If a number of applications that are supposed to be compatible with Mac OS X fail to launch, you should consider reinstalling Mac OS X. You can do this without losing your existing system settings or installed documents and software. Just use Panther's Archive and Install option, and check Preserve Users and Network Settings to keep your configuration essentially intact. I cover the entire installation process in glorious detail in Chapter 2.*

TIP: *One possible cure for an application that quits or another oddity is to remove the application's preference file. Like the Classic Mac OS, a corrupted preference file can cause an application to stop running or refuse to launch. You'll find these files in your personal or Users Library folder, in the folder labeled Preferences. Although many preference files look normal, or at least normal to users of older Mac OS versions, some carry a "com" prefix, after which you see the name of the company that made the product, such as com.apple. Then you see the name of the program the preference file is for, and then you'll see a .plist suffix. So the preference file for Apple's Mail application is known as com.apple.mail.plist.*

The Classic Environment Fails to Run

Do you have Mac OS 9.1 or later installed? The Classic feature simply won't support any earlier version of the Mac OS. In addition, many third-party system enhancements won't run in this setting. The best way to run a Classic System Folder is to configure it to be lean and mean. I cover the subject in more detail in Chapter 15.

NOTE: *The Classic environment works best with Mac OS 9.2.1 or later (9.2.2 was the version shipping at the time this book was written). In addition to offering better performance, improved boot time, and improved stability, some of the Classic quirks (such as the missing-cursor symptom) are eliminated, so it's worth updating from, say, 9.1.*

If setting up an Apple-only System Folder fails to resolve the startup problem, consider reinstalling your Classic Mac OS using the original system CD or DVD that came with your Mac. On recent Macs, you'll find the Classic installation file that can also restore other software that came with your computer. If you are using an older Mac with separate Mac OS 9 installation CDs and you have applied a system update, you'll need to do a clean installation (click Option on the first Installer screen). Then, apply any system updates you've received. Don't forget that when you do a clean installation of your Classic Mac OS, you'll also have to transfer your system settings (for your ISP and Internet software) and third-party software from your older or previous System Folder to your newly installed System Folder.

18. Troubleshooting Panther

NOTE: *Beginning with the Power Macs that shipped in August, 2002, there is no custom installer for Mac OS 9. It's strictly a part of the System Restore application that is used with your Restore CDs.*

Related solution:	Found on page:
Getting Reliable Performance from Classic Applications	328

Solving Network Access Problems

Although Panther has enhanced networking capability, that doesn't mean everything will work perfectly all the time. Here are some ways to handle common network problems:

- *Settings don't change*—You do not have to restart your Mac whenever you switch network configurations, but doing so doesn't hurt. In addition, you may want to redo the settings in the Network pane of the System Preferences application, just in case you missed something the first time out. Chapter 8 has more information on this subject.

- *Networked Macs and printers are not available*—Reopen your Network pane and make sure AppleTalk is turned on and you've given your Mac a name that's unique on your network. If everything is properly configured, check your network cables and hub configuration. Also make sure the other Macs on the network can recognize your Mac or other devices on the network. If other Macs encounter similar problems, complete network troubleshooting is in order. For a large system, you should contact your network administrator for further assistance.

NOTE: *AppleTalk can only be activated for one networking setup at a time. This means, for example, that if your Mac also has AirPort hardware, you'll have to choose between AirPort and built-in Ethernet to support AppleTalk devices.*

- *Windows networking software doesn't run*—If you're using such programs as Thursby Systems' DAVE or MacSOHO, you should contact the publisher directly about support for Panther. You can also use Panther's expanded built-in Windows networking features, which are described further in Chapter 8.

Related solution:	Found on page:
Fixing Network Access Problems	194

Login Window Shakes

If you enter a username and password and the window shakes when you try to log in, it means the name or password you entered is not correct. The solution is to reenter the login information and make sure each keystroke is accurate. If the symptom happens with another user, you may need to reset his or her password.

NOTE: You should make sure you are correctly typing lower case and upper case letters. The login window will show if caps lock is engaged.

Here's how to do it:

1. Login under your Administrator's account.

2. Launch System Preferences, and then open the Accounts pane.

3. If it's closed, click the padlock icon and enter your administrator username and password.

4. Click the name of the user whose password you want to change, and then the Password button. The dialog shown in Figure 18.3 appears.

5. Enter the new password, and click Save to store the settings.

6. Choose Quit from the System Preferences Application menu, or press Command+Q.

7. If necessary, log out again and log in under that user's new password.

Desktop Folder Contents Aren't Visible Under Mac OS 9.x

You place a file or folder on Panther's desktop, but when you reboot under Panther, the item is not there. What's wrong?

The answer is that the desktops for the two operating systems are totally separate. The contents of one are not mirrored on the other. If you've installed Mac OS X on the same volume as Mac OS 9.1, you'll

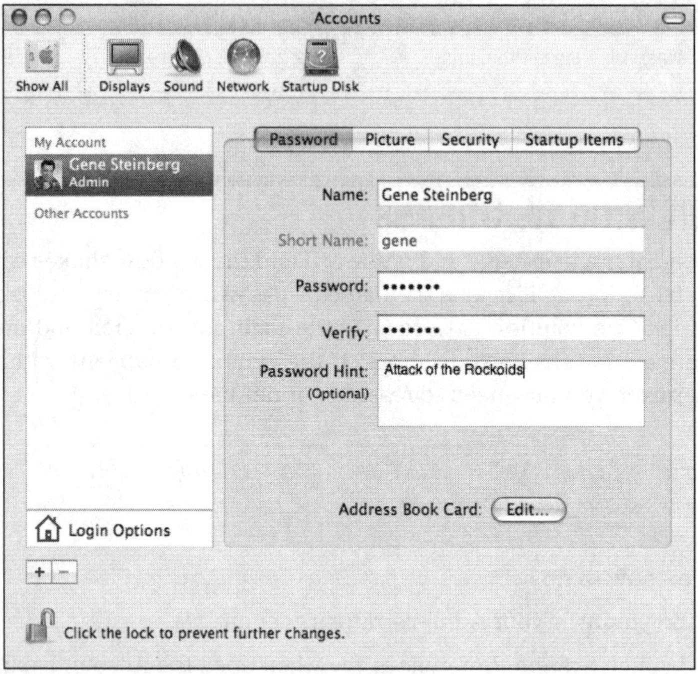

Figure 18.3 Edit a user's password here.

find a workable solution. There's an alias on your Mac's hard drive labeled Desktop (Mac OS 9). When you open that folder, you'll see a folder that contains all of your Classic Mac OS desktop items. If the desktop is on another drive, just access that drive from a Finder window, and you'll see a folder labeled Desktop that contains the items you want.

Panther Won't Boot after You Deleted a File by Mistake

When you run your Mac under Mac OS 9, by default you'll see the following files at the top or root level of the hard drive on which Panther is installed (plus any additional files or folders you've placed on the top level of the drive):

- Applications
- Applications (Mac OS 9)
- Library
- mach

- mach.sym

- mach_kernel

- System

- System Folder

- Users

If you delete something from the Panther Applications folder, that application is no longer available. In addition, deleting a user's folder removes that user from the system. Do not attempt to remove any of the files labeled *mach*, or the files in the folder labeled *Library* or *System*, because removal will prevent Panther from running. Should the worst happen, you will have to run your Mac OS X Installer CD to reinstall the system. If you haven't installed any maintenance updates (such as the one from 10.3 to 10.3.1, and so on), you can perform a regular installation to preserve your system-related settings. Otherwise use the Archive & Install option. I cover all this in complete detail in Chapter 2.

Solving Other Common Panther Problems

Here are other problems you might encounter with Mac OS X. They usually have solutions, but some may not be as easy as you'd prefer:

- *The screen remains dark when booting from the Installer CD*— Panther only supports graphics cards and chips from ATI Technologies, IX Micro, and NVIDIA. If you're using a graphics card from a company such as Formac, contact the manufacturer directly about a Panther–compatible version.

NOTE: *If you are using a Voodoo graphic card from 3dfx Interactive, you are probably out of luck. With the departure of the company after selling its assets to rival NVIDIA several years ago, the likelihood that driver updates will be produced are slim. Fortunately, Mac OS X–compatible graphics cards are not terribly expensive. The ATI Radeon 7000, which outdoes the fastest Voodoo card in virtually all respects, was selling for less than $129 when this book was written. In addition, Formac informs me that their ProFormance3 card is compatible with Mac OS X, although it doesn't provide 3D acceleration (which is, in essence, the core of the Mac OS X graphical experience).*

- *The printer isn't recognized*—Panther should recognize most laser printers. However, ink jet printers and some USB-based laser printers may require special drivers to work. Drivers for such makes as Canon, Epson, HP, and Lexmark ink jets are provided with Panther. In addition, Gimp-Print, a set of open source printer drivers, is part of the standard Panther installation.

18. Troubleshooting Panther

These drivers support a number of additional devices, particularly older models, with nearly full support for all features. If your printer remains unsupported, you'll need to contact the manufacturer about the availability of driver updates. A good place to look is the company's Web site. If none are available, the devices will work only for Classic applications. Maybe it's time to buy a new printer.

- *The scanner won't scan*—This issue is the same as the printer not being recognized. It is up to the manufacturer to deliver a device driver that will function. Out of the box, Panther's Image Capture application supports a small number of consumer and SOHO models from Epson. If you cannot locate a Mac OS X–compatible version for a specific make and model, you should see if the software for a similar product in the manufacturer's line runs. Quite often, scanner drivers recognize a number of different models.

TIP: One possible solution if your scanner maker doesn't have a Mac OS X driver is a shareware program, VueScan, from Hamrick Software (*www.hamrick.com*). This nifty application comes in versions for the Classic Mac OS, Mac OS X, Windows, and even Linux, and supports dozens of flatbed and slide scanners from all the major makers, such as Agfa, Epson, HP, Microtek, and Umax. If you crave more professional features, consider SilverFast from LaserSoft (*www.lasersoft.com*), which not only supports nearly 200 scanners, but provides features that rival many imaging editing programs.

- *You cannot burn a CD*—Panther supports a number of third-party FireWire and USB CD burners in addition to Apple's own drives. This support allows you to use the Finder-level CD burning feature with a number of mechanisms. But a number of drives aren't supported (and this is especially true for SCSI-based CD burners), in which case, you'll have to ask the manufacturer of the product about Mac OS X–savvy software. Or, just reboot under your Classic Mac OS.

TIP: The latest versions of Roxio's Toast and CharisMac's Discribe both support CD burning under Mac OS X. These product will recognize most any CD or DVD burner, including Apple's.

- *Documents won't print*—You send a document to the printer, and the printer's icon appears in the Dock. But it disappears just as quickly, and your document hasn't printed. The first thing to check is your print queue. To do that, launch the printer's application, which is placed in the Printers folder inside your personal Library folder when you set up the printer on your Mac (see Figure 18.4). If you see a toolbar icon labeled Start Jobs in the

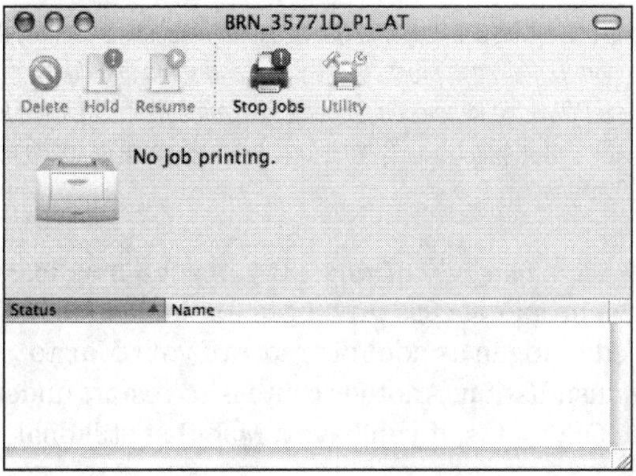

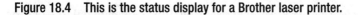

Figure 18.4   This is the status display for a Brother laser printer.

print queue window, the one that bears the name of your printer, click it. It means that the print queue was stopped for some reason. Usually this will fix the problem (it has to be checked for each printer you use). If this doesn't work, try turning the printer off and on, recheck printer cables and, if all else fails, check with the maker's Web site or versiontracker.com for updated drivers.

NOTE: When you set up a printer, you can also opt to create a desktop icon, which gives you full time access to your printer's queue. Chapter 8 will show you how this is done.

- *You can't use a digital camera*—Apple's Image Capture and iPhoto applications support a wide variety of cameras from most major makers. If your device isn't supported, check with the manufacturer about what options you might have with regard to image capture software.

- *Input device features are not recognized*—Panther has built-in support for the second button and the scroll wheel on most input devices, but others require special software, especially if extra buttons and scroll wheels are included. You'll need to contact the publisher about compatibility issues.

- *Not all drives are recognized*—Panther provides standard support for most popular removable and fixed storage devices, such as Imation and Iomega drives and devices from EZQuest, LaCie, Maxtor, OWC, QPS and SmartDisk. If the product you want to use won't run, the manufacturer is your best resource for assistance.

18. Troubleshooting Panther

NOTE: If your storage device is connected courtesy of a SCSI adapter card, contact the maker of the card about Mac OS X support. Not all such products will work, and some that due may require the installation of a new ROM chip to function properly. Also remember that some PCI cards aren't compatible with the Power Mac G5's PCI-x feature, because some cards do not support what is known as 3.3V signaling.

- *You can't install Classic applications*—If you get a message that you don't have the proper access privileges for such an installation, you will need to log in as administrator of your Mac to perform such an installation. Another route is to restart under your Classic Mac OS; that is, if you have a Mac that still dual boots, of course.

- *The Dock freezes*—On occasion, the Dock may fail to work, or open applications will not have the telltale arrow beneath their icon. Unfortunately, the Dock isn't recognized in the Force Quit window, so you can't quit it that way. The solution is to use the Activity Viewer application, which is located in the Utilities folder. With Activity Viewer launched (see Figure 18.5), locate and select Dock. Now choose Quit Process from the toolbar, and

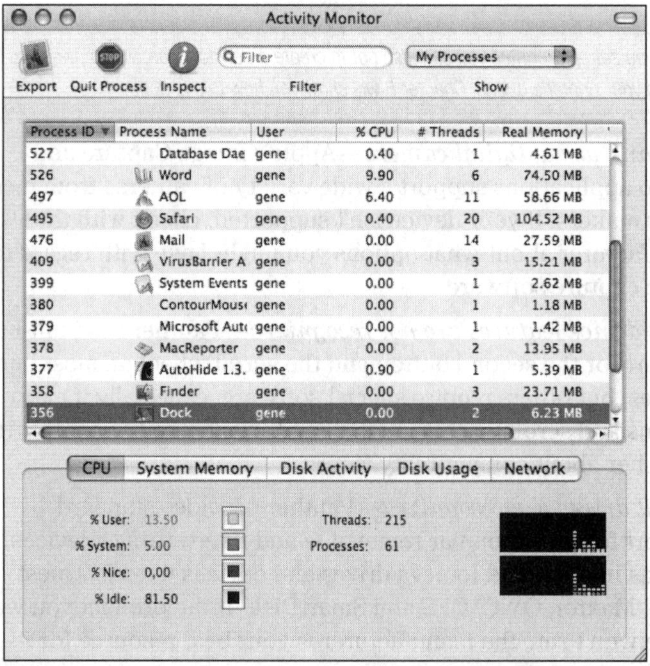

Figure 18.5   Use Activity Viewer to quit a system process that isn't recognized by the Force Quit function, such as the Dock.

then choose Quit in the Quit Process dialog box. Within seconds, the Dock will disappear and relaunch itself, after which it should run normally. If it doesn't, restart your Mac.

- *You can't delete a file*—When you try to empty the trash, you get a message that the trash is in use, or that you don't have permission to zap a file. If this happens, remove the item from the Trash, and, with the item selected, call up the Finder's Get Info window. Use the Ownership & Permissions feature to make sure that your user name is listed as owner of the file. You may have to OK a password prompt first, though. If that doesn't work, put the item back in the trash, locate the Terminal application in the Utilities folder and launch it. With Terminal open, type "sudo rm –rf .Trash" and press Return. Enter your administrator's password and press Return again. All the files in the Trash will be discarded (although you may have to open and close a Trash window to see the empty icon).

TIP: *A quick way to fix permissions problems with Mac OS X files is to use Disk Utility. With the program open, click on the First Aid tab, select your startup drive, and click on Repair Disk Permissions. In almost every case, you'll see a few permissions fixed, but sometimes there will be a long list. Regardless, with permissions fixed, you should no longer run into problems deleting and moving files that are not in Mac OS X's System folder. It doesn't hurt to restart after permissions are repaired, but it isn't required. You may perform the same functions with third-party utilities, such as Cocktail (my favorite) and Panther Disk Cleaner. These little applications simply put a pretty face on Unix functions, and they can handle a host of system maintenance chores without you having to fret over them.*

WARNING! *As with any Terminal action, there's no opting out. When you engage a command, the Unix core of Mac OS X will do the deed—and that, as they say, is that. Also, be sure to allow a short time for all files to be deleted before quitting Terminal; otherwise some files may still be there when you recheck the Trash.*

Performing System-Level Disk Diagnostics

Although Panther is built upon a solid Unix core, you seldom need to explore the underbelly with the Terminal, although I've given you a few hints here and there. For example, many of the diagnostic chores can be done utilizing the basic tools that come with Panther.

For example hard-disk management is done with a new, combined application called Disk Utility, found in the Utilities folder. It combines Disk First Aid and Drive Setup. Unfortunately, the version offered with Mac OS X cannot examine or repair damage to your startup drive. Although your drives are checked every time you boot your Mac, as an ounce of prevention, you can also perform a disk diagnostic by rebooting with your Mac OS X CD and accessing Disk Utility from the Installer's application menu. If you don't have your system CD readily at hand, here's another alternative—a disk-checking process that allows you to explore the depths of Mac OS X and have your Mac run in a fashion you never expected.

Here's what to do:

NOTE: There's no way to provide illustrations of this process with the standard screen shot. The information provided, however, should be clear enough. Don't be alarmed by what you see; this is the way Mac OS X is designed. Just bear in mind that doing a disk repair from the command line is no more effective than running Disk Utility on a drive. However, it is a useful exercise if you want to explore the depths of Mac OS X.

---

1. Restart your Mac.

2. As soon as the restart process begins, press Command+S, which is a shortcut to put your Mac in what is known as *Single User Mode*. What you see is only vaguely reminiscent of the DOS prompt accessed under Microsoft Windows. You see a true Unix command line, and if you thought DOS looked different, it doesn't hold a candle to what you see here.

3. With the command line displayed, a mélange of text appears. At the bottom of the text is a **localhost#** prompt. Type the following command (and don't forget the space before the hyphen [-]):

```
fsck -y
```

NOTE: If your hard drive is "journaled," which is part of the standard Panther installation, add the command –f to force checking. And, by the way, I don't recommend turning off journaling, which you can do without affecting your data. It provides an important extra ounce of drive protection, because it stores drive actions in a database. That way if you crash during a save operation, it can roll back to the previous directory status, which at least helps prevent files from being corrupted.

---

4. Press Return. Over the next minute or two, a series of status messages appear that are not dissimilar from those you'd see in

Disk First Aid. These messages indicate the progress of the disk check. You'll also see an indication that the disk is being repaired, if this is necessary. When the disk check is finished, the **localhost#** prompt returns.

5. If the drive is shown as "modified," meaning drive damage was repaired, repeat the process until the drive comes up as OK.

NOTE: If you have a recent Power Mac, with multiple cooling fans, don't be surprised if you find them working full force while this disk check process is being performed. That's because the operating system's management features for those fans isn't operational in this mode, and they do not automatically quiet down. This is particularly noticeable on the Power Mac G5, which has all of nine cooling fans to handle the needs of its powerful processor and other subsystems.

---

6. It's time to restart and return to the comfort of the familiar Aqua interface. Type the following:

```
reboot
```

7. Press Return. The screen darkens, and the Mac's startup chord sounds. Then the familiar Mac OS X startup screen appears.

Setting Root Access

Under rare circumstances, a software publisher may ask that you access the root or super user mode to diagnose a problem. Usually the administrator's password is sufficient to gain this access, but the password will be rejected unless you enable this feature.

To solve this problem, follow these steps:

1. Go to the Utilities folder and launch the NetInfo Manager application (see Figure 18.6).

2. Go to the Domain menu, choose Security, and select Enable Root User from the submenu.

3. Enter the password for the root user in the password prompt and then reenter it when requested. When it's entered, root access will be enabled or reset for your Mac, and you'll be able to use the full scope of available administration tools.

18. Troubleshooting Panther

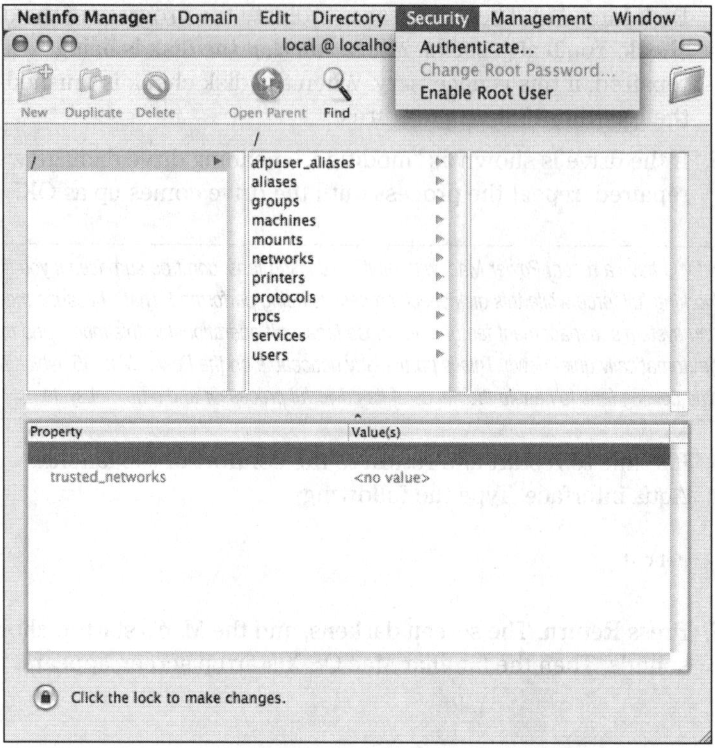

Figure 18.6   The NetInfo Manager is a useful network administrator's tool.

WARNING! *Unix mavens say enabling root access presents a security risk because all parts of your computer are available. You can even trash system files with impunity, so use this process only as a last resort. Most users of Mac OS X will never need to use this feature.*

4. Once you've finished running under Root mode, reboot under your regular user's account, open NetInfo Manager, and choose Disable Root User from the submenu. Authenticate when requested. That will shut down root access, and I'd suggest this be done right away.

Monitoring System Use to Check for Conflicts

From time to time you'll need to examine how your Mac is running to help a software publisher find the source of a conflict.

Here's a way to see how programs are using system and memory resources, using the Terminal application:

1. Go to the Utilities folder and launch Terminal.

2. With Terminal open, type the command "top" and press the Return key. You'll see an interactive display showing how resources may be using CPU or RAM on your Mac (see Figure 18.7). This information can help a software publisher see if there's the potential for trouble.

3. Launch Console, also located in the Utilities folder. This program will display a log of system activities (see Figure 18.8) that a publisher can use to trace the possible cause of a crash or other performance problem. The log can be saved or printed for later review.

NOTE: *If your Mac is the victim of a kernel panic, information about it and what brought it about will appear in the log.*

TIP: *Like other Unix-based operating systems, Mac OS X is designed to perform system maintenance and update processes between 3:15 A.M. and 5:30 A.M. each day. The process includes updating and cleaning out system database and log files. If your Mac isn't running at that hour, you may find that performance dips over time, or the logs become huge. One solution to this dilemma is a shareware application, Macaroni, which comes as a preference*

```
●○○                   Terminal — top — 80x24
Processes:  62 total, 2 running, 60 sleeping... 212 threads          10:55:39
Load Avg:  0.38, 0.38, 0.27     CPU usage:  8.0% user, 13.7% sys, 78.3% idle
SharedLibs: num =   120, resident = 58.7M code, 4.23M data, 19.9M LinkEdit
MemRegions: num = 13003, resident =  285M + 17.7M private,  457M shared
PhysMem:    173M wired,  266M active, 1.21G inactive, 1.64G used,  369M free
VM: 7.82G + 84.7M   77689(1) pageins, 9025(0) pageouts

  PID COMMAND      %CPU   TIME   #TH #PRTS #MREGS RPRVT  RSHRD  RSIZE  VSIZE
 1044 screencapt   0.0% 0:00.03   1    27    31   220K   968K   916K   155M
 1042 top         19.3% 0:01.26   1    17    26   336K   496K  1.80M  27.1M
 1039 bash         0.0% 0:00.02   1    12    15   156K   976K  1.30M  18.2M
 1038 login        0.0% 0:00.02   1    13    37   140K   488K  1.96M  26.9M
 1037 Terminal     0.0% 0:00.42   3    61   145  1.49M  21.9M  15.3M   226M
  764 AppleModem   0.0% 0:00.23   2    64   110   840K  19.4M  2.82M   221M
  706 modemd       0.0% 0:00.02   1    18    22   216K   424K   560K  27.1M
  680 efax         0.0% 0:00.27   1    12    18   136K   484K   388K  17.8M
  666 Internet E   0.8% 0:33.48   6    86   341  12.5M  45.9M  26.2M   264M
  651 pppd         0.0% 0:00.10   1     9    21    52K  1.11M   188K  27.3M
  650 pppd         0.0% 0:00.03   1    15    21    80K  1.11M   832K  27.3M
  568 SystemUISe   1.6% 0:20.15   1   180   169 1.02M- 22.6M+ 4.80M-  226M
  534 SecurityAg   0.0% 0:00.08   2    73   134  1.74M  22.0M  4.95M   225M
  529 AppleSpell   0.0% 0:00.26   1    37    37   704K  9.76M  1.78M  36.3M
  527 Microsoft    0.8% 0:04.08   1    66   132  2.06M  12.8M  4.61M   218M
  526 Microsoft   10.4% 17:18.26   6   189   535  48.8M   226K  74.7M   494M
```

Figure 18.7   Terminal is used to access Panther's Unix core directly.

18. Troubleshooting Panther

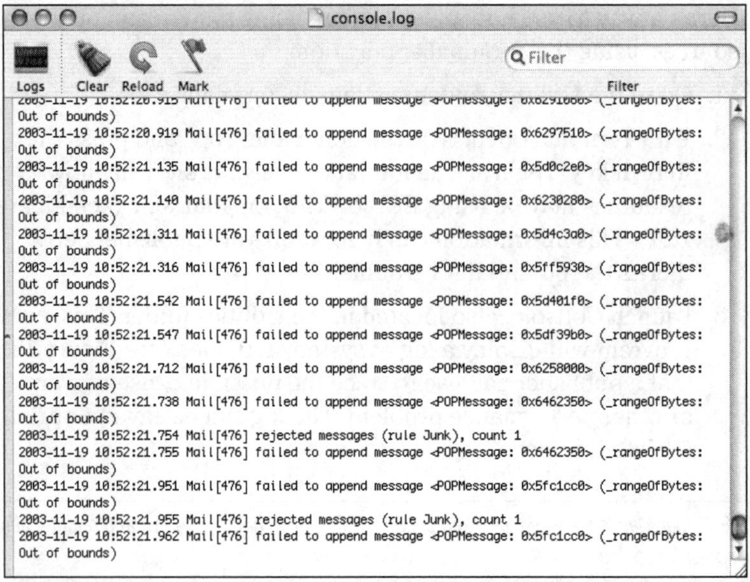

Figure 18.8   Console logs system operations and is a useful tool to diagnose software conflicts.

panel component that can be configured to run all those maintenance processes automatically. You don't have to keep your Mac running at the appointed hour, so you can save on your electric bill. Other options include Cocktail and Panther Cache Cleaner, which can be configured to perform other tasks, such as permissions repairs, and make minor interface changes to the operating system.

A Fast Introduction to Panther's Unix Environment

In Brief

The friendly Aqua interface of Panther holds hidden treasures. Deep within its bowels exists what some might regard as another universe. To enter this Twilight Zone of the operating system world, you need only launch a simple application and enter a few text-based commands.

So far in this book I've introduced you to a few command line solutions to a few vexing problems with Panther. In large part, though, access to Darwin, the Unix core of Panther, is strictly optional. Panther comes with a rich set of graphical tools that you can use to access many of the features you need to configure and manage your Mac. In addition, Unix mavens the world over have been toiling day and night to provide pretty Aqua front ends to hidden features and present them as system extras that can add additional Dock positioning choices, text smoothing, and other interesting possibilities.

If you're an experienced Mac user, perhaps you attempted to toil in the back doors of the Mac with ResEdit. However, the Terminal application (see Figure 19.1) located in the Utilities folder is far more powerful and encompassing. Terminal gives anyone with administrative access to a Mac direct control of Darwin's command line interface and the ability to harness the power of Unix to move files, manage services, and tell the computer how to function.

NOTE: Even if you don't have administrator's access, you'll be able to do some things in Terminal but you will be limited to commands that encompass your access level.

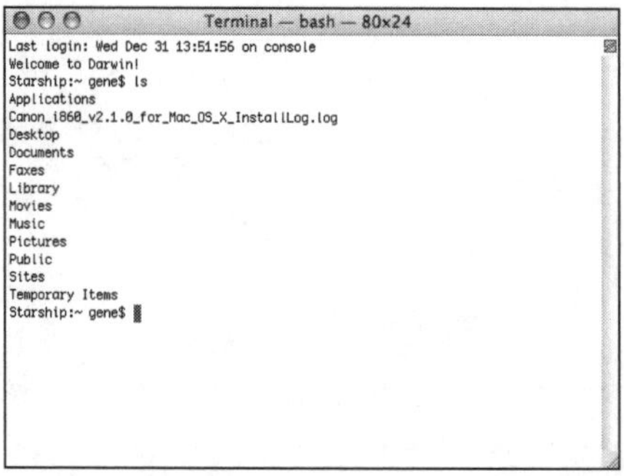

Figure 19.1 Apple's Terminal application is your "stargate" to the world of Unix.

When you first launch Terminal, you enter the world of Unix in all its glory. With Terminal open, you'll see your username followed by a dollar sign ($). This is the first stop on your voyage into the world of the command-line interface (CLI). If you've lived your life in the graphical user interface world, a CLI takes some getting used to. It is far less forgiving than the safe, graphical world Aqua provides. When you engage a command, there will be no turning back. You won't find a prompt giving you the chance to opt out. So, until you learn the ropes, proceed with caution.

When you get used to typing a command rather than pointing and clicking, you may find that using the CLI is far faster for some functions. However, it requires a lot more attention to detail because every keystroke you type is a literal request to do something.

NOTE: If you are experienced at Unix, you'll see that this chapter is meant strictly for beginners. If you know your way around the command line under Unix, you'll be pleased to discover that most or all of your favorite commands will work without alteration under Panther. It's very common for Linux users to attend conventions with Apple laptops in tow because OS X can give them the command-line tools they need, plus key productivity applications, such as Microsoft Office, all in a single product, without having to switch to another operating system.

Looking at the Nuts and Bolts of Darwin

Terminal is a shell interface. A shell program offers a set of utilities and commands that let you write executable scripts to automate certain tasks, much like AppleScript. Shells also act as the buffer between you and the bare operating system, making your life a bit easier.

When you launch Terminal, you access the bash shell. This is one of the more popular shell programs and is a good choice for most users, because it is fairly simple to master and is extremely popular in the Unix world. If you're a power user, you'll be pleased to know that such shells as zsh, csh, tcsh, and plain old share also available for Panther. Each of these shells has its fans and detractors, but a description of the plusses and minuses of these programs is way beyond the scope of this book. If you are interested in exploring the Unix environment in more detail, you should read a library reference work on the subject. One informative example is O'Reilly's *Learning Unix for Mac OS X Panther.*

When you launch Terminal, the first thing you'll see is the ubiquitous $ that indicates you are running the bash shell. From this prompt, you can type in the first command. Let's start with a command that lets you examine the contents of your personal Users file and folder directory: **ls**.

WARNING! *When I say that Unix is literal-minded, I'm very serious. You need to be careful when you type commands and filenames because every character must be accurate. Unix is also case sensitive. You can easily wipe out the contents of your drive if you do the wrong thing, so the watchwords are "be careful."*

When you have typed "ls-", press the Return or Enter key to execute the command. Looking at the results, you should see a list of all the files and folders in the current directory.

To take things a bit further, perhaps you'd like to see a list of all the files, their security settings, and such interesting data as file size and commercial and modification dates. To do so, add the –l switch or modifier to the **ls** command, just as I did in Figure 19.2.

Just type **ls** –l and press Return or Enter. You should now see an expanded list showing the number of files in each folder.

By using the up and down arrows, you can scroll back and forth through the commands you've used. This is a very useful feature if you've entered a particularly long and complex command and you'd like to use it again. It's also helpful in the event you made a mistake and want to fix the error rather than repeat the command. With all the modifications, some Unix commands can be long and complex; an easy fix is often the best way to proceed.

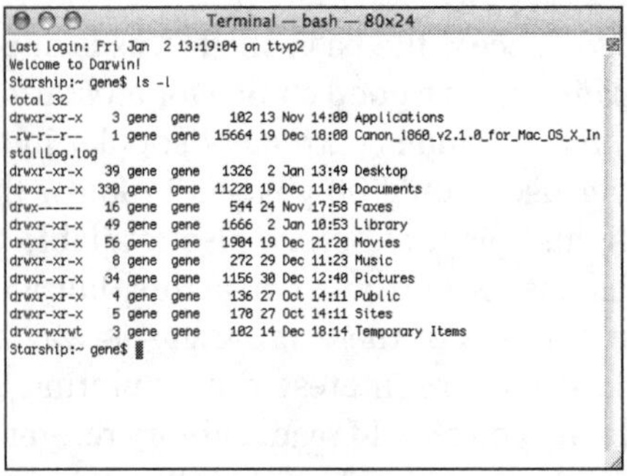

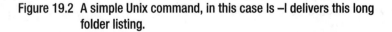

Figure 19.2   A simple Unix command, in this case ls –l delivers this long
folder listing.

TIP: *Don't forget that you can cut the commands from a Web site or e-mail message and paste them into Terminal. That way you can get the command correctly and not have to fret over making a mistake. Of course I assume that the command you're typing is correct.*

Introducing the Autocomplete Feature

The bash shell offers a really nice feature (also present in some of the other Unix shells) known as *Autocomplete*. This feature—reminiscent of the one you find in such applications as Microsoft Entourage, Internet Explorer, Apple's Mail, and Safari—lets you simply type in the first few letters of a filename or folder name or directory path and press Tab. Autocomplete then attempts to fill in the rest of the name of the command. If two or more names match the letters you've typed, Autocomplete fills in the remaining letters to the point where the different versions diverge; then it beeps.

Here's an example: Suppose I want to go to a directory that contains the files for my latest science fiction novel. I type something like **cd /Users/gene/Ro** and then press the Tab key. The tcsh shell fills in the remaining characters so that I see **cd /Users/gene/Rockoids.** As soon as I press Return or Enter, I'm taken to the proper directory. On the other hand, if more than one file or folder name begins with *Ro* in my home directory (such as Rockoids and Rockoids2_the_coming_of_the_protectors), pressing Tab makes Autocomplete fill in everything up to *Rockoids* and then beep to let me know it has found two or more files or folders that match my criteria.

NOTE: *Unix doesn't believe in being spaced out. What I mean is that Unix doesn't believe in word spaces. If you need one in a file or directory name, use an underscore instead, just as I've done here.*

What do I do next? To go to the Rockoids2_the_coming_of_the_protectors directory, I type "2" so that the names are no longer ambiguous, and then press Tab again. Autocomplete shows **cd /Users/gene/ Rockoids2_the_coming_of_the_protectors**, and I can press Return or Enter to jump to that directory.

Running Software from the Command Line

We're all accustomed to just double-clicking on a document or application to launch it. In contrast, running programs from the command line can be a bit of a trick if you've never done it before. When you type a command name and press Return or Enter, Unix searches the directories specified in its path to see if they contain a file whose name matches what you typed in. If it finds such a file, it will launch the application.

However, Unix doesn't search the directory you are currently in. So it's very common for new users to mistakenly launch or execute the wrong application. To launch a file in the directory you are currently in, you can preface the command with a period followed by a slash (*./*) to force Unix to execute only files in the local directory. You can also preface the filename with the whole path. For example, to launch the setup or installation program for a game you downloaded, you would switch to the directory that holds the file using a command similar to **cd /Users/ gene/downloads/reallyawesomegame**.

NOTE: *Don't forget to press Enter each time you want to engage a command. Also, don't use the period at the end of the sentence. It's just there in the interests of good grammar (otherwise my publisher's copy editors would object).*

Once you're in that directory, you could use the command **./setup** or **/Users/gene/downloads/reallyawesomegame/setup** to execute the setup utility.

WARNING! *Most experienced Unix users prefer to use the full path when executing applications rather than the ./ shortcut, because it's more reliable and less prone to error. In addition, you will sometimes find that you cannot execute a file even if you are the owner and have full control of it. The problem is that you have not set the permissions on the file to allow execution. To fix this situation, use the* **chmod** *command to set the execute rights. The full command is* **chmod +x** *followed by the filename.*

On Backing Up Files and Folders

It is very possible to back up files via the Unix command line, using the copy and move commands mentioned in the "Immediate Solutions" portion of this chapter. But this process has its limitations. For one thing, many older Mac files, especially Classic applications, come in two parts—a data fork and a resource—but Unix doesn't recognize the latter. So, if you copy a file via the command line using the **cp** (Copy) or **mv** (Move) command, you'll end up with a file that is not quite the sum of its parts.

This result presents no problem if you're just copying regular document files or Panther native applications. If you need to copy a Classic application or file related to your Classic system software, forget the command line and use the Finder instead.

TIP: If you enjoyed trying the Terminal tips listed here, you'll find additional information at http://homepage.mac.com/x_freedom/tips/terminal.html.

The Short List of Popular Command-Line Features

To further acclimate you to Panther's Unix environment, here are some common and very useful commands and the functions they perform. To make them easier to use, I've grouped similar commands together, even though they are not in alphabetical order:

NOTE: A number of the commands I use here require that you first enter your administrator password in the Terminal command line. After you do that and press Enter, you'll be able to activate these functions.

- **cd** *(change directory)*—The **cd** command lets you switch directories, provided of course that you have the rights needed to access that directory. For example, **cd /Users/gene/Rockoids** will take you to the Rockoids directory located inside the my home directory (to use an example on my own Mac). Likewise, **cd ..** will move you to the directory one level above the one you're currently in.

- **cp** *(copy)*—This command allows you to copy a file or directory from one location to another. You can also use the **cp** command with wildcards (an asterisk) to move only those file(s) that match certain criteria. For example, the command **cp cd /Users/gene/Rockoids/Chap* /Users/gene/Rockoids_backup** will copy (not move) all files that start with *Chap* from my Rockoids directory to my backup folder.

- **mv** *(move)*—This command is used to move (not just copy) files from one location to another. The command **mv /Users/gene/Rockoids/Chap* /Users/gene/Rockoids_backup** will transfer and not copy files that begin with the word *Chap* to the target directory.

TIP: *The **mv** command is also used to rename files. For example, to rename a file named Chapter40 to Chapter41, use the command **mv** Chapter40 Chapter41.*

- **chgrp**—This command changes the group associated with a file. For example, as administrator, you can change the group listed for a file or directory from one user to another. To change a file's group to authors, if the file is currently assigned to a different group, use **chgrp authors [*file or directory in question*]**.

- **chmod** *(change file permissions)*—This is an extremely powerful command that you use to set the access rights for your files and directories. Although this is easy to do in the Finder's Show Info window, in the Privileges category, **chmod** is far more encompassing. What's more, it can be a saving grace in the event you encounter problems with permissions on a file or folder—a dreaded warning that you don't have the right to access, change, or copy a file (a not-uncommon event in Panther). You can also use **chmod** to change the permissions on a large number of files and directories quickly, using wildcards.

  For example, you can limit the ability of others in the authors group to change certain files, but still let them read the files. Here's the command I would use to modify those file permissions: **chmod o=r /Users/gene/Rockoids/Chap***. The end result? This command sets the file permissions for all files that start with "Chap" in the directory **/Users/gene/Rockoids** to read-only status, for everyone but me as owner of the file and those in the group associated with the file or directory. You can use this command in the same fashion to let others read but not executive or modify your files.

- **chown**—This command changes the ownership of a file. As administrator of your Mac, you can use this command to switch ownership of a file or folder from one user to another. Say you wanted to switch ownership of a file created by another user. Just type the command **chown [*username*] [*name of file*]**. A press of the Return key makes you, or the person named in the command, the owner of that file or folder.

NOTE: *If you must change permissions for a file or folder, you aren't confined to the command line. The Finder's Get Info has a very capable Ownership & Permissions feature that will provide easy access to all or most of the changes you need to make within a simple-to-use graphical interface. But doing it by the command line is probably more fun, so long as you're enthusiastic about learning the ins and outs of the command line.*

- **ln** *(link)*—The Unix variant of an alias is known as a *symbolic link*. This command, when used with the name of a file, creates a symbolic link to that file. You can use it in much the same fashion as an alias to access that particular file. For example, suppose I want to create a symbolic link to a file named Rockoids in my root or top directory. To begin with, I use the command **cd /** to switch to the root directory. Now, I type **ln /Users/gene/ Rockoids Rockoids**. The result is a symbolic link named Rockoids that will access the folder named Rockoids on the root directory of my Mac's hard drive.

- **ls** *(list directory)*—In combination with the **ln** command, you can use this function to create a link to a specific directory.

- **less**—Enter this command plus the file name, and you'll be able to browse the contents of a file without modifying it.

NOTE: *If the file isn't a text file, you will be informed that the file may be binary and asked if you want to view it anyway.*

- **pwd**—This simple command displays the directory you are currently in.

- **mkdir**—This is the command line equivalent of the New Folder command in the Finder and in Open and Save dialog boxes. To create a folder called Rockoids2 in my home directory, I enter this command: **mkdir /Users/gene/Rockoids2**. When I open a Finder window, a folder appears in the location in which I established it via this command.

NOTE: *To use a word space for your new folder, you would, for example, specify the name* **Rockoids_2** *in your* **mkdir** *command line. When you view the new folder in the Folder, it will have a normal word space.*

- **rmdir** *(remove directory)*—This command is rather destructive because it removes whole directories. Fortunately, it can delete a directory only if the directory has no files in it. Unix does offer some protection against deleting the wrong files.

- **rm** *(remove)*—Use this command with extreme care, because, as I said before, there's no turning back in Unix. The **rm** command deletes files. There is no corresponding undelete command. For example, to remove a file named ooops from my home directory, I'd use the command **rm /Users/gene/ooops**.

- **more**—This is a command similar to **less** that allows you to look at the contents of a file without changing it. You will not be warned, however, if you're trying to view a binary file. The command **q** can be used to exit the file.

- **passwd**—Want to change your password? Type this command, and you'll be prompted for your current password. Once you've entered that, you can enter your new password (but type it carefully, because you won't even see the number of characters displayed in the Terminal prompt).

Immediate Solutions

Repeating Commands

From time to time, you'll find it necessary to state a command a second time, perhaps to enter some additional commands to customize what you're trying to do.

To repeat the command you just activated, press the up arrow so that **ls –l** appears once again at the command prompt, and press Return or Enter. The bash shell is smart, and it retains a history of most or all of the commands you've entered since you began your Terminal session (the number depends on its configuration). In addition, you can save the session as a text file for later access if you want to review what you did.

Using Panther's Command-Line FTP Software

Several flexible Aqua-based FTP applications are available, such as Fetch and Interarchy, and you can FTP access via the Connect to Server feature in the Finder's Go menu. However, the tools in Panther's command line are quite flexible.

TIP: *For a comprehensive list of available Mac OS X FTP software, check out www.versiontracker.com.*

In this exercise, you will have a chance to check Id Software's FTP site for available updates for Quake III, the famous 3D game used by dedicated gamers and to benchmark graphic cards. Here's how it's done:

1. Launch Terminal from the Applications folder.

2. When you download files from the FTP site, no doubt you'll want them on your desktop for easy access (otherwise they go to the root level of your Users or Home directory). Type "cd desktop" in the Terminal window to change the location.

3. To connect to the remote site, enter the command **ftp** followed by the name of the site, in this case **ftp.idsoftware.com**. The result, shown in Figure 19.3, will be a request for you to enter your name.

4. Enter "anonymous" to gain guest access. In the password prompt, enter your email address.

NOTE: Not all sites allow anonymous or guest access. If you cannot enter a site in this fashion, you will need to contact the company or administrator for the proper access credentials.

---

5. To see a list of available files, enter the command **ls** or **dir**. Use the **cd** command, as needed, to burrow through the file directory.

---

*NOTE: If you know the entire path to get to the directory you want, you can type it instead, separating each directory in the hierarchy with a slash. Here's an example: **/idstuff/quake3/mac**.*

TIP: Because the name of the file or directory must be entered exactly, using upper- and lowercase as needed, you can copy the name from the Terminal window and paste it when needed to be sure it's accurate.

---

6. When you've located the file you want to retrieve, enter the command **get** followed by the name of the file. In the example shown in Figure 19.4, I wanted to retrieve an update for Quake 333. Thus, I entered the command **get uake3-132.pkg.sit**. After the command has been given, file retrieval will take a few seconds to begin. When it's finished, a Transfer Complete message will appear, including both the time it took to retrieve the file and the speed (bytes per second).

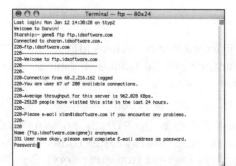

Figure 19.3 Access an FTP site via Panther's command line interface.

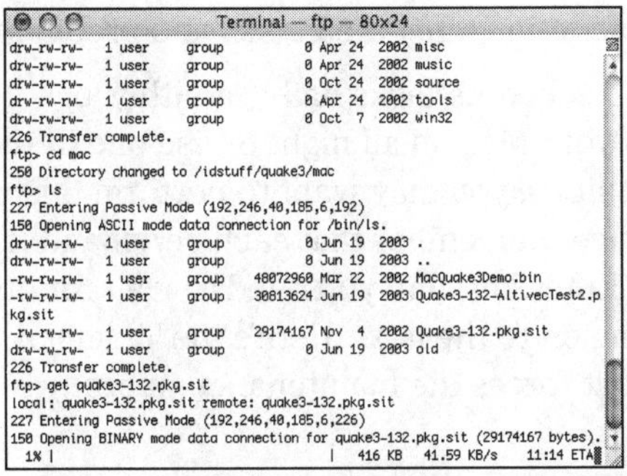

Figure 19.4 Here the download is still in progress.

TIP: *Sending and receiving files to a remote FTP site is one way to test the speed of your Internet connection, free of the constraints of the Web. However, if a site becomes busy, the speed ratings may not reflect the potential. If you can access a site that allows both file uploads and downloads, it's best to test performance during the wee hours of the morning.*

---

7. To send a file, you use the command **put** followed by the location and name of the file. Bear in mind, though, that commercial FTP sites usually do not allow uploads without permission, except where special folders are set up for those files.

Performing System Maintenance Using Terminal

As you learned in Chapter 18, Panther, like other Unix systems, performs regular system maintenance and update tasks during the wee hours of the morning. This is done to clear out old cache and log files. If you don't do it, your Mac will still operate, of course, but you risk slower performance. It's also a good idea to run the repair desk permissions every so often, so the convoluted assemblage of file read and write permissions can be sorted out.

You can perform the system maintenance tasks using graphical utilities, ranging from Apple's own Disk Utility for permissions to third-party programs such as Cocktail, Macaroni, MacJanitor, and Panther Cache Cleaner for the rest of the batch. These programs simply call the same Unix tools that you can access using the command line. However, if you want to really explore the Unix capabilities of Panther, you will want to try every possible tool directly, as I'm doing here.

Here is the Terminal alternative for scheduled tasks and prebinding:

- *Scheduled tasks*—You can schedule tasks daily, monthly, or weekly. If you don't keep your Mac on all night or use one of the graphical maintenance utilities, you may want to perform this regular system maintenance. Remember that each command is followed by pressing the Enter key, and you need to wait for one to complete before moving on to the next. Here's the Terminal command for each one that forces the maintenance or *cron* routine to run:

  sudo periodic daily

  sudo periodic weekly

  sudo periodic monthly

- *Prebinding*—When you finished installing Panther or when you run another system installer or update, no doubt you see a message about "optimizing" the system. What is actually happening is a prebinding operation. According to Apple Computer, "Prebinding is the process of computing the addresses for symbols imported by a framework or application prior to their use. Resolving these addresses before their use reduces the amount of work performed by the dyld tool at runtime and results in faster launch times for applications." This simply means that applications launch a little faster if prebinding is performed. Usually this is done upon installation or when a program is run, but if you want to do it manually to force the process, type this command in the Terminal (you'll have to provide your administrator's password, of course):

  sudo update_prebinding -root / -force

Surfing the Net

In Brief

Surfing the net without fuss or muss is a hallmark of the Mac user experience. With Panther, Apple has delivered better Web performance, extra features, and a brand new default Web browser. This chapter focuses on ways to enhance your Internet experience. You'll learn how to take advantage of Apple's new Safari Web browser and several other browsers you may not have heard about. You'll also discover how to enter the fast lane and divest yourself of a dial-up connection.

An Introduction to Broadband

Broadband Internet access has likely arrived in your neighborhood despite plenty of bumps along the road due to the technology industry's woes. With broadband, your online experience will never be the same. Most of you are getting offers in the mail or deposited in your front door with promises of huge speed increases over the conventional modem. Claims such as, "Experience full-motion video and high-quality stereo sound" and "Retrieve files in seconds" abound.

Although broadband technology is getting better each year, the situation isn't quite perfect. You may call up a service that has been marketing its powerful promises only to find out the service is not available in your neighborhood yet, although this is largely becoming the province of smaller cities.

I can't promise that I can help you get broadband service any faster, but in this section, I'll cover the various technologies you'll be able to access on your Mac with Panther.

NOTE: Getting online at high speed is only part of the equation. If you already have an ISP, you may or may not be able to continue to use the service when you switch to broadband. Some of these ISPs don't offer faster access, and others are still fighting with cable TV companies for open access. Don't be surprised if you have to switch providers and e-mail addresses when you trade up in performance.

Here is a short list of some of the technologies that provide broadband. I'm not recommending any particular service, beyond listing the common advantages and disadvantages.

- *DSL*—Short for *Digital Subscriber Line*, this service allows your phone line to do double duty. First, it handles phone calls and faxes just as it does now. But it can also carry high-speed digital data to and from your Mac, without affecting the use of your phone in any way. Compared to what you get with a 56Kbps modem (which seldom gets you speeds over 50Kbps, and usually a lot less), basic DSL starts at around 256Kbps and generally delivers up to 1Mbps (megabits per second). Speeds are higher and extremely expensive with business-oriented services. The consumer-oriented variant, *ADSL* (the *A* is for *asymmetric*), throttles the upload speed to something far less—usually around 128Kbps. The reasoning is that most folks, except those who need to send large files all the time, perform far fewer upstream tasks than downstream tasks. Therefore, they won't suffer much from the speed sacrifice. Like other broadband services, DSL connects with a standard Mac Ethernet network, using a special device that acts like a modem to send and retrieve digital data from your phone line.

> **NOTE**: Another variation of DSL technology is VDSL, short for Very High Speed Digital Subscriber line. It's used by such companies as Qwest Communications to deliver cable TV and high-speed Internet to homes. However, the service has been slow to catch on, and its future is uncertain, especially since Qwest has been partnering with satellite TV providers to deliver digital TV.

- *Cable modem*—Here the same cable from which you receive cable TV broadcasts can give you high-speed Internet access. Speeds are potentially even higher than DSL, up to 3Mbps and more for higher-tier services. The downside is that access to the network is shared among a group of several hundred users on a single node or segment. If many folks are accessing the Internet at the same time that you are, performance can slow down to speeds that may not be much greater than regular DSL, unless the cable service has enough capacity in a specific node or section of the network. Upload speeds are usually throttled to 128 or 256Kbps. An interface device, the cable modem, is used to bring the signal from the cable line to your Ethernet network.

> **NOTE**: Some cable modem services offer a hybrid or telco service. Such a system uses an analog modem built into the cable modem that offers 33.6Kbps maximum uploads using a regular phone line. Although this may be the only way the service is available, other services offer the hybrid service as an intermediary step to sign up customers while they finish rewiring a neighborhood. Once the wiring is done (assuming it ever is), customers are moved to the higher-cost full service and the preliminary service is discontinued.

- *Wireless Internet*—Do you live in a city or small town where broadband seems years away, or may never come because the work required is too great or the population density just isn't enough to support cable modems or DSL? If so, you might consider the third choice—wireless. Whether by satellite disk, such as the service offered by Directway Satellite Internet, or land-based transmitters, these services offer options that are otherwise unavailable. They may cost more, and they may not give the same level of performance as a cable modem, but they may be the only option.

NOTE: *A common way of getting broadband is the Wi-Fi hot-spot, which is simply a location such as a restaurant, coffee shop, or airline terminal that is outfitted with transmitters supporting either the 802.11b or 802.11g standards. Although some hot spots are free, such as the ones run by airports or Starbucks, others charge fees for the service. Either way, you just equip your Apple laptop with an AirPort or AirPort Extreme adapter and you're ready to roll.*

- *Future technologies*—Determining the technologies of the future is a highly speculative matter, but many are betting that even faster services will emerge, using all fiber-optic cabling or other new technologies. Since rewiring smaller communities with the needed fiber optic cable may cost too much, some companies are experimenting with delivering broadband via the power lines or by long-range Wi-Fi systems. This is a field that has yet to fulfill its promise but the potential rewards to computer users are immense. No doubt some day you'll have a fast enough service to download an entire movie in a few minutes, rather than hours.

Panther Web Browsers Profiled

At one time, Mac users either used Microsoft Internet Explorer or Netscape to access the Web. The browser landscape, however, has become quite crowded in the Mac universe in recent years. Plentiful choices abound, and I'll review the most compelling options in this section.

Apple Safari

A new kid on the block emerged in 2003 called Safari. While it's not the first browser produced by Apple (the long discontinued Cyberdog holds that distinction), Safari (see Figure 20.1) is not only as fast or faster than other browsers, it fits with Apple's model of using industry standard software and technologies.

NOTE: *Cyberdog was part of OpenDoc, a technology that was designed to be document- rather than application-centric. If this standard caught on, you'd have separate components that would load as you needed to work on different areas of your document, such as a graphics module for illustration and a word processing module for a manuscript. The same document could be used for e-mail and Web access. For what it's worth, I still have my official Cyberdog beta tester's shirt and I wear it on occasion.*

Safari's page rendering engine is based on KHTML and KJS software from the KDE open source project. As a result, Apple, like thousands of developers around the world, will make changes to the engine and deliver them back to the open source community. If you're a member of Apple's developer program, you can even take advantage of its WebCore, which is software that allows you to embed the Safari rendering engine in your own software. This is already done in the latest versions of OmniWeb from OmniGroup, which is profiled later in this chapter.

Here are the basic features of Safari 1.1, which shipped with Panther as the default browser:

- *Tabbed browsing*—This feature lets you group multiple pages with little tabs to separate one from the other. That way you don't have to confront multiple windows or constantly click forward and back buttons when moving from one site to another.

Figure 20.1   Safari has most of the features you want in a powerful browser.

- *Google integration*—Google is perhaps the most powerful search engine on the planet. AOL and other ISPs have integrated this feature and it's also part of Safari. The Search window on the right end of Safari's toolbar lets you call up Google to find the Web content you want.

NOTE: Some of you might prefer another search engine. If you do, check what Sherlock offers among its Internet search capabilities. It's always possible a future version of Safari, however, will extend its reach beyond Google.

- *SnapBack*—When you access a site either from the regular address window or the search window, you'll see a tiny arrow at the right pointing backwards. Click that arrow and you'll be returned to the first page of a site. SnapBack really simplifies navigation through many layers of a Web site back to the starting point. This feature may be the one that really sets Safari apart from the competition.

- *Popup blocker*—Popups *are* the bane of the Web surfer's existence. You click on one site, and tiny windows pop up above or beneath that page. The popup blocker feature, also available in other browsers, let's you block popups before they intrude on your privacy. I will cover this subject in more detail in the Immediate Solutions section of this chapter.

NOTE: When choosing a browser, you may want to prepare yourself for having to turn off popup blocking from time to time. Some commerce sites require that you leave it off, otherwise you won't be able to log in. If this is the case, you might want to complain to the site that you'd rather use their services with less intrusive methods.

Microsoft Internet Explorer

After being the number one browser on the Mac for a number of years, Microsoft Internet Explorer (see Figure 20.2) is now lodged in maintenance mode. This means that changes will only be made to fix serious bugs or security leaks. It now occupies second place on new Macs because of Safari. On the other hand, Internet Explorer still comes with Panther and it is still needed for some Web sites that don't display properly with other browsers.

Here are the most significant features of version 5.2.3 of Internet Explorer:

- *Search Assistant*—This feature takes a task-based approach to locating information on the Internet. You click the Search button,

Figure 20.2   Internet Explorer has remained essentially unchanged for several years.

select the category of the search, and then enter the search request in the text field. You can easily switch among search engines if the first doesn't deliver the results you want.

Related solution:	*Found on page:*
Enhancing Internet Searches	160

- *Auction tracker*—If the online auctions from services such as eBay and Yahoo! interest you, this new feature (see Figure 20.3) lets you enter the information about the auctions in which you participate. If someone exceeds your bid for a particular item, you're notified via a browser display (or even by e-mail). You can then decide whether to return and change your bid.

- *Scrapbook*—This is my favorite feature. You can store a full Web page, including the artwork, on your Mac. That way, even if the page is removed from the site, or the site is taken offline, you can still access the content you want for later review.

Figure 20.3   Internet Explorer's auction tracker makes it possible to know when you need to increase your bid.

iCab

Eternally previewed, but not quite released, iCab (see Figure 20.4) is a slim Web browser from a German-based software publisher. Although iCab doesn't always render pages as accurately as other browsers, it has lots of features that might be worth looking at.

Figure 20.4   iCab is a worthy alternative to the big guys.

TIP: You can download a copy of the latest version of iCab from ***www.icab.de.***

Following is a list of major iCab features that are designed to differentiate this program from the pack:

- *Support for current Web standards*—The publisher of iCab claims support for current Web standards, including HTML 4.0 and Cascading Style Sheets Level 2 (CSS2). In addition, iCab provides extra support for specific Internet Explorer and Netscape extras, such as the Netscape **<BLINK>** command (which can be used to flash a title).

- *Support for older Macs*—In addition to the Mac OS X edition of iCab, another version can actually run on any Mac using System 7.0.1 or later with 4MB free RAM; even Macs with a 68020 processor are supported. Only Opera can match iCab's support for older Macs. Such support may make it possible for you to deploy this browser on an entire network consisting of Macs with widely varying hardware and system setups.

- *Cookie filters*—Most Web-based cookies serve a useful purpose, such as letting you track your visits to a Web site to ease navigation. iCab enhances cookie management with more extensive options, such as letting cookies expire at the end of a session.

Netscape

Although it's glory days are past, Netscape 7.1 for Mac OS X (see Figure 20.5) still remains popular with loyal users who prefer to keep themselves free of Microsoft software. Like Netscape Communicator for the Classic Mac OS, Netscape is not just a browser, but actually a suite of Internet applications.

Here are a few examples from the huge feature set of Netscape 7.1:

- *User-customizable sidebar*—The busy sidebar puts your favorite sites and features front and center for easy access. Additional default tabs can be added, and Netscape offers extra options at its Web site.

- *Built-in e-mail client*—Unique among the browsers described in this chapter, Netscape includes a full-featured e-mail client (see Figure 20.6) that can manage multiple accounts and even AOL e-mail (with full support for your AOL address book).

- *Built-in Instant Messaging*—AOL's popular AIM client is also part of Netscape so you can stay in touch with your online buddies. Support for AOL's ICQ service is also part of the

Figure 20.5   Netscape 7.1 remains the most feature-complete Web browser.

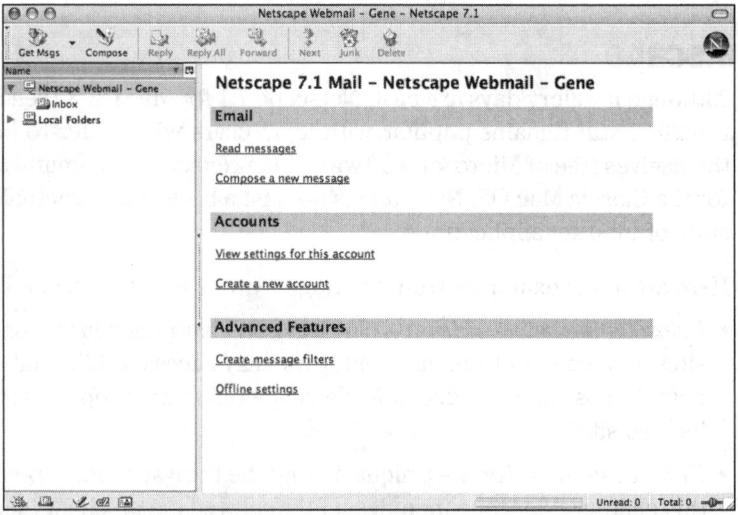

Figure 20.6   Manage all your e-mail with Netscape (including AOL) without the need for any other application.

package, but connections must be made separately, which means an AIM member cannot directly communicate with an ICQ member, even if you have accounts on both services.

NOTE: *You can, if you prefer, use iChat to contact both AOL and AIM users, and mac.com members instead. Nothing forces you to use the chat client or any other component of Netscape if you just want to use its browser.*

- *Tabbed browsing*—This nifty feature can open separate links in a single window, and you just have to click a tab to jump from one to the other.

NOTE: *Those who examine feature sets may remind me that Opera had this feature first, and other browsers are adding it at a fever pitch. A good feature is always worth copying.*

If you want to use a somewhat leaner, purer version of Netscape, you might want to try Mozilla, which previews new technologies before they are rolled into its commercially-oriented brother. An even purer application, offering the same "Gecko" rendering engine but without the extra baggage, is available in two other browsers: Camino and Mozilla Firebird. These two programs are simply browsers without e-mail, chat clients, and the rest. If you want to learn about the latest versions of these applications, and even download nightly builds, which are development versions that are apt to be somewhat buggy, pay a visit to the Mozilla organization at **www.mozilla.org/**.

OmniWeb

It may come as a surprise to some of you that Netscape wasn't the first Web browser for the Mac. Several others came earlier, including OmniWeb from OmniGroup, which was originally developed for NeXTSTEP and is regarded as the first widely-distributed browser. Like Apple's Safari and Netscape's Camino, OmniWeb is distinguished by being developed in Apple's Cocoa programming language and features a decidedly different interface (see Figure 20.7) with some very unique features.

TIP: *You can easily get the latest versions of iCab, Netscape, OmniWeb, and Opera from a popular Web site that tracks and links to the latest software updates. Just point your browser to **www.versiontracker.com**. In addition to these programs, you'll find a healthy collection of software for both the Mac OS 9 and Mac OS X user environments.*

OmniWeb 5 uses the same rendering engine as Apple's Safari but that's where the similarities end. Here's what I mean:

Figure 20.7   OmniWeb 5 is the latest creation from an experienced developer of NeXTSTEP software.

- *Tab browsing with thumbnails*—As shown in Figure 20.7, OmniWeb's answer to tabbed browsing uses miniature or thumbnail images of a page to make it easier for you to find the one you want. You can even drag and drop them from their display drawer to new positions for more convenient access.

- *Workspaces*—A workspace might be considered a collection of the sites you visit during a single section. You can create multiple workspaces for different needs, such as finance sites, entertainment sites, and, of course, Mac sites. Once this is done, you can make a snapshot of a workspace to return to the same pages whenever you want.

- *Site preferences*—Normally, when you set viewing preferences for a browser, such as font size, file download location, and whether to accept cookies and popups, it applies to all the sites you visit. Until you change them again, that is. OmniWeb 5 lets you customize the way you want to interact with each site, so you don't have to repeatedly jump to the preferences box. This is a big time saver.

- *Unique bookmark features*—In addition to storing your favorite sites, OmniWeb 5 lets you share the bookmarks to others on your network courtesy of Mac OS X's Rendezvous feature. OmniWeb's Shortcuts feature lets you specify a keyword to apply to a specific bookmark, and when you type that shortcut, the site loads right before your eyes.

NOTE: At the time this chapter was written, OmniWeb 5 was still under development, so the features you are reading about in this chapter could change somewhat in the final version.

Opera

Norway-based Opera Software claims Opera for Mac OS X (see Figure 20.8) offers superior support for emerging Web standards and speedier browser display.

NOTE: Fastest browser? I am just citing the publisher's claim. Independent tests have been inconclusive, but that's how benchmarking goes.

The following description covers version 6.0.3, the version available when this book was written:

- *Superior Web standard support*—All Web browsers tout their support for the various World Wide Web Consortium (W3C) standards. Opera's publishers list a full range, including CSS1, CSS2, XML, HTML 4.01, and more.

- *Super-fast rendering engine*—Everyone claims to do this better. Opera displays the time it takes to retrieve a Web site, so you can easily do the comparisons yourself and put the claims to the test. Don't forget that Apple also claims Safari is faster.

Figure 20.8   Available for a number of operating systems, Opera claims to be the fastest browser on the planet.

- *Zooming*—A pull-down menu lets you select a zoom factor for a Web page, as you would in a word processor. The settings range from 20% to 1000%. Panther's smooth font rendering makes text look great, but graphics will, naturally, suffer as their size increases.

- *Direct access to search engines*—Click on a down arrow and get a list of popular search engines (which you can customize) for convenient searches for the Web-based information you want.

- *Tabbed browsing*—This feature appeared in Opera first, but is also being used in Apple's Safari and other browsers. It allows multiple browser windows to be accessed by clicking a tab, rather than a new window. It's a great saver of screen real estate, especially on a smaller display.

NOTE: *Opera Software was developing a new Mac version of its flagship browser application at the time this book was written. New features will include a powerful e-mail engine and other features similar to what is already offered on Windows and other platforms.*

Mac Internet access is a highly simplified process: You launch your browser and you connect. But behind those simple actions are many more considerations to get the maximum value from your online experience and steps you can take to get the maximum stability from your surfing experience. We'll look at these issues in the next section.

Immediate Solutions

Deleting Browser Caches

A Web browser uses a *cache*, consisting of a single file or several files, to store the artwork retrieved from a Web site. Whenever you call up the site, the contents of the cache are compared with the site, and only new artwork is downloaded. This process can speed up Internet performance, sometimes dramatically. But if performance bogs down or you find that your browser is crashing, the next step is to delete the cache.

WARNING! *A separate set of cache files is stored in each user's Preferences folder, inside his or her Library folder. If you remove the cache files while logged in under one user account, those files won't be removed for the others. However, the administrator can do a search of all user folders with Sherlock to find and remove all the caches.*

The following sections describe how to delete the caches in some of the browsers described in this chapter.

TIP: When you empty a Web cache, all the artwork will be removed. As a result, the browser must retrieve it again. You won't see a performance gain until the browser retrieves the site for a second time. And don't forget, the steps described here must be repeated for all users of your Mac unless the administrator performs them manually via a file search.

Killing the Cache in Safari

You can't customize the size of Safari's cache, so deleting it is basically a two-step operation. All you have to do is choose Empty Cache from the Safari menu, choose Empty from the acknowledgement prompt, and, within seconds, the cache files will be deleted. Nobody makes it simpler.

Killing the Cache in Internet Explorer

Internet Explorer has a more traditional way of emptying the cache. Here's how to how to perform that task:

1. With Internet Explorer running, go to the Application menu and choose Preferences.

2. In the Preferences panel, scroll to Web Browser and click on the disclosure triangle to expose the settings under this category.

3. Click on the Advanced category, which produces the dialog box shown in Figure 20.9.

4. Click Empty Now to delete the contents of the cache file. Because Internet Explorer stores its entire cache in a single file, IE Cache.waf, this process should take only a second.

5. Visit your favorite sites and see if the appearance or performance improves after the site is visited for the second time.

6. If performance doesn't improve, delete the actual cache file. You'll find it in the Preferences folder inside the Library folder, which is, in turn, located in the Users folder bearing your login name. Look for a folder labeled MS Internet Cache or Explorer for this file.

Killing the Cache in iCab

The process of emptying iCab's Web cache under Panther is the same as in the Classic versions. Just follow these steps:

1. With iCab running, go to the Application menu and choose Preferences.

2. Click the icon labeled Cache, as shown in Figure 20.10.

3. To delete the cache, click the Clear Cache Now button.

4. Click the close box to dismiss the Preferences dialogs.

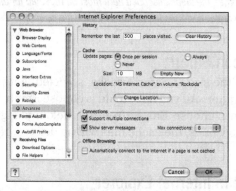

Figure 20.9   Empty the cache and perform some additional operations in this dialog box.

Figure 20.10   iCab's cache removal options are fairly straightforward.

5. Visit your favorite sites and see if the appearance or performance improves.

Killing the Cache in Netscape

Netscape's cache-killing process is, like the others mentioned so far, pretty straightforward:

1. Launch Netscape, go to the Application menu, and choose Preferences.

2. Click the arrow next to Advanced so it points downward (or leave it alone if it's already that way).

3. Click Cache to bring up the dialog box shown in Figure 20.11.

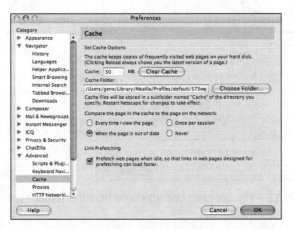

Figure 20.11   Clear Netscape's cache from this dialog box.

NOTE: Despite the fact that AOL for Mac OS X uses Netscape as its browsing engine, it doesn't share the Web cache. To remove the cache under AOL, you need to choose Preferences from the application menu and click on the WWW icon. Finally, click the Empty Cache Now and then OK to close the dialog box.

4. Click Clear Disk Cache to zap the cache files. As an extra ounce of prevention, you may also want to click Clear Memory Cache, which also removes the artwork cached in memory.

5. Click OK to close the Preferences dialog box.

NOTE: At the time this book was written, OmniWeb 5's user interface wasn't finished, so the organization of preferences wasn't 100% certain. In the previous version, all you had to do was choose Flush Cache from the Tools menu.

Killing the Cache in Opera

Here's how to empty the cache in Opera:

1. With Opera open, bring up the Preferences dialog box from the Application menu.

2. Click History And Cache to bring up the dialog box shown in Figure 20.12.

3. Under Disk Cache, click Empty Now to remove Opera's cache files.

4. Click OK to dismiss Opera's Preferences dialog box.

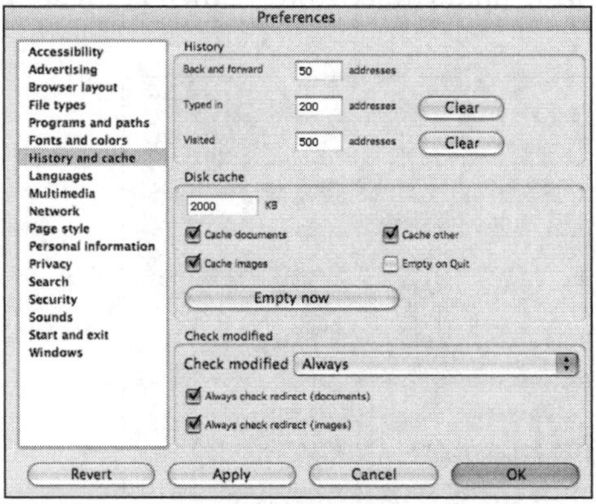

Figure 20.12   You can clear Opera's cache from this rather busy window.

Determining Whether a Larger Cache Is Necessary

The standard Web cache is usually 5MB to 10MB (it was 2MB in the version of Opera examined for this book and 50MB for AOL and the standalone version of Netscape). You can easily increase the cache to a higher figure if you prefer by accessing a browser's Preferences as described previously. Before you do so, however, consider that having a Web cache that's too large may be counterproductive. For one thing, if the browser spends additional time checking the contents of the cache before accessing an updated site from the Web, performance may actually be slower.

However, if you frequently access a large number of Web sites with plenty of artwork, a setting of 15MB or even 20MB may be useful; iCab sets its cache at a maximum of 30MB, and no appreciable slowdown results. Your mileage may vary. If you choose to reduce the size of a cache, however, empty it first.

Using Bookmarks to Get There Faster

Over time, you'll come across Web sites you'd like to visit on a regular basis. The best way to keep track of these sites is to save them as bookmarks. Each browser has a different name for its bookmarks feature. For Internet Explorer, it's called Favorites; for iCab, it's the Hotlist; and Safari and OmniWeb uses the traditional name, Bookmarks (as do Netscape and Opera).

In each case, you'll find a menu with the name of the bookmarks feature. To add a page to your bookmarks, access that menu and use the command to add the current page. You may see a confirmation message that you must OK in order for the page to appear on the list.

Removing a bookmark involves opening the list, selecting the bookmark, and then pressing the Delete key or choosing Delete from the Contextual menu or Edit menu. (The process varies from browser to browser.) Again, you'll usually need to OK a prompt to delete the entry.

Ridding Yourself of the Popup Curse

You know the scene: You open a Web site and just as the page appears another window jumps up at you, right in front of the window you are viewing or behind it. I have seen sites spawn several of these intruders and they are very annoying. I have better things to do than dismiss a bunch of them every time I want to visit a site, and, frankly, I tend to avoid such places unless they are absolutely needed.

To combat this problem you can use a built-in popup blocker. Here's a brief look at how to access the built-in popup blockers in various Mac Web browsers:

NOTE: In the trade, a browser window that appears above the page you opened is a pop-over. The window that appears beneath is a pop-under. I prefer to call them pop-annoying.

- *Safari*—Blocking popups with Safari is easy. Go to the File menu and select Block Popup Windows. This option will remain checked while the feature is active.

- *Netscape*—The process is a bit more complicated in Netscape. Choose Preferences from the Netscape (application) menu, and expand the arrow under Privacy & Security. Once that's done, click on Popup windows and check the box labeled "Block Unrequested Popup Windows." Netscape will also play a sound when a popup is blocked. You can specify which pages are immune from popup blocking in the preferences dialog. These would tend to be commerce sites that produce extra windows for information or ordering.

- *Opera*—Choose Preferences from the Opera menu, select Windows, and click on the option labeled Refuse Popup Windows. There are two more options: One to allow popup windows and the other to open them in the background so you can keep them out of site until you have a chance to inspect them. With Opera, click Apply to change a preference before dismissing the dialog.

NOTE: At the time this book was written, the preference settings for blocking popups in OmniWeb 5 weren't final. But the usual methods, as outlined in other applications, above, are expected to apply.

A Short Introduction to Tabbed Browsing

Even if you have dispensed with popup windows, you still may find yourself with lots of open browser windows. That's because some sites specify that a blank page open when you click a link to another page. Supposedly that makes the path back to the original site somewhat easier because you just have to click on another window rather than a navigation arrow. But there's still another way of handling this stuff—tabbed browsing (see Figure 20.13). Whether in Safari, Netscape, or Opera, the plan is the same. A bunch of tabs appear at the top of the window. Click a site to go there directly using the exact same window. In a sense, then, tabbed browsing works like the Finder, because it lets you reuse a single browser window for all the content you want.

NOTE: As you read in the section on OmniWeb's new tabbed browsing feature, this program uses tiny thumbnails in a side window to display the various sites you've called up.

While different programs may have variations on the theme, few do it as simply as in Safari. Just open the Preferences box from the Safari menu, choose Enable Tabbed Browsing. To add a tab, choose New Tab from the file menu and load a site. Would could be easier?

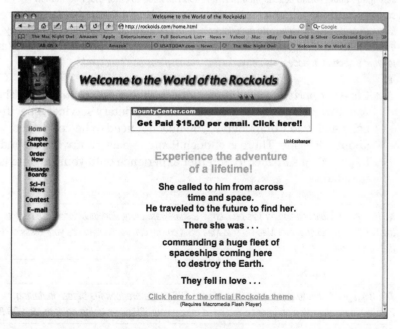

Figure 20.13   A bunch of tabs are used to keep browsing simple in Safari.

Internet Connection Problems

Because of its support for open standards, Panther should, in theory, offer a faster and more reliable browsing experience. But nothing is ever perfect, so here's a list of some of the most frequent problems and what you can do to resolve them:

- *You cannot get online with a cable modem or DSL.* Some ISPs may require special software to connect. You'll have to contact the service to see when a Panther–compatible version is available, or whether other connection options can be found. In the meantime, check whether your service will give you a static set of IP access numbers, which might get you connected when you enter them via the Network pane of the System Preferences application.

NOTE: The need to use special software is usually theoretical. Such services as AOL, CompuServe 2000, Juno, NetZero and MSN have special dialing software. But most services dispense with such things and allow you to use Internet Connect for dialup.

TIP: Some cable providers require entering a dedicated modem ID address in your network settings to allow you to access their network. You will need to enter that information correctly in order for you to connect to that service; the Mac OS X Setup Assistant and the Network preference panels both include a place for you to put this information. Others may even require use of a special application to log in; you will have to contact the ISP directly as to what's needed to access its networks if the usual steps don't succeed.

- *Classic applications may not run with dial-up connections.* The watchword is to try first. Aside from proprietary services, specifically AOL and CompuServe, you may not need to be concerned about this issue. There is enough Panther–savvy software around to provide a satisfactory Internet experience until your favorite is updated.

NOTE: One possible solution for this problem is a shareware utility, PortReflector, which reflects the TCP/IP connections from Mac OS 9 to Mac OS X so you can continue to use your Classic dial-up program.

TIP: It's a good idea to retain a backup of your TCP/IP Preferences file before installing Panther to avoid problems in case you need to use your ISP when going back to Mac OS 9.

- *Artwork changes from browser to browser.* This issue is due to the inexact nature of the way a browser interprets a page and is a chronic problem (and the source of endless headaches) for Web authors. Despite claims from each publisher that its browser supports standards better than the competition, expect differences. If you want to view a site in a particular way, you may want to stick with the browser that presents it the way you like. Another possibility is to report a display problem to the publisher of the browser application, so it can examine the situation and see if it can do anything to update the program for better display.

- *A site is not accessible.* This may be the fault of the site itself or of Internet congestion and not your browser or connection. The first possible solution is to click the Refresh or Reload button on the browser, so that the site is retrieved again from scratch. Another possible solution is to log off from your ISP and then reconnect. If neither step resolves the problem, try to access the site again at a different time.

- *A site's artwork is distorted.* One possible solution is to just refresh or reload the page, which delivers the site from scratch. If that fails to resolve the problem, follow the steps in the earlier section "Deleting Browser Caches" to empty the Web cache. If doing so doesn't resolve the issue, it may be the fault of the Web site itself, so there's nothing you can do but complain to the Webmaster.

TIP: *If you use the embedded version of a browser as supplied with AOL or CompuServe 2000, go to the Preferences dialog box of either application. Scroll to the WWW category and uncheck the Use Compressed Images option. This setting keeps AOL and its sister service from converting the Web artwork to a proprietary format and delivers a more accurate rendering of Web artwork and photos.*

- *Download speeds vary.* It is normal for the speed of a file download to vary somewhat, whether you have a dial-up connection or broadband. This is a normal part of the process; sometimes, it's a problem with your connection or with congestion on the part of the Web server hosting the site. However, if download speed bogs down, you may want to stop the download and try again. If you have a dial-up connection, you may also want to log off and then reconnect; however, if all other services run at normal speed, there may be nothing you can do to resolve the problem.

- *Internet Connect doesn't support your modem.* Most Macs that can run Mac OS X already come with an Apple internal modem, so this may not be a serious issue for you. But, if you have a different modem, feel free to experiment with a similar make or model, or just use Hayes Compatible. Most modems that support standard setups will probably function in a satisfactory manner. If you still do not get acceptable performance, contact the manufacturer of the modem directly for suggestions.

- *Dial-up connection fails.* You try to log in and don't succeed. Should this happen, verify the information you placed in the Internet Connect application. Review Chapter 8 for information on how to set up this program to work with your ISP. If the information is all right, try to connect once again. If the connection still fails, contact your ISP and see if it is doing system maintenance or can offer you alternate connection numbers.

- *The browser crashes.* With Panther, you do not need to restart your Mac whenever a program freezes or suddenly quits. You can continue to work, and even try running the application again. Because some of the applications for Panther are beta versions, check with the publisher's Web site for newer versions. You should also read Chapter 18, which covers a number of ways to troubleshoot Panther.

- *Java applets don't run.* Although Panther incorporates the very latest Java technology from Sun Microsystems, not all Web browsers were working properly with Java applets when this book was written. This was particularly true of iCab and Opera, both of which were in public beta form. If you run into a problem, first try the site in Microsoft's Internet Explorer, since it remains a standard for most sites, and if it works there, check the Web site run by the publisher of your preferred browser (or **www.VersionTracker.com**) for information about an updated version that might fix the problem.

Exploring Panther's
E-Mail Software

In Brief

Can you imagine life without e-mail? Each day, hundreds of millions of messages cross the Internet on their way to folks across the world. For many people, postal or snail mail seems a distant memory.

Businesses, small and large, depend on office e-mail to transfer information. This is becoming increasingly common, even if the recipient sits in an adjacent office or cubicle. In fact, e-mail has sometimes replaced the practice of actually speaking with a nearby coworker.

NOTE: *Another common practice is the use of instant messaging in lieu of conversation, and I'll get into that in Chapter 22, when I discuss Apple's iChat AV.*

Introducing Panther Mail

From it's humble beginnings, Mac OS X's e-mail application (see Figure 21.1) has become a powerful program with loads of features including an extremely effective spam filter.

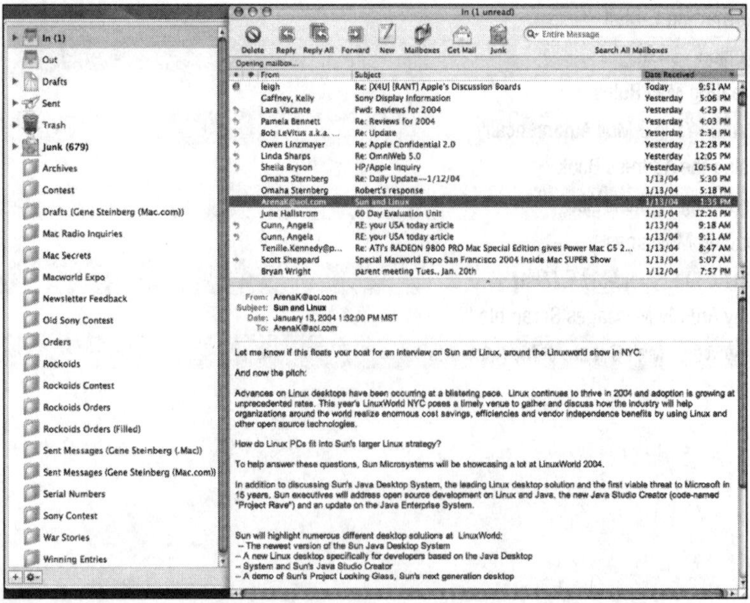

Figure 21.1   Apple's e-mail client is clean, uncluttered, and lightning-quick.

Apple's e-mail software is called Mail. It descended, in part, from the simple program that shipped with the NeXTSTEP operating system, the precursor to Mac OS X. If you compare Mail with its rivals, including he ones you have to pay for, you may actually find Mail to be equal or superior in terms of features and performance.

NOTE: *The features that make a good e-mail application vary. Some users might prefer Microsoft Entourage, Eudora, or one of the others. For years, I stuck with Claris E-mailer, even though it was discontinued several years ago and only runs in the Classic environment under Mac OS X.*

Here's a brief list of Mail's important features:

- *Spam filtering*—This is the number one feature. Spam is the bane of the personal computer user's existence, and Mail provides a sophisticated method of flagging spam and getting it out of your way. Using a feature Apple calls "latent semantic analysis," both subject and content are analyzed for suspicious messages. The feature has been enhanced for Panther, and now uses an ISP's own spam flagging features to expand its capabilities. You'll learn more about this feature later in the chapter.

- *Multiple user accounts*—Do you have home and office user accounts or different e-mail addresses for business and personal use? Mail lets you configure the program to handle all of them. You can set it to log in at specified time intervals so you're never out of touch. In addition, other users who work on your Mac can configure their own settings and store their own collections of e-mail without having access to anyone else's e-mail.

- *Microsoft Exchange Support*—Microsoft's groupware software is the most popular business-oriented e-mail system. Thus, it makes sense to be able to connect without having to buy extra software. Apple's Address Book will handle your Exchange contact list but you won't find support for calendars or task reminders, unfortunately.

NOTE: *Neither AOL nor CompuServe 2000 mailboxes are supported, and that is not expected to change. Time Warner continues to use its own proprietary method of storing and processing e-mail. For now, your best e-mail options beyond these applications are AOL Communicator and Netscape.*

- *Safari-based HTML display*—Mail uses the same browsing engine as Safari for speedy display of embedded pictures and artwork. Even better, the feature is automatically turned off for messages that are marked as junk. That way, spammers won't get confirmations that you've read their filth when you open one of these messages.

- *Message threading*—Those of you who frequent newsgroups are probably familiar with the ability to thread messages, which is simply grouping all messages in a single topic together. The grouping is done in Mail and it is easy to navigate. Click a down arrow to see all of the messages in a thread.

- *Pointers to replies*—If you receive a message and you really aren't sure what you said even though part of your original comment was quoted, this feature will help considerably. Click the tiny pointer at the left of a message label and you'll see your original e-mail in all its glory. This feature works pretty much the same way as it works in Microsoft Entourage.

- *Spellchecker*—If you turn on the spellchecker option for interactive checking as you write an e-mail, words with potential spelling problems are flagged in red. Otherwise, you can spell-check manually before you send a message.

- *Message searching*—Messages can be searched by sender, recipient, subject, or content. This is a powerful tool that you can use to find information quickly in the messages you've stored.

NOTE: *Whenever e-mail awaits you in the Mail application, the icon for the program in the Dock will display a number specifying the number of messages that remain unread.*

Reviewing Other Panther E-mail Choices

I don't want to create the impression that Mail is your only choice after you install Panther. Of course Mail is free and is set up as the default e-mail client (unless you upgrade from a previous installation where another application was selected). What's more, I have a personal affinity for Mail's marvelous spam filter, which has made my online experience far more pleasant.

But there are other e-mail clients that you should consider. Here's a brief look at other options. I'll ignore the basic e-mail features that they all share, such as multiple user accounts, the ability to import messages from other programs, and message filtering. Instead, I'll focus on some of the unique attributes that are worth considering if you're looking for alternatives.

Entourage X

Entourage X is part of Microsoft's Office version X for the Mac business application suite (see Figure 21.2). It is not just restricted to e-mail and newsgroup messages. It is a full-featured personal information manager that includes a calendar and task and event reminders. The major features of Entourage include:

NOTE: At press time, Microsoft announced Entourage 2004, which will include such useful features as the Project Center. According to Microsoft, the new version will offer an easy way to read and stay abreast of e-mails, files, contacts, meetings, and other tasks connected with a single project and share that information with your clients.

- *Rich content*—Similar to a feature that is supported in Mail and AOL's e-mail, you can insert graphics and photos within the body of your message. Entourage X also works with sounds and video clips.

- *Spam filter*—Entourage X has a decent filter to check and flag spam. The sensitivity of the spam filter can be adjusted to lessen flagging of messages you do want to retrieve. In addition, you can set up exceptions, so that certain messages are not labeled as "junk." While it's not quite as sensitive as the one in Panther's Mail application, it is a usable alternative.

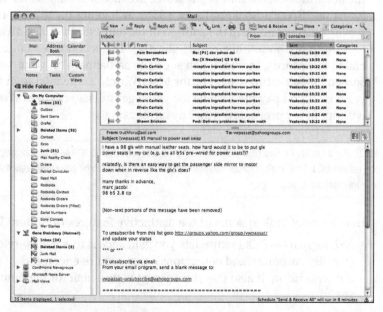

Figure 21.2   Entourage X packs a number of powerful contact management features.

- *Exchange Support*—Entourage X matches Mail's ability to handle your Exchange mail and contact lists, and it adds the ability to support individual and group calendars and reminder notices. If you need these additional elements, this is your only Panther alternative.

- *Tri-pane calendar*—You can view your appointment and event calendar by month, week, or even workweek. You are also able to put tasks that are due or overdue in a separate pane for easy organization.

NOTE: If you prefer Apple's Mail application, you can get the calendaring functions courtesy of Apple's iCal. You'll learn more about iCal in the next chapter.

Eudora Pro

Eudora Pro is a perennial favorite. It is one of the earliest Mac e-mail applications. You can download and install the latest version of Eudora Pro (see Figure 21.3) from the publisher's Web site (**www.qualcomm.com**) without paying a license fee. But the user license comes in three levels, depending on whether you want to upgrade to a paid version. The first, Lite, is roughly equivalent to the Eudora Lite software used on Macs for years. You get full use of the software, except that key features are disabled such as the ability to use Secure Sockets Layer (SSL) in logging on to an e-mail server, placing photos in the address book, and using the MoodWatch feature (more about this feature shortly). The second free option is called Sponsored, in which you see little ad banners on your e-mail screen. Most features, except for MoodWatch, are available in this version. If you pay the license fee you'll get full use of the software without being presented with any advertising.

NOTE: The ad mode for Eudora is not super-intrusive, and you're not pestered with annoying pop-up windows. So if you opt for all the features but would rather let the advertisers pay the bills, this isn't a bad way to go.

Here's a brief look at some of the distinctive features of Eudora Pro:

- *SSL support*—This feature lets you gain access to e-mail services (usually corporate and educational) that require encrypted authentication. It also lets you encrypt your e-mail for maximum security.

Figure 21.3　This is the ad-laden version of Eudora Pro.

- *MoodWatch*—Have you ever written a message in which you expressed anger over a person or situation, and then regretted what you wrote after your message had been sent? The MoodWatch feature can be set to flag language that may be offensive or inflammatory, and delay sending the message to allow a "cooling-off" period. That way, if you decide that you were just a little too over-the-top in your message, you can revise the message before it's sent. This is a great way to keep friends and business contacts when the going gets tough.

- *Photos in Address Book*—AOL users have enjoyed this feature for a while—the ability to insert someone's photo in your personal address book.

- *Usage stats*—Am I serious? Yes. This feature helps you keep track of your daily e-mail traffic. I just hope most of your e-mail isn't just spam.

- *Drag and drop nicknames*—You can use this feature to give your e-mail contacts a friendly, or not-so-friendly, moniker. Let's say your brother's address is fredxab340993@whatisitmail.com (and I hope that's not a real address). Rather than have to enter that address, you can simply use the name you knew him by as a child, say "smart a—" (my publisher insisted I take out the remaining letters in that word).

NOTE: Apple's Address Book application also lets you store photos as you'll discover later in this chapter.

Netscape

Netscape remains unique among the programs discussed here because it integrates the browser, e-mail client (see Figure 21.4), and Web authoring and chatting software in a single application.

Here are the basic features of the e-mail component of Netscape 7.1 for Mac OS X:

- *AOL support*—This is a feature that is not likely to be found in any other Panther application, other than AOL's own client software and AOL Communicator (which is essentially the e-mail component of Netscape). It allows you to retrieve your AOL e-mail in the same fashion as you can retrieve e-mail from any other online account.

- *Separate mailbox for each account*—This feature lets you easily sort messages from your various Internet accounts without having to configure an all-new mailbox for each address.

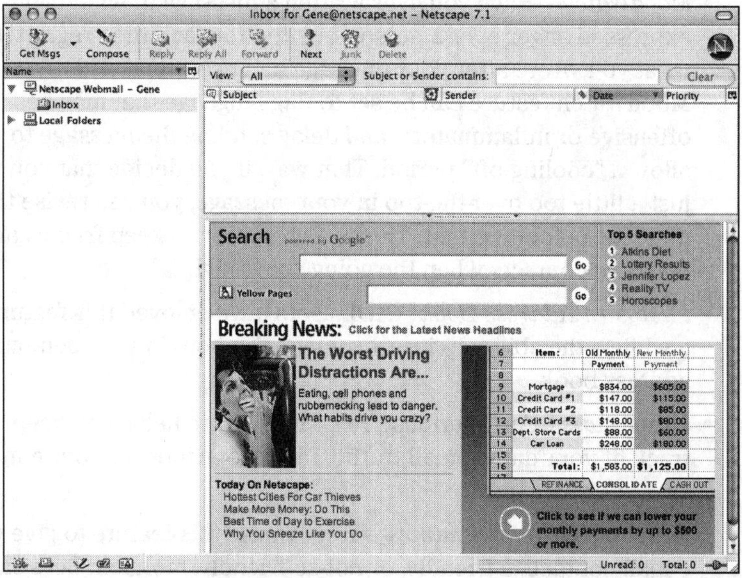

Figure 21.4   Netscape 7.1's e-mail window is similar to the one available in prior versions of the program.

Mailsmith

The e-mail applications I've mentioned so far share the ability to display rich text and show pictures and graphics. Mailsmith, which emanates from Bare Bones Software, shares one big thing with BB Edit, the text-editing tool that comes from the same company. It displays your messages in text, period (see Figure 21.5).

Aside from not supporting HTML display, here's a brief look at what Mailsmith can do:

- *Powerful security*—Mailsmith uses PGP 8.0 or later to encrypt and sign your e-mails, and to verify your incoming messages. If you are in a business where sensitive communications are required, this is an essential feature.

- *Database support*—All your messages are kept in the software's own database for efficient storage and backup of your e-mail.

PowerMail

This unique e-mail client emerges from the development labs of CTM Development of Geneva, Switzerland. Its stock-in-trade is a cross-platform e-mail engine, which is designed to offer good performance and extensive import and export options. It's also one of the rare

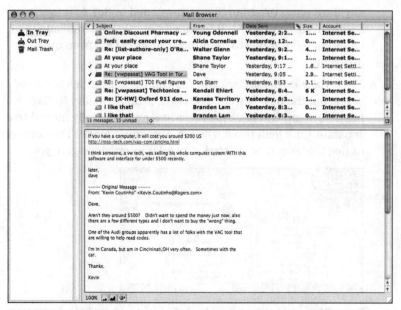

Figure 21.5   Mailsmith is a powerful, but text-based e-mail client.

applications that still runs in the Classic environment. PowerMail is a good choice if you need to deploy the same e-mail software to users of your older and newest Macs.

Other E-mail Possibilities

Other e-mail clients include AOL, CompuServe 2000, and MSN. These clients provide access software that only works with the service alone and not any other online services. If you prefer to use one of these specialized programs and you need to access your e-mail from other services, check to see if that ISP has a WebMail feature. Most do, even AOL, for that matter. The downside of Web-based e-mail is that it tends to be slow even if you have broadband access.

Comparing Mail with the Competition

Even though Mail is the default e-mail program for Panther, there are plenty of other choices. So how does Mail rate when you compare it to Microsoft Entourage, Netscape, Eudora, and all the rest?

Here's the short list of features that shows how Mail compares:

- *Separate address book*—Mail includes a separate program, Address Book (see Figure 21.6), for managing your address list. It is designed to serve as the contact list not just for Mail, but for any third-party program that is developed to link to it (such as SmithMicro's FAXstf X). It is linked directly with Mail and provides limited options to import the address lists from other programs.

- *Powerful message filtering*—You can establish rules for messages, but the best feature, bar none, is Mail's ability to flag possible spam and have the messages automatically moved to a separate Junk mail filter, when in Automatic mode. The contents of that folder can be deleted at regular intervals to give you

Figure 21.6   Use this program to configure an address book for messages.

enough time to double-check for a mistake. It stands head and shoulders above what Entourage can do, although AOL Communicator does offer a fairly decent alternative.

- *Lacks newsgroup support*—Entourage and Netscape can retrieve Usenet newsgroup messages. Mail can't. If you are interested in this option, look for a Panther-savvy news-reading program to support your needs.

TIP: Two very useful options for reading newsgroup messages are NewsWatcher-X, the Carbon update to the popular free newsgroup application, and Thoth from Brian Clark, author of YA-NewsWatcher. The latter, however, is demoware, and the downloadable version is crippled in key functions, such as saving updates to subscribed newsgroups, unless you buy a user license. Thoth, however, is worth the modest fee and is a favorite among many users. A third option, MT-NewsWatcher, is favored by many because of its superior ability to multitask. Even better, it's free.

- *No automatic connections*—Microsoft's Outlook Express and Entourage can both be configured to check e-mail at regular intervals, even if either program isn't open, by launching and establishing your Net connection. Mail can recheck for messages on a regular basis only when it's running.

- *No support for AOL e-mail*—As mentioned earlier, only Netscape and its subset, AOL Communicator, can retrieve AOL e-mail. If you wish to access your AOL messages otherwise, you have to log on to the AOL Web site (**www.aol.com**) with your browser and access its AOL Anywhere feature.

- *Exchange support*—Other than Entourage, only Mail, working in concert with Address Book, can manage your Microsoft Exchange messages and contact lists. There's no support for calendaring or task reminders, however. But half a loaf is pretty good if you don't need the other features.

- *Performance*—The Panther version of Mail is a lot faster than the one in Jaguar and previous versions of Mac OS X. This means large numbers of messages can pour into your mailboxes rather than trickle in, as with some other programs.

If you've worked with other e-mail programs, you'll find that setting up and using Mail is pretty straightforward, and the differences aren't all that significant. Even better, some of the initial setups, for your default e-mail account, are done as when you configure the Mac OS X Setup Assistant. The "Immediate Solutions" section covers the basics of using this application.

Third-Party Spam Blockers

Mail has a powerful spam blocker. AOL Communicator can do a decent job too, but Entourage's spam filtering is rather weak. You can, of course, choose an ISP that has a server-side spam guard, but if the one you have doesn't do the job and you don't want to switch services, other options are available:

- *Spam blocking software*—The most popular spam blocker is SpamSieve, which offers a powerful Bayesian spam filtering scheme that is supposed to work with all or most e-mail clients and Apple's Address Book. Another option is Spamfire from Matterform Media. As with all programs of this type, download the free or demo versions and see how well they work in your environment before you buy a user license.

- *Challenge-response*—Some of your business contacts may already be using this method. You send a message to someone, and the response says you have to connect to a Web site and enter information to prove you're not a spambot (an e-mail server sending junk messages). Once you do that, the message goes through. There are several firms that offer this service. Among the most Mac friendly is Mailblocks (**www.mailblocks.com**), which offers several levels of service, depending on your message volume. As with a spam-blocking program, you'll want to try a service like this to see if it is worth the benefits (some methods may be annoying to some recipients).

NOTE: *As a historical side note, the late CEO of Mailblocks, Phil Goldman, is known in the industry for not only for being one of the founders of WebTV, but for his contributions to the early Mac operating system. When he worked at Apple Computer, he was one of the authors of Multifinder, the original multitasking method used on Macs.*

Immediate Solutions

Setting Up Your Mail User Account

When I gave you a guided tour of the Mac OS X Setup Assistant in Chapter 2, I explained how to enter your e-mail settings during the initial setup of the new operating system. However, if you need to change those settings or add an extra user account, follow these steps:

NOTE: If you provided your e-mail account information when you ran the Mac OS X Setup Assistant, everything should be setup correctly. You can edit your account information as needed or add any additional ISP accounts you want.

1. Launch the Mail application.

2. Go to Mail's Application menu and choose Preferences. The dialog box shown in Figure 21.7 appears.

3. Click the Accounts icon and then the + icon at the bottom of the dialog, in the accounts category, as shown in Figure 21.8.

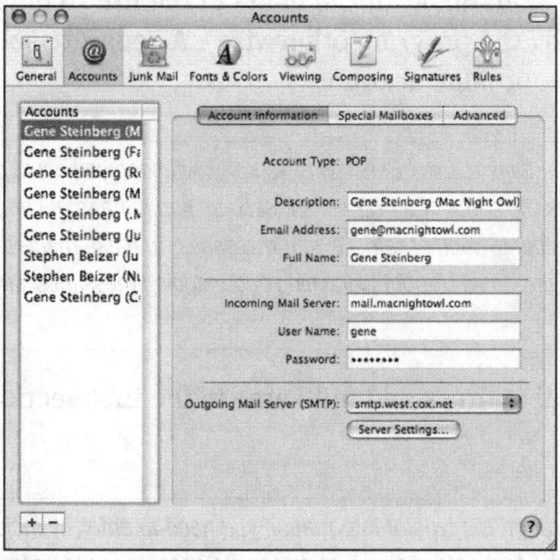

Figure 21.7   Set up and manage Mail's settings from this screen.

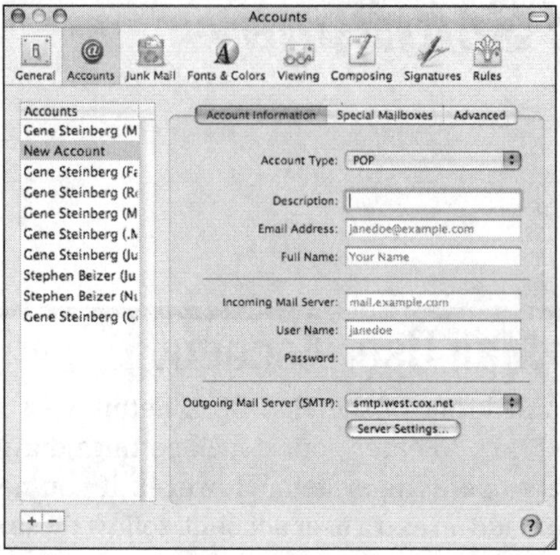

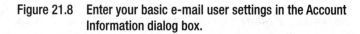

Figure 21.8 Enter your basic e-mail user settings in the Account Information dialog box.

NOTE: If your Mac is set up with multiple user accounts, each user can configure Mail separately to handle his or her accounts and e-mail from that user account. The information isn't available to any other users unless they log in to the same account.

---

4. Under the Account Type category, choose the type of e-mail account you're establishing (usually a POP account, although some ISPs support IMAP instead) and provide a description, such as "Work," "Personal," or the name of the ISP (a default will be entered by the program otherwise). A separate selection is provided for your .Mac account.

NOTE: Not sure what account settings to use? Check with your ISP. Although you could possibly guess at some settings, such as the name of a POP server (such as pop.[ISPname].com), one wrong entry will make it impossible to send or retrieve your messages. To make matters more confusing, some ISPs use the label "mail" for both incoming and outgoing messages, such as mail.earthlink.net.

---

5. Enter your e-mail address and full name in the first section of the dialog box.

TIP: Apple helps guide you through the type of information you need to enter by including gray text prompts in most of the text entry fields that disappear once you enter information.

6. Under Incoming Mail Server, enter the name of the mail server from which you retrieve your e-mail (usually your ISP's, unless you have other e-mail accounts you want to use). Insert your username and password as needed to connect to your ISP.

7. In the final category you need to enter the name of the Outgoing Mail Server (SMTP) of your ISP if it's not already listed. You also need to enter authentication (if required) or password account information. To store that information, simply click on the popup menu and choose Server Settings.

8. In the dialog box that appears, enter the name of the server. If authentication is required, click on the Authentication pop-up menu and specify which authentication scheme you want. (The normal setup is Password.) Next, enter your username and password.

NOTE: *Your remaining choices are Kerberos Version 4, Kerberos Version 5 (GSAAPI), and MD5 Challenge-Response. Which do you need? That depends on the e-mail server's setup, and you'll need to check with your ISP or systems administrator for that information.*

9. Click OK to accept the server settings.

10. When your settings in the Account Information button are complete, close the window and click Save on the next prompt to store the settings. Or, if you prefer, click the Special Mailboxes button (see Figure 21.9) to further customize your settings. The following options are provided:

   - *Sent*—Click on the pop-up menu to select when or if sent messages are erased. The default is Never, but you can have them zapped after a day, week, month, or whenever you quit Mail.

WARNING! *Once a message is erased from Mail, it cannot be recovered so choose your erase options carefully. Try to be conservative and let your messages hang around a little longer since they likely won't consume huge hunks of hard drive space.*

   - *Junk*—Once you put Mail's Junk Mail filter in Automatic mode (I'll cover the subject in more detail later in this chapter), suspicious messages will be deposited in a Junk mailbox. You can opt to have them erased at the same intervals as your Sent mail.

   - *Trash*—Once you delete messages, they are placed in a Trash folder and can be erased at the intervals you select.

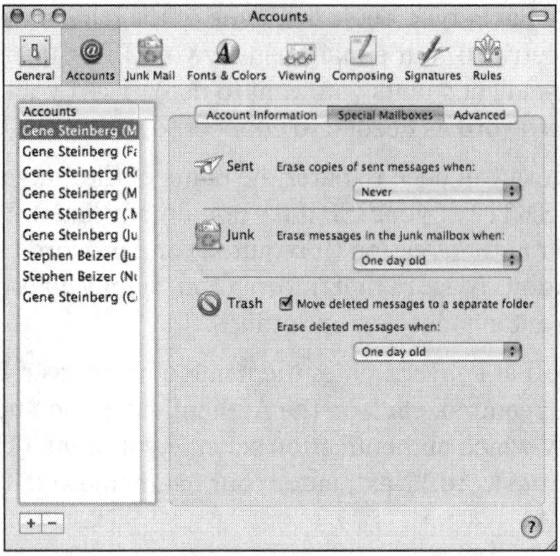

Figure 21.9   Choose how your Sent, Junk, and Trash mailboxes process messages.

NOTE: *What interval should you choose? That depends on how long you need your Sent mail. For the other options, a day or a week should be sufficient to give you a chance to review and move messages that were labeled as Junk or trashed by mistake.*

---

11. All done? Here's your final set of options. To see them, click on the Advanced button (see Figure 21.10) to see setup information under these categories:

  • *Enable This Account*—This option is normally checked by default. You can disable a user account if you don't want to retrieve messages from it for a while.

  • *Include This Account When Checking For New Mail*—For whatever reason (perhaps the account is only used rarely), you may choose not to check for a specific e-mail account when new mail is automatically accessed.

  • *Remove Copy from Server After Retrieving a Message*— Messages can be left on the server for a week, month, or removed when mail is retrieved via Mail. If you access e-mail from multiple Macs, you may want to leave your messages alone for a period of time to allow you to access the same e-mail from both computers.

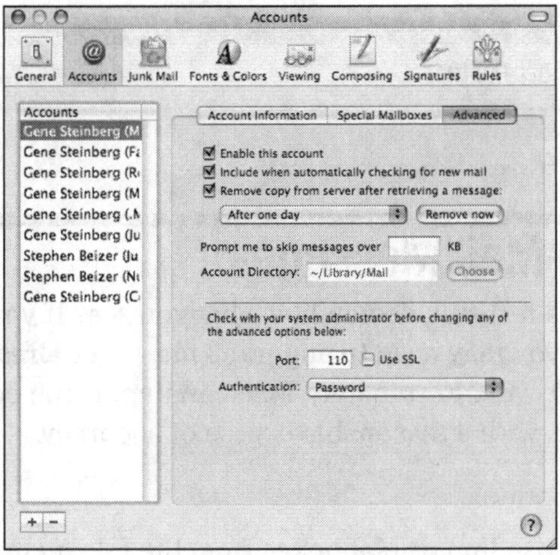

Figure 21.10 This setting controls how your e-mail account runs.

21. Exploring Panther's E-Mail Software

NOTE: The Remove now option clears messages right away. It's a useful option if you have a lot of stored mail and need to clear out your mailbox, as most ISPs have a limit on messages or storage capacity (5MB is common). It's also important in some setups because your ISP may not purge older messages. In this case people will get a Mailbox Full message when trying to contact you. No, it's not meant as a dodge to escape bill collectors.

- *Prompt Me To Skip Messages Over*—Specify a size if you don't want to look at large messages or those with large attachments right away.

- *Port*—This setting is entirely based on the requirements of your ISP or network system. Normally it's best to leave the default entry. The other options, such as Use SSL (Secure Sockets Layer) and Authentication, depend entirely on the requirements of the e-mail system you're using.

NOTE: If you're not sure what settings to enter for your e-mail options, contact your ISP for the proper access information. The settings will vary considerably, depending on an individual service's setup.

12. When your settings are complete, close the window and click Save on the next dialog to store your settings.

Related solution:	Found on page:
Setting System Preferences Under Panther	47

Importing Your E-Mail Messages

After you've given Mail a test run, do you like what you see? If you'd like to keep using Mail, you may need to import all messages already stored in your other software. Fortunately, Mail can import the contents of those mailboxes with a reasonable degree of accuracy.

Here's how to use that option:

1. With Mail open, choose Import Mailboxes from the File menu to bring up the import assistant shown in Figure 21.11. Click the right arrow to proceed or the left arrow (when not grayed out) to recheck your settings.

2. Choose the e-mail client from which you want to import messages. The Standard mbox files option is used to import e-mail from unsupported programs, so long as you can save those messages in this industry standard format. You'll want to check the export features for your e-mail program to see if mbox is supported. As you progress through the dialog boxes, click the right or "next" arrow to proceed. When you select an e-mail client and the category of data you want to import, you'll see an acknowledgment such as the one shown in Figure 21.12.

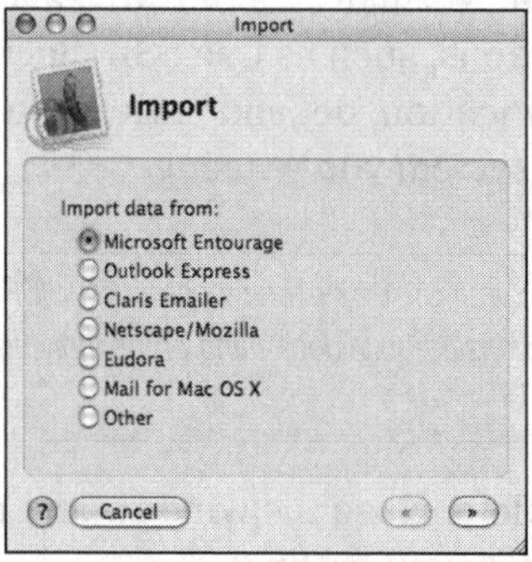

Figure 21.11   Begin the e-mail import process in the Import Mail boxes dialog box.

Figure 21.12   Mail notifies you that the selected e-mail client, Entourage, in this case, will be launched as part of the import process.

NOTE: This process must be repeated for each e-mail program you're using. In addition, the mailboxes will all be placed in separate message folders; there's no way to put them together except by manually dragging and dropping them into the proper location.

3. After you've selected the mailboxes that apply to the e-mail application (see Figure 21.13), select the ones you want to convert and click the right arrow to proceed. By default, all of the folders in the e-mail application that you're importing will be checked.

4. You'll see a progress bar showing the number of messages being retrieved. When the import process is complete, click Done to wrap up the process and dismiss the dialog box.

5. If the list of mailboxes isn't displayed, choose Show Mailboxes from the View menu. You'll see additional folders in your Mail drawer that match the ones in your e-mail program. Click on

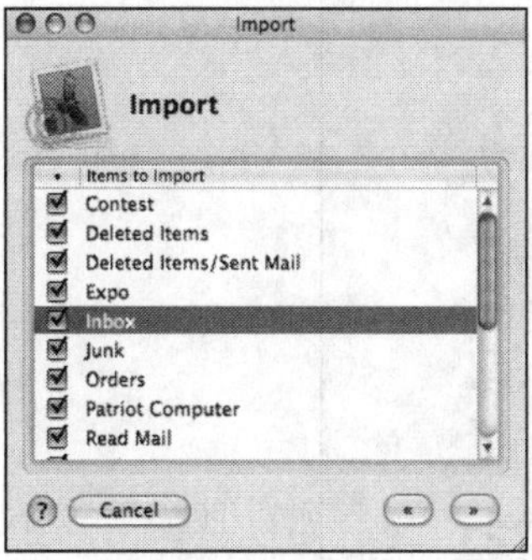

```
● ● ●            Import
       Import

   •  Items to import
   ☑  Contest
   ☑  Deleted Items
   ☑  Deleted Items/Sent Mail
   ☑  Expo
   ☑  Inbox
   ☑  Junk
   ☑  Orders
   ☑  Patriot Computer
   ☑  Read Mail

   ?  ( Cancel )        ◄  ►
```

Figure 21.13   Once you've selected mailboxes, a click of the right arrow will begin the import process.

any of them to finish the process. Mail will update its database to incorporate the messages you've imported.

TIP: *If you have an e-mail application not supported in Mail's Import feature, or if the import process goes badly, you may want to try AppleScript import tools that promise better-quality imports. Click on the AppleScript logo in Mail to bring up a menu of some fascinating possibilities to expand the power of the program.*

Customizing Mail's Toolbar

Extending the Finder-like display of Mail, you can easily customize the toolbar in the same fashion as the Panther Finder. To make these changes, follow these steps:

1. With Mail open, choose Customize Toolbar from the View menu. The display shown in Figure 21.14 will appear.

2. To add icons to the toolbar, click and drag them to the desired location in the toolbar.

3. To remove an icon, drag it off the toolbar and it will disappear.

4. To restore the default set of icons, click and drag the Default Set icons to the toolbar.

5. Click Done to store your settings.

Figure 21.14   Click and drag the items you want to the toolbar.

Composing a New Message

To write a new message in Mail, follow these steps:

1. Click on the Compose button, which brings up a blank e-mail screen.

2. Type the recipient's e-mail address in the To field (such as mine, **gene@macnightowl.com**). If you enter the name of more than one recipient, separate the names with a comma. If the e-mail address you're looking for is in your Address Book, click the Address button to bring up that program so you can add the names you want.

> *NOTE: As you type the address, Mail will consult your Address Book and the messages you've sent and received, and attempt to auto-complete the address for you. If the correct name is selected, click Tab or Enter to move to the next field.*

3. To send courtesy or carbon copies to other recipients, place their addresses in the CC field, separated by commas.

> *NOTE: A third addressing option, BCC, sends a blind carbon copy to recipients. None of the recipients will see the names of those in the BCC field. By default, this option is turned off, but you can activate it by going to the Message menu and choosing Add BCC Header, or press Command+Shift+B. Once you've added an address field, it will apply to all new messages you create unless you use the very same option to remove the field.*

4. Enter a topic for your message in the Subject field. You can move through fields with the Tab key or reverse the motion with Shift+Tab. This is the same behavior you find in any e-mail program.

5. Type the text of your message. If the spellcheck feature is turned on (and it is by default), you'll see spelling errors flagged in red.

6. When you've completed your message, click the Send button to speed it on its way.

7. To work on the message again at a later time, go to the File menu and choose Save As Draft. The message will be stored in your Drafts mailbox for later updating.

> *NOTE: By default, the messages you send are saved in the Sent folder in your personal mailbox. This and other settings for the messages you write are saved under Mail Preferences when you click the Compose button. In this settings panel, you can also specify a different location for sent messages.*

21. Exploring Panther's E-Mail Software

Answering a Message

When you receive messages, they'll show up in your Inbox. Just clicking on a title is sufficient to see the contents in the bottom pane of the Mail application window. New messages are signified by a blue button at the left of the message's title.

Once you've finished reading a message, you might want to write a reply. To do so, click the Reply button to bring up a response window, shown in Figure 21.15.

NOTE: If the message went to more than one recipient, you have the option to reply to the original sender or, by clicking Reply All, to everyone who received the message, including those listed in the CC field.

When you've finished writing your message, click Send to whisk it on its way. (You must be connected to your ISP for this to work, of course.)

Quoting Messages

When you reply to a message, it's customary to quote relevant portions of the message to which you're responding. The normal way to do this is to first select the material that you wish to quote, and then click Reply. The quoted portion will show up in your response window.

Figure 21.15   Write your answer in the response window.

WARNING! *If you don't select the portions of a message to be quoted, the entire message will appear in the response window. If you're responding to a long message, seeing so much material can be irritating for the recipient. It's better to quote just enough of the message so the recipient knows precisely what your response is about.*

Spellchecking Your Messages

Mail excels in its ability to automatically check your spelling as you type, marking words with questionable spelling in red (see Figure 21.16).

Here's how you can handle Mail's powerful spellcheck features:

1. When Mail flags a word whose spelling is in question, you can either make your correction as you proceed, or Control+click the word to see a contextual menu with your spellcheck options (see Figure 21.17).

2. From the contextual menu, you can choose a different spelling from the list of suggestions, or have the spellchecker ignore or learn the word as it's spelled. When you specify a different spelling for the word, it will be replaced automatically.

3. To perform a batch spellcheck, simply choose Spelling from the Edit menu, and then Spelling from the submenu. Or, press Command+:.

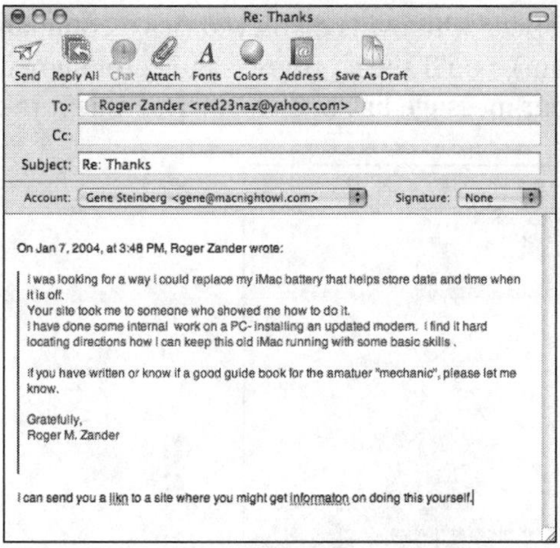

Figure 21.16   Where would your long-suffering author be without the ability to fix his spelling errors? Probably still suffering.

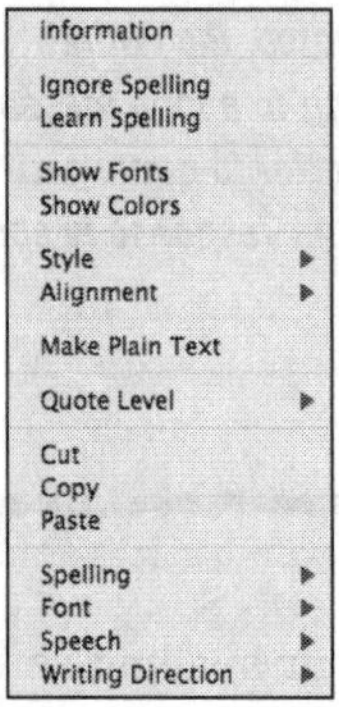

information

Ignore Spelling
Learn Spelling

Show Fonts
Show Colors

Style   ▶
Alignment   ▶

Make Plain Text

Quote Level   ▶

Cut
Copy
Paste

Spelling   ▶
Font   ▶
Speech   ▶
Writing Direction ▶

Figure 21.17   Correct the word or leave it as is.

Sending E-Mail Attachments

When it comes to attaching one or more files with your e-mail, you'll find the process in the Panther version of Mail is at once simple and complex. This might sound like a contradiction in terms but let me explain.

To attach a file to your e-mail, follow these steps:

1. Open a New Message window.

2. Click the Attach button to produce an Open dialog box, shown in Figure 21.18.

3. Select one or more files to send, and click the Choose File button.

4. Continue to prepare to send your message, and then click Send. If the Activity Viewer window is displayed (it's a command in the Window menu), you'll see a progress indicator showing how much of your message has been sent. The time it takes to

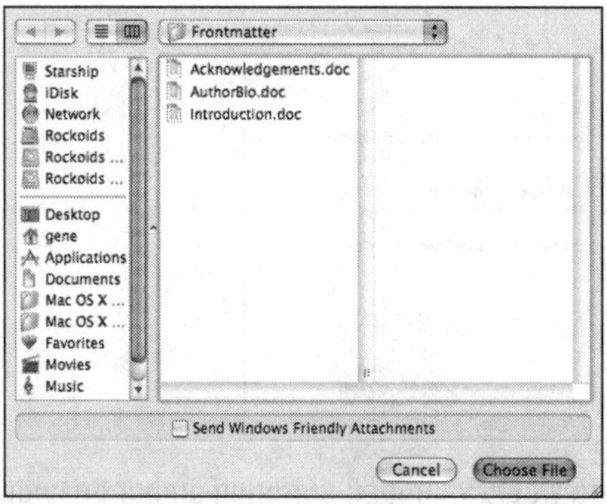

◀ ▶   ≡ ⬚   📁 Frontmatter   ▼

💾 Starship   📄 Acknowledgements.doc
💿 iDisk   📄 AuthorBio.doc
🌐 Network   📄 Introduction.doc
📁 Rockoids
📁 Rockoids ...
📁 Rockoids ...

🖥 Desktop
👤 gene
🅰 Applications
📄 Documents
💽 Mac OS X ...
💽 Mac OS X ...
💛 Favorites
🎬 Movies
🎵 Music

☐ Send Windows Friendly Attachments

(Cancel)   (Choose File)

Figure 21.18   Select a file to ride along with your e-mail.

transfer depends on the size of the file you wish to send and the speed of your Net connection.

When sending attachments, you'll need to consider a few items to make sure your files reach their destination intact:

- *Make sure your recipient can open it.* If your attachment was created in a particular application, you should check whether the recipient has the same program, or a program that can handle that type of document. For example, if you're using Microsoft Word, a Windows user with a recent version of the program can read the document. In addition, many other programs can read Word documents. However, more specialized software, such as QuarkXPress, requires that the recipient have the same program on hand. To be sure, you might want to select Send Windows Friendly Attachments in the Attach dialog box before you select your files.

- *Name Windows files properly.* Whereas the Mac OS doesn't need a file extension to identify the type of file, Windows does. The file types are entered as three-letter extensions. Common names include .doc for a Word document, .jpg for a JPEG file, and .gif for a GIF picture.

21. Exploring Panther's E-Mail Software

TIP: Some programs, such as Word and recent versions of Adobe Photoshop, can be set to automatically append the proper extension for a file. Panther's Finder and native programs are savvy about proper file extensions, but it never hurts to double-check.

- *Be careful about compressing files.* Whereas Mac users can handle files compressed in the industry-standard StuffIt format, users of Microsoft Windows generally use Zip files (although there is a StuffIt version for Windows, as well). If you know your files will be read by both Mac and Windows users, the best way to handle it is with Panther's built-in Zip compression ability. Just select the files you need to compress from the Finder, and choose Creative Archive from the File menu, Action menu, or context menu. That's what I used to handle the cross-platform needs of my publisher while writing this book.

- *Avoid sending multiple attachments to AOL users.* AOL's e-mail servers have problems decoding e-mail with more than a single attachment. Just send one attachment with each message. Or, for convenience, consider using a compression program to combine the attachments into a single file. You'll also get the added benefit of being able to send a smaller file.

- *Watch out for file-size limits.* You may run into problems with large attachments. As mentioned, some services, such as AOL, limit attachments to 2MB from sources outside the service. Others can be as high as 10MB (EarthLink) or 5MB for such broadband services as Cox High Speed Internet.

Forwarding E-Mail

No doubt you've received a message that you'd just love to send along to a third party, whether a friend or business contact. To send that message intact, or with some annotations of your own, just follow these steps:

1. With your new message open, click Forward. A new message window will appear with all the text in the original message quoted.

2. Address the message in the appropriate field.

3. Add text before or after the message you're forwarding, if necessary.

4. Click Send.

WARNING! *It's really bad manners to forward to a third party a message that the original sender might not want to disseminate. If you have any concerns about doing so, contact the original sender and ask if it's all right to send it elsewhere; if need be, specify the names of the intended recipients.*

Adding E-Mail Signatures

It's always a good idea to use a signature on e-mail, in the same fashion you'd use it on physical or snail mail. Although you can certainly enter a signature manually, you can easily store it in Mail so that you can use it regularly.

Here is how to set up a list of stored signatures:

1. With the Mail application open, go to the Application menu and choose Preferences.

2. Click the Signatures button.

3. In the Signatures dialog box, click Create Signature and type the text for the signature you want to use.

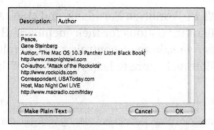

Figure 21.19 This is indeed my actual signature.

4. Enter the signature's description in the Description box (see Figure 21.19).

5. Follow the preceding steps to add extra signatures as needed.

6. With all your new signatures set up, click OK. Then, click the Active column next to the name of the signature to make it active. From here on, you can specify the signature to use from the Signature pop-up menu.

TIP: *If you are sending a message to a recipient who might not be able to see e-mail formatted with rich text, which will show Web links and formatted text, click the Composing icon and select Plain Text from the Default Message Format pop-up menu. Doing so will affect not just your signatures, but your entire message until the setting is changed.*

Formatting E-Mail

The hallmark of a twenty-first century e-mail client, Mail gives you a fairly decent set of formatting controls to handle the style of your messages. With a message window open, click the Format menu to choose font style, font size, and text orientation, such as left or centered. If the recipient may not be able to see a styled message in all its glory, choose Make Plain Text from the Format menu.

Blocking Spam

When I read that spam now consumes over 56% of all incoming messages, I couldn't say I was terribly shocked. Even with a Federal law in place, you can't expect simple solutions. Some services do have their own spam blocking capability, such as those provided by

BrightMail to such ISPs as AT&T WorldNet, EarthLink, and MSN. AOL and other services offer still other options for their members. However, if your ISP isn't using server-side spam controls, you can rely on Mail's powerful Junk Mail filtering feature to help you get rid of these annoying pitches.

NOTE: So how did a lunchmeat product become connected with junk messages? It all dates back to that wonderful British comedy troupe, Monty Python's Flying Circus. In one skit, an unwary diner tries to place an order at a restaurant, only to find that everything they offered had SPAM in it. Even quoting the skit wouldn't convey the madcap humor. You'd have to watch the actual sketch, often broadcast on cable TV, to really appreciate those comic geniuses. Now let me go out and buy a SPAM candy bar for dessert.

Here's how to use the spam blocking feature:

1. When you first run Mail, spam mail is flagged and listed in light brown. Without going into the significance of the color choice, this lets you separate the real from the suspicious.

2. If you see a message that isn't spam, just click on it to open the message in Mail's bottom pane, where you'll see a Not Junk button. Click that button to tell Mail that the message is not to be flagged that way, and it'll store the change in its database.

3. If Mail misses a spam message, select it and choose Mark from the Message menu and select As Junk Mail from sub-menu or just press Command+Shift+J.

4. After you've had a chance to play with this feature for a while and train Mail, you can opt to have Mail deposit the stuff in a separate folder. All that's necessary is to open Preferences from the Mail menu, click the Junk Mail icon, and choose Move It to the Junk Mailbox (Automatic), as you see in Figure 21.20.

NOTE: Did I forget something? Well, for normal use, just leave all the standard options checked. If you find that Mail suddenly starts making lots of mistakes, open Mail's preferences, choose Junk Mail, and click Reset. Once you click Yes on the confirming dialog, all the training information in Mail's database is wiped out. This should seldom be necessary unless you get a positively huge amount of spam and run into problems. Of course you have to train it all over again, but sometimes there's no choice.

---

5. You can use Mail's preferences to specify when or if the contents of the Junk mailbox are going to be deleted, as I described in the section presented earlier entitled "Setting Up Your User Account."

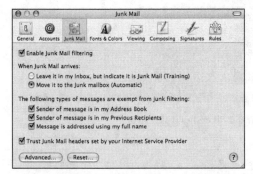

Figure 21.20   I'm pulling out all the stops here to lessen my e-mail load.

WARNING! No filter is perfect. Mail will make a mistake from time to time, so it's a good idea to check the Junk folder every day or so to make sure that messages you want aren't being improperly labeled as Junk. If you find such a message, just open it, and click Not Junk to keep it from being flagged incorrectly again. You can then drag the message into another mailbox so it isn't deleted by mistake. If Mail fails to flag spam, follow the steps in Step 3 above. The training process is never complete, even when in Automatic mode.

Creating Mail Rules

Panther Mail's Junk Mail filter actually uses a set of rules to handle suspicious messages. You can click on Advanced in the program's Junk Mail preferences to see what it does, or modify the settings if you feel comfortable with such things. You can also create your own e-mail processing rules, specifying custom steps to store and sort e-mail messages. Such rules will help you organize messages for later review or disposal. Although this feature isn't as powerful as the filtering options provided by other programs mentioned in the "In Brief" section of this chapter, it's nonetheless quite useful.

Here's how to create your very own mail rule:

1. With the Mail application open, choose Preferences from the Mail Application menu.

2. Click the Rules button. In the setup pane that appears, click Add Rule to bring up the setup dialog box shown in Figure 21.21.

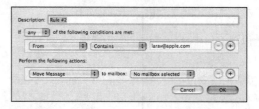

Figure 21.21   You can create an e-mail rule here.

NOTE: By default, an e-mail rule has been created for Apple's own regular newsletters. You can click the Remove buttons in the Mail preference box to dispose of them, or just uncheck the Active buttons to make them hibernate until you need them.

3. Under Description, give your e-mail-sorting rule a name. By default, the name given will be Rule #1, Rule #2, and so on.

4. In the Criteria pop-up menu, select the field that applies to that specific rule, such as To, From, Subject, and so on.

5. If you need to add another category, click the plus sign for each additional criteria you want to add. You can, for example, use the second pop-up menu to select the criteria that triggers the rule, such as whether the message Contains, Does Not Contain, Includes, and so on.

6. Type the word or phrase that field must contain to trigger the rule. For example, if all messages from someone named **grayson@rockoids.com** are to be stored, you'll enter that information for this particular rule.

7. Click the plus sign to add actions to fine-tune what happens when the criteria is met. You will be able to do such things as change the color of a flagged message, play a sound, transfer it to another mailbox or, if need be, delete it.

8. When you're finished, click OK to store the rule and then close the Mail Preferences window. From here on, any e-mail that matches the rule criteria will be stored as you've selected. You can create different rules for different messages to provide a full range of options for storing your messages.

NOTE: Although these sections concentrate strictly on Panther's Mail program, many of the steps described here can also be applied to the rule setting capabilities of other e-mail programs. You can't transfer them 100%, but you can use the logic rules here in such programs as Entourage, Eudora, and Netscape to make them automate different things. When I set up Mail, for example, I migrated from Entourage and was able to recreate my most powerful mail processing rules within minutes just by careful comparison and simple experimentation.

21. Exploring Panther's E-Mail Software

Getting Your E-Mail Automatically

When you first use Mail, it automatically checks for your e-mail on all active accounts at regular intervals. You can change this option if you want to only retrieve e-mail manually.

Here's how to adjust the option:

1. With Mail open, go to the Application menu and choose Preferences.

2. Click Accounts and select the account for which you want to change the setting.

3. In the resulting setup window, click the Advanced button, and then check or uncheck the Enable This Account (it's checked by default).

4. Choose another account or click the General icon to proceed. You'll have to click Save in the next dialog to store your new settings. From here, you can choose the Check For New Mail pop-up menu to look for new messages in your active accounts at a given interval (normal is five minutes) or manually.

5. The last setting allows you to select a sound from the pop-up menu that will notify you when a new message is received (I like Glass, but you can select None if you don't want to be disturbed). Click the close box after you've made your changes to complete the process.

NOTE: The General preference panel in Mail is, by the way, the only official way to change your default e-mail clients under Panther. The separate Internet preference panel is gone. That means, even if you prefer Mailsmith or Eudora, you still have to set that default in Mail. So now you know.

Using the Address Book

Mail has the ability to remember the addresses in letters you've sent and it will put up a list to auto-complete when you begin to type an address. However, there's a lot more to this. You can also keep a repository of regular contacts in a companion application, called Address Book, that can store your commonly used e-mail addresses, or just to keep a record of your regular contacts. In addition, you can import your contacts from other e-mail programs if you decide to migrate from another program.

21. Exploring Panther's E-Mail Software

NOTE: Address Book is compatible with programs that use the vCard format. It is also used for SmithMicro's FAXstf X and SmileOnMyMac's Page Sender, two popular Mac faxing applications.

To use this program, perform the following steps:

1. If you want to access a contact from Mail, choose Address Panel from the program's Window menu. This lets you select or search specific contacts for messages.
2. To directly access Address Book, click on the application icon from the Dock or Applications folder (listed in the Finder's default Sidebar).
3. In the Group menu, click on the category that describes your contact: All, Buddy, Home, Favorite, or Work.
4. To create a new contact, click New Card in the File menu. Enter the information in the appropriate contact fields in the Address Card window (see Figure 21.22). Each contact category is clearly labeled, so you know where to put the information.

NOTE: The fields identified by up and down arrows can be changed. Just click on the arrows to choose another category or Custom to build a new information category from scratch.

5. When the address card is filled in, it will automatically be stored in the All group, with your other contacts. If you want to put it in another group drag it into that group.
6. If you want to create a custom group, select New Group in the File menu and give the category a name.

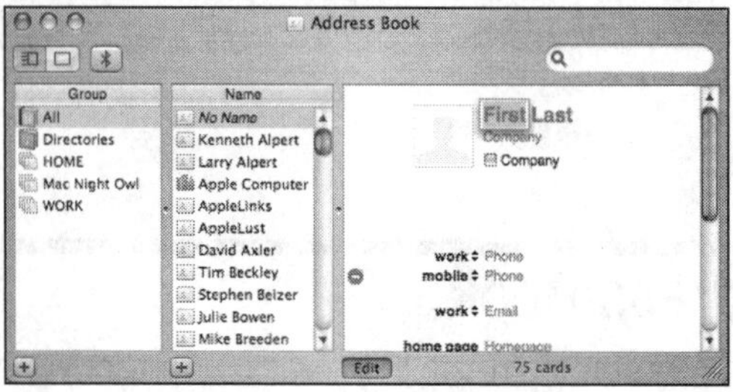

Figure 21.22 Fill in the blanks to set up a new contact.

NOTE: You can attach any single address card to multiple groups, or even create new groups as needed to organize your contact list.

7. Click OK and click Save to store the settings.

8. Repeat the preceding steps for each individual or group you wish to store.

NOTE: To delete an address book entry, click on it and press Delete. You'll see an acknowledgement dialog box, where you have to click Yes to remove the contact.

9. Once you've completed an address card for a contact, you can click on the name and see the basic contents in the Preview window at the bottom of the Address Book window.

Importing Contact Lists

You do not have to redo your entire address book once you've switched to Mail. A reasonably adept Import feature will let you import basic information from other e-mail programs. To use the feature, follow these steps:

1. Go to your e-mail program and use the options available (if any) to export your address book as vCards or an LDIF file.

NOTE: Address Book can, after a fashion, export contacts. Just select one or more contacts, choose Export vCard, and you'll be able to save them in a format that can be read by other programs that support the vCard feature. You'll want to check the import options of your chosen software.

2. With Address Book open, choose Import from the File menu and either vCard or LDIF from the submenu to bring up an Open dialog box shown in Figure 21.23.

3. Select the exported address book file you want and click Open. The list you selected will be added to your Address Book, using nearly the same fields as the original.

NOTE: If Address Book can't parse the fields, a dialog box will open in which you can select the proper destination fields for your data from a pop-up menu. If the address book entries don't come through accurately, you will need to select them in Address Book, click the Edit button, and adjust them as necessary.

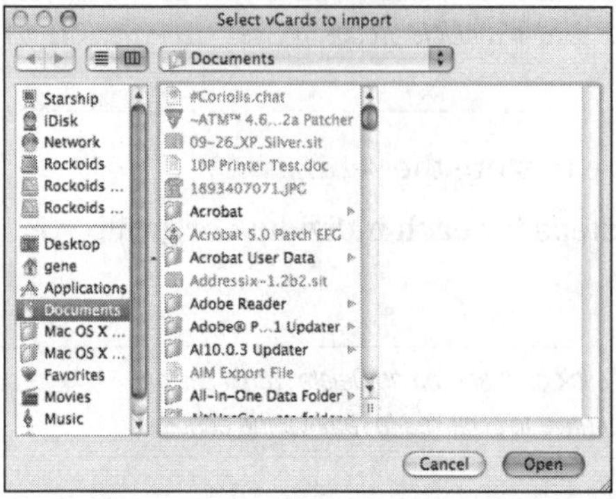

Figure 21.23   Choose the address book file from the Open dialog box.

Finding Messages

Did you ever wonder what you said in that message you sent to a client a week earlier? Or, perhaps you want to find out if you sent your aunt a birthday gift or you just need to recheck the acknowledgment letter you got from a dealer so you can track the progress of an order. Mail delivers two ways to find that message.

The first is ultra-simple if you have the client's response at hand. If you see a backwards-pointing arrow at the left of the message listing, click on it to see the letter you sent.

But that's not all. You don't have to depend on the response to find messages. You can also use Mail's powerful search engine to locate what you want. You can search by the message's header, such as the From and To information; by its subject; or by content. An individual mailbox, which you select, can be searched or you can opt to search all your mailboxes. Here's how to run a search:

1. With Mail running, locate the mailbox you want to search and click on its name in the Mailboxes drawer.

NOTE: *Mail indexes the contents of text messages, but you cannot search for text placed within an image or a file attachment of any kind.*

---

2. Click the pop-up menu next to the magnifying glass icon to choose the category of the search. The Entire Message category covers headers, subject, and body.

3. Enter the word or phrase that describes your search in the Search field of Mail's Edit menu.

4. If a match is found, you'll see it displayed in a results window.

5. If your search ends up with the wrong result or no result, consider these options to refine your search request:

- *Include All Words*—A search request that reads "Cars and Ford," for example, will look for e-mail that contains these words. Use the word "and" between each word in your search.

- *Include One Word Or The Other*—If you enter—"Cars and Ford," Mail will look for matches that contain either word.

- *Use Either Or*—If you enter—"Cars and (Ford or Cadillac)," material in the first category will be located, as well as either of the items entered within the parentheses.

Why Can't I Send My E-Mail?

This information really applies to all e-mail applications and not just Panther Mail. If you encounter any difficulties getting your e-mail to go out to its recipients, consider these remedies:

- *Are you really connected?* Make sure that you are actually connected to your ISP. If you're using Internet Connect for a dial-up connection, open that application and look at the status screen to make sure a connection has been made. If you've activated a system menu for Internet Connect on your menu bar, the connection bar above the phone icon should remain solid. If it flashes, a successful connection hasn't been achieved. If you're connected but your e-mail still won't work, click Disconnect to log off. Then, when the button changes to Connect, click it again to log in. If you're using a broadband connection to the Internet, such as a cable modem or DSL, you may want to try accessing a Web site to see if you have a connection. If you are connected via dial-up, or see no indication that your broadband connection is offline, contact the ISP directly for further help.

- *Message saved as a draft?* Maybe you clicked the wrong button when you wrote your message. To handle this problem, click on the Drafts mailbox, double-click the message to double check its content, and then click Send.

- *E-mail sent via wrong account?* If you have several e-mail accounts, you'll have an Account pop-up menu in your message that will allow you to select the account that will send your message. The account listed will always be the one listed first in your preferences, or the one used in any message you have selected in your mailbox. If you want to change the default account, just open Mail's preferences and drag the account you want to become the default to the top of the list. It will also be first in the pop-up menu.

- *POP server's port number is incorrect.* Open Mail's Preferences window and click the Account button. Click on the name of the account you're using to display the Account Information. Next, click the Advanced button and remove the entry at the bottom of the dialog box next to Port. Once you OK all the settings, Mail sets the proper number automatically when you again make your connection (assuming your ISP follows standard e-mail protocols).

- *Yes, it's your ISP's fault.* Sometimes the fault lies with the service that provides your Internet connection. Check its Web site or call the ISP for information about maintenance or system-related problems.

NOTE: On one occasion, I was unable to access the mail servers for one of my accounts. The technical support people gave me a different setting for its mail servers, and, once the changes were made, I was able to retrieve my e-mail without further trouble. In addition, sometimes an ISP will change its server settings without giving proper notice to its subscribers (that is, in fact, what happened to me).

Why Are My Messages Scrambled?

Normally, Mail formats all your messages in Multipurpose Internet Mail Extensions (MIME) or Rich Text Format. That way, you can use text styles, color, embedded graphics, and Web links in your messages. Keep in mind, however, that not all e-mail programs can read these added frills.

To remove the formatting option, just open a new message window, and then go to the Format menu and select Make Plain Text. That should take care of this problem.

NOTE: Although such older e-mail clients as Claris E-mailer won't interpret Rich Text in messages, it usually provides the text along with the core HTML code (the latter sometimes as an attached file). As a result the messages are, at least, readable.

Why Won't Mail Check All My Accounts?

If you want Mail to automatically check for e-mail from a specific e-mail account, you must make sure the account is active and that it is accessed when you check for e-mail. Here's how to confirm these settings:

1. Open Mail's Preferences window by choosing that option from the Application menu.

2. Click on the Accounts icon, select the e-mail account, and click the Advanced button.

3. Make sure the Enable This Account option is checked. It is set that way by default, you might have unchecked it to test a preference or to temporarily disable the account.

4. Close the Mail Preferences window and click Save in the next dialog to store you settings. You can also repeat the operation first with your other accounts to make sure it is enabled.

With the settings configured properly, Mail should be able to retrieve your messages automatically from all active accounts.

Related solution:	Found on page:
Using Internet Connect for Dial-Up Networking	185

Exploring Apple's Digital Hub Applications

In Brief

Your Mac consists of a lot more than just the hardware and the operating system. Beginning a trend that was later echoed by other companies in the PC industry, Apple CEO Steve Jobs offered a visionary look at taking the company beyond the box during his Macworld Expo keynote in January 2000 in San Francisco. Instead of just selling computers, displays, peripherals, and the Mac OS, Apple wants to deliver additional user experiences that make the platform more compelling. This vision was later refined as a "digital hub" strategy, in which the personal computer was meant to be the hub of your digital lifestyle, which extended to such devices as camcorders, handheld computers, music players and mobile phones. Panther is designed to enhance the ability to mate with such devices.

Over time, Apple introduced a slew of so-called "i" (or digital hub) applications that range from a simple video editing application, iMovie, to iSync, a program that works with your iPod music player, Palm Pilot, cell phone and even another Mac, to keep your calendar and contact information current.

In addition, Apple introduced a suite of Web services to help expand your digital lifestyle to the Internet. These services were first introduced as iTools, a collection of special features that could only be accessed by users with Mac OS 9 or later installed (although some features can be used by folks who have older versions of the Mac OS or computers with other operating systems installed). However, free Web services are a dying breed and Apple finally morphed iTools into .Mac, a subscription-based service.

NOTE: *Another of Apple's "beyond the box" efforts is a different sort of box, the iPod. Introduced in November 2001, the iPod is a miniature jukebox player that mates with iTunes to help you take your tunes on the road. This clever little device also does double-duty as a small FireWire backup drive for your Mac. It is a favorite among young and old, works on both Mac and Windows PCs and has become, on the basis of dollar sales figures, the number one music player in the world.*

The core features of .Mac include the famous mac.com e-mail address, 100MB of online storage, backup and virus protection software, plus an assortment of value-added extras, ranging from additional services and software, to discount coupons, all designed to enhance the value of the package. When you buy a new Mac or install Panther, you get a 60-day free trial.

An Overview of Apple's Digital Hub

At the heart of Apple's digital hub offerings are a number of applications with a consistent look and feel that allow you to organize and simplify your lifestyle. Here's a brief look at what they do. I'll cover them in more detail in the Immediate Solutions section of this chapter.

- *iCal*—Help manage your busy schedule with this simple desktop calendar (see Figure 22.1). Whether you need a reminder about that doctor's appointment next week or that critical conference with a business associate, iCal can help. The calendars can be printed or shared if you have a .Mac membership or have access to a web server with WebDAV enabled. In case you're wondering, WebDAV is short for "Web-based Distributed Authoring and Versioning," and it's a method for handling files on remote Web servers.

NOTE: *Apple doesn't synchronize its digital hub software releases with its operating systems. In January 2004, iLife '04 was introduced at the Macworld Expo in San Francisco. In addition to updating the existing applications, Apple introduced a clever music editing program, GarageBand, which has taken off big time. It may indeed become the tool with which the next great music act produces a hit recording.*

- *iChat AV*—Have a one-on-one online conversation with users of AOL, CompuServe or AOL Instant Messenger, or with folks who subscribe to .Mac. The coolest features of this instant messaging application include the ability to put chat text in bubbles and use custom "buddy" icons, even your own photo, to identify yourself when you're online. But the real power is support for microphones and cameras, which allows you to use the program as telephone or teleconferencing system (see Figure 22.2).

NOTE: *Since popular services such as MSN and Yahoo use different instant messaging systems, you cannot access users of these services via iChat. Some day we might see compatibility among the various messaging services, but there was no solution on the horizon when I wrote this book and I see no rush to make this happen.*

- *iDVD*—If you are among the millions who own a DVD player, no doubt you've wondered whether you can use it to show your family videos. Using Apple's iDVD solution, you can. Edit your movie in iMovie, then build a custom navigation menu in iDVD

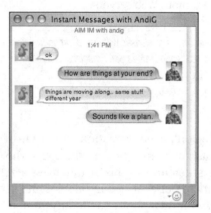

Figure 22.1   Organize your digital life with iCal.

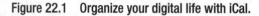

Figure 22.2   Chat bubbles and TV pictures fill your iChat window.

and in a short while, you'll have a high-quality DVD that can be played in almost any player (except the really old models).

NOTE: *Unless Apple changes its methodology, iDVD officially supports only a Mac with a built-in SuperDrive, which is Apple's parlance for the CD/DVD burners supplied with some of its new computers. The third-party internal DVD burners that are of the same make and model that Apple uses will probably work. But other models and external CD/DVD drives do not work with iDVD. The makers of these products usually supply their own software, and you should check out the features of that software to see if it meets your needs.*

- *iMovie*—One of Apple's original digital hub applications, this is a smooth-as-silk video editing program that gives your movie a professional spit-and-polish without a steep learning curve. Just drag and drop a clip here, add a title and transitions (special effects that smooth the passage from one scene to another), and you have a video ready to save as a QuickTime movie, copy back to your camcorder, or save in a form that can be used by iDVD.

- *iPhoto*—Organize the photos you've taken on your digital camera or uploaded from your scanner. iPhoto (see Figure 22.3) lets you perform simple editing functions. You can resize, rotate, and remove that red eye effect (so you don't look as though you've had one too many or been up all night). Your pictures can be printed on your color printer, or you can order up professional prints and even high-quality photo albums that will fit beautifully on any cocktail table. You can also post your photo album on your .Mac Web site.

- *iTunes*—Rip (import) songs from your music CDs, assemble tracks from music downloads, and compile them into custom music mixes to play on your Mac, dub onto a CD, or download to your iPod or other music player. iTunes also includes the ability to rate your music and sort your play list by how frequently the music is played. You can also listen to a number of Internet-based

Figure 22.3 iPhoto helps you fix up and organize your digital photo library.

radio stations and talking books through Audible.com. But the most significant feature of this program is support for the iTunes Music Store (see Figure 22.4), where you can sample and purchase hundreds of thousands of tunes from both the major recording companies and independent labels.

NOTE: *iTunes for Windows is meant to be identical in the basic look, feel, and feature-set as the Mac counterpart. That way, if you must use a Windows computer from time to time, you can still enjoy the benefits of iTunes.*

An Overview of .Mac Features

When you sign up for .Mac, you get a fairly extensive suite of Web-based features and software. Here's a brief look at what's available as of the time this book was written.

- *E-mail*—Create an e-mail address with a mac.com domain. You can use any e-mail application, other than AOL and CompuServe 2000, and you'll receive a prestigious mac.com e-mail address, reflecting your commitment to your favorite computing platform. A great feature of this e-mail service is a 15MB storage limit,

Figure 22.4   Apple's Music Store offers simple downloads of your favorite tracks and albums to millions of Mac and Windows users.

higher than you get from most ISPs. So if you need to send a large file to a business contact, this may be the way to do it. (I had to use my mac.com account to send some of the larger files for this book to my publisher.)

NOTE: *Apple's .Mac is not meant to replace your ISP; you still need an Internet account to access these services. In addition, AOL's proprietary e-mail system makes it impossible to send e-mail via the Mac.com address.*

- *iDisk*—Apple gives you 100MB of storage space at its Web site when you opt for a full subscription; it's limited to 20MB during the free trial period. You can use iDisk for backups, your personal Web sites, or to make files available to friends, family, and business contacts. Apple also lets you purchase extra storage space (up to 1GB) for an annual fee.

- *HomePage*—Would you like to build a Web site, but don't want to learn a new application or hassle with HTML coding? No problem. Apple's HomePage feature lets you build your personal Web site with an iCal calendar, iPhoto album, iMovie home videos, résumés, and more in just three convenient steps, all in a matter of minutes. Once your site is set up, it is hosted by Apple's Web site. The feature is similar to those offered by such services as AOL and EarthLink. And, like other free Web sites, it can be accessed by anyone with Internet access; it's not restricted to .Mac users or even to Mac users.

NOTE: *Such free no-hassle Web builders as HomePage aren't designed for a full-fledged business site. They are fine for a personal page, a family photo album, or even for posting your résumé. But if you wish to do business on the Web, the best way is to use a professional Web-authoring program (such as Adobe's GoLive or Macromedia's Dreamweaver) and then get a regular "dot.com"-style custom domain name via a commercial Web hosting service.*

- *iCards*—Send personal greeting cards or business announcements using a convenient array of photos and artwork. iCards also features a fairly decent selection of fonts and color styles.

- *Backup*—As I said in Chapter 16, regular backups are crucial if you want to recover your files in the event something goes wrong with your Mac. Backup works with your Mac's optical drive, your iDisk, or most external drives.

- *Virex*—A long-time favorite of many Mac users, McAfee's Virex, which is covered in more detail in Chapter 18, is bundled with a .Mac account.

NOTE: *The best thing I can say about the versions of Virex that were bundled with .Mac is that you don't pay any extra for a copy. On the other hand, unless the program inherits some new features in versions to come, you'll get a far better virus protection solution with Intego's VirusBarrier or Norton Anti-Virus. The automatic scanning features of the latter pair are among the enhancements that will make your life simpler and more secure.*

- *Value-added Extras*—From time to time, Apple has offered additional "Member Benefits" for .Mac members to entice new signups and raise the percentage of renewed subscriptions. You'll find such things as computer games, productivity software for download or at discount, online training sessions for Mac OS X and other subjects, and discounts on a variety of third-party products. Among the items I checked out as of the latter part of 2003 was a free subscription to VersionTracker Plus, the well-known site that tracks new software releases and updates, free Blogging software, free software from Aladdin Systems, and discount coupons for Apple stores in Australia, Europe, and Japan (which is great if you travel a lot). You'll find the latest perks under the Member Benefits category at the .Mac Web site.

NOTE: *Blogging? In case you haven't kept up with the news, blogging is a shortcut for Web Logging, the biggest online craze in recent years, where you can post your personal diaries for all to see. Try it; you'll like it!*

Immediate Solutions

Some of Apple's digital hub applications (such as iDVD and iMovie) are worth a full chapter by themselves. Fortunately, these programs come with complete Help menus (and sometimes a tutorial) that will easily guide you through the basics of using these applications.

In this section, I'll cover some of the other digital hub features offered with Panther.

Using iCal

Are you ready to get organized? Apple's iCal makes it simple, even for folks like me whose Mac display is covered with little, yellow sticky-notes and reminders.

Let's look at the basics of how iCal works.

Creating New Calendar Events

1. Launch iCal, which will open in the default month view.

2. Click on Day or Week at the bottom of the calendar window (sorry, this doesn't work when you view your calendar by the month).

3. First, click on the name of the calendar to select it. The default styles are Home and Work.

4. Point the mouse at the time an event will begin, and click and drag to the end of your event as I've done in Figure 22.5.

NOTE: If you mess up and set the wrong time, you can click and drag your event to a different location. Double-click on the event's start time, or click on the "i" or Info icon at the bottom right of the calendar window, to bring up the Event Info window. Here you can change the duration, or its status, such as whether the event is tentative, confirmed, or cancelled. You can also move the event to a different calendar.

Creating a New Calendar

1. With iCal open, double-click on the white area below the list of calendars, or just click on the plus symbol ("+") at the bottom left of the calendar window.

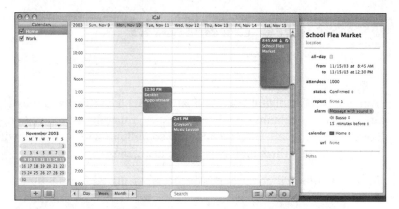

Figure 22.5   Click and drag and instantly create a calendar event.

2. Name your calendar in the way that suits your needs, such as school or club reminders, or whatever applies.

3. Following the instructions above, you can now populate your new calendar with events.

More iCal Features Summarized

I can only give you the bare essentials of iCal's capabilities in this chapter. You'll find the application intuitive and easy to master. Here's the short list:

- *Guest Invites*—To invite your family, friends, or business associates to an event, just click on the People icon at the bottom right of the calendar window. Your Address Book contacts list will appear. Once you've brought up the list, drag the names of your contacts to the actual event in your calendar. You can use the Event Info window, available by double-clicking on the event time, to send invitations, after clicking on the People icon.

- *To Do Lists*—In addition to event reminders, you can also create a To Do list to help organize and prioritize daily tasks, such as your shopping list or cleaning up that messy office. The feature is available via the pushpin button at the bottom right of the calendar window. Click on the button and enter your tasks in the To Do Items window. You can also rate To Do items in order of importance, courtesy of the Priority pop-up menu.

- *Navigation Arrows*—Click the navigation arrows to move back and forth through a calendar. The diamond button is used to display today's date, in case the rush of events has made you momentarily forget.

- *Calendar Sharing*—Once you've set up a calendar, choose Publish from the calendar menu to share it on your .mac Web site or another Web server.

Setting Up iChat AV

Instant messaging has become a world unto itself. Teens use it to "talk" to their friends, and the rest of us use it for relaxation or to stay in touch with business contacts. Businesses use them for inter-office communication.

NOTE: *Several years ago, I visited AOL's headquarters in Dulles, Virginia. While talking with some of my friends there, I noticed they used instant messaging to talk with co-workers instead of using phones. Here is a case of a company using its own product to interact. Since AOL's merger with Time Warner, I do not know if that habit spread to the rest of the company, although the unsavory aftermath might have made some of the company's employees think twice, I suppose. I should also point out, though, that I saw the same reliance on instant messaging over at CNET's San Francisco headquarters.*

You can use iChat AV to communicate with other Jaguar or Panther users on your network. In order to use iChat for Internet-based communication, you need an account with AOL or AOL Instant Messenger (AIM or a mac.com e-mail address). The latter comes with a .Mac subscription. If you don't subscribe to .Mac or AOL, you can set up an AIM account at AOL's web site at: **www.aim.com/index.adp?promo=208884&aolperm=h**. Once you have a user name for iChat, you can set up the software in just a few seconds following these instructions:

NOTE: *Rendezvous chats and regular iChat conversations are totally separate. They show up in separate chat windows, and the participants in one cannot participate using the other chat method unless it's supported on their computers, and/or they have a supported online account.*

---

1. Launch iChat from the Dock or from the Applications folder.

2. When the Welcome To iChat screen appears, click Continue to bring the first setup screen (see Figure 22.6), where you can enter your name, the type of account (Mac.com or AIM), and the account name and password.

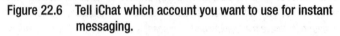

Figure 22.6   Tell iChat which account you want to use for instant messaging.

NOTE: If you don't have an AOL or AIM account, you can sign up for Mac.com right from the iChat Welcome dialog.

3. Click OK when you're ready to write or talk.

4. If you want to access Mac OS X's Rendezvous networking feature to communicate with other Mac users on your network, click yes at the Rendezvous prompt (see Figure 22.7).

NOTE: Rendezvous messaging only works with other Macs running Mac OS X 10.2 or later. It will not let you network with users of early Mac operating systems. I'll let you know more about this great "zero configuration" networking feature in Chapter 8. If you passed that chapter by because it seemed a little too arcane for you, please try it again. Networking under Panther really isn't all that hard once you learn the basics.

5. Once your setup is done, your personal Buddy List will appear. If you already have an active AOL or AIM account, it'll be populated by your full list of online contacts (see Figure 22.8).

6. To add another name to your Buddy List, click the plus symbol at the bottom of the Buddy List window, choose the contact's AOL, AIM, or Mac.com user name from your Address Book window and click on Select Buddy.

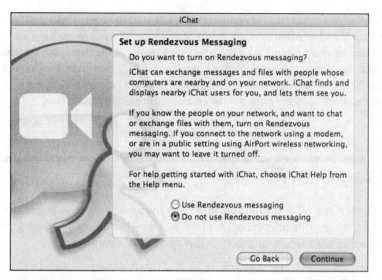

Figure 22.7   Click yes only if you have other Jaguar or Panther users on your network.

Figure 22.8   Double click on a name to send that person a message.

7. If the name isn't stored in your Address Book list, click New Person to bring up a dialog box. You can now enter the member's user name, and, if you wish, enter additional information, including a photo, to store in the Address Book.

8. Click Add to put the name in your Buddy List and repeat the above steps to add more contacts to your Buddy List.

WARNING! *Be careful about entering the name of a new contact in your Buddy List. You must use the actual online or, as AOL calls it, screen name, and not a person's real name. If you enter the wrong name, it will point to the wrong person. You cannot rename someone to make them easier to identify, otherwise your buddy list will point to the wrong person. Since my AOL screen name is Gene, you can understand that I'm often the victim of mistaken identity because many members overlook these simple requirements.*

Using iChat AV

Once iChat AV is configured, you'll see the name darken in your Buddy List when your online contact logs in. Once the contact appears, just double click on the name to bring up an iChat window.

NOTE: *Even though the official name of the product is iChat AV, which distinguishes it from the older version that doesn't support audio or video communication, Apple still lists the copy in Panther as iChat, but it also bears version 2.0 or later, which is the key to figuring out what you really have.*

Just enter your chat text in the bottom text field, and press Return or Enter to send it on its way. Chat text will appear in little cartoon-like balloons (as you see in Figure 22.9).

The little icons at the bottom of the chat window allow you to show or hide a Buddy, change text to bold or italic, add a smiley or other emoticon (a little symbol that express emotion), or send a file attachment to your online contact.

Figure 22.9   It's not Donald Duck or Bugs Bunny, but your author and an online friend having a friendly conversation.

iChat AV also includes the following features:

- *Online telephony or video conferencing*—Just pick up Apple's iSight or any camera that hooks up to the FireWire port (including a regular digital camcorder), and you'll be able to have an audio or video conference with anyone using a similar setup (see Figure 22.10). How do you know what your buddies have? Simple, just look at the telephone and/or camera icon and click the appropriate one to begin the chat. It's that simple. The voice of your contact will be heard in your Mac's speaker.

WARNING! *The video feature of iChat isn't going to work unless you have a broadband Internet connection, such as cable, DSL, or some sort of wireless technique. While a normal dial-up modem connection is fine for audio communications, the wider bandwidth of video won't function. Fortunately, iChat AV is smart enough not to initiate a video conference if your Internet access isn't fast enough.*

TIP: *If you want to hear your buddy's voice clearly, don't rely on the tiny speaker of a Power Mac. While the iMac and Apple laptops might provide decent sound, get yourself a really good set of speakers. You'd be surprised how good it can sound, far better than the voice quality of the typical phone.*

- *Automatic chat logging*—Just open iChat's Preferences box from its application menu, click the Messages icon, and choose Automatically Save Chat Transcripts. That way you can have an online business meeting.

Figure 22.10   Here I am talking with Apple Computer's iChat product manager, Kurt Knight, about the company's latest product releases. Ignore that ugly dude in the tiny thumbnail picture, because I cast a bad reflection.

- *Set up a chat room*—If you want to speak with several people at once, select New Chat from the File menu. With the chat window opened, click the plus or Add button at the bottom of the list of chat participants, and select the buddies you want to invite. When you press Return they'll receive a chat invitation. If they accept your invitation, their names will appear among the Participants in your chat room.

- *Custom buddy photos*—Use your photo to identify yourself, as I've done in Figure 22.9. The feature is supported in Apple's Address Book, where you can easily drop in a contact's picture.

- *Configure chat balloons*—The Messages preference panel in iChat also lets you change the color of your chat balloons or pick a different typeface to display chat text.

- *Protect your privacy*—It's not uncommon to get online solicitations from folks you didn't want to contact. If you get offensive or irritating messages, or just don't want someone to know when you're online, click the Privacy icon in iChat's preferences window and enter the name of those users you want to block. You also have the option of only allowing those users you specify to see when you're online. That provides the utmost in online privacy.

Hints for Chatting Safety

I'd like to say that it's perfectly safe for you to talk to strangers online because you can easily strike up friendships with people from around the world. While that's probably true for the most part, you should be very cautious because the online world is a little bit crazy.

This is especially true if you give your kids instant messaging access. I've assembled a few safety tips to help you protect yourself:

- *Limit a Child's Internet Access*—AOL and MSN, for example, have Parental Controls that allow you to give your child a custom online environment that caters strictly to his or her age group. You can reduce access to sites and pose limits on instant messaging. The most important limitation is to block messages from people not in someone's Buddy List. That keeps out strangers.

- *Monitor a Child's IMs*—No, I don't mean read the conversations. A child is allowed to a certain degree of privacy, so long as parental rules are followed. But AOL and MSN let you create logs of a child's online access, so you know the names of the people they contact and when the conversations took place. So if homework isn't being finished on time, you'll know why and what to do about it.

TIP: *If you don't use a service with Parental Controls, consider the Norton Internet Privacy application in Norton SystemWorks or Intego's ContentBarrier to restrict online access. You can get these utility programs from your Apple dealer.*

- *Don't Allow Online Strangers Into Your Home*—Someone writes to your child (assuming access isn't blocked) and says they are the same age. They agree to meet. What do you do? Well, limit those meetings to a public place, and be present. This will help you be certain the other person is really a child and not an adult. And don't be afraid to ask to speak to the child's parents, to get a sense whether you should allow such a meeting.

- *Block Online Harassment*—From offers of sexually-oriented content to general online harassment, people may guess your instant messaging handle and annoy you. If you haven't blocked strangers from contacting you, you can still stop harassment on a case-by-case basis. Simply use your instant messaging software's privacy feature. In iChat AV, for example, you can block someone right from a message invite screen or later on, using the Privacy pane in the Preferences dialog box (see Figure 22.11).

Using iPhoto

Digital cameras are fast becoming a staple in the home or office of both amateur and professional photographers. It's now possible to get a high quality picture without spending a king's ransom on a camera. If you take lots of digital pictures, wouldn't it be nice to have a

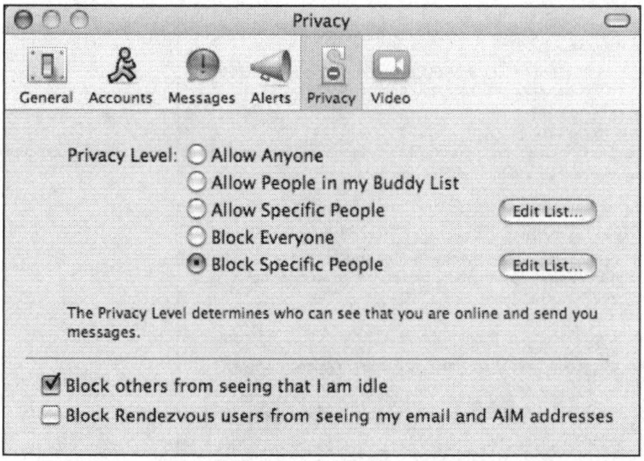

Figure 22.11 Here you can choose whether people you don't know can contact you, and keep a listing of blocked buddies.

convenient way to organize your libraries? That's the logic behind Apple's iPhoto).

When you install Panther, iPhoto comes along for the ride, and it's placed, like other applications, in the Applications folder (there's also a Dock icon for it when you do a clean install). When you first launch iPhoto (see Figure 22.12), you'll have the option to decide whether iPhoto will open whenever you connect a digital camera to your Mac. If you say No, Image Capture will run instead.

Here's a brief look at iPhoto's features:

- *Simple editing*—While it won't replace a dedicated image editing program, such as Adobe Photoshop, you can handle a few basic touch-ups in .Mac (see Figure 22.13). You can adjust brightness and contrast, resize and crop, convert to black and white, or eliminate the red-eye effect. These features are sufficient for most family photos.

- *Organize your library*—You don't have to confront a confusing mess of pictures. Create custom albums for family functions, vacations, corporate events, and so on. You can import photos from the most popular digital cameras (check **www.apple.com/iphoto/compatibility/** for the latest listing), or use your scanner to handle photo prints.

- *Create a printed photo album*—You can create high-quality, professionally bound and printed, coffee table-style photo albums

Welcome to iPhoto!
iPhoto is your best choice for importing, organizing and sharing your digital photos. Best of all, you don't even have to download any software. Just plug in your camera.

Optimized for Mac OS X.
iPhoto was engineered to take advantage of the speed and power of Mac OS X so you can do more with your photos, faster.

No Drivers Necessary.
iPhoto does not require any additional drivers or software, so you can begin enjoying your digital photos the second you plug your camera in.

So Many Ways to Share
Send photos via e-mail, print them on your home printer or create your own professional-quality photo books. iPhoto lets you do more with your favorite shots.

Do you want to use iPhoto when you connect your digital camera?

Use Other   Decide Later   Use iPhoto

Figure 22.12   Would you like iPhoto to open whenever you connect your camera?

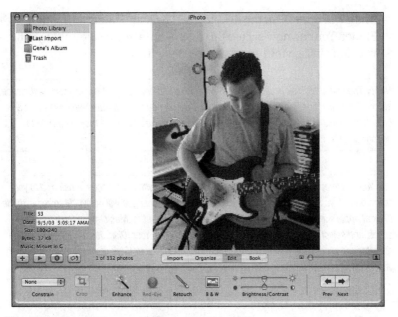

Figure 22.13 Handle simple touch-ups in iPhoto.

at a modest price, through Apple's publishing partner. This is a
great way to catalog important family or corporate events.

---

*NOTE: You can, if you prefer, make your own album, using a color inkjet printer. Just take your
prints to the local copy center, and select a custom binding. But Album's photo album solution is
so elegant you might prefer it.*

- *Extra features*—Your iPhoto library can be published at your
  .Mac Web site, e-mailed to your online contacts, or sent out for
  professional, lab-quality photo prints via an online retailer. A
  finished photo library can also be converted to a QuickTime
  movie or used as a screen saver or desktop background.

Using the iDisk Feature

One of the more useful functions of .Mac is iDisk. When you become
a paid subscriber, you get 100MB of online storage space to use as
you wish, for backups, for documents you need to exchange with your
business contacts, or to post your personal Web site. Here's how to
use the feature.

From the Panther Finder, choose iDisk from the Go menu or press
Command+Option+I. Within a few seconds, the icon for your personal

iDisk will appear on the desktop and be listed under Computer in the Finder. You can now access this disk in the same fashion as any other— you can share, view, send, and retrieve files.

NOTE: *The speed of iDisk access depends on several factors, not the least of which is the speed of your SP connection. It's slow going with a dial-up connection, but reasonably swift with a broadband hookup. In addition, network congestion at Apple's Web site may contribute to performance slowdowns.*

TIP: *You can keep your iDisk on your desktop all the time, with a local copy transferred to your Mac's hard drive for fast access. Whenever you're online, changes will be synchronized with the iDisk at Apple's .Mac Web site. To activate this feature, open the .Mac pane in System Preferences, and select the option labeled Create a Local Copy of Your iDisk. Just remember that the time it takes to copy the contents to the Internet version of your iDisk depends on the speed of your Internet connection. With dial-up access, it can tie up your connection for quite a while.*

However, your iDisk isn't exclusive to your Mac running Mac OS 9 or X. You can access your files from any PC running the Linux or Windows operating system if it uses a WebDAV client application.

Here's how it's done:

1. From the PC, launch your Web browser and enter the following URL: **http://idisk.mac.com/*username*** (where you enter your .Mac account name), as shown.

2. Enter the password from the login prompt (see Figure 22.14).

If you need more storage space, you can click on the Upgrade button at Apple's iDisk page and increase disk storage from 100MB all the way to 1GB. You'll want to consult the Upgrade Storage page for current pricing information.

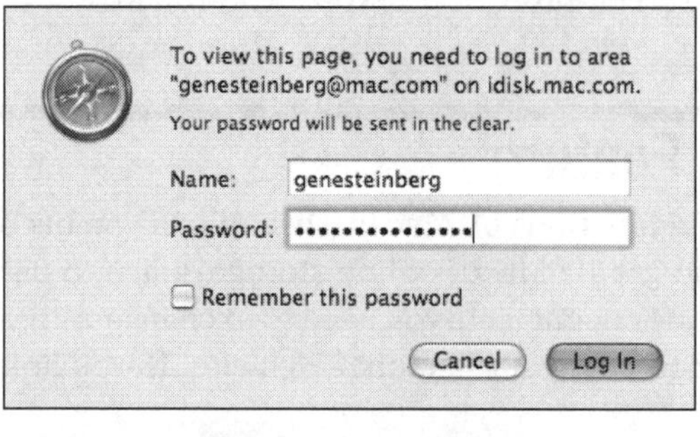

Figure 22.14 Go ahead and connect.

Index

J

K

T